CHÂTEAU PONTET-CANET
Ferran ADRIÀ

CHÂTEAU BATAILLEY
Juan Mari ARZAK

CHÂTEAU GRAND-PUY-LACOSTE
Émile JUNG

CHÂTEAU LYNCH-BAGES
Thierry MARX

CHÂTEAU LYNCH-MOUSSAS
Kiyomi MIKUNI

CHÂTEAU DAUZAC
Jean-Pierre MOULLÉ

CHÂTEAU D'ARMAILHAC
Anthony SICIGNANO

CHÂTEAU DU TERTRE
Wylie DUFRESNE

CHÂTEAU HAUT-BAGES LIBÉRAL
Michel PORTOS

CHÂTEAU PÉDESCLAUX
Marc MENEAU

CHÂTEAU BELGRAVE
Vangelis KOUMBIADIS

CHÂTEAU DE CAMENSAC
Bock-Ryo HAN

CHÂTEAU COS LABORY
Emilio GARIP

CHÂTEAU CLERC MILON
Alexander ZAITSEV

CHÂTEAU CROIZET-BAGES
Manjit SINGH GILL

CHÂTEAU CANTEMERLE
Peter KÖRNER

CHÂTEAU D'YQUEM
Dominique ANSEL & Daniel BOULUD

CHÂTEAU LA TOUR BLANCHE
Martín BERASATEGUI

CHÂTEAU LAFAURIE-PEYRAGUEY
Georges BLANC

CLOS HAUT-PEYRAGUEY
Alain DUTOURNIER

CHÂTEAU DE RAYNE-VIGNEAU
Alex ATALA

CHÂTEAU SUDUIRAUT
Annie FÉOLDE

CHÂTEAU COUTET
Sergio HERMAN

CHÂTEAU CLIMENS
Pierre GAGNAIRE

CHÂTEAU GUIRAUD
Jean-Georges VONGERICHTEN

CHÂTEAU RIEUSSEC
Hiroyuki HIRAMATSU

CHÂTEAU RABAUD-PROMIS
Tetsuya WAKUDA

CHÂTEAU SIGALAS-RABAUD
Christian SINICROPI

CHÂTEAU DE MYRAT
Fulvio PIERANGELINI

CHÂTEAU DOISY DAËNE
David KINCH

CHÂTEAU DOISY DUBROCA
Peter GOOSSENS

CHÂTEAU DOISY-VEDRINES
René REDZEPI

CHÂTEAU D'ARCHE
Michel GUÉRARD

CHÂTEAU FILHOT
Yu BO

CHÂTEAU BROUSTET
Hans VÄLIMÄKI

CHÂTEAU NAIRAC
Alain SOLIVÉRÈS

CHÂTEAU CAILLOU
Heinz WINKLER

CHÂTEAU SUAU
Roberta SUDBRACK

CHÂTEAU DE MALLE
Vincent ARNOULD

CHÂTEAU ROMER DU HAYOT
Claus-Peter LUMPP

CHÂTEAU ROMER
Bruno OTEIZA & Mikel ALC…

CHÂTEAU LA…
Chris SALANS

GRANDS CRUS CLASSÉS

Sophie Brissaud, a recipe creator, writer, and journalist, has written many books on cooking, wines, and teas, collaborating with the greatest chefs. In 2004, she was awarded the Antonin Carême prize for food writing.

Wine journalist Jancis Robinson writes a weekly column in the *Financial Times* and updates her own website dedicated to the world of wine. She is a counsellor for HRM Queen Elizabeth II's personal wine cellar, and she cowrote the famous *World Atlas of Wine*, among other books.

Nicholas Lander is a restaurant critic for the *Financial Times*; he is also a broadcaster for the highly popular BBC programme *MasterChef*.

A journalist for the weekly French magazine *Le Point*, Jacques Dupont is particularly notorious for two much-awaited yearly issues: "Spécial Bordeaux Primeurs" in May and "Spécial Vins" in September.

Photo reporter Cyril Le Tourneur d'Ison's images may be seen in many international magazines, covering subjects such as world heritage sites, the environment, humanitarian issues, and wine. In 1990, he received the World Press award for his report on the people of the Indus region in Pakistan.

Iris L. Sullivan is a culinary photographer whose work has appeared in books and magazines around the world. She travels extensively in China and Japan, and has published several books. She was awarded the Antonin Carême prize for her book on honey.

Texts Sophie Brissaud

Translation Roxane Compagne, Maria Grazzini, Rupert Hasterok and Thomas de Kayser

Editor Nathalie Chapuis

Corrections Julie Houis

Photographs of the châteaux Cyril Le Tourneur d'Ison, except pages 35 top left, 36–37, 75 top and bottom right, 94, 95, 187 right, 254, 255, and 330 by Guy Charneau

Photographs of the recipes Iris L. Sullivan

Collaboration on the recipes Nathalie Nannini, Coco Jobard and Alain Cirelli

Styling of the recipes Nathalie Nannini

Layout Sophie Compagne/Albert&Cie

Cataloging-in-Publication Data has been applied for and may be obtained from the Library of Congress.
ISBN 978-1-58479-877-4

© 2009 Éditions de La Martinière, Paris

Published in 2010 by Stewart, Tabori & Chang, an imprint of ABRAMS. All rights reserved. No portion of this book may be reproduced, stored in a retrieval system, or transmitted in any form or by any means, mechanical, electronic, photocopying, recording, or otherwise, without written permission from the publisher.

Printed and bound in China
10 9 8 7 6 5 4 3 2 1

Stewart, Tabori & Chang books are available at special discounts when purchased in quantity for premiums and promotions as well as fundraising or educational use. Special editions can also be created to specification. For details, contact specialmarkets@abramsbooks.com or the address below.

ABRAMS
THE ART OF BOOKS SINCE 1949

115 West 18th Street
New York, NY 10011
www.abramsbooks.com

www.grand-cru-classe.com

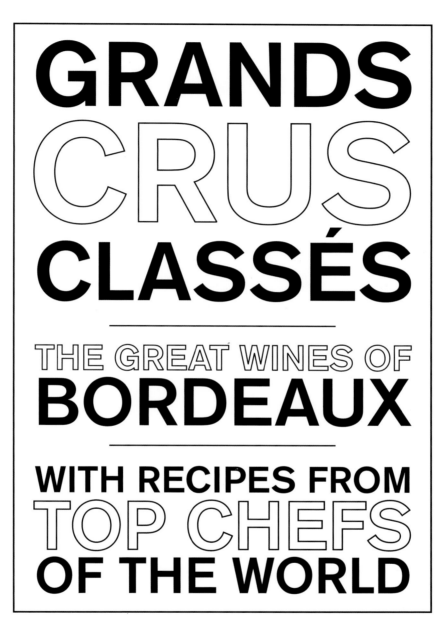

GRANDS CRUS CLASSÉS

THE GREAT WINES OF BORDEAUX

WITH RECIPES FROM TOP CHEFS OF THE WORLD

Texts by Sophie Brissaud
Photographs by Cyril Le Tourneur d'Ison & Iris L. Sullivan
Preface by Jacques Dupont
Introduction by Jancis Robinson & Nicholas Lander

STEWART, TABORI & CHANG, NEW YORK

"Draw me a sheep!" was the Little Prince's challenge to the aviator. Antoine de Saint-Exupéry found a solution by sketching a box in which the Little Prince could imagine a sheep of his own design.

To speak of the crus classés, to consider the reasons for their international renown, to explain their preeminence among the ranks of the world's great wines, the ruse employed by Saint-Exupéry would seem the best approach. Show not a box, but simply a château, some vines and a bottle, then let imagination do the rest, thus avoiding any risk of disappointment, frustration or misunderstanding. Obviously, there is the terroir: one can always fall back on the terroir when at a loss to explain the difference between the three Léovilles or the two Pichons.

"Draw me a terroir"? This is a little more challenging. You have to sketch the soil with more or less clay and gravel—those small, round stones that are so simple to draw—and occasionally a solid base of limestone. There should be a slight slope, too, just a modest incline: the Médoc and the Sauternes region are not the Alps. There's no need for a steep grade to drain rainwater away from the vines. However, here things become a little complicated. Often, to channel away the water it is necessary to dig ditches, to install drains, to intervene and modify the natural environment.

Thus, to draw the terroir it is also necessary to include in the picture the image of a person, perhaps wielding a pick. Is this person big or small? If small, this would mean that in drawing a terroir it is nature, the soil, sun and rain that play the major role. If, by contrast, the person is the prominent element in the drawing, this clearly suggests the human factor is most important. This proposition is certain to arouse strong feelings among those for whom a bottle of wine is the expression of Nature's spirit, those who believe that without the blessing of a host of divine influences there would be no Yquem, no Palmer.

Without denying the importance of place, weather, soil and subsoil, and the northerly location of the vineyards—"Where difficulties abound, but where the inimitable is created," according to œnologist and winemaker Denis Dubourdieu—it can be argued that the human element has been essential. Simply put: elsewhere, it could be worse; without dedicated people, it simply could not be. Of course, one must acknowledge the noble importance of their physical contributions: the work in the vineyard, selection for quality, drainage of vine parcels, construction of cellars . . .

Often, however, one fundamental activity is overlooked: commerce. "If you cannot sell your wine, of what use is a great vineyard?" asked the agronomist Olivier de Serres in Théâtre d'agriculture et mesnage des champs, published in 1600. The humorist Alphonse Allais felt that cities would be better if they were situated in the countryside away from cities, but if one pursues this idea and imagines Bordeaux sans river, sans estuary, sans port, set on an inaccessible plateau far from any means of communication, there would be no crus classés. Commerce, in both its forms—the exchange of goods among people and the exchange of their values—has been a major factor in the worldwide appreciation of the crus classés. This was true well before the year 1855 and its classification; it has been even truer since.

Today, where is one most likely to find the owners of these châteaux? In airports. Each year they travel thousands of kilometres, taking with them the box of Antoine de Saint-Exupéry, the box of imagination. Each grand cru bottle holds a bit of French culture, several lines of Voltaire, some advice from Escoffier, a recipe by Joël Robuchon and more. Commerce has made gastronomy a vast, global affair, richly spiced and deeply coloured, which readily crosses national barriers. Like the great diplomats of the past, the crus classés speak every language; they find easy concord with every style of cuisine. These are wines of great humility: they accompany without dominating, an achievement we may attribute to human intervention and the natural elements. However, their ability to achieve the incomparable is due to human intervention alone.

Jacques Dupont

CONTENTS

SOMMELIER BIOGRAPHIES

Éric BEAUMARD

Several years of experience as a cook—in particular for Olivier Roelinger, the Michelin-starred chef at the Maison de Bricourt in Cancale—led Eric Beaumard to become a sommelier. Excelling in this domain, he won the title of Best Sommelier in France in 1992 and 1997, Best Sommelier in Europe in 1994, and finally the silver medal in the Best Sommelier in the World competition in 1998. Since 1999, Beaumard has been the wine director at the prestigious Le Cinq restaurant in the Four Seasons Hôtel Georges V, one of the finest addresses in Paris.

Serge DUBS

Born in Strasbourg, Serge Dubs discovered the world of wine in 1972 at the Alsatian restaurant Auberge de l'Ill in Illhaeusern, which has earned three Michelin stars for more than 40 years. With daily exercises to develop his palate and sense memory, he became Best Sommelier in Alsace in 1974 and 1976, while working at the Parisian three-star restaurant Laserre. He continued on this path to become Best Sommelier in France in 1983 and took the European title four years later. With a well-developed competitive spirit, he triumphed at the contest for Best Sommelier in the World in 1989. Since 1976 he has been the Master Sommelier at Auberge de l'Ill, the restaurant where he made his debut.

Andreas LARSSON

Andreas Larsson began his gastronomic career as a chef, a natural choice for this Swede with an appreciation for good food. An interest in the pleasures of wine developed during a trip to France, and in 1998, at the age of 28, he took his first step towards becoming a sommelier. For three consecutive years he was voted Best Sommelier in Sweden, then in 2004 became Best Sommelier in Europe, before reclaiming the national title once again. Since 2006, he has been Chief Sommelier at the restaurant Pm & Vänner in Sweden. In 2007, Larsson won the title of Best Sommelier in the World. He says that for him, wine is more than his profession; it is his passion.

Markus del MONEGO

Born in Switzerland but of German parentage, Markus Del Monego learned the sommelier's art in 1988 at the Four Seasons Hotel in Hamburg. His passion for wine led him to pursue an international career, aided by an impressive talent for languages (German, French, English and Italian). He has earned numerous titles, and in 1998 he became the first German to achieve the ultimate accolade of Best Sommelier in the World. Del Monego has not stopped there: today he is the owner of caveCo GmbH in Essen and consults across the globe.

Virginia PHILIP

Having developed an early interest in the world of wine, Virginia Philip began studying the subject upon entering college and her passion led to work in an upstate New York vineyard. After finishing her studies in 1989, she worked as a sommelier at restaurants across the country before becoming Chief Sommelier at The Breakers in Palm Beach, one of the finest hotels in the United States. In November 2002 she became the tenth woman in the world to earn the prestigious Master Sommelier distinction, and three weeks later she won the title Best Sommelier in the United States.

Olivier POUSSIER

From his arrival at the Tecomah hotel school in Jouy-en-Josas, Olivier Poussier felt a strong attraction for the world of wine. This led him on an itinerary that took him to such fine restaurants as Tour d'Argent, Pavillon Ledoyen and Manoir "Aux Quat'Saisons" in United Kingdom. With unflagging effort, he achieved the title of Best Sommelier in France in 1989. World vice-champion at the sommeliers competition in 1995, he attained the illustrious title of Best Sommelier in the World in 2000. Since 1993 he has been Chief Sommelier at the world-famous restaurant Lenôtre and has consulted for the Accor hotel group and Air France.

Yoichi SATO

After completing university studies in his hometown of Osaka, Yoichi Sato settled in France for three years, during which time he began to study the sommelier's art. After a brief spell in Tokyo, he returned to Europe and honed his talents in such great restaurants as Enoteca Pinchiorri in Florence, then Taillevent and Robuchon in Paris. His experiences at these prestigious establishments led him to open his own restaurant, Maxivin, in the Roppongi district in central Tokyo. In 2005 Yoichi Sato entered the demanding competition staged by the 6,000-member Japan Sommelier Association, and was honoured with the title of Best Sommelier in Japan.

Franck THOMAS

Culinary studies led Franck Thomas to pursue a career in wine, and in 1993 he earned his professional sommelier's diploma. After winning the title of Best Sommelier in Provence, he continued this impressive achievement by accumulating the titles of Meilleur Ouvrier de France, then Best Sommelier in France, and finally ascending to the rank of Best Sommelier in Europe in 2000. Franck Thomas considers wine to be a philosophy and has sought to share its wisdom with others throughout the world.

Savor this work, which unites the history of the 1855 classification
with the imaginations of the world's top chefs, a magic encounter of flavors and savoir faire,
of great talents and great terroirs.

Philippe CASTÉJA
President of the Conseil des Grands Crus Classés 1855
(Médoc & Sauternes)

Editor's note: This book presents the châteaux that figure in the 1855 Bordeaux Classification
that are members of the Conseil des Grands Crus Classés en 1855 (Médoc & Sauternes).

INTRODUCTION

What an honour it is for us to be invited to write an introduction to a book that combines so many of the aspects of life that give us the greatest pleasure.

We fully realise how lucky we are to earn our livings by respectively eating and or drinking, and to have the even greater fortune to occasionally do those activities together, in some of the most beautiful corners of the world. When the food and the wines are some of France's finest, in some of the most beautiful wine properties that exist, then truly our cup runneth over.

A very significant proportion of the greatest wines we have experienced have been made on the estates featured in this book, which of course adds enormously to the sense of pride and enthusiasm with which we approach the task of providing an introduction to it.

The 1855 Grands Crus Classés of Bordeaux (Médoc and Sauternes) are the envy of the world in the respect they command as measured by their market value but also, more importantly as far as we are concerned, by their ability to deliver unrivalled nuances, savour and complexity after decades in bottle.

The wines described in this book are quintessentially wines for the dining table. Even if some of the world's keener wine enthusiasts and students are tempted nowadays to open great Bordeaux in a noisy bar, night-club or, more intently perhaps, in a classroom, these wines are designed as a foil for food—dishes carefully chosen to complement their intricacies.

But such are their nuances and, often, delicacy, that it can be difficult for even keen amateurs to match suitable dishes to great Bordeaux. This is just one reason why this book is so useful. We lovers of fine food and wine can therefore use this book as a food and wine matching guide at our own dining tables, or when choosing dishes in a restaurant.

That of course is but one of the book's charms. The briefest glance at it shows how much sheer visual pleasure can be derived from its well-designed pages. Here is a thoroughly appetising and up-to-date guide to many of the Bordeaux region's architectural treasures.

The texts that introduce each château are also designed to capture the spirit of each of these very different properties, their often- fascinating history, and the special attributes they try to communicate in every bottle.

Some of our most memorable meals have been shared with members of the Conseil des Grands Crus Classés en 1855, in some of the most distinctive dining rooms of châteaux all over the Bordeaux region—whether it be an all-Yquem lunch at the great premier grand cru classé in Sauternes or a dinner with wine merchants from around over the world around the hospitable table at Château Margaux.

In our experience the food served in Bordeaux châteaux tends to be almost exclusively French and fairly classical, but we salute the Grands Crus for being more adventurous in this book. Embracing the great chefs—and what a roll call of famous names—of America, Asia, Australia and all over Europe is just what they should be doing today. The Bordelais sell their wines to connoisseurs in every corner of the world and are increasingly demonstrating that they are prepared to travel from Seattle to Sydney via Shanghai in order to introduce their wines to the swelling ranks of fine wine lovers everywhere. Meanwhile, lovers of the good life everywhere are tending to explore a wider and wider range of different cuisines.

It is only fitting therefore that the recipes here range from Tetsuya Wakuda of Sydney's Blue Cheese Bavarois with Sauternes Jelly to Ferran Adria of El Bulli's enigmatic Turtledoves with Chocolate Air—far outside the confines of strictly French cuisine. This collection of recipes is truly cosmopolitan. We expect of course the roster of France's finest chefs to be found in these pages, but our eyes were caught by other, more exotic members of the world's gastronomic aristocracy. The Walnuts and Dried Berries proposed by the talented young René Redzepi of Noma in Copenhagen with Château Doisy-Védrines is intriguing to say the least. Also with Sauternes, Château La Tour Blanche in this case, Martín Berasategui of San Sebastian nominates Celery Ice with slices of mango and a compote, while Bruno Oteiza and Mikel Alonso of Biko in Mexico City suggest something they call "100% Cotton Foie." Surely even the most experienced cooks and travellers will find much to learn from this book.

Just flicking through the recipes brings back happy memories of great meals we have enjoyed on our own travels: Alex Atala of D.O.M. in São Paulo with his Priprioca-scented Milk Custard with Lime and Banana Ouro Ravioli; Alexander Zaitsev of Pushkin in Moscow with his Chicken Offal Pâté and Mushroom Caviar; Peter Goossens of Hof Van Cleve's Caramel Apple; Carlo Cracco's intriguing Veal Kidney with Sea Urchins; not to mention the host of American chefs—coast to coast, from Chez Panisse to Le Bernardin via Charlie Trotter in Chicago. Not to mention the distinctly anglophile choice of Neil Perry of Rockpool in Sydney—with English-bred lamb—and our very own Fergus Henderson of Saint John restaurant in London and his choice of Pot-roasted Should of Lamb. Lamb and Bordeaux, after all, combine to give us one of the great classic food and wine pairings.

Bordeaux is a thoroughly modern city nowadays, albeit with a strong (and recently refurbished) historic personality. This book is just one particularly appetising piece of evidence of the way some of its most important people and products are adapting to the world around them.

Although, fortunately, the famous terroirs of the Médoc and Sauternes ensure that the wines described in here, no matter how the wine world develops, will always carry their own particular imprint of Nature.

Jancis Robinson and Nicholas Lander

MÉDOC

CHÂTEAU LAFITE-ROTHSCHILD

PAUILLAC

VINEYARD SIZE	107 hectares
VINE DENSITY	9,000 stocks per hectare
AVERAGE AGE OF VINEYARD	40 years
AVERAGE PRODUCTION	45,000 cases
SOILS AND SUBSOILS	fine, deep gravel mixed with aeolian sand on a Tertiary limestone subsoil
GRAPE VARIETIES	Cabernet Sauvignon 70% Merlot 25% Cabernet Franc 3% Petit Verdot 2%

On August 8, 1868, when Baron James de Rothschild acquired the Château Lafite, the place already had a long story behind it. It had begun in the 17th century in the hands of the famous de Ségur family. Later, the 1855 Classification awarded it the rank of First of First Growths in the Médoc, but 40 years earlier, the wine broker Lawton, writing the first classification of Médoc wines, had already placed Lafite at the top, pointing out that "the position of its vines is among the finest in the Médoc" and that its wines were "the most superb." And indeed, the formal perfection of the gravel hills that rise around the château is impressive. The exit from the cellar into the vineyard, framed by two vertical walls, offers a sudden, striking view: the vine rows pointing to the sky look like the tightened strings of some heavenly musical instrument.

The vineyard—70 percent Cabernet Sauvignon, 25 percent Merlot, 3 percent Cabernet Franc and 1 percent Petit Verdot—borders that of Duhart-Milon, another classified growth managed by the same team, with Charles Chevallier at the helm. "But while Duhart-Milon is a Pauillac, Lafite is a Lafite," says Christophe Salin, general manager of the Domaines Barons de Rothschild. The estate's cooperage, which employs five men, produces 2,000 barrels every year for the Domaines' wine properties. The fermentation is led in magnificent thermoregulated oaken vats.

A château visit is an initiatory journey. The long, tunnel-like vaulted cellars are bathed in a quiet, velvety darkness reminiscent of Romanesque church crypts. They alter our sense of time, reminding us of our humble human status in relation to what has come before us. While deeply absorbed in meditation, you suddenly emerge into the Chai 2000 for an immediate mental shock. Huge, subterranean, circular, mimicking a giant

spaceship or a Mycenian necropolis, this amphitheatre—with a capacity of more than 2,000 barrels—was conceived by Ricardo Bofill in 1987. The matt grey of the bare concrete, lit by a zenithal oculus, throws you into the future after your descent into the cellars immersed you into the past.

There is a source of life here, an elusive but tangible fountain of youth. It was already known back in the 18th century, when Mr. de Richelieu, Governor of Guyenne, was prescribed the wine of Lafite by his physician. "Maréchal," King Louis XV said to him when he returned to Paris, "you look 25 years younger than you did when you left for Guyenne." It also shows through the beautiful photograph of ecstatic vine harvesters—all bright colours and joyful energy, raising their arms with clippers in hand—that was the Domaines Barons de Rothschild's New Year's greeting card in 2009. The nose and lip piercings in the photo had shocked a few recipients. "Why, life is—just that!" was Christophe Salin's answer.

"Life" is indeed the right term—and perhaps the key to the mystery—to describe Lafite-Rothschild. In the glass, Château Lafite-Rothschild is profound, bewitching and deeply spiritual, more a wine of revelation than of meditation. It claims the sovereignty of mind over matter. "Whatever happens, all the wines of Château Lafite smell of almond and violet," according to an expert. But Lafite is so much more than fragrances: it is an artefact born from the inner depths of the earth and of the heart, a wine with mysterious connections, which, helped by our senses first, then by our emotions and thoughts, lead us into the oceanic sensation of our presence in the world.

1. Château Lafite-Rothschild. Records show the existence of the medieval seigneury of Lafite since the 14th century.

2. Inside the château.

3. The main gate.

Next pages: the Chai 2000, a gigantic round barrel cellar built in 1987 by the Catalan architect Ricardo Bofill.

Squab Breast with Cocoa Tuiles, *Cherries and Cocoa Barbajuans*

Yannick ALLÉNO

Le Meurice - Paris, France

SERVES 4

The barbajuan dough

1½ cups (200 g) flour

⅔ cup (15 cl) white wine

¼ cup (20 g) cocoa powder pinch of salt

The squab

4 squab, about 1⅛ pounds (500 g) each, untrussed, with their livers

1 red bell pepper

⅛ pound (50 g) foie gras terrine

⅛ pound (50 g) chicken livers

20 cherries, such as Bing

unsalted butter

2 tablespoons sherry vinegar

2 tablespoons maple syrup

1 lemon

1 head celery

The cocoa tuiles

2 cups plus 1 tablespoon (250 g) confectioners' sugar

⅔ cup (75 g) flour

1 tablespoon cocoa powder

¼ cup (5 cl) water

7 tablespoons (95 g) melted unsalted butter

4½ tablespoons (50 g) cocoa nibs (finely chopped cocoa beans)

For the barbajuan dough: Mix the flour, white wine, cocoa, and salt into a smooth dough and form into a ball. Wrap in plastic wrap and refrigerate for 4 hours.

For the squab: Cut off the thighs from the squab and set aside. Trim each of the breasts, still on the bone, into a "boat" shape.

Peel, seed and dice the bell pepper. Stew it slowly in a covered pan and then refrigerate.

For the cocoa tuiles: Mix the confectioners' sugar, flour and cocoa. Add the water and the melted butter and stir until smooth. On a parchment paper–lined baking sheet, drop the batter in very thin 4-inch (10-cm) disks. Sprinkle with the chopped cocoa beans and bake for 5 minutes in a 350°F (177°C) oven. Set aside 4 of the tuiles.

For the stuffing: Dice the meat from the squab legs. Dice the foie gras, and chop the chicken livers and squab livers. Mix the chopped livers, diced leg meat, diced foie gras and 1¼ ounces (50 g) of the diced bell pepper.

For the ravioli: Roll the barbajuan dough into 2 large sheets. Make ravioli using the dough and the stuffing made above, and set aside 16 ravioli.

For the garnish: Slit 16 of the cherries around the stone and remove the stone. Carve out the inside of the 4 remaining cherries.

Chop the cherry trimmings and the scooped out cherry flesh and stew them over low heat with a little butter, 1 tablespoon of sherry vinegar and 1 tablespoon of maple syrup.

Cut the lemon zest into a fine julienne and blanch it in boiling water.

Sauté the carved-out cherries in a little butter, and deglaze the pan with the remaining sherry vinegar and maple syrup, before adding a few drops of lemon juice. Fill each carved-out cherry with the cherry marmalade and add a bit of the julienne of lemon zest.

Peel and trim the celery with a potato peeler and cook in boiling water. Using a paring knife, trim the sticks into a thinner shape and cut 1³⁄₁₆-inch (3-cm) disks from them with a round cutter.

For the presentation: Roast the pigeon breasts for 5 minutes in an oven and let them rest for 5 minutes. Reheat the celery disks and the cherries. Fry the barbajuans in hot oil.

In the middle of each plate, place 4 celery disks in a line, add 4 stuffed cherries and dot each cherry with a barbajuan. Carve out the squab breast meat and arrange it on the plates, adding pieces of the cocoa tuiles.

CHÂTEAU LAFITE-ROTHSCHILD BY YOICHI SATO, BEST SOMMELIER OF JAPAN, 2005

The greatness of Lafite-Rothschild needs no introduction; its flawless potential, revealed with time, is well known. The 2000 vintage is remarkable in its intensity and magnificence. When tasting this wine I am deeply impressed by the château's unflagging pursuit of excellence.

CHÂTEAU LATOUR

PAUILLAC

VINEYARD SIZE	80 hectares
VINE DENSITY	9 900 stocks per hectare
SOILS AND SUBSOILS	The terroir of L'Enclos is composed of three main pedologic entities: clayey gravel, gravelly sand and marley clay
GRAPE VARIETIES	Cabernet Sauvignon 75 % Merlot 23 % Cabernet Franc 1 % Petit Verdot 1 %

As you enter the Pauillac appellation coming from the south, you cannot miss that round tower with a dome-shaped roof on the right (*tour* in French), but this one, a 17th-century dovecot, never had a military purpose. Of the original tower of Saint-Maubert that gave its name to the property and dominated the estuary during the Hundred Years War, nothing is left.

The history of wine at Latour began in 1718, when the Marquis Nicolas Alexandre de Ségur, notoriously known as "the wine prince," exploited the vineyard as one of his estates, which also included Lafite and Calon. When Thomas Jefferson discovered Latour in 1787, a barrel of its wine already cost 20 times the price of a run-of-the-mill Bordeaux, a success that was confirmed later by the 1855 Classification.

In 1963, the descendants of the Marquis de Ségur sold 75 percent of Latour's shares to two British companies. A second wine, Les Forts de Latour, was created alongside the First Growth. In 1964, one of the first stainless-steel vathouses in France was installed here (the first one having been built at Château Haut-Brion in 1961). In 1993, François Pinault acquired Château Latour. The third wine, audaciously christened "Pauillac," dates from this period.

All around the château lay the historical heart of the estate, L'Enclos, the 47 hectares producing the great wine. The whole vineyard covers 80 hectares, with a planting of 75 percent Cabernet Sauvignon, 23 percent Merlot, 1 percent Cabernet Franc and 1 percent Petit Verdot. In 2001, smaller vats replaced the 1964 stainless-steel vats in order to improve the plot selection. The First Classified Growth is aged for 18 months, in 100 percent new French oak barrels from 11 different cooperages. Only the two first wines benefit from the characteristic wrapping in white silk paper, while an authentication code engraved on the bottle is common to the three growths.

"The sense of beauty that reigns here is of a stark, almost Cistercian nature," explains Frédéric Engerer, manager of Château Latour. "Fifteen years ago, when I first arrived here, I tried to set the myth aside in order to understand exactly where in the world I was standing. Just try this: stand beside the tower and look all around. You will grasp a mysterious presence and realise that you are on a truly soulful and profound geographical spot. The vines give this place its tension, its purpose, its spine. And all is expressed in a strong, simple and stately way."

"François Pinault," Engerer adds, "likes to go straight to his goals, using time as a means of action and giving back every single thing he received. The wine is like him. When young, it sticks to an intense and austere expression, but it gives back a hundredfold if given some time to develop. It is a joyful, uncomplicated wine—a wine of flesh and generosity, which never lets you down. It endures and lasts; it is more Ingrid Bergman than Marilyn Monroe."

This artful merging of bare, raw earthiness and creative abstraction is the very power that underlies great wines. The great mural painted in the courtyard with Gironde mud expresses that idea very directly, as a tribute to the terroir, the region and, through that, the people of Médoc, "a people of hunter-gatherers, attached to their land," says Engerer admiringly. "They have managed to preserve their way of passing down their culture through generations. I feel tremendous respect for these families who took care of this terroir and developed it, from a modest amount of knowledge and technical means, to reach the extraordinary viticultural quality we now enjoy. Here, in Médoc, the soul is the essential factor. And why should it be otherwise? Growing vines here is like cultivating bonsai trees."

1. The round 17th-century dovecot marks the surroundings of Lafite.

2. A delicate white silk paper wrapping is the distinctive mark of Château Latour.

3. Château Latour's stainless steel vathouse.

Next pages: The vineyard of Latour looks at the Gironde from close by, as do many of the greatest Médoc classified growths.

Slow-roasted Spiced Shoulder of Lamb,
Paimpol Fresh White Haricot Beans

Éric BRIFFARD

Le Cinq - Paris, France

SERVES 4

The lamb shoulder

one 3⅛ to 3½-pound (1.4 to 1.6 kg)
Pauillac lamb shoulder

3½ tablespoons olive oil

½ cup (10 cl) lamb stock or water

The aromatics

3 large onions, diced

2 carrots, diced

1 celery stalk

1 bouquet garni (thyme, rosemary
and parsley stalks)

½ head garlic

sprig of fresh rosemary

The spice and herb mix

1 heaping tablespoon coriander seeds

1 level tablespoon cumin seeds

1 teaspoon Madras curry powder

1 level tablespoon fine salt

1 teaspoon black peppercorns

8 sprigs thyme

2 sprigs rosemary

2 chopped garlic cloves

The fresh Paimpol bean stew

⅓ pound (150 g) fresh seasonal
white haricot beans, shelled

1 carrot

½ onion, studded with 2 cloves

1 tomato

3 garlic cloves

1 small bouquet garni

2⅛ ounces (80 g) blanched smoked
bacon rind

savoury

4 tablespoons (50 g)
unsalted butter (½ stick)

coarse salt

fine salt

freshly ground black pepper

For the lamb shoulder: Ask your butcher to tuck back the meat on the bone and to saw the shoulder bone.

Using a sharp knife, cut off the silver skin, but keep the fat on the meat to keep it moist and fragrant during cooking. Set the trimmings aside. Season the shoulder with salt and pepper.

Preheat the oven to 165°F (75°C).

Heat the olive oil in a Dutch oven. Gently brown the shoulder in the oil for about 10 minutes on all sides. Add all the aromatics, stew for about 10 minutes, then add the spice and herb mix. Add the lamb stock or water. Cover the Dutch oven and bake for 12 to 15 hours (low-temperature cooking).

For the bean stew: Blanch the beans, cover them with cold water and bring to the boil. Drain and cool in cold water. Then put the beans in a Dutch oven with the carrot, the onion, the tomato, the garlic, the bouquet garni, the bacon rind and the savoury. Cover with cold water, add a moderate amount of salt and cook, covered, for about 30 minutes. Check for doneness by squeezing a bean between your index and thumb.

Discard the aromatics, and cut the carrot and bacon rind into small dice. Return them to the beans with the butter and a touch of chopped garlic. Simmer for 15 minutes, then taste and correct the seasoning.

For the presentation: When the meat is done, remove it from the cooking pot and place it on a serving dish with the aromatics. Set aside.

Shortly before serving, roast it for 15 minutes in a 425°F (220°C) oven or under the grill (broiler) until golden.

CHÂTEAU LATOUR BY ÉRIC BEAUMARD, SILVER MEDAL, BEST SOMMELIER OF THE WORLD, 1998

The terroir here is truly exceptional, and can be considered a "world heritage site" for Cabernet Sauvignon, producing one of the purest expressions of this varietal. On one visit to the château I viewed an excavation among the vines showing the soil profile of the "Clos," the heart of the Latour vineyard. In my mind's eye I can still see the pure blue clay, several metres deep, which was laced with a fine web of roots. Here the conditions are perfect for Cabernet Sauvignon to give birth to wines that have shown a rare consistency of quality over the years and an unequalled capacity for ageing.

CHÂTEAU MARGAUX

MARGAUX

SÙPERFICIE	82 hectares
DENSITÉ DE PLANTATION	10,000 stocks per hectare
ÂGE MOYEN DU VIGNOBLE	35 years
PRODUCTION MOYENNE	12 500 cases
SOLS ET SOUS-SOLS	80% Quaternary gravel and 20% clay-limestone
ENCÉPAGEMENT	Cabernet Sauvignon 75 % Merlot 20 % Cabernet Franc et Petit Verdot 5 %

What makes the greatness of a great wine? Keeping aside all hopes of explaining an ever-elusive enigma, it may be noted that First Great Classified Growths all share a common feature: each one sums up the characteristics of its appellation. Lafite, Latour and Mouton summon all of Pauillac into their typicity, Haut-Brion is the quintessence of Graves and Yquem the expressive synthesis of Sauternes. Greatness is manifested through classicism, and classicism is the coherent display of a style. Château Margaux, all charm and delicacy, all tannins singing in harmony, is the Margaux style itself.

"We are not the masters of these great wines", says Corinne Mentzelopoulos, owner of Château Margaux, voicing the spirit that runs through the whole estate. "We stand humble before them." All the people who work at Margaux have the same sparkle of serene admiration in their eyes. This is a *place*, in the strongest sense of the word; a place that exerts its charm onto anyone who lives there.

Château Margaux is a collection of exceptional circumstances layered together. There, in the 18th century, Mr. Berlon laid the bases of modern winemaking by starting the practice of plot-by-plot harvesting. In 1810, the estate, under the impulse of Marquis de La Colonilla, was constituted into a one-of-a-kind urban complex: a homogenous and socially autonomous winemaking village built around the Palladian-style château. A fully functional illustration of the utopian urbanist trend of the late 18th century, a genuine wine-dedicated phalanstery was then created: vathouse and cellars, artisans' courtyard, harvesters' hall, worker's houses—the perfectly organised compound is painted a beautiful ochre yellow, saturated in late afternoon by the slanting Médoc daylight. All around, the estate's 262 hectares are comprised of one-third vineyards, one-third meadows and gardens and one-third woods.

The château, Corinne recalls, is the crowning touch of the vineyard, born from it and conveying its image. The theatricality of the architecture is meant to honour and serve the terroir—a terroir in which her father, André Mentzelopoulos, then the owner of the Félix Potin grocery stores, had put all his faith when he purchased the estate in 1977. Château Margaux had just gone through some difficult years, and very few in Paris believed in his new endeavour. But Mr. Mentzelopoulos's visionary spirit was instrumental in resurrecting the estate, through ambitious replanting and the building (then quite innovative) of underground cellars in order to preserve the beauty of the Classified site. When the successful 1978 vintage came along, justifying his efforts, he felt comforted and the following years confirmed that rebirth.

The mythology of Château Margaux is among the richest in the world of wine. Better than a wine, it is a magic potion, as testify its enchanting sensuous, tender and elegant notes resting on a complex and refined framework. The actress Margaux Hemingway once confided to an interviewer that she got named after the bottle of Château Margaux her parents had drunk on the night she was conceived, thus opening the road to thousands of little Margaux girls the world over. This wine could have been Tristan and Iseult's favorite. In William Styron's *Sophie's Choice*, lovers pour it to celebrate their union, and in Junichi Watanabe's *Paradise Lost*, they share it to inscribe their love into eternity. All references to passion, pointing out to the profoundly erotic nature of this wine, which borders on the mystical dimension of love.

1. *The château's monumental facade, of a Palladian style rarely seen in France, is a grand ceremonial setting meant to serve the terroir and the vineyard.*

2. *The vineyard of Château Margaux covers one third of the 260-hectare estate.*

3. *The barrel cellar, supported by gigantic pillars, is built in the same neoclassic style as the château's.*

Next pages: meadows, vines, winemakers' village and, crowning it all, the château: the whole estate of Château Margaux is summed up in one picture.

Noisettes of Quercy Lamb Saddle, Black Truffle and Potato Gratin

Pierre CARRIER & Pierre MAILLET
Hameau Albert 1er - Chamonix-Mont-Blanc, France

SERVES 8

The lamb

2 Quercy lamb saddles

3 ounces (80 g) black truffle (3 to 4 truffles)

The gratin

2⅝ pounds (1.2 kg) agria potatoes (or any firm-fleshed potatoes)

2 medium onions

2⅛ cups (50 cl) chicken stock

1 cup (25 cl) lamb jus

salt and freshly ground black pepper

For the lamb: Cut out the filets from the lamb saddles and cut them into two to obtain 8 portions. Refrigerate.

Carve twenty-four ¼ x 1¼-inch (5-mm x 3-cm) sticks into the truffle, and chop the rest. Using a larding needle, insert 3 truffle sticks into each portion of lamb.

For the gratin: Peel the potatoes and soak them in cold water to prevent discolouring. Peel and finely slice the onions. Cut the potatoes into very thin slices using a food processor or a mandoline.

Butter a 6 x 12-inch (15 x 30-cm) ovenproof dish. Cover the bottom with a layer of potatoes, season with salt and pepper, then scatter some of the reserved chopped truffle over the surface and cover with a layer of onion. Add more salt and pepper. Repeat the layering three times, finishing with a layer of potatoes. Pour the stock over and bake in a 250°F (120°C) oven for 3 hours.

When cooked, remove the dish from the oven, cover the gratin with a wooden board and press down vigourously. Let cool. When cold, unmould the gratin and cut it into thirds crosswise then into eighths length-wise, making equal-size portions.

To cook the lamb: Lightly score the lamb noisettes on the fatty side, season them with salt and pepper and sear them in foamy butter, as slowly as possible, until the core temperature is 133°F (56°C). Meanwhile, fry the potato cubes in butter to brown them on all sides.

For the presentation: On each plate, place 1 lamb noisette and 3 cubes of truffled potato. Add the lamb jus with the remaining chopped truffle mixed in.

CHÂTEAU MARGAUX BY OLIVIER POUSSIER, BEST SOMMELIER OF THE WORLD, 2000

For more than 20 years, thanks to a team led by Paul Pontallier and the support of Corinne Mentzelopoulos, Château Margaux has produced a succession of exceptional wines of unequalled purity and refinement. The main wine is a privileged assemblage of Cabernet Sauvignon and Merlot, with a touch of Cabernet Franc and Petit Verdot. There is no limit to the superlatives that can be used to describe the level of quality attained by Château Margaux.

CHÂTEAU MOUTON ROTHSCHILD

PAUILLAC

VINEYARD SIZE	84 hectares
VINE DENSITY	8,500 stocks per hectare
AVERAGE AGE OF VINEYARD	50 years
AVERAGE PRODUCTION	160,000 bottles
SOILS AND SUBSOILS	80% gravel and 20% clay-limestone
GRAPE VARIETIES	Cabernet Sauvignon 83% Merlot 11% Cabernet Franc 5% Petit Verdot 1%

Great wines are always a lot more than the contents of their bottle, however wonderful these are. They are precious, multi-layered cultural artefacts that belong to a country's history in the same right as its finest monuments. They have the power of taking in their trail many other masterpieces of beauty and knowledge. Great historical wines have the quintessential power of gathering civilization around them, and Mouton Rothschild shows that power more than any other.

The mere mention of the wine irresistibly summons mental images—for instance the famous labels created each year, since the end of World War II, by a different artist; also the magnificent works—paintings, sculptures, glasswork, tapestry, jewellery—kept at the exceptional Museum of Wine in Art, whose collections were brought together by Baron Philippe de Rothschild and his family over the years. His daughter, Baroness Philippine, likes to insist on this particular artistic status of the château, which she nurtures and embellishes year after year.

"My father," she says, "took care of this beloved place of his for 70 years of his life, and I am pursuing his work. The soul of Mouton? I would describe it as based on two entities: first, a Great Classified Growth born from an exceptional terroir, and second, a place of art and beauty. We who are in charge of those great wine estates are not their masters. They do not belong to us. Born from the soil and from the work of men, they are entrusted to us by time and we nourish them as well as we can. A great wine is a universe in itself; each vintage is different from one year to another but also from one château to another. This is the great diversity of the Médoc. And Mouton's strong personality is a daily reminder of how lucky we are to live on such a wonderful terroir."

The story that unites Château Mouton Rothschild and Baron Philippe (1902–88) bears all the characteristics of a love story. He, indeed, struggled passionately to have his wine rightly promoted as First Growth instead of Second, as it was classified in 1855. In 1973, his efforts were rewarded, and the château's motto, *Premier ne suis, second ne daigne, Mouton suis* (First I am not, Second I will not, Mouton I am), was changed to *Premier je suis, second je fus, Mouton ne change* (First I am; Second I was; I, Mouton, do not change). The Baron also invested his passion into bringing innovative improvement to the world of wine, for instance, exclusive bottling at the château, instead of selling it in barrels. Designed by the cubist painter Jean Carlu, the Mouton Rothschild label of 1924 was the brilliant symbol of a practice that became a general rule and a guarantee of quality.

Château Mouton Rothschild is the property of Baroness Philippine de Rothschild and her children, and placed under the responsibility of Philippe Dhalluin and Hervé Berland, respectively technical and commercial manageing directors for the châteaux of the family-owned Baron Philippe de Rothschild SA Company. The 84 hectares of vineyards are planted with 83 percent Cabernet Sauvignon, 11 percent Merlot, 5 percent Cabernet Franc and 1 percent Petit Verdot. Cabernet Sauvignon dominates in the blending with a little more or less than 80 percent. The wine ferments in magnificent wooden vats and is aged in 100 percent new oak casks for 19 to 22 months.

As is usually the case with First Great Classified Growths, Château Mouton Rothschild is representative of its appellation to the point of being a synonym for it. Noble and flamboyant, it rests on the fertile duality of great Pauillac wines: a dense, deep framework supporting a luxuriant, smooth and delicate fruitiness with charming, singing tannins. This harmonious fusion of opposites evokes a philosophical, alchemical process—a secret of eternal youth.

1. During your visit, you will encounter this 18th-century Bacchus: at Mouton, art is around every corner.

2. Each year, a different artist gets to design the grand vin's label.

3. The vineyard of Mouton.

4. A statue of Bacchus closes the perspective of beautiful wooden vats set in a double line.

Next pages: the 100-metre-long barrel cellar of Mouton Rothschild.

Caramelised Quail,
Truffled Potato Purée

Joël ROBUCHON
La Table de Joël Robuchon - Paris, France

SERVES 4

The quail

2 quail, about ⅔ pound (300 g) each

a little peanut oil

2 teaspoons (20 g)
unsalted butter (¼ stick)

fresh sliced black truffle

arugula

vinaigrette

The syrupy sauce

1 tablespoon soy sauce

1 tablespoon acacia honey

1 garlic clove, chopped

1½ teaspoon olive oil

fleur de sel

freshly ground black pepper

The purée

⅔ pound (300 g) ratte potatoes,
unpeeled and thoroughly scrubbed

6 tablespoons (80 g)
unsalted butter (¾ stick)

1 cup (25 cl) warm milk

salt

Ask your butcher or poultry vendor to prepare the quail without trussing them.

For the syrupy sauce: Pour the soy sauce, honey, finely chopped garlic and olive oil in a deep dish. Whisk well until combined, then refrigerate.

For the purée: Put the unpeeled cleaned potatoes into a saucepan, cover with cold water, and add salt. Bring to the boil and cook for 30 minutes over medium heat. When the potatoes are cooked, peel them and pass them through a potato ricer, adding the fresh butter and the warm milk all the while. Season with salt to taste.

For the quail: Season the inside and outside of the quail with salt and pepper. In a sauté pan, heat the peanut oil and butter, add the quail and brown them on all sides. Set them aside to cool on a rack.

Discard the fat from the sauté pan and return the quail to the pan over very low heat. Baste them with the syrupy sauce for 4 to 5 minutes, until they are quite brown and crispy all over.

For the presentation: Carve the legs and the breasts with a sharp knife. Arrange them on the plates in a nice pattern. Add a quenelle of potato purée. Scatter sliced truffle over the plates and add some jus. Garnish with a few arugula leaves, seasoned with vinaigrette.

CHÂTEAU MOUTON ROTHSCHILD BY MARKUS DEL MONEGO, BEST SOMMELIER OF THE WORLD, 1998

Every drop of this wine reveals the enchantment felt by the young Philippe de Rothschild for that magical terroir that put him under its spell. His vision of what a great wine should be led him to develop such revolutionary ideas as bottling each vintage's entire harvest at the château. Philippe's daughter, Philippine, carries on his pursuit of quality as she watches over this exceptional patrimony. Today it is she who enchants us with these bottles, which continue to display the work of a great artist each year. This wine brings together qualities that seem, at first, to be contradictory: power and elegance, opulence and freshness, complexity and subtlety. This is the eternal wonder of Mouton Rothschild.

CHÂTEAU HAUT-BRION

PESSAC

VINEYARD SIZE	48.35 hectares
VINE DENSITY	10,000 stocks per hectare
AVERAGE AGE OF VINEYARD	36 years
AVERAGE PRODUCTION	12,000 cases
SOILS AND SUBSOILS	gravelly soil, clayey-gravelly subsoil
GRAPE VARIETIES	Merlot 45.4 % Cabernet Sauvignon 43.9 % Cabernet Franc 9.7 % Petit Verdot 1 %

"And here [I] drank a sort of French wine, called Ho Bryan, that hath a good and most particular taste that I never met with," wrote Samuel Pepys in his diary on April 10, 1663. But his noble king, Charles II, had not waited for him; he had already been treating his guests with generous torrents of *Hobriono* [sic] for a few years, as his cellar book from 1660 testifies. Both king and diarist had discovered the first Grand Bordeaux of history, or New French Claret as Londoners called it then. This new type of wine, bound to gradually replace the palus clarets that had been enjoyed by British wine drinkers, is the child of Arnaud III de Pontac, lord of Haut-Brion and the first great wine prince. In 1677, John Locke described Haut-Brion in these terms: "a little rise of ground, lying open, most to the west. It is nothing but pure white sand, mixed with a little gravel. One would imagine it scarce fit to bear anything. . . ." Nothing indeed, except for a certain fruit-bearing creeping plant that needs to send its roots as deep as possible into the soil in search of nutrients and cool humidity. The long suffering of the vine plant on gravelly soils has begun and modern viticulture is getting ready to spread out its wings.

Haut-Brion is the château of first times: first *grand cru*, first great wine to be exported under its own name, first graftings, first serious study of the soil characteristics in relation to the quality of wines and first appearance of the notion of the wine château. This pioneering spirit is still alive at Haut-Brion, from the sophisticated grape- cloning system and the careful attention devoted to barrel -making (a branch of the cooperage operates on the premises) to the painstaking maturity tests performed in the in-house laboratory. Without Haut-Brion, wine of Graves, the great Médoc wine saga from the 18th century to today would not have been the same. It was therefore only natural that the 1855 Classification awarded it the rank of First Growth. Thomas Jefferson had preceded

it in 1787, listing it with the other "first reds,"–Château de La Fite, Château Margaux, La Tour Ségur (Château Latour) and Haut-Brion–in the very order of their future ranking.

The feeling of deep respect that seizes every visitor to Château Haut-Brion is owed to the certainty of witnessing a living, sensitive tradition. One does not run a château or a terroir; one is run by it. HRH Prince Robert of Luxembourg shows this humble and dedicated approach through his management of the estate. This great-grandson of the famous New York financier Clarence Dillon, who bought the vineyard in 1935 and created the wine estates that bear his name, speaks about his wine in precise and earnest terms, expressing great fondness for this estate where he grew up. "Haut-Brion is a wine of secrecy," he says, "endowed with depth and elegance. Meditative and intellectual, it requires a little effort to be understood. Marketing that sort of wine is no easy task. As a matter of fact, it does not fare extremely well in massive tastings, unless you offer some time to ponder over it. Haut-Brion never does it the easy way, it always seeks profundity."

Complex and delicate, Haut-Brion is perfectly adapted to the table. Prince Robert points out that the art of good eating has always been taken very seriously at Château Haut-Brion, as is the art of pairing wine with great food. He recalls that the Prince de Talleyrand-Périgord was the owner in the early 19th century. And as he says that, he takes you through the château kitchen, where a superb loin of farm-raised Bigorre pork is being trussed. The words "living, sensible, tradition" come to mind.

1. This is the château where stainless-steel vats were first used, in 1961. Those seen here were installed in 1991 and designed by Jean Delmas.

2. Inside the château Haut-Brion.

3. In the barrel cellar, solid wood beams are supported by stone columns.

Next pages: At Haut-Brion, the notion of wine château appeared for the first time in history. The château cherishes the memory of its pioneer, Arnaud III de Pontac, the very first "prince of Wine."

Challans Duck
with Hibiscus and Orange Marc

Alain PASSARD
L'Arpège - Paris, France

SERVES 6

The duck

6 small duck magrets

The sauce

⅓ cup (60 g) sugar

2⅛ ounces (60 g) dried hibiscus flowers

3⅓ cups (80 cl) warm water

2 whole cloves

pinch of nutmeg, pinch of cinnamon,
pinch of star anise, all powdered

7 tablespoons (100 g) salted butter

2 tablespoons balsamic vinegar

3 tablespoons soy sauce

The garnish

2 organic oranges

1 glass freshly squeezed orange juice

½ cup (10 cl) extra virgin olive oil

fleur de sel

12 small young red beets,
cooked with their skins on

melted salted butter

For the duck: Slit the skin of the magrets in a crisscross pattern to help them melt during cooking and become crisp.

Broil the magrets, keeping them rare. Let them rest between 2 warmed plates for a few minutes to render blood, which you should set aside for binding the sauce.

For the sauce: Blend 3 tablespoons (40 g) sugar with ⅓ ounce (10 g) hibiscus flowers, then pass through a *tamis* (fine-mesh sieve). Set aside the hibiscus sugar.

Meanwhile, in a large saucepan, steep the remaining hibiscus in hot water with the spices and the remaining sugar for about 30 minutes. Pour through a cloth-lined sieve and reduce by half. Whisk in the butter to mount the sauce, then add the soy sauce and balsamic vinegar. Finally, bind the sauce with the reserved duck blood.

For the orange marc: Cut the oranges into pieces, leaving the peel on, and blend them into a fine purée with the orange juice. Pour this into a saucepan, add the olive oil and cook over low heat for about 10 minutes. Season with some fleur de sel.

To caramelise the magrets: Sprinkle the magrets lightly with the hibiscus sugar and place them under the grill (broiler) until the sugar is melted and golden. Season with fleur de sel.

For the presentation: Pour the hibiscus sauce onto the plates. Add the caramelised magrets, a quenelle of orange marc and a few cooked beets, brushed with melted salted butter.

CHÂTEAU HAUT-BRION BY MARKUS DEL MONEGO,
BEST SOMMELIER OF THE WORLD, 1998

This prestigious growth, situated on a unique terroir within the city, has been an innovator since its inception, and permanent research is fundamental here. An impressive property, it has given major impetus to the world of wine through the commercialisation of its wine by name since 1660, vinification in stainless-steel tanks since the 1960s, and the clonal selection of its vines today. This innovative genius has produced a wine for long keeping, with abundantly fine and complex aromas, and a powerful body that is elegant and fresh.

CHÂTEAU RAUZAN-SÉGLA

VINEYARD SIZE	62 hectares
VINE DENSITY	10,000 stocks per hectare
AVERAGE AGE OF VINEYARD	35 years
AVERAGE PRODUCTION	120,000 bottles
SOILS AND SUBSOILS	fine, deep gravel
GRAPE VARIETIES	Cabernet Sauvignon 55 % Merlot 40 % Petit Verdot 4 % Cabernet Franc 1 %

The Château Rauzan-Ségla now appears in a renewed state of youth, adorned with climbing rose bushes and stately old trees. It is indeed one of the oldest wine châteaux in the Médoc: in 1661, Pierre de Rauzan, a famous Bordeaux trader and member of the Parliament, took Château Margaux and Château Latour in tenant farming. He decided to build his own house on this estate, in the rustic style of Périgord mansions. During the two following centuries, the wines of Rauzan acquired an excellent reputation which reached its peak at the end of the 18th century; Thomas Jefferson was not the least of its lovers. That did not prevent the estate from being divided into three in 1763; one third became Rauzan-Gassies while the two remaining parts, which include the château, remained Rauzan-Ségla.

In 1903, when the owner Frédéric Cruse decided to rebuild the château, he hired the architect Louis Garros, who worked from the existing style. A few remaining parts of the building were incorporated into the whole. Rauzan-Ségla should be admired at sunset, when the light strikes the smooth blond stone walls almost horizontally, giving it a golden shine and lighting up the well-trimmed lawns like velvet. It is no mystery that the Maison de Chanel, owned by the Wertheimer family, as soon as it acquired the château in 1994, wished to restore its original grace. The renovation was done following the 1904 building plan, and the result shows a tasteful harmony. American interior designer Peter Marino created a decor where all the objects, pieces of furniture and fabrics look like they were picked at different times through the decades, brought back from a trip or cherished like an old souvenir. Nothing is original—even the antique floorboards were imported—but everything has a look of domestic familiarity, and sometimes of refined wear.

John Kolasa manages this lovely estate with a precise hand. As he lifts a heavy load with two fingers, he explains that drinking red wine on a regular basis makes him strong. Not many Scotsmen can boast French spoken with such a perfect Médoc accent—a gift from local gravel and vineyards, and an illustration of the uncommon rooting power of the Bordeaux land, which proves as good for men as for the vine.

In 1971, soon after he arrived in Bordeaux, John was trained in all wine-related activities by Mrs. Janoueix, a wine trader from the nearby Corrèze region. From 1987 to 1994, he worked at Château Latour as commercial manager. He began to oversee the Rauzan-Ségla vineyard soon after Chanel acquired the place. "My first serious vintage," he says, "was 1995. When I arrived, I found the vine rows set wide apart for machines to run through—I gained one whole hectare by remodelling the vineyard. Dampness in the ground was ruining much of the wine's personality, so I drained the soils, which caused the vines to plunge their roots deeper into the gravel." John treats the vineyard with integrated pest control, does not weed the rows and ploughs them deeply. "Chanel likes to preserve traditional skills," he explains.

The fine, deep gravel terroir of Rauzan-Ségla is planted with 55 percent Cabernet Sauvignon, 40 percent Merlot, about 4 percent Petit Verdot and a touch of Cabernet Franc. The ageing in barrels is carried on for 18 to 20 months. "Petit Verdot," says John, "gives texture, density, complexity and a touch of velvet to the wine." Throughout the vintages, John maintains the deep, mysterious sensuality and notes of violet that characterise this wonderful Margaux.

1. In the Margaux daylight, the château Rauzan-Ségla watches over its vineyard.

2. The barrel cellar of Rauzan-Ségla.

3. Racking is a gentle technique for wine clarification. The clarity of the wine is checked through the glass by candlelight.

Lamb Ballotines
in Goat Milk, Straw and Hay

Heinz BECK
La Pergola - Rome, Italy

SERVES 4

The goat milk (prepare 1 day ahead)
2⅛ cups (50 cl) fresh goat milk
⅓ pound (150 g) hay
thyme
basil
rosemary
1 teaspoon (⅛ ounce) (5 g) powdered red seaweed

The vegetables
12 artichokes
extra virgin olive oil
juice of 1 lemon
a little dry white wine
½ cup (10 cl) vegetable stock
10 tomatoes
peeled and chopped garlic
thyme
basil
rosemary

The ballottines:
1⅜ pounds (650 g) lamb leg meat
1 scant cup (20 cl) lamb stock
a few spinach leaves for serving
salt and freshly ground black pepper

For the goat milk: Steep the hay and the herbs in the goat milk for at least 24 hours.

For the vegetables: Trim 9 artichokes, removing the outer leaves and the choke. Quarter them and season them with olive oil, salt, and lemon juice. Put 6 of them into a sous-vide bag, seal the bag and cook for 30 minutes at 195°F (90°C). Blend into a smooth purée.

Sear the 3 remaining artichokes in olive oil. When they are slightly coloured, add salt, a little white wine and the vegetable stock. Continue cooking until they are tender. Let cool.

Boil the tomatoes for a few seconds, quarter them and peel them. Remove the seeds. Arrange them on a baking sheet and season with olive oil, thyme, basil and rosemary. Bake in a 180°F (90°C) oven for 4 hours.

Trim the 3 remaining artichokes. Finely dice their hearts. Fry them in 320°F (160°C) oil until crispy. Remove them with a finely slotted spoon and drain them on paper towels.

For the ballottines: Bone the lamb and butterfly it. Cut it into ⅓-pound (150-g) pieces. Place each piece between plastic wrap and beat it with a mallet until ¼ inch (5 mm) thick. Season lightly with salt and pepper.

In the middle of each lamb slice, arrange some artichoke purée, diced artichoke hearts, and slow-roasted tomatoes (keep a few for garnishing).

Fold each lamb slice into a small parcel (ballottine). Insert the ballottines into a sous-vide bag, adding olive oil and seasonings. Seal the bag. Plunge it for 10 seconds in boiling water, then cook for 5 hours in 285°F (140°C) water Remove from the bag and glaze them with the lamb stock.

For the presentation: Place the ballottines, the remaining tomatoes and some spinach leaves in a deep dish. Sprinkle with remaining fried artichoke hearts. Strain the goat milk, bring it to a simmer and pour it onto the dish. Wait for the milk to set before serving.

CHÂTEAU RAUZAN-SÉGLA BY MARKUS DEL MONEGO, BEST SOMMELIER OF THE WORLD, 1998

Since its acquisition by the Chanel group, we have witnessed the rebirth of a great growth! This property, Margaux's "sleeping beauty," has been awakened by a very talented team who know how to bring out the terroir's potential. Judicious vineyard management, meticulous selection during harvest and rigourous assemblages produce a wine with a delicate bouquet and unique taste, beautiful aromatic concentration and great finesse.

CHÂTEAU RAUZAN-GASSIES

MARGAUX

VINEYARD SIZE	30 hectares
VINE DENSITY	1,000 stocks per hectare
AVERAGE AGE OF VINEYARD	40 years
AVERAGE PRODUCTION	15,000 cases
SOILS AND SUBSOILS	fine, deep Günzian gravel
GRAPE VARIETIES	Cabernet Sauvignon 54% Merlot 40% Petit Verdot 5% Cabernet Franc 1%

If the history of Château Rauzan-Gassies began in 1766, its wine has a longer history. At the end of the 17th century, the famous Margaux wine estate of Pierre de Rauzan, a member of the Bordeaux Parliament, had already been separated from the vineyards of Desmirail and Marquis de Terme. This time, through marriage, two-thirds of his property went to the Barons de Ségla while the remaining third kept the name Rauzan-Gassies. The master of Rauzan left his heraldic mark on the stylish bottle label: two spread wings on top of cascading grapes. Mr. de Rauzan could be proud of his wine production, which he sold personally in London, and which was classified as Second Growth in 1855.

When Paul Quié—a Bordeaux trader who settled in the Paris wine market of Bercy—bought Château Rauzan-Gassies in 1946, the decision was in line with a coherent program of vineyard purchase: this passionate winemaker wished to have every type of local terroir at his disposal. Thus, he also acquired Château Croizet-Bages in Pauillac and Bel-Orme-Tronquoy-de-Lalande in Saint-Seurin-de-Cadourne. But the very diversity of soils that can be found at Rauzan-Gassies could have sufficed to make him happy, for the 30 hectares that compose the vineyard are scattered on the communal lands of Margaux and Cantenac, giving Château Rauzan-Gassies a wide range of terroir types that are translated in the wine into a remarkable complexity. The blending is also nuanced: 54 percent Cabernet Sauvignon and 40 percent Merlot, with Petit Verdot and Cabernet Franc making up remaining 10 percent in equal parts. A careful work on the plot selection and on the planting is the necessary consequence of such diversity. Since 2001, Mr. Quié has given the reins of the vineyard to his children, Anne-Françoise and Jean-Philippe.

In the Quié family, where all decisions are made in a collegial manner, a straightforward approach is appreciated. The cellars and vathouse have been renovated in a modern, streamlined style. A few bronze sculptures, including a life-size horse (the Quiés love horses), adorn the welcoming courtyard. What the Quiés search for above all is the finesse of great Margaux wines; hence the delicacy of Château Rauzan-Gassies's structure, the firm confidence of its robust tannins awaiting their maturity. Upright and distinguished, these wines show a serene self-respect that inspires respect and wonder. "We strive to develop a pure fruitiness, a soft, never dry expression of wood and a gentle aromatic persistency."

Anne-Françoise Quié insists on the importance of viticultural transmission. Here, winemaking leans on the skills of the maîtres de chai of past generations, whose precious insight has been confirmed by time. On the shelves in the tasting room, antique log books and vineyard registers show physical evidence of that respect. Their faded colours—the dark red of wine, the light viridian of Bordeaux mixture—are in harmony with their theme, while their pages display pen-scribbled notes where practicality mingles with poetry: plot names (Jarre-Maca, Mayne de Jeannet, Derrière-Moneyres, Devant-Beaucourt), grafts, work in the vineyard, weather details. Such books are probably kept at most châteaux, but it is no accident that, at Rauzan-Gassies, they are exposed to every visitor's view.

1. The memory of the estate is written in these antique vineyard registers kept in the tasting room.

2. The origin of Château Rauzan-Gassies is related to Pierre de Rauzan, a member of the Bordeaux Parliament, who gave it his name.

3. Bringing out the best in the terroir: the fine, deep Margaux gravel soils give the wine of Rauzan-Gassies its elegance and aromatic density.

Squab with Hijiki Seaweed Sauce, *Matsutake Mushrooms and Fennel Seed*

Charlie TROTTER
Charlie Trotter's - Chicago, United States

SERVES 4

The roasted mushrooms

2½ cups (250 g) matsutake mushrooms, cleaned and stems removed

2 sprigs thyme or rosemary

½ cup (50 g) chopped Spanish onion

1 tablespoon olive oil

⅓ cup (8 cl) water

salt and freshly ground black pepper

The seaweed sauce

1 cup (30 g) dried hijiki seaweed, soaked in water overnight

1⅔ (40 cl) cups reduced meat stock

1 tablespoon sesame oil

1 tablespoon mirin

2 teaspoons tamari sauce

The mushrooms and turnips

1 cup (150 g) thinly sliced matsutake mushrooms

2 tablespoons (28 g) unsalted butter

½ cup (10 cl) water

8 baby turnips, peeled and tops trimmed

The squab

2 squabs, trussed

2 tablespoons grape seed oil

2 tablespoons fennel seeds

1 teaspoon fresh thyme leaves

salt and freshly ground black pepper

For the roasted mushrooms: Preheat the oven to 325°F (165°C). Place the mushrooms, herb sprigs, onion, olive oil and water in a roasting pan and season with salt and pepper. Cover with a piece of aluminum foil and roast for 30 to 40 minutes. Let cool in the juices.

Combine the roasted mushrooms with the water and any juices that remain in the roasting pan and purée until smooth. Season to taste with salt and pepper.

For the seaweed sauce: Drain the hijiki, measure out ½ cup and set aside. Purée the remaining hijiki with the meat stock reduction, sesame oil, mirin and tamari. Pass through a fine-mesh sieve. Set aside.

For the mushrooms and turnips: Sauté the sliced mushrooms in 1 tablespoon of the butter in a sauté pan over medium heat for 2 minutes, or until tender. Season to taste with salt and pepper.

Place the turnips in a sauté pan with 1 tablespoon of the butter and cook over medium heat for 10 minutes, or until caramelised. Season to taste with salt and pepper. Set aside.

For the squab: Preheat the oven to 400°F (200°C). Season the squab with salt and

pepper. Sear the squab with the grape seed oil in a hot sauté pan over medium-high heat for 2 minutes on each side, or until golden brown. Sprinkle with the fennel seeds and roast for 10 minutes, or until cooked to medium. Remove from the oven and let rest for 3 minutes.

For the presentation: Just prior to serving, warm the roasted mushroom purée in a small saucepan. In another small saucepan warm the seaweed sauce.

Remove the breasts from the bone and cut each breast in half. Season to taste with salt and pepper. (Reserve the remaining parts of the squab for another use.)

Spoon the matsutake mushroom purée in a large triangle in the centre of each plate. Spoon the seaweed sauce in a large triangle just overlapping the mushroom purée. Arrange the mushroom slices over the sauces, and place 2 pieces of squab breast in the centre of the plate. Sprinkle the reserved hijiki seaweed and thyme leaves around the plate, and finish with freshly ground black pepper.

CHÂTEAU RAUZAN-GASSIES BY YOICHI SATO, BEST SOMMELIER OF JAPAN, 2005

This wine has a unique character, expressed by the slight astringency it often shows on the palate. At the moment it can be difficult to find wines that develop a certain flowing character with age; however, this one—alone among Margaux wines—shows well among those heartier types. With its very ripe tannins, this wine would be even better if we could get it in magnum.

CHÂTEAU LÉOVILLE-POYFERRÉ

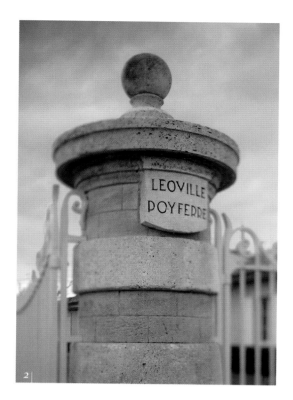

VINEYARD SIZE	80.3 hectares
VINE DENSITY	8,500 stocks per hectare
AVERAGE AGE OF VINEYARD	30 years
AVERAGE PRODUCTION	18,000 cases
SOILS AND SUBSOILS	Garonne gravel on Mindelian I and II gravels
GRAPE VARIETIES	Cabernet Sauvignon 64 % Merlot 26 % Petit Verdot 8 % Cabernet Franc 2 %

Between 1638 and the end of the 18th century, the three Léoville estates—Poyferré, Las Cases and Barton—were one large property called Mont-Moytié. The place had been named after its founder, Jean de Moytié, a wine trader and a member of the Bordeaux Parliament whose wine was one of history's first Grands Crus de Médoc. In 1740, Mont-Moytié was acquired through marriage by Alexandre de Gasq, who renamed it Léoville (or Lionville) after his first estate on the right bank of the Gironde.

Starting from 1775, on a still homogenous Léoville, the heirs of Alexandre de Gasq were selling their wines under four distinct names: d'Abadie, Chevalier, Lascaze and Monbalon. After the French Revolution, the property status of the land had become notably more complex than before. In 1840, the vineyards of the former Mont-Moytié were divided between the heirs. One of the daughters yielded her rights to her own daughter, who had married the Baron Jean-Marie de Poyferré de Cerès, born of a noble Armagnac family. He had, some time before, absorbed the name Léoville d'Abadie into his own wine production. Thus was born the Léoville-Poyferré wine estate, whose château remains divided between two properties, a chimney shaft marking the boundary in the courtyard.

In 1865, after fighting a fierce war against powdery mildew and going through several difficult vintages, Baron de Poyferré sold the estate to the Lalande et Erlanger, a family of bankers and wine traders. They were followed by the Lawtons, who kept the estate until 1920, when it was acquired by the Cuveliers, a family of wine traders from the northern French city of Haubourdin. Today, the Cuveliers still own the Château Léoville-Poyferré, with Didier Cuvelier at the helm since 1979. "All the different Saint-Julien types of soils may be found here," says Cuvelier. "Hence the beautiful balance, power and tenderness in the wine, and its consistent elegance even through the hotter, reputedly atypical vintages such as the

astonishingly fresh-tasting 2003. Our vineyard covers 80 hectares of Garonne gravel, planted with 64 percent Cabernet Sauvignon, 26 percent Merlot, 8 percent Petit Verdot and 2 percent Cabernet Franc." Château Léoville-Poyferré is aged from 18 to 20 months in 75 percent new French oak barrels.

"In 1979, when I arrived here," Cuvelier adds, "there were 32 hectares of wasteland. Since then, I have spent my time improving the facilities and the vineyard." Cuvelier devotes his attentive care to all his wines, both the Great Classified Growth and the second wine, Moulin Riche, as well as Pavillon de Poyferré, which he describes not as the third wine but as "a second wine to the two others."

Didier Cuvelier is a remarkable advocate of the excellence and unique character of Médoc wines. As a joint effect of passion and knowledge, he makes the peculiar geography of the region sound very simple when he speaks about it. His arguments for the enduring pertinence of the 1855 Classification are just as clear and convincing: "A few years ago, when all the Médoc Great Classified Growths were gathered for a blind tasting, the classification was identically reproduced, except for one detail—one Fifth Growth had risen up into the top fifteen." To further the demonstration, he summons climatology and pedology: "During the great cold wave in the winter of 1985, the only vineyards whose feet never froze were those of the Great Classified Growths. And if the Gironde's waters rose by 30 feet, they would be the only ones to emerge."

1. In every detail, the stainless steel vathouse at Château Léoville Poyferré shows the attention that the owner, Didier Cuvelier, devotes to technical facilities.

2. Léoville-Poyferré is one of the estates that were created from the division of the former Léoville, also known as Mont-Moytié.

3. The cellars of Léoville-Poyferré.

4. On the white walls of the tasting room, handwritten notes are left by visitors.

Fricassée of Bresse Chicken
with Morels

Paul BOCUSE

L'Auberge du Pont de Collonges - Collonges-au-Mont-d'Or, France

SERVES 4

The mushrooms

1 ounce (30 g) dried morel mushrooms

½ cup (10 cl) Madeira

2½ chicken stock cubes

The chicken

one 4-pound (1,8 kg) Bresse chicken, cut into 8 pieces

¼ pound (100 g) fresh mushrooms

6 small shallots

3 sprigs tarragon

½ cup (10 cl) Noilly-Prat

2 cups (50 cl) dry white wine

1½ tablespoons (20 g) softened butter

2½ tablespoons (20 g) flour

2 cups (50 cl) crème fraîche

For the mushrooms: Cover the morels with warm water in a bowl and let them soak for 30 minutes. Drain and halve each morel length-wise. Pour the Madeira in a saucepan and boil it down entirely. Add the morels and ½ cube of chicken stock. Cover with water and cook for 40 minutes, uncovered, over medium heat.

For the chicken: The chicken cut into 8 pieces comprises 4 pieces of breast meat and 4 pieces of dark meat (leg and thigh). Salt the chicken on the flesh side.

Trim the mushroom stalks, rinse and pat dry the mushrooms and finely slice them. Rinse tarragon, pat dry. In a Dutch oven, pour 1 cup (25 cl) water, the Noilly and the white wine. Add the tarragon, shallots, mushrooms and 2 remaining stock cubes. Bring to a fast boil, add the chicken and cook for 12 minutes, uncovered.

After 12 minutes, remove the white meat and let the dark meat cook for 13 more minutes.

Knead the butter with a spatula, add the flour and mix well (what you obtain is a beurre manié). Remove the last pieces of chicken from the Dutch oven. Discard the tarragon. Boil down the cooking stock entirely, then add the beurre manié and the crème fraîche and cook for 5 minutes, stirring.

Put the chicken back into the Dutch oven. Roll the chicken pieces in the sauce to coat, and let them reheat. Drain the morels and add them into the Dutch oven with a little chopped fresh tarragon leaves.

For the presentation: Divide among warm plates and serve immediately.

Château Léoville-Poyferré by Olivier Poussier, Best Sommelier of the World, 2000

Owned by the Cuvelier family for almost a century, Château Léoville-Poyferré has achieved ever-greater success since the 1990s. With convincing results drawn from a terroir worthy of its Second-Growth status, this property has rejoined the ranks of Saint-Julien's greatest wines.

CHÂTEAU LÉOVILLE BARTON

SAINT-JULIEN

VINEYARD SIZE	50 hectares
VINE DENSITY	9,000 stocks per hectare
AVERAGE AGE OF VINEYARD	32 years
AVERAGE PRODUCTION	22,000 cases
SOILS AND SUBSOILS	gravelly soils on a clayey subsoil
GRAPE VARIETIES	Cabernet Sauvignon 73% Merlot 23% Cabernet Franc 4%

In 1722, a 27-year-old Irishman from County Fermanagh disembarks at Bordeaux. His name is Thomas Barton, but he soon will be nicknamed "French Tom" as a consequence of the successful business he will lead on the Continent. By 1725, he is already at the head of a trading house, but his one son, William, prefers to dwell on the Irish family estate. When his father dies, in 1780, William inherits the trading house and the Irish property, as well as £60,000 to share between his six sons. Only the fourth, Hugh, will choose to be involved in the family business, his five brothers pursuing other interests. During the French Revolution, though, William finds it wiser to spend most of his time in Ireland, giving the storm a chance to settle.

When William dies in 1793, he leaves the entire management of the family's interests to Hugh. Hugh runs the business from a relative distance. In 1821, he finds himself fortunate enough to purchase a wine estate. First he acquires Langoa, in Saint-Julien-Beychevelle, and a few years later, in 1826, increases his properties by buying one quarter of the vast Léoville estate, confiscated by the state during the French Revolution. In Ireland, he also builds the manor of Straffan House, which will become the family home.

The Bartons, already mentioned as owners by the 1855 Classification, still own the two estates of Léoville Barton and Langoa Barton, a remarkable case of successful heritage transmission for two full centuries. After Hugh, three generations followed at the head of the vineyards, but Ronald Barton (1902–86) was the most dedicated of all to the family's French affairs. Since Hugh, he was the first Barton to take thorough care of the estate and also the first one since "French Tom" to spend most of his time in France. In 1983, he passed the properties to his nephew Anthony, who runs them today, with the help of his daughter, Lilian. Born in County Kildare in 1930 and arriving in Bordeaux in 1951, Anthony started his career in the family's wine trading house, but he soon preferred to settle on the vineyard. "I always was a country chap," he says, "and in the country I meant to stay."

The vineyard of Léoville Barton, north of the Saint-Julien appellation, covers 50 hectares of gravel on a clayey subsoil, with a planting of 73 percent Cabernet Sauvignon, 23 percent Merlot and 4 percent Cabernet Franc. Much of it consists of aged vines, to which a special team of winemakers is dedicated.

Château Léoville Barton is a dense, complex, tense wine, built on an admirable framework. Classic and timeless, it merges the masculinity of Pauillacs with the fruitiness of Saint-Juliens. "The simpler the cooking," Anthony confides, "the better it suits great wines." He goes on to enumerate the pairings that he finds most appropriate—traditional cuisines, simmered dishes, red meats grilled on dried vine shoots or roast fowl like duck or squab—classic associations for a wine whose strong and rich texture evokes cooked black fruit, cocoa, forest floor and precious leather.

1. Here and there, a few stone lions recall the origine of the name Léoville Barton. The ancient domaine of Léoville was also known as Lionville.

2. In the vineyard, a generous proportion of aged vines plays a substantial part in the wine's exceptional depth and personality.

3, 4. The cellars and vathouse of château Léoville Barton.

Spice-glazed Mallard Duck, Red Cabbage with Figs

Marc HAEBERLIN
L'Auberge de l'Ill - Illhaeusern, France

SERVES 4

The red cabbage and figs

1¾-pound (800 g) red cabbage

pinch of sugar

3 tablespoons red wine vinegar

½ pound (200 g) onions

8 dried figs

½ cup (10 cl) olive oil

1 cup (25 cl) red wine

½ cup (10 cl) Port

3 slices fresh ginger

salt

The duck

½ cup (30 g) Sichuan peppercorns

⅓ cup plus 1 tablespoon (30 g) coriander seeds

1 tablespoon (10 g) cumin seeds

4 green cardamom pods

2 mallard ducks, plucked, gutted, and trussed

7 tablespoons (150 g) acacia honey

1 tablespoon soy sauce

2 tablespoon dry sherry

2 garlic cloves

salt

For the red cabbage: The day before: Cut the cabbage into quarters and remove the stem. Finely mince the cabbage, add the sugar, vinegar and some salt. Mix well and macerate overnight.

The next day: Preheat the oven to 300°F (150°C). Peel and finely slice the onions. Finely dice the figs. Heat the oil in a Dutch oven, brown the onions in it, add the macerated cabbage and the figs. Add the red wine and Port, then the ginger. Cover, place the Dutch oven in the oven and bake for 1½ hours until the cabbage is very tender.

For the duck: Using a small food processor or a coffee grinder, reduce the Sichuan pepper, coriander, cumin and cardamom to a fine powder. Mix this powder into the honey, soy sauce and sherry. Add the whole peeled garlic cloves.

Preheat the oven to 410°F (210°C). Season the ducks with salt and pepper inside and outside. Set aside 2 tablespoonfuls of the spiced honey mixture, then brush the ducks with the remaining mixture. Place the ducks into an ovenproof dish, put them into the oven and roast for 20 minutes. Remove them from the oven and let them rest for 15 minutes.

Brush the ducks with the reserved 2 tablespoons of spiced honey glaze, return them to the oven and roast for 10 more minutes.

For the presentation: Before serving, mix the cabbage and figs, and taste and correct the seasoning. Serve the carved ducks on a serving dish, presenting the carved breasts in a fan shape. Serve the cabbage and figs on the side.

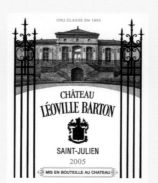

CHÂTEAU LÉOVILLE BARTON BY SERGE DUBS,
BEST SOMMELIER OF THE WORLD, 1989

This château helped establish Bordeaux's reputation for greatness and has continued to uphold it over the centuries. Here, an ideal gravel terroir extends across a superbly situated outcrop, giving birth to wine of great character and personality. Its tannins lightly caress the palate, evoking such descriptions as fine, well bred, chewy, flavourful, ample and rich. The bouquet is spontaneously expressive, with aromatic nuances of black truffle, black-leaf tobacco and pepper, which emphasise the complexity and richness of an exceptional terroir. This wine offers great sensual pleasure, the stuff that dreams are made of.

CHÂTEAU DURFORT-VIVENS

MARGAUX

VINEYARD SIZE	60 hectares
VINE DENSITY	7,000–8,000 stocks per hectare
AVERAGE AGE OF VINEYARD	25 years
AVERAGE PRODUCTION	150,000 bottles
SOILS AND SUBSOILS	Quaternary Garonne gravel on a sandy-clayey matrix
GRAPE VARIETIES	Cabernet Sauvignon 76% Merlot 20% Cabernet Franc 4%

The Château Durfort-Vivens is easily located as you enter Margaux from the South. In the 15th century, it belonged to the powerful Durfort de Duras family, who also owned the "noble hill of Margaux", now Château Margaux. Two centuries later, the land was a property of the Chevalier de Lascombes, whose family sold it later to the Monbrison and Vivens families. In 1785, when Thomas Jefferson wrote his own classification of Bordeaux wines, he placed Durfort right after Lafite, Latour and Margaux, next to "Rozan" and Léoville–a choice that would to be confirmed by the 1855 Classification. Meanwhile, in 1824, the Vicomte de Vivens became sole master of the estate and gave his name to the château.

In the late 1930s, the Ginestet family added Durfort-Vivens to their own properties, which already included the Château Margaux. The main shareholder, a Mr. Léonce Récapet, was the grandfather of Lucien Lurton, himself the creator of a famous dynasty of Bordeaux winemakers and notably the father of Gonzague Lurton, owner of Château Durfort-Vivens since 1992.

The "Lurton touch"–based on painstaking care in winemaking, a strong sense of finesse and personal style and a dedication to excellence–may be found wherever a member of this family is at the helm. As early as 2001, Gonzague, in addition to the existing wooden vats, installed stainless-steel vats of various capacities in order to refine the plot selection. Fermentation is carried by microplots: all the distinct pedologic entities are processed individually and put in barrels in separate lots.

The estate covers 60 hectares of Günzian and Mindelian gravels planted with 76 percent Cabernet Sauvignon, 20 percent Merlot and 4 percent Cabernet Franc. "Initially," says Gonzague, "we believed we were standing on a homogeneous terroir, but we still could not figure out why, within a short distance on the same type of soil, we could record a differ-

ence of several days in optimal maturity. So we drilled throughout the vineyard and found out that the subsoil was far more diversified than we thought. Gravel dominated in most of the samples, but their matrix varied from sand to clay.

"Good wine is first and foremost made in the vineyard. As the harvesting time grows near, we rely solely on tasting the grapes to decide on the harvest date. The alcoholic fermentation and the extractions are modulated differently for each vat according to the quality and style of the grapes. And once the wine is in barrels, it never moves. We have two cellars, one for even years and one for odd years, so that the wines remain undisturbed during the ageing. We rack from barrel to barrel without any mechanical treatment or brutal oxidation of the wines. The barrel cellars are insulated and inert, which allows natural temperature and hygrometry control through ventilation. We use air from the outside as well as spraying through an automated system connected to probes. The ageing varies; we have no readymade rules–there again we rely on tasting. In 2003, we aged the wine for 14 months, and in 2005, for 22 months. We work surgically, on small details and tiny variations, as precisely as possible, hoping to respect the identity of our terroir and of our wines. The cutting-edge technology that we use remains at the service of tradition and authenticity."

In practice, all of this means that the sheer beauty of this both wise and intuitive winemaking should translate into pure pleasure in the glass. The "malo" fermentation carried in oak brings fullness and smoothness to the wines, polishes their tannic structure and guarantees a rich aromatic palette. Durfort-Vivens is a miracle of freshness, minerality and elegance. Lengthy and powerful, it gives out distinguished notes of Oriental spices, black pepper and touches of ginger on a red fruit framework. Is this a classic Margaux or a modern one? The question is irrelevant: the ideally balanced, modern aromas offered by this wine are carried through long roots from the deep layers of the Margaux tradition.

1. *Fitted with both stainless steel and wooden vats, the vathouse of Château Durfort-Vivens is managed with great attention to plot selection: each vat gets individual treatment.*

2. *The gravel soil of Durfort-Vivens, homogeneous in appearance, actually rests on an astonishingly diversified basement.*

3. *In the cellar, nothing troubles the wines' long sleep from the beginning to the end of their ageing.*

Roe Deer and Cèpe Mushrooms,
Victoria Plums, Spring Onion and Carrots

Per BENGTSSON
PM & Vänner - Växjö, Sweden

SERVES 4

The roe deer filet

1⅓ pounds (600 g) roe deer filet

1½ tablespoons (20 g) unsalted butter

The garnish

4 fresh cèpe mushrooms

sprig of thyme

3 carrots

4 spring onions, cleaned, greens attached

fresh thyme

cold-pressed canola oil

2 Victoria plums

salt and freshly ground black pepper

The sauce

10 white peppercorns

2 shallots, finely chopped

oil

½ teaspoon ground Sichuan pepper

½ cup (10 cl) Port

½ cup (10 cl) white wine

1⅔ cups (40 cl) heavy roe deer stock

For the sauce: Blanch the white peppercorns 8 times in boiling water. Sauté the shallots in oil until transparent. Add the white peppercorns, Sichuan pepper, Port and white wine. Reduce by two-thirds and add the deer stock. Reduce by half, and then strain. Set aside and keep warm.

For the filet: Tie up the filet with butchers' twine. Sauté the filet in a pan with the butter until it is golden brown on all sides, then finish the meat in an oven at 210°F (100°C) until it reaches an internal temperature of 120°F (50°C). Let rest.

For the garnish: Clean the mushrooms and cut them into small cubes. Sauté in a hot frying pan with oil and thyme, then drain them on paper towels.

Run 1 carrot through a vegetable juicer, and grate the remaining 2 on a grater. Boil the grated carrots in the carrot juice, covered, over low heat for 10 minutes. Remove the lid and let all the liquid steam away, stirring constantly. Season to taste with salt and pepper.

Clean the spring onion and bake it aluminum foil with some thyme, canola oil and salt at 220°F (110°C) for 30 minutes.

For the presentation: Cut the plums into small cubes, and place them gently in the strained sauce for 2 minutes. Add the mushroom cubes right before serving.

Arrange 3 slices of roe deer filet on each of the plates, and add a bit of the sauce. Place the textured carrot nearby in a circle, top with a braised spring onion and serve.

CHÂTEAU DURFORT-VIVENS by Andreas Larsson, Best Sommelier of the World, 2007

A stylish Margaux that's not built on opulence or flesh, a wine whose classic and fresh structure needs patience. This Margaux is based on a high proportion of Cabernet that adds a certain austerity in its youth but with age it blossoms and displays a great purity and freshness. Even if it has gained some flesh over the last years, it is by no means a "show off" wine that will win blind tastings; this is a wine that should be drunk over a great meal by Bordeaux and Margaux aficionados.

CHÂTEAU GRUAUD LAROSE

SAINT-JULIEN

VINEYARD SIZE	82 hectares
VINE DENSITY	8,500 stocks per hectare
AVERAGE AGE OF VINEYARD	45 years
AVERAGE PRODUCTION	250,000 bottles
SOILS AND SUBSOILS	Quaternary Garonne gravel deposited over 700,000 years ago
GRAPE VARIETIES	Cabernet Sauvignon 61% Merlot 29% Cabernet Franc 5% Petit Verdot 5%

"This terroir of reddish-brown gravel has always made me dream," says the affable Jean Merlaut. "Before I owned this château, I would often go by a roundabout way just to see it. I am very sensitive to soils." By way of demonstration, he decidedly pushes you into a perilous spiral staircase leading to the top of a turret. You have not just risked breaking your neck for nothing, as the view is indeed fantastic. The large roofs of the cellars and vathouse and the vine plots stretch in huge planes hatched with fine parallel lines, whose axes sometimes cross and sometimes follow one another. This pure beauty—the architecture of vines prolonging the architecture of stone and tiles—recalls antique perspective, and this interaction of repetitive lines seems to play a celestial music.

Around 1725, Joseph Stanislas Gruaud created in Saint-Julien the vast estate of Fonbedeau, which was to become Gruaud Larose. In 1757, it had more or less reached its current expanse of 82 hectares. Jean-Sébastien de Larose inherited it in 1771, before a group of associated buyers purchased it in 1810 and gave it the name it bears now. One of them, Baron Sarget, created its motto: "The king of wines, the wine of kings." Soon afterward, the property was divided into two. It remained so until 1935, when the wine trader Désiré Cordier restored Gruaud Larose to its initial state. From 1993 to 1997, the château belonged to the Alcatel-Alsthom company. Since 1997, Jean Merlaut has owned it.

The greatest things are often given small names. In the long-gone days of wisdom when good wine was used as preventive treatment, Château Gruaud Larose was simply called Larose and one glass could be served as an elixir of youth. For instance, Sido, Colette's mother, speaks to the village priest in *La Maison de Claudine* (1922): "But at the mass, when you force us to kneel down, I have two or three quiet moments to think of my own business. I think about our girl looking a little pale these days, and about fetching a bottle of Château Larose

from the cellar so that she does not catch green sickness." Another example: at the Paris bistro Le Châteaubriand, an antique patch of painted wall, dating approximately from Colette's childhood, may still be seen above the counter. It reads: "St-Émilion 5 francs – St-Julien 5 francs – St-Estèphe 5 francs – Château-Larose 5 francs." This king of wines was treated like an appellation in its own right.

As is usually the case with people who study the vine closely, Jean Merlaut speaks in simple, witty words: "Making wine is like cooking. It is all about balance and small details. Ploughing the vineyard four times a year, organic composting, bud pruning, leaf stripping, thinning out, all that upstream work allows us to reduce the need for green harvest. Though I cannot prove it, I am persuaded that plants have a memory. As long as they are correctly pruned, after a few years they adapt, by their own decision, to the yield you expect from them."

When in the presence of a superior growth, the splendour of the wine and the splendour of the place that produces it are synthesised in the glass. The crystal can hardly contain the thoroughbred that is Gruaud Larose. Woodsy fragrances; fresh and fragrant red fruit travelling through time; dense, smooth and spicy notes; and the perfect roundness of tannins entice you into lengthening this moment of delight. In the château's bottle cellar, Jean Merlaut cautiously picks up one of the two oldest relics, marked with the 1815 vintage; the ruby colour is perfectly preserved. Colette's mother was right: what better prescription could a doctor write?

1. Under the groined vaults of the cellar, the barrels are still fitted with the glass plugs that allow the wine to overflow.

2. The thin parallel lines of the roofs and vineyard, seen from the top of the tower, sometimes cross and sometimes follow each other.

3. The classic facade of Château Gruaud Larose.

Wok-fried Wagyu Beef Cubes
with Morel Mushrooms

Chan YAN-TAK
Lung King Heen - Hong-Kong, China

SERVES 4

The beef

½ pound (250 g) Japanese wagyu beef,
cut into cubes

The vegetables

⅔ ounce (20 g) dried morel mushrooms

⅛ pound (50 g) bai ling mushrooms

⅛ pound (80 g) honey beans

⅔ ounce (20 g) spring onion

⅔ ounce (20 g) red bell pepper

1 tablespoon light soy sauce

¼ cup (5 cl) oil

⅔ cup (15 cl) Chinese rice wine

1¼ cups (30 cl) chicken broth

⅛ cup (3 cl) oyster sauce

1 teaspoon sugar

1 teaspoon cornstarch

For the beef: Cut the wagyu beef into cubes, place them in a bowl and season with the light soy sauce, a bit of oyster sauce, sugar and a little cornstarch. Set aside while preparing the other ingredients.

For the vegetables: Soak the dried morel mushrooms in water for 20 minutes, then drain. Trim the stalks of the bai ling mushrooms. Trim the honey beans. Set aside.

Cut the spring onion into pieces, and slice the bell pepper into cubes.

For the stir-fry: Heat the wok over medium-high to high heat, and add 2 tablespoons of oil. When the oil is hot, add the beef and stir-fry until the redness of the meat is gone and the beef is half-cooked. Remove the beef from the pan, and drain the oil.

Heat the wok again with another 2 tablespoons of oil, add the spring onion and red pepper, and stir-fry for 2 minutes.

Add the dried morel mushrooms, bai ling mushrooms and Chinese rice wine and stir.

Return the beef to the pan, and add the reserved 2 tablespoons of chicken broth, the remaining oyster sauce, sugar and cornstarch. Stir for another minute to combine. Heat through and serve hot.

CHÂTEAU GRUAUD LAROSE BY VIRGINIA PHILIP,
BEST SOMMELIER OF THE UNITED STATES, 2002

Known for producing some of the best wines, even during the most difficult vintages, this wine is consistently a beautiful and well-crafted wine. On the nose, both red and black fruits of cassis, cherry, plum and blackberry are predominant. Full-bodied and a bit powerful, the palate carries over the black cherry, black raspberry and cassis with chewy cigar, smooth tannins and a long, elegant finish.

CHÂTEAU LASCOMBES

MARGAUX

VINEYARD SIZE	84 hectares
VINE DENSITY	10,000 stocks per hectare
AVERAGE AGE OF VINEYARD	35 years
AVERAGE PRODUCTION	40,000 cases
SOILS AND SUBSOILS	deep Quaternary gravel (fourth terrace) from the Günzian and Mindelian eras
GRAPE VARIETIES	Merlot 50% Cabernet Sauvignon 45% Petit Verdot 5%

Depending on which side you approach Château Lascombes, your first impression of it may be quite different. The place, like the wine, is all shadows and light. Shadows as you enter the shady garden through a monumental, slightly intimidating ironwork gate. The vine-clad facade, a neo-renaissance mansion built in 1867, smells strongly of gothic romanticism. Light as you discover it from the warehouse side, where a vast, welcoming lawn greets you, framed at its end by the brighter face of the château and a lovely terrace shaded by enormous plane trees. The doors and shutters of the elegant vathouse and cellars are painted in a refined shade of lilac, the emblematic colour of Château Lascombes.

The estate owes its name to the chevalier Antoine de Lascombes, who established it in the 17th century. At the end of the 18th century, his descendant Jean-François de Lascombes, councilor at the Bordeaux Parliament, dedicated much passion and his considerable wealth to the making of a first-class wine—and successfully so. In 1855, Château Lascombes was classified as Second Growth. During the decades that followed, the estate passed through several hands, including those of Alexis Lichine in the 1950s. Since 2001, Château Lascombes has been owned by Colony Capital and directed by Dominique Befve, who used to work at Château Lafite-Rothschild. Michel Rolland is the wine consultant. "It was quite a challenge to take over this château," says Mr. Befve. "I found it in a seriously run-down state; we had to start again from scratch."

Covering 207 acres, it is one of the largest estates in the Margaux appellation. Being relatively scattered, it offers an interesting diversity of soils: gravel, clay-gravel and clay-limestone. An in-depth study of the soil has been undertaken for each plot, resulting in a thorough reorganisation of the vineyard. The planting makes Lascombes distinctly different from other Médoc Classified Growths: Merlot takes up half

of it, Cabernet Sauvignon following with 45 percent and Petit Verdot with 5 percent. "The terroir rules," says Befve. "Half of our soils are clay-limestone, and Merlot likes clay-limestone. This is a job of passion: decisions need to be made according to the gifts of Nature. Our blending should reflect her demands as closely as possible."

In order to extract the tannins from the grapes with the utmost precision, Befve applies cold pre-fermentation maceration, a new technique that consists of cooling the lightly crushed crop for eight days in the vat with an injection of carbon dioxide ice. This method achieves an intense and stable colour and improves the aromatic complexity.

The cellars are also indisputably one-of-a-kind—not only because of the spectacular blue light that illuminates them. The casks are mounted on Oxoline racks and regularly rotated, a precaution that prevents oxidation and keeps the lees in suspension. This ageing on the lees, which may be likened to a batonnage, takes up 4 months of the 18 to 20 months of the ageing in casks.

Not surprisingly, the result of such careful extraction is reflected in the concentration, the richness and the velvety texture of the wines of Château Lascombes. Their dark, inky robe bears the mark of the meticulous and original work done on the lees. Lascombes is an opulent, distinguished wine, with smooth and silky notes reminiscent of a wood fire and black tulip. Among the reputedly feminine great Margaux wines, this one is certainly the manliest of all.

1. Château Lascombes, as seen from the garden gate. The château was built in 1867 by barrister Chaix d'Est-Ange.

2. The entrance to the château from the cellar courtyard.

3. In the cellar, a knob of sulphur is burned to sterilize a barrel. The rack system that supports the barrels allows for regular rotation to prevent oxidation and keep the lees in suspension, thus helping to achieve the wonderful, rich and smooth texture of the wines.

White Tuna and Japanese Kobe Beef,
Fresh Kimchi, Yuzu–Brown Butter Emulsion

Eric RIPERT

Le Bernardin - New York City, United States

SERVES 4

The tuna

four 2½-ounce (70-g) white tuna steaks

four 2-ounce (50-g) Kobe beef filets, cut into 2 x 3-inch (5 x 7.5-cm) pieces

fine sea salt

freshly ground white and black pepper

The kimchi marinade

½ teaspoon fine sea salt

½ teaspoon xanthan gum

½ teaspoon Espelette pepper

pinch sugar

½ cup (12 cl) lemon juice

1 teaspoon garlic, peeled and thinly sliced

1 tablespoon Gochujang, Korean hot pepper paste

½ cup (12 cl) extra virgin olive oil

The BBQ sauce

1 tablespoon garlic, peeled and sliced

1 teaspoon ginger, peeled and sliced

½ cup (70 g) onion, grated on a box grater

½ cup (125 g) white miso paste

½ cup (125 g) Sunchang Gochujang hot pepper paste

½ cup (125 ml) Japanese rice wine vinegar

2 tablespoons mirin

2 tablespoons soy sauce

½ teaspoon sesame oil

1/4 cup (6 cl) ginger oil

The kimchi vegetables

4 Napa cabbage leaves, kept long but ends trimmed

6 butternut squash batonnets

12 Asian pear batonnets

The yuzu–brown butter emulsion

4 tablespoons (50 g) unsalted butter (½ stick)

3 tablespoons fumet (reduced from 6 tablespoons)

3 tablespoons yuzu juice

2 tablespoons white miso paste

freshly grated yuzu zest

1 tablespoon thinly sliced chives

fine sea salt

freshly ground white pepper

For the kimchi marinade: Mix together the salt, xanthan gum, sugar and Espelette and set aside. In a blender, combine the lemon juice, garlic and hot pepper paste. Slowly drizzle in the olive oil. Add the reserved dry ingredients and emulsify. Refrigerate until ready to use.

For the BBQ sauce: Combine all of the ingredients in a blender. Blend and strain through a chinois. Refrigerate.

For the kimchi vegetables: Blanch the Napa cabbage leaves and butternut squash separately in boiling salted water; plunge into ice water and drain. Refrigerate until ready to use.

For the yuzu–brown butter emulsion: Melt the butter in a pot over medium-high heat. Brown the butter by keeping it over medium heat, whisking occasionally, until all of the milk solids in the butter are very dark, but not burned. Set aside.

Warm the fumet and add the yuzu juice, miso paste and zest. Using a hand-held immersion blender, slowly add the brown butter to the liquid in a steady stream. Season to taste with salt and pepper. Keep warm.

For the tuna: Preheat the grill to medium-high heat. Season the white tuna on both sides with salt and pepper. Grill until the tuna is just medium-rare in the centre.

For the beef: Meanwhile, heat two sauté pans. Season the beef on both sides with salt and pepper; brush 1 teaspoon BBQ sauce on each filet, coating both sides. Quickly sear the filets in the pan, turning them once, so that each side is browned and the meat is medium.

For the garnish: Marinate the cabbage leaves, butternut squash and Asian pear with a little kimchi marinade and warm in a small pan.

For the presentation: Arrange a cabbage leaf on the top half of each plate. Draw a thin line of BBQ sauce horizontally across the bottom half of each plate. Place a beef filet over the BBQ sauce. Place the white tuna offset and slightly overlapping the beef filet on each plate.

Arrange 2 squash batonnets and 3 pear batonnets on top of each piece of white tuna. Stir the thin sliced chives into the yuzu–brown butter emulsion and spoon over the white tuna.

CHÂTEAU LASCOMBES BY ÉRIC BEAUMARD, SILVER MEDAL, BEST SOMMELIER OF THE WORLD, 1998

This château brings back memories of my beginnings in this profession, when I was a young man working at a wine shop in Rennes, where I stacked cases of Lascombes 1978 and 1979. Since changing ownership in 2001, the property has developed a new spirit of achievement as shown by significant investments in the vathouse and barrel cellars in order to better understand and express the vineyard's character. Today, the wines produced here are defined by their smoothness and balance.

CHÂTEAU BRANE-CANTENAC

MARGAUX

VINEYARD SIZE	85 hectares
VINE DENSITY	6,666–8,000 stocks per hectare
AVERAGE AGE OF VINEYARD	35 years
AVERAGE PRODUCTION	150,000 bottles
SOILS AND SUBSOILS	deep Quaternary gravel (fourth terrace)
GRAPE VARIETIES	Cabernet Sauvignon 55% Merlot 40% Cabernet Franc 4.5% Carmenère 0.5%

Lovely in its simplicity, the château Brane-Cantenac is set in a quiet park, surrounded by the vineyards of the Plateau de Brane, itself a part of the vast Plateau de Cantenac. In the 18th century, when the château belonged to the Gorce family, its wines were already famous. By the time of the French Revolution, their prices almost equaled those of the first growths. In 1833, the last descendant of the Gorces sold the estate to the Baron de Brane, nicknamed "the Napoleon of wine," who left his name to the château. Since 1992, Brane-Cantenac has been the property of Henri Lurton, assisted by Christophe Capdeville (estate manager), Charles de Ravinel (vineyard manager) and Corinne Conroy (marketing and communication manager). Jacques Boissenot is the consultant œnologist.

Henri Lurton knows every square metre of his vineyard by heart; he has been on this spot since 1986, when his father Lucien still managed the estate. Obviously, though, it takes more than 23 years on the land to know so many of its secrets. Henri is, quite simply, a lover of the terroir. He insists on showing you not only his vine plots, but sections of them, pointing out the finest soil variations.

"The geological history of this place," he says, "is related to a meander of the Garonne, formed during the Quaternary. Where the river's course was the strongest, it left those large pebbles. On the Plateau de Brane, which is the historical heart of the estate, the deepest layers of gravel (10 to 12 metres) are rich in clay. They have an excellent draining power, but they also hold in the water in sufficient quantity throughout the year, while being compact enough to limit the plant's water absorption. Hence the controlled vigour in the vines and the silky, round tannins they produce in the wines. Gravel soils from later periods are found in another zone, behind the château's park. The wine from those plots shows a more assertive tannic character. Finally, there is a third section of the vineyard close to the Château du Tertre, where again we find gravel of the same period as those on the Plateau de Brane.

"We make the wine on 85 hectares with 55 percent Cabernet Sauvignon, 40 percent Merlot, and the remainder in Cabernet Franc. My father was a Cabernet Sauvignon man—but the soil, not the grape variety, is the most important element. The microplot layout here is quite a wonderful thing. Some plots include up to three different types of soil."

In 1999, Henri renovated the cellar buildings, adding to them a modern extension with natural materials: wood is everywhere, from the large sliding shutters that delimit the vathouse to the beautiful wooden vats, which are closely adapted to the plot selection.

Henri devotes special care to the purity of the harvest. Having been selected the first time at the vineyard on mobile tables, the grapes are sorted three more times at the vathouse. After de-stemming, the smallest remaining bits of stem and leaf are eliminated by hand. "Regarding maturity," Henri adds, "we have often been the last to harvest. We do like to wait for the best possible tannic maturity. Which does not mean 'overripe.' The harvests of the 1980s, when grapes—particularly Merlots—were picked too late, are long gone."

Château Brane-Cantenac is a wonderfully balanced wine with plenty of personality. It shows all the desirable characteristics of Margaux: a nose of violets, notes of black currant and other black fruit, an intense and deep colour. The attack is ample, the tannins are velvety and the finish is lengthy and distinguished. This wine is celebrated for its bouquet and never lacks charm in its youth, though its elegant structure increases with age.

1. The simple chartreuse of Brane-Cantenac, home of the Lurton family, stands in a vast green park.

2. Morning mist, a frequent sight in the Médoc.

3, 4. The winemaking facilities of Brane-Cantenac combine wood and stainless steel—a good example of a two-material vathouse whose varying capacities allow to refine the plot selection.

Pears, Beans and Bacon

Nils HENKEL
Dieter Müller - Bergisch Gladbach, Germany

SERVES 4

The bacon and stock

1⅛ pounds (500 g) fresh unsmoked bacon

1 scant cup (20 cl) water

1 scant cup (20 cl) brown veal stock

1 shallot

1 garlic clove

1 bay leaf

10 peppercorns

a few coriander seeds

2 sprigs savoury

pinch of nitrite salt

pinch of ground cumin

pinch of caraway seeds

lemon zest

The beans

¼ pound (100 g) flat green beans

2 tablespoons savoury butter

2 tablespoons broad beans

The savoury mousse

1 shallot

3 cultivated white mushrooms

1½ tablespoons canola oil

3 tablespoons Riesling

1 scant cup (20 cl) chicken stock

5 sprigs savoury

pinch of lecithin

salt and freshly ground black pepper

The savoury sauce

1 thinly sliced shallot

1½ tablespoons ruby Port

3½ tablespoons pear juice

1 scant cup (20 cl) reduced bacon stock

3 sprigs savoury

½ teaspoon crushed caraway seeds

xanthan gum, optional

pear jelly

warm pear preserves

a few pieces of raw pear

grilled lardons

For the bacon and stock: Trim the bacon and remove the skin. Bring the trimmings and bones to a boil in a scant cup (20 cl) of water with the remaining ingredients. Reduce to a simmer and cook over low heat for 1 hour. Strain the stock and let it cool.

Put the bacon and the stock into a sous-vide bag, seal and cook for about 36 hours in a bain-marie kept at 150°F (65°C). Let cool, then dice the bacon into 2-inch (5-cm) cubes. Reduce the stock and keep it aside for the savoury sauce.

For the beans: Blanch the green beans in boiling salted water, keeping them al dente, then cool them under cold running water. Trim them to exactly 5½ inches (14 cm) and cut them length-wise into a fine julienne. Brush 4 strips of parchment paper with some of the savoury butter and lay the beans on them in 2 x 5½-inch (5 x 14 cm) rectangles. Brush again with some savoury butter.

Blanch the broad beans in boiling salted water. Cool under cold running water and set aside.

For the savoury mousse: Chop the shallot and mushrooms and sauté them in canola oil. Deglaze with the wine. Add the chicken stock and savoury sprigs, bring to a boil, and then let rest off the heat for 20 minutes. Add salt, pepper and a small pinch of lecithin. Set aside and keep warm. Just before serving, blend in a Thermomix at 160°F (70°C) until you obtain a smooth mousse.

For the savoury sauce: Sweat the thinly sliced shallot in butter, deglaze with the Port and pear juice and then add the bacon stock. Add the savoury, caraway and pepper, bring to a boil. Remove from the heat, let rest for about 30 minutes. Bring back to a boil, then strain. If needed, bind the sauce with a pinch of xanthan gum. Season with salt and pepper.

For the presentation: Shortly before serving, heat the diced bacon (lardons) to 140°F (60°C), season with salt and pepper, then sear it lightly on all sides. Reheat the bean rectangles on their paper for about 3 minutes in the oven and slide them onto the plates, removing the paper. Reheat the broad beans in a little savoury butter, and season with salt and pepper. Scatter the broad beans nicely among the plates. Dot each cube of bacon with a cube of pear jelly, and put in a warm oven for 1 minute. Put 1 cube of bacon and 1 quenelle of warm preserved pear on each plate with raw pear, and finally add the savoury sauce and a small cloud of savoury mousse. Scatter each plate with small, crispy lardons and serve.

CHÂTEAU BRANE-CANTENAC BY FRANCK THOMAS,
BEST SOMMELIER OF EUROPE, 2000

The focus of Brane-Cantenac's prestigious history is an incomparable soil, the object of long study by the greatest specialists. Historically renowned as one of the the Médoc's finest, the terroir at Brane has earned the property its longstanding reputation as "first of the seconds." The vineyards around Cantenac produce wines that are among Margaux's most severe, and the longest to reach maturity. Brane-Cantenac is no exception; even in less-rich vintages, the wines need several years in bottle to develop fully. The firm nature of Cantenac's Cabernets will disappear with an older vintage and will afford a memorable experience.

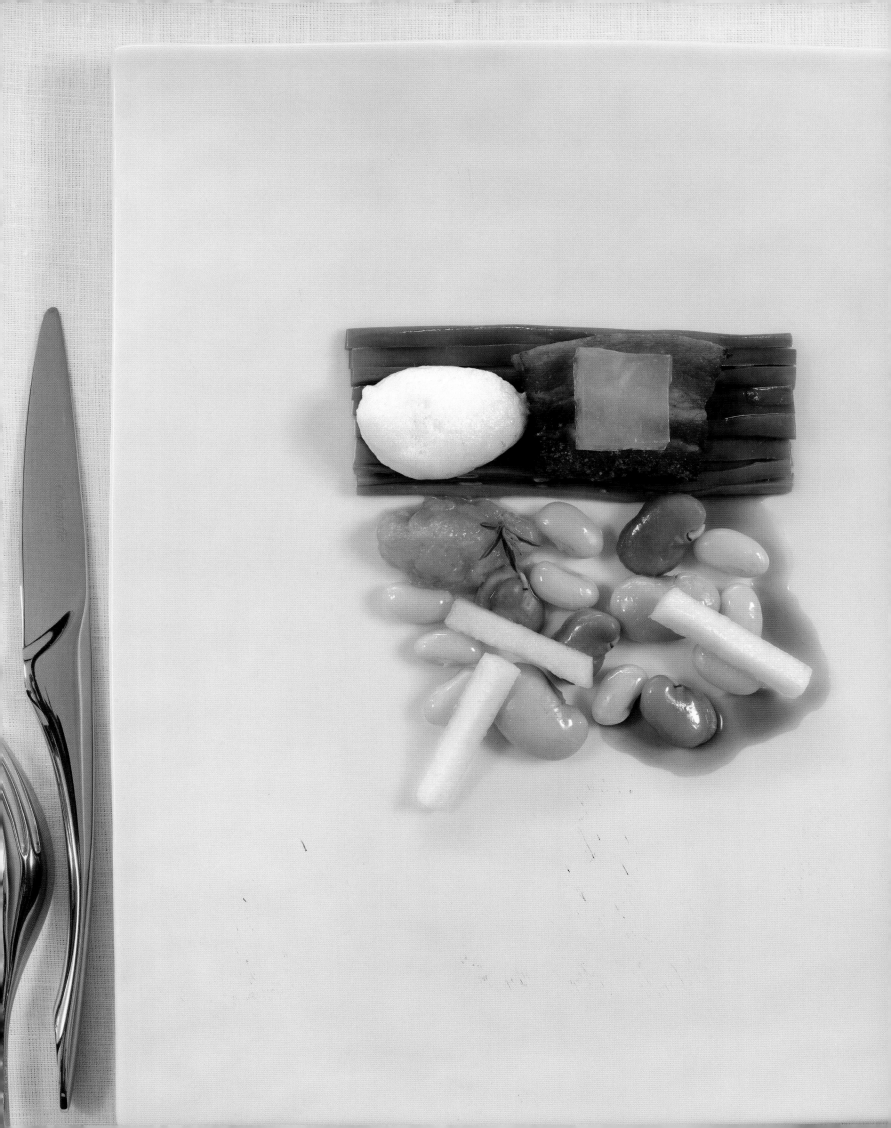

CHÂTEAU PICHON-LONGUEVILLE

PAUILLAC

VINEYARD SIZE	73 hectares
VINE DENSITY	9,000 stocks per hectare
AVERAGE AGE OF VINEYARD	30 years
AVERAGE PRODUCTION	25,000 cases
SOILS AND SUBSOILS	Garonne gravel
GRAPE VARIETIES	Cabernet Sauvignon 62% Merlot 35% Cabernet Franc 3%

In 1851, when Baron Raoul de Pichon-Longueville built his château, the wish to go unnoticed did not seem to be his main concern. Rigorously symmetrical, facing you with a decided look, the building bears high its two side towers as a knight carries his spear in a tournament. You think you are looking at the château, but it looked at you first. The fairy-tale castle, interpreted by 19th-century romanticism, finds one of its most flamboyant expressions here.

This strong aesthetic statement, which crowns an exceptional terroir, did not keep Pichon-Baron—as it is often called—from experiencing some difficulties during the 20th century. In 1987, the AXA Millésimes group acquired the château with two objectives in mind: to raise this great classified growth back to its rightful quality level of "super-second" and to reorganise the vineyard and facilities. Architects Patrick Dillon and Jean de Gastines restored the château and surrounded it with a monumental set of winemaking buildings whose style borrows from Egyptian temples, Mycenian necropolises and sword-and-sandal movies. The most recent achievement, completed in 2007, is an underground barrel cellar built under a large pond. The circular vathouse is built around a central colonnade inspired by Romanesque church choirs and lit by an oculus at the zenith—a sanctuary for a great wine. In the adjacent tasting room, Christian Seely, Manageing Director of AXA Millésimes, brings up one of his favourite conversation topics: terroir.

Seely takes after his father, James, with whom he wrote the reference book Great Bordeaux Wines. Before he found himself at the helm of two Great Classified Growths—Pichon-Longueville in Pauillac and Suduiraut in Sauternes—he watched over the destiny of Quinta do Noval Ports for seven years, thus improving his experience of great landmark wines. Through a clear-sighted and enthusiastic discourse, he declares himself convinced that vine cultivation is a long-term occupation. Such is the paradox of Great Classified Growths: being purchased by a large group, when that happens, does not rob them of their poetic nature. On the contrary, one could say that being objects of poetry at heart is what makes them a profitable business. "In Médoc, during the last few years," says Seely, "there was a tremendous push for quality. The current yield of Pichon-Longueville is half of the quantity that was produced in the 1990s. Whatever the classification level, all Great Classified Growth owners strive to make the best possible wine. And the strength of these growths is the distinct personality of each château."

And where does Pichon-Longueville's personality lie? "In the amazing variety of its types of soil," answers Seely. "73 hectares of fine, deep Garonne gravel on highly diversified plots, planted with 62 percent Cabernet Sauvignon and 35 percent Merlot. The beautiful undulating hills southwest of Pichon are the heart of our terroir, the soil that gives the wine its distinctive character. One of the greatest soils in the world." Seely, though, is modestly omitting to mention how skilfully and wisely he restored Pichon-Longueville's natural nobility and buoyancy—rich, fleshy, fresh, full-bodied, bursting with red fruit, the wine never ceases to amaze. In the glass, it asserts its joy to be alive, as does Seely when he speaks about it. A fine example, among many others, of the perfect match between a great wine and the people who make it.

1. The stainless steel vathouse of Pichon-Longueville is famous for its elegant and modern lines.

2. The château is a perfect specimen of Neomedieval architecture of the Romantic era.

3. Egyptian obelisks, Doric pediments, Ionic volutes—all elements of an architectural program of Minoan-like monumentality. Whole eras of antiquity are brought together into the cellars of Pichon-Longueville.

Pot-roasted Shoulder of Lamb

Fergus HENDERSON
Saint John - London, United Kingdom

SERVES 4

1 shoulder of lamb, on the bone
20 shallots, peeled and left whole
20 garlic cloves, peeled and left whole
a splash of olive oil
a bundle of thyme and rosemary
½ bottle of white wine
1 quart (1 l) light chicken stock
sea salt and freshly ground black pepper

For the lamb: Chop, leg, best end of lamb are all splendid, but a slow-roasted shoulder of lamb. . . ahhh! A piece of meat with a truly giving nature.

In a roasting pan deep and wide enough to hold the shoulder of lamb, brown the shallots and garlic in oil. Lay the herb bundle of joy in the pan and put the shoulder of lamb on top. Pour on the white wine and stock. Season the shoulder liberally with salt and pepper.

Cover with foil and place in a gentle oven at 250°F (120°C) for 3 to 4 hours, as always keeping an eye on it and poking it with a small, sharp knife to check if it's done. Uncover at this point, if not colouring, and if you want the liquids to reduce. I leave that choice to your personal taste.

As far as cooking meat goes, shoulder of lamb is one of the best-behaved joints and you don't even have to know how to carve. It is a case of attack.

CHÂTEAU PICHON-LONGUEVILLE BY MARKUS DEL MONEGO,
BEST SOMMELIER OF THE WORLD, 1998

The prestigious name of Pauillac exerts an incomparable fascination over connoisseurs, due in great part to wines like this. Blessed with an exceptional terroir and benefiting from modern vinification techniques, this property has become the ambassador for a style of Pauillac that joins innovation with tradition. This wine is full of complex aromas and powerful tannins that are silky and opulent in character, all in balance with the freshness that is the hallmark of a great wine.

CHÂTEAU PICHON-LONGUEVILLE COMTESSE DE LALANDE

PAUILLAC

VINEYARD SIZE	87 hectares
VINE DENSITY	9,000 stocks per hectare
AVERAGE AGE OF VINEYARD	35 years
AVERAGE PRODUCTION	16,000 cases
SOILS AND SUBSOILS	gravel on clay
GRAPE VARIETIES	Cabernet Sauvignon 45% Merlot 35% Cabernet Franc 12% Petit Verdot 8%

At the end of the 17th century, the famous vineyard owner Pierre de Rauzan bought a vast estate of "forty fine gravelly plots" in Saint-Lambert, near Pauillac. His daughter, Thérèse, later married Jacques de Pichon-Longueville, the first president of the Bordeaux Parliament. In 1850, when Baron Joseph de Pichon-Longueville passed away, his property was divided between his five children; two-fifths went to his two sons and three-fifths to his three daughters. One of the young ladies, Sophie, was a painter and a poet, trained under Baron Gérard. Many of her works can be seen at the château. But only Virginie, Comtesse de Lalande, had a passion for winemaking. The absence of children finally caused the estate to be divided between two heirs; Raoul took the men's share and Virginie, the women's. The charismatic countess then set out to make her own wine under her own label. The venture proved a total success, confirmed by the 1855 Classification. The two resulting estates, often called Pichon-Baron and Pichon-Comtesse (or Pichon-Lalande), still stand facing each other on either side of the D2 road.

In 1925, the property was purchased by the Bordeaux traders Louis and Édouard Miailhe. When Édouard's daughter, May Éliane de Lencquesaing, took over the direction of the vineyard in 1978, she revived a tradition that had been started by Countess de Lalande. In the course of 30 years of rigorous management, all the while producing a continuous series of splendid vintages, she enlarged and restructured the wine-making facilities, prolonged the underground cellar and ordered a second one from the architect Bernard Mazières. Then she installed a bottling zone and a storage warehouse, two brand-new state-of-the-art vathouses and a vast reception space called L'Orangerie. She also remodelled the park and the panoramic terrace with a view of the Gironde. Aside from that, over the years, she gathered a magnificent collection of antique and modern glasswork that may be admired at the château's museum. This passion for glass is explained not only by the natural affinity between contents and container, wine and glass, but also by the humble nature of their origin—sand for the glass, gravel for the vine.

In 2007, May Éliane de Lencquesaing chose the Louis Roederer company as her successor. Gildas d'Ollone, her nephew, who has been manageing the estate since 1991, is still at the helm since the property has been purchased by the famous Champagne house. "It is in Roederer's style," he explains, "to preserve the human capital."

The 87 hectares of vines, located south of the Pauillac appellation, are gathered into a rather homogeneous estate. This great wine is composed of 45 percent Cabernet Sauvignon, 35 percent Merlot, 12 percent Cabernet Franc and 8 percent Petit Verdot. The fine-tuned alchemy produced by this unusual planting plays a substantial part in Pichon-Lalande's unique aromatic complexity and, by enhancing its femininity, sets it apart among the Pauillac Great Classified Growths. Smooth, racy, elegant and amazingly persistent, the wine has a soft and velvety mouthfeel and expresses a delicate voluptuousness. The aromatic palette typically includes violet, mulberry, cinnamon, black currant and vanilla. Many tasters, captivated by its uncommonly fine tannins, are tempted to use textile terms—silk, velvet, satin—when describing this exceedingly charming wine, whose memory lingers in your heart for a very long time.

1. The château Pichon-Lalande obviously appears as the feminine equivalent of Château Pichon-Longueville Baron, which faces it. While the latter expresses vigourous masculinity, the former displays a poetic, womanly grace.

2. The terrace of the château offers a splendid view over the Gironde and surrounding meadows.

3. Within those walls, Countess Virginie left her strong aura and her charming portrait.

Roast Bresse Pigeon
with Fresh Peas

Michel ROUX

Le Gavroche - London, United Kingdom

SERVES 6

The white chicken stock

Makes about 4 quarts (4 l)

**4⅜ pounds (2 kg) chicken bones
or wing tips**

1 calf's foot, split

5 quarts (5 l) water

1 onion

1 small leek

2 celery stalks

2 sprigs thyme

6 parsley stalks

The pigeons

**6 Bresse pigeons,
¾ to 1 pound (400 to 450 g) each**

olive oil

The vegetable garnish

18 baby onions

1 large carrot

about 3 cups (400 g) shelled fresh peas

**9 tablespoons (120 g) unsalted butter
(1 stick plus 1 tablespoon), cubed**

⅝ pound (275 g) smoked bacon

1 cup (22.5 cl) chicken stock

1 round lettuce, shredded

salt and freshly ground black pepper

For the the chicken stock: Place the bones and calf's foot in a large saucepan, cover with the water, and bring to the boil. Skim off the scum and fat that rises to the surface. Reduce the heat, add the remaining ingredients, and simmer for 1½ hours, skimming occasionally. Pass through a fine sieve and leave to cool. This can be kept in the refrigerator for up to 5 days, or frozen.

For the pigeons: Preheat the oven to 450°F (230°C). Season the pigeons inside, then smear them with olive oil and sprinkle with salt. Place in a hot roasting pan over high heat and brown the birds all over. Turn them on to their backs and roast in the oven for 12 minutes; the meat should be rosy pink. Remove from the oven, turn them breast side down so the juices permeate the breast meat, cover with aluminum foil and set aside to rest in a warm place for 15 minutes before serving.

For the vegetable garnish: Peel and trim the baby onions. Peel and cut the carrot into 1³⁄₁₆-inch (3-cm) long batons. Cook the onions, carrot batons and peas in boiling salted water until just tender. Refresh in ice-cold water and drain well. Cut the bacon into thin batons and blanch for 1 minute in boiling water; drain well.

Melt 1 tablespoon of butter in a wide saucepan. When it foams, add the bacon and cook until it begins to brown. Add the onions and cook for a further 3 minutes, rolling them around the pan from time to time. Then add the peas, carrots and 1 cup (22.5 cl) chicken stock and simmer for 10 minutes.

For the presentation: Season well, then add the butter a little at a time, shaking the pan so that it emulsifies and thickens the sauce. Just before serving, fold in the shredded lettuce leaves. Serve with the pigeons.

CHÂTEAU PICHON-LONGUEVILLE COMTESSE DE LALANDE
BY YOICHI SATO, BEST SOMMELIER OF JAPAN, 2005

Each time I taste this wine, its aromas and taste reveal the same flavourful oriental notes. Its steady, constant aroma evoking the heart of a mahogany forest, its lightness and even its rich astringency combine to create a deliciously long finish on the palate.

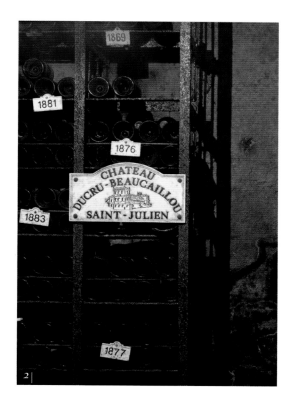

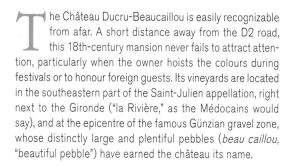

CHÂTEAU DUCRU-BEAUCAILLOU

SAINT-JULIEN

VINEYARD SIZE	75 hectares
VINE DENSITY	10,000 stocks per hectare
AVERAGE AGE OF VINEYARD	35 years
SOILS AND SUBSOILS	Günzian gravel on a Gironde-type hill bordering the estuary
GRAPE VARIETIES	Cabernet Sauvignon 75% Merlot 25%

The Château Ducru-Beaucaillou is easily recognizable from afar. A short distance away from the D2 road, this 18th-century mansion never fails to attract attention, particularly when the owner hoists the colours during festivals or to honour foreign guests. Its vineyards are located in the southeastern part of the Saint-Julien appellation, right next to the Gironde ("la Rivière," as the Médocains would say), and at the epicentre of the famous Günzian gravel zone, whose distinctly large and plentiful pebbles (*beau caillou*, "beautiful pebble") have earned the château its name.

It is an accurate choice: the large yellow stones showing through the clayey sand of the plots nearest to the château are indeed a fine sight. And it is always a delight to hear Bruno-Eugène Borie, the owner, talking precisely and passionately about his terroirs: "Here, close to the estuary, the microclimate is generated by the Gironde, whereas on the other side of the road it is conditioned by the Beychevelle marshes or by the Mouline, a small stream that runs through the appellation from west to east, bordered on either side by some fine Médoc gravel hills. On the 215 hectares covered by our estate, 100 are planted in the Saint-Julien appellation, including 75 for Château Ducru-Beaucaillou and Croix-de-Beaucaillou. The remaining 25 hectares constitute the Château Lalande-Borie, created by my father in 1970. The planting for Ducru-Beaucaillou is 75 percent Cabernet Sauvignon and 25 percent Merlot.

"Around the château and nearly all the way to the river, our subsoil is clayey, slightly ferruginous and very cool, so that the vine's vegetative cycle is smooth and regular. The vine is never overstressed from contrasting temperatures and the grapes ripen without interruption. This gives our Great Classified Growth of Ducru-Beaucaillou its particular style, all freshness and elegant tannins. Even in the scorching 2003 summer, they never lacked any coolness."

The notion of "right place" is important to Borie. As an example, he chooses the Templar church of Bernos, in the Médoc village of Saint-Laurent, a magical place, he says, through its outlines, its setting and its spirit. Borie elaborates, "Many traditional places are conceived that way. Country people used to refer to them as 'places where the stones go to sleep.' In vineyards and in fields, there are spots where migrating skylarks settle and other spots, close by and looking quite the same, where they never do. What is the logic behind that? We have no clue. And the same phenomena may be observed with some microplots and the distinctive influence they exert on wine."

The spectacular assets of Ducru-Beaucaillou are not restricted to the château. The large, recently built cellars, with a springboard-shaped porch roof emerging from a large swell of turf-covered soil, are rightly famous. Likewise, the old cellars and the tasting room are decorated in a contemporary style. This lively visual impression, paired with the golden yellow colour—much loved by Borie—on the walls and on the wine label, echoes the powerful energy and distinction of the wines of Ducru-Beaucaillou. Its unconditional lovers claim that this is the wine they would bring along on a desert island. However, if you are tempted by such an experiment, be warned: Ducru-Beaucaillou is a gastronomy wine, good food being another passion of Borie's. As proof of that, the magnificent, beautifully furnished kitchen of the château is likely to impress the most demanding professional chef. Huge cauldrons for harvest feasts are still in place, in working order. Borie will also proudly lead you to the vast vegetable garden where all the household's produce is grown. If you need to take Château Ducru-Beaucaillou to a desert island, do not forget either a corkscrew or your lunch. A foie gras–stuffed woodcock terrine should do the trick.

1. *The Château Ducru-Beaucaillou was founded in the 18th century and remodelled in the 19th century.*

2. *The bottle cellar contains treasures which demonstrate the great ageing capacities of this Saint-Julien.*

3. *In many parts of the château, including the cellars, the aesthetic harmony leans towards contemporary art.*

Woodcock and Foie Gras Terrine

Jacques THOREL

L'Auberge bretonne - La Roche-Bernard, France

one 12 x 14-inch (30 x 10-cm) terrine
5 woodcocks (not hanged!)

The gratin filling

¼ pound (125 g) chicken livers
or calf's liver

⅔ ounce (20 g) fatback bacon

¼ pound (125 g) pork loin

1 shallot

sprig of thyme

½ bay leaf

1 scant cup (20 cl) red wine

The ground filling

¼ pound (100 g) duck meat
(about 1 thigh)

½ pound (200 g) pork belly

¼ pound (100 g) duck foie gras

The diced filling

½ pound (250 g) duck foie gras

The seasonings
(per 2¼ pounds, or 1 kg, of filling)

1 crushed juniper berry

fresh thyme blossoms

2 teaspoons fleur de sel

2 teaspoons freshly ground black pepper

½ teaspoon ground allspice

2½ teaspoons Madeira

2½ teaspoons Cognac

2½ teaspoons sherry

2 tablespoons truffle juice

For the woodcocks: Bone each of the woodcocks, setting aside the breast meat, thigh meat, and the offal.

For the gratin filling: Remove the gall bladder from the chicken livers and halve them. Finely dice the fatback bacon and the pork loin. In a sauté pan, sweat the chopped shallot and the fatback bacon with the thyme and bay leaf. Add the chicken livers and pork loin and sauté until medium-rare. Season with fleur de sel and pepper, deglaze with the red wine. Reduce the jus. Roll the meats and the foie gras in the jus, and immediately remove from the heat. Set the meats aside on a plate. When the filling has cooled completely, remove the thyme sprig and bay leaf. Process the filling in a blender, and then pass it through a tamis (a fine-mesh sieve) until it is perfectly smooth.

For the ground filling: Pass the duck thigh meat, the pork belly, the foie gras and the woodcock offal through a meat grinder fitted with the medium disk.

For the diced filling: Dice the woodcock breast meat and the foie gras into even ½-inch (1-cm) cubes.

Assembling the terrine: In a large dish, mix the gratin filling with the ground filling. Add the diced stuffing. Weigh the filling and season accordingly, then fill the terrine. Cover with parchment paper and bake for 2 hours in a bain-marie, in a 212°F (100°C) oven. The terrine is done when the temperature in the centre is 160°F (70°C). Refrigerate the terrine for 2 days before serving.

CHÂTEAU DUCRU-BEAUCAILLOU BY OLIVIER POUSSIER,
BEST SOMMELIER OF THE WORLD, 2000

This Second Growth, owned by the Borie family, is produced with consistent quality making it especially suited for long ageing. Year after year, these wines are vinified with care every step of the way, from the vineyard to the cellar. The resultant wines, whose rich, profoundly elegant breeding only emerges after a decade of patience, can easily claim close kinship with the First Growths of the Médoc.

CHÂTEAU COS D'ESTOURNEL

SAINT-ESTÈPHE

VINEYARD SIZE	91 hectares
VINE DENSITY	10,000 stocks per hectare
AVERAGE AGE OF VINEYARD	30 years
SOILS AND SUBSOILS	Quaternary gravel on a clay-limestone subsoil
GRAPE VARIETIES	Cabernet Sauvignon 70% Merlot 28% Cabernet Franc 2%

Saint-Estèphe is a wine that likes to keep it under cover. Not out of a wish to deceive us, but in order to keep intact the surprise of its spicy brilliance underneath a so-called austere and monarchal appearance. The wine is a voluptuous body concealed in a monk's frock, a lover of good living who uses seriousness as a protective screen and whose sense of humour is deadpan. But Cos d'Estournel, for one thing, does not feel any need for shyness. As is the case with all Great Classified Growth châteaux, it has to be praised for telling it like it is and fully manifesting its true nature. But this one goes a bit further, anticipating all questions and emphasising its self-expression through architecture, making a show of itself, affording itself every luxury—because it is pure luxury.

Discovering the Château Cos d'Estournel for the first time always gives a slight shock, especially when the late afternoon sun hits the golden sandstone frontally, splashing copper, saffron and turmeric shades all over it; outlines the slightest shadow on this uncanny, delicately chiselled facade; makes the bizarre pagoda-roofed bell towers glisten and all the chinoiserie, Indian, African exotic mannerisms of the building vibrate. To top it all, this château is not even a château.

Built around 1830 by the eccentric Louis-Gaspard d'Estournel, this folly (in the architectural sense of the term) is simply a cellar and a vathouse, and never was designed to be a house. "Quite cheerful-looking . . . and rather in the Chinese style," as Stendhal wrote, this is a palace dedicated to the glory of wine, celebrating the international success of Cos d'Estournel, a wine that was loved by the Maharajahs and many other crowned heads. The harmony between the Oriental destiny of Cos d'Estournel and its warm, spicy, intensely aromatic character is obvious in the glass, but the château itself proclaims it, embodying the wine to the perfection. With rich curry and toasted cumin notes with a touch of cardamom, Cos d'Estournel is designed for the spice-marinated grilled meats and complex layered tastes of Mughal cooking. Fresh, crisp fruit, black or red cherry, is also passionately present. With age, the wine develops tones of coffee, liquorice, bay leaf, black pepper and warm fur.

The modern rationality of the methods used to make this flamboyant wine, now a property of the Domaines Reybier, demonstrates once again the crucial importance of the terroir, the only factor really holding that promise of fire, fruit and spice. Recently, another page of Cos d'Estournel's history was turned: under the pagoda roofs, architect Jean-Michel Wilmotte, here again displaying his love of architectural transplants, has just installed an impressive, partly underground vatroom and cellar complex. The alignment of conical brushed stainless-steel vats, filled by gravity-trough mobile vats set on elevators, produces an amazing science-fiction decor hidden below the château and a mind-boggling feeling of time clash in iceberg mode: one-tenth visible centuries-old chinoiserie, nine-tenths submerged futuristic steel and glass. However, whether at ground level or below, Cos d'Estournel stays true to its own style, a theatricality that speaks the truth, a culture of excess that never goes too far.

1. Visually striking, tronconical brushed steel fermenting vats stand in regular lines in the ultramodern cellars designed by Jean-Michel Wilmotte.

2. The inimitable Château Cos d'Estournel—a neo-Chinese folly devoted to the exclusive glory of wine.

3. In the basement of the newly built facilities, the barrel cellar is supported by glass-inlaid pillars.

Potato and Truffle Emulsion

Jean-Georges KLEIN
L'Arnsbourg - Baerenthal, France

SERVES 10

The potato emulsion

½ pound (230 g) potatoes
¼ cup (6 cl) potato cooking water
⅛ cup (3.5 cl) Baena olive oil
⅓ cup (7 cl) heavy cream
truffle oil
Guérande fleur de sel
salt and freshly ground black pepper

The truffle disks

twenty 4½-inch (11-cm) wax paper disks
truffle oil
⅓ pound (150 g) black truffles
(3 to 4 truffles)

For the potato emulsion: Cook the potatoes in boiling water and drain, reserving some of the cooking water, and peel them.

Blend the potatoes with a bit of their cooking water, adding olive oil and cream. Season with salt and pepper and pass through a fine-mesh sieve.

Pour the purée into a 3-cup (¾-l) siphon, add a gas cartridge, shut the siphon and shake it vigourously. Keep it at a temperature of 140°F (60°C).

For the truffle disks: Brush a wax paper disk with truffle oil. Cover with thin slices of truffles, overlapping them, and cover with another wax paper disk brushed with oil. Repeat with the remaining ingredients and wax paper disks.

For the presentation: Siphon out the potato mousse into shallow, round soup plates. Peel off the paper and lay a trufle disk onto the mousse. Run each plate under the broiler for a brief moment just before serving, and sprinkle with truffle oil and fleur de sel.

2005

COS D'ESTOURNEL
SAINT - ESTÈPHE

CHÂTEAU COS D'ESTOURNEL BY SERGE DUBS, BEST SOMMELIER OF THE WORLD, 1989

This flamboyant and prestigious Saint-Estèphe terroir has a centuries-old talent for consistently producing wines with aristocratic charm, proud character and fine breeding. This great Bordeaux growth has remained firmly rooted in its ancient, delightfully stony gravel, while making the most of modern techniques. Dense and full, with a tannic streak of great class joined by a refined, subtle bouquet.

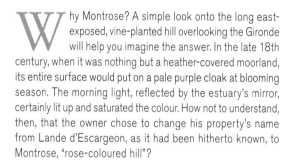

CHÂTEAU MONTROSE

SAINT-ESTÈPHE

VINEYARD SIZE	68 hectares
VINE DENSITY	9,000 stocks per hectare
AVERAGE AGE OF VINEYARD	35 years
AVERAGE PRODUCTION	18,000–20,000 cases
SOILS AND SUBSOILS	Pyrenean gravel on a clayey subsoil
GRAPE VARIETIES	Cabernet Sauvignon 65% Merlot 30% Cabernet Franc 4% Petit Verdot 1%

Why Montrose? A simple look onto the long east-exposed, vine-planted hill overlooking the Gironde will help you imagine the answer. In the late 18th century, when it was nothing but a heather-covered moorland, its entire surface would put on a pale purple cloak at blooming season. The morning light, reflected by the estuary's mirror, certainly lit up and saturated the colour. How not to understand, then, that the owner chose to change his property's name from Lande d'Escargeon, as it had been hitherto known, to Montrose, "rose-coloured hill"?

In order to appreciate the full beauty of the Montrose site, you have to approach it from the riverside—preferably in the morning, when the rising sun lights it up and polishes it. The view that you discover then is one of those that gives you a feeling of fulfilment and stimulates the joy of living. The vineyard appears ideally situated between sun, air and water. The west winds dry it up neither more nor less than it needs, the fine gravel drains excess moisture and the nearby river tempers the climate. A perfect location if there ever was one.

Montrose is, first and foremost, a unique place—68 hectares of a perfectly homogeneous land. In the late 18th century, this former property of Alexandre de Ségur belonged to a Mr. Théodore Dumoulin. And when Dumoulin decided to bring the moor into cultivation and grow vines on it, he was acting as a visionary, for Montrose was classified as Second Growth in 1855. However, the transformation of Montrose into a true viticultural village was brought on by the following owner, Mathieu Dollfus, who reorganised and modernised the estate, building houses for the winemakers, as well as corrals and stables for oxen and horses. Showing extensive care for his employees, he bore the cost of their health expenses and shared the estate's profits. The Charmolüe family, who bought the property from him, succeeded in maintaining the quality of this Great Classified Growth through the 20th century.

In the spring of 2006, the brothers Olivier and Martin Bouygues acquired Château Montrose. Even before being an investment, it was a love story. "I discovered Château Montrose through friends in the United States," says Martin Bouygues. "I liked it so much that I bought many vintages of it for my personal cellar. So, when I found out I had the opportunity to buy the property, I did not think twice." The new management is done with great respect for the estate's history; the pretty 19th-century chartreuse still retains its modest, country-house appearance. Regarding the wine, the skills and experience of Jean-Bernard Delmas, the son and grandson of wine-estate managers who was born at Château Haut-Brion, were called upon.

"Terroir," says Delmas, "is what gives the wine its soul. It can be credited for three-quarters of the job. Wine is not made in the cellar: it is made in the vineyard." He advocates a gentle style of winemaking, avoiding brutal pumping and racking, and fine-tuning the ageing process by carefully adjusting the proportion of new and one-year-old barrels.

Château Montrose is a noble and masculine wine, endowed with a sunny sensuality. But it can also be caressing, with a gentle attack, smooth fruitiness and a silky finish. Its expression is always confident, yielding notes of saffron, tobacco, aromatic herbs and cedarwood. Although it was cut out for lengthy ageing, it nevertheless enjoys a lovely fullness in its youth. "A great wine should always be good, whatever its age," says Delmas. "There is absolutely no harm in making wines that can be drunk young."

1. *A mere heather-covered moor until the late 18th century, this land was later converted into one of the finest vineyards of the Médoc.*

2. *"Terroir", says Jean-Bernard Delmas, "is where the soul of wine resides." In the 19th century, Montrose was organised as a genuine winemakers' village.*

3. *The old-fashioned vathouse, where wooden vats are set upon masonry jambs.*

4. *Heat-retaining, draining, regulating soil humidity and vine rooting—gravel is the gold of Médoc.*

Braised Veal Sweetbread
with Fennel and Lemon

Éric FRÉCHON
Le Bristol - Paris, France

SERVES 4

The sweetbreads and jus

2¼ pounds (1 kg) veal sweetbreads
(4 sweetbreads)

⅔ pound (300 g) boned veal breast

1 sliced carrot

1 finely sliced onion

1 bouquet garni

a few sprigs of dried fennel

3½ tablespoons (50 g) unsalted butter

salt and freshly black ground pepper

The garnish

2¼ pounds (1 kg) fresh fennel bulbs

3½ tablespoons (50 g) unsalted butter

1 preserved lemon

1 teaspoon fennel seeds,
slightly crushed

2¼ pounds (1 kg) medium-size
young carrots

2⅛ cups (50 cl) orange juice

½ pound (200 g) dry gingerbread,
blended into fine crumbs

salt and freshly ground black pepper

For the jus: Cut the veal breast into pieces and brown them in butter in a large pan with the carrot, onion and bouquet garni. Add water to barely cover, add the dried fennel and a little salt and simmer for 3 hours. The jus should be concentrated. Strain it and set it aside. You should get about 2⅛ cups (50 cl).

For the sweetbreads and jus: Preheat the oven to 300°F (150°C).

Blanch the sweetbreads briefly in boiling water and peel them. Season them with salt and pepper and brown them in butter in a sauté pan, over moderate heat. When golden brown, take them out of the pan and deglaze with some of the veal jus, scraping the bottom of the pan with a spatula. Put the sweetbreads back into the sauté pan, add the jus and roast in the preheated oven for 7 to 10 minutes.

For the garnish: Trim the fennel bulbs and cook them for 5 minutes in boiling salted water. Cut them into quarters, and then brown them in butter in a sauté pan.

Finely dice the preserved lemon and add it into the pan with a little veal jus and the fennel seeds.

Cook the carrots in orange juice and butter. When tender, drain them well and roll them in gingerbreadcrumbs.

For the presentation: Arrange the carrots on the serving plates, place the fennel around them and place 1 sweetbread on the carrots. When in season, a fennel blossom may be added for decoration. Serve the remaining jus in a gravy boat.

CHÂTEAU MONTROSE BY ANDREAS LARSSON,
BEST SOMMELIER OF THE WORLD, 2007

This is the epitome of a classic Bordeaux with its eyes in the future. I was always intrigued by the austerity of the northern Médoc, the density of the Cabernet-based wines and the unique structure that manages to combine dark ripe fruit, concentration, yet with a moderate alcohol and an always present freshness. Add to that the exquisite perfume that emerges with age, spices, cigar box, leather, cassis and minerals. And then the length—where on Earth can you get this lingering aftertaste? Remarkably precise and complex, just what makes Bordeaux a Bordeaux!

CHÂTEAU KIRWAN

MARGAUX

VINEYARD SIZE	37 hectares
VINE DENSITY	10,000 stocks per hectare
AVERAGE AGE OF VINEYARD	30 years
AVERAGE PRODUCTION	7 500 cases
SOILS AND SUBSOILS	fine gravel on a clay-limestone plateau culminating at 23 m above the Gironde
GRAPE VARIETIES	Cabernet Sauvignon 45% Merlot 30% Cabernet Franc 15% Petit Verdot 10%

In the 17th century, the château that was to be later known as Kirwan was named Domaine de La Salle, a small seignory that depended on the Château d'Issan and guarded the entrance to the river. In 1710, Renard de La Salle sold the property to Sir John Collingwood, an Englishman who was the first to develop a proper vineyard on the estate. His son-in-law, Mark Kirwan, an Irishman from Galway, gave his name to the château and made the wines famous. After losing his property during the French Revolution and recovering it under the French Consulate, he finally added the vineyards of Ganet to his own estate—then still named La Salle—obtaining the 37-hectare layout that was known at the time of the 1855 Classification and has not changed since.

Château Kirwan was sold several times during the 19th century, until shortly after the Classification, when it was bought by Camille Godard, the deputy mayor of Bordeaux. Born into a family of botanists and patrons of the arts, Godard designed the splendid 2-hectare garden, bore the first artesian well in the Médoc, planted the rose garden and built the greenhouse and wine cellars. The romantic grace of the Kirwan estate owes a lot to him. And since the railroad happened to run next to his château, he took the opportunity to build his very own little train station.

When Camille Godard died, he left Kirwan to the city of Bordeaux, which soon went looking for someone to take it over. Schyler and Schroeder, a company of German-born wine traders, were granted exclusive distribution rights after 1900, then bought the estate in 1925. Eight generations later, the Schyler family still owns the château.

A sensuous and elegant wine, Château Kirwan was mentioned in 1780 by Thomas Jefferson, who spelled it "Quirouen" and placed it "second in quality behind Margaux, La Tour, Haut-Brion and La Fite." Its blend of 45 percent Cabernet Sauvignon, 30 percent Merlot, 15 percent Cabernet Franc and 10 percent Petit Verdot shows a rare balance, the four main Médoc varietals being used in more equal proportions than elsewhere in the peninsula. Petit Verdot plays a substantial part, bringing colour, potency and a velvety texture, while the highly diversified fine gravel soil on a clayey subsoil brings strength and complexity. A mature, silky and spicy wine, often praised for its notes of tobacco, curry powder, ripe black fruit and forest floor.

"Making a great wine," explains Philippe Delfault, the general manager of Château Kirwan, "means staying as close to the terroir and the vineyard as possible. In Kirwan's case, the renovation had to be done in several successive stages. First a reorganisation of the vineyard and a remodelling of the plots were done in the 1960s, resulting in a global improvement in quality. The second stage was in the 1990s, with the advice of consultant œnologist Michel Rolland. And the third turn was taken after 2000, when we worked with increased precision to make the most of the terroir variations and establish a finer plot selection. Winemaking became a keyboard play, an extensive set of keys at our disposal. This combinatorial art is the strength of Bordeaux. A recent trend perhaps, but leaning on the skills of many Médoc maîtres de chai from past generations.

"What do we get? The very essence of the Bordeaux terroir. A delicate framework where Petit Verdot is the master beam, Cabernet Sauvignon is all the remaining framework, with Cabernet Franc giving frankness and lengthiness—and Merlot filling the roof space."

1. The lovely park of Château Kirwan was created by Camille Godard, who owned the château during the second half of the 19th century.

2. At left, a vertical press. After alcoholic fermentation, press wines, which will be used in the blend, are extracted from the marc.

3. The barrel cellar of Château Kirwan.

English-bred Lamb Saddle
with "Our Ratatouille" and Cumin Mayonnaise

Neil PERRY
Rockpool - Sydney, Australia

SERVES 8

The lamb stuffing (makes ¼ pound/125 g)

8 garlic cloves
1/3 cup (7.5 cl) chicken stock
pinch of chopped rosemary and thyme
pinch of freshly ground cumin seeds
breadcrumbs
extra virgin olive oil
lemon juice
sea salt and freshly ground white pepper

The lamb loin

1 lamb saddle (barrel)
olive oil
butchers' twine
sea salt and freshly ground white pepper
⅔ cup (15 cl) olive oil
2¼ sticks (250 g) unsalted butter
4 garlic cloves
4 sprigs thyme
2 lemons
2 teaspoons freshly ground cumin

The vegetables (makes 1⅓ pounds/600 g)

6 eggplants, cut into ½-inch (1-cm) dice
olive oil
1 cup (25 cl) basil leaves
1 cup (25 cl) parsley leaves
2 brown onions, finely diced
6 garlic cloves, finely diced
10 anchovies, finely chopped
8 red bell peppers, cut into small dice
10 tomatoes, blanched, peeled and seeded
⅛ cup (24 g) capers packed in salt, rinsed
sea salt and freshly ground black pepper

The tomato jam (makes ½ pound/250 g)

8 plum tomatoes, cored
olive oil
½ small brown onion, finely diced
1 garlic clove, finely diced

sea salt
⅛ cup (3 cl) red wine vinegar
⅛ cup (31 g) superfine sugar

cumin mayonnaise (½ pound/250 g)

For the lamb stuffing: Bring the garlic, stock, herbs and a pinch of salt to a boil in a saucepan. Simmer until most of the stock has reduced and the garlic is soft, adding stock if necessary.

Pound finely with a pestle, then add the cumin. Add breadcrumbs to bind and olive oil to slightly loosen. Season with salt, pepper and lemon juice.

For the lamb loin: Remove both filets from the loins. Roll the flesh off and reserve the carcass for stock. Cut along the spine, remove the loin, trim off skin and sinew and put in sheet pan.

Trim all sinew from the fat and cut to ¼-inch (½-cm) thickness. Pound out with a meat tenderiser. Place the loin and filets and season with salt and pepper. Spread with the stuffing and roll up with ½ inch (1 cm) overlapped. Truss at ½-inch (1-cm) intervals to form a long sausage. Do the same with the other loin. Vacuum-pack with salt, pepper and olive oil. Cook in a 125°F (52°C) water bath for 3 hours. Plunge into ice for 3 hours. Refrigerate.

For the vegetables: Lightly salt the eggplants for 15 minutes, then rinse and pat dry. Heat the olive oil in a pan and fry the eggplant dice until golden. Remove and drain on paper towels.

Reheat the oil and fry the basil and parsley; drain on paper towels Combine the eggplant, capers and herbs together in a bowl. Heat fresh oil in the pan; sauté the onion, garlic and anchovies with a pinch of salt until soft. Add the bell peppers and cook until soft, then add to the bowl with the eggplant. Warm 3 tablespoons of olive oil in a pan and gently fry the capers. Remove from the heat when lightly crisp and add to the bowl. Dice the tomatoes, add to the bowl and season with salt and pepper.

For the tomato jam: Place the tomatoes on a baking sheet with olive oil and roast at 300°F (150°C) until very soft. In a heavy-bottomed pot, sweat the onion and garlic in olive oil with a pinch of salt until soft. Pass the tomatoes through a food mill into the pot, add the vinegar and sugar and slowly reduce until thick. Blend in a high-speed blender until smooth.

To cook the lamb: Before serving, heat olive oil in a pan and add the lamb loins. Roll the loins in the pan over medium heat for 5 minutes to turn the fat a golden colour. Add the butter, garlic and thyme and foam, basting over the heat for 5 more minutes until brown and crisp. Rest the loins for 10 minutes. Warm the vegetables and tomato jam together.

For the presentation: Divide the vegetables among 8 plates. Slice the lamb into medallions and place on the bed of vegetables. Season the lamb with lemon juice, salt, pepper and a drizzle of olive oil. Spoon the mayonnaise on top and scatter the plate with freshly ground cumin.

CHÂTEAU KIRWAN BY VIRGINIA PHILIP, BEST SOMMELIER OF THE UNITED STATES, 2003

With the outstanding 2000 and 2003 vintages, Kirwan is regaining the reputation it deserves. With a considerable amount of Merlot in the blend, Château Kirwan never accounts for more than 65 percent of the harvest. The wine has the typical black fruit profile of Margaux and is considerably tight and powerful in the more youthful vintages. The structure and nose become more perfumed and elegant with time, showing its potential to age.

Château d'Issan

MARGAUX

VINEYARD SIZE	53 hectares
VINE DENSITY	8,500 stocks per hectare
AVERAGE AGE OF VINEYARD	35 years
AVERAGE PRODUCTION	30,000 cases
SOILS AND SUBSOILS	gravelly clay
GRAPE VARIETIES	Cabernet Sauvignon 65% Merlot 35%

The Great Classified Growth estates of the Médoc are a fascinating subject for lovers of 19th-century architecture. If many of their châteaux are built in a tasteful neoclassical style, with a few Palladian touches here and there, the region has its share of exotic follies, romantic neo-medieval manoirs or buildings that could have inspired Edgar Allan Poe to write a short story or two. In that context, the Château d'Issan, with four centuries of age, is a rare bird: it is not everyday that the Médoc offers you a fairytale castle.

If you encounter it at the end of the long and straight alley that goes through the vineyard, you will first discover a monumental compound encircled by a ditch. The 17th-century entrance porch dramatically opens through a courtyard onto the château's facade. The lovely gardens owe more to the French Renaissance than to the classic style: long-necked stone lions stare half in fury, half in fun, and a small round tower that completes the decor seems perfect for locking up princesses. The only element missing is a dragon or a prince. The interior of the château is lavishly furnished and decorated with rare antiques, beautiful canvases, old books, hunting trophies and touching family memorabilia, all adding to this intensely human, melancholy grace.

Issan is one of the oldest wine estates in the Médoc. In 1152, its wines were served at the wedding of Eleanor of Aquitaine and Henry Plantagenet. Later, the château successively belonged to the Ségurs, the Salignacs and the La Vergnes until the Chevalier d'Essenault, a councilor at the Bordeaux Parliament, tore down the old château and built the one we now admire. In 1866, Gustave Roy restored the château and the gardens, built the cellars and vathouse, dug an artesian well to irrigate the vineyard and promoted his wine among a few celebrities of his time; the emperor Franz-Joseph of Austria was quite a fan of Château d'Issan. However, shortly before 1914, the Roys left the estate and a period of decline followed. When the Cruses, a family of Bordeaux wine traders of Danish origin, bought the château in 1945, Issan had no more than 2 hectares left in cultivation.

Since 1994, Emmanuel Cruse, with the help of technical manager Éric Pellon, has devoted himself to the resurrection of the family property and takes passionate care of this beautiful terroir bordering the Gironde: 120 hectares including 53 hectares of soft gravel hills planted with 65 percent Cabernet Sauvignon and 35 percent Merlot. Cruse's sense of humour and friendly, lively conversation give a warm touch to this dream-like château. He has no intention, he declares, to run an American-style winery. Making the wine of Château d'Issan, to him, is serving the purpose of a deep, delicate, soulful style whose finesse and classic harmony have inspired the château's motto, *Authentically Margaux*. For a few years, he has been focusing on improving the tannic structure and achieving a perfect Cabernet Sauvignon typicity. "Cabernet Franc?" he says. "It fares better on the right bank. Unlike Petit Verdot, which I intend to try soon. Recently, I tasted a drop of it from a vat: what a taste! Pure fruit, plum jam. Hard to ripen, but when it does—I would describe it as a super–Cabernet Sauvignon and a super-Merlot. A blending booster." Since the conversation is now on taste, what style of cooking does Cruse like to pair with his wines? "The real thing!" he answers. "For me, there are no taboos in cooking. True cuisine may be any style as long as it is well made and tastes good. Oh—and I love duck."

1. *A lovely park, laid out more in the Renaissance style, surrounded by a turreted wall and a ditch—the Château d'Issan clearly came out of a fairy tale.*

2. *In the main salon, books, artwork and objects left by previous generations make up a beautiful, warm and touching interior.*

3. *This 17th-century stone portal, lost in the vineyard, materializes the estate's boundaries.*

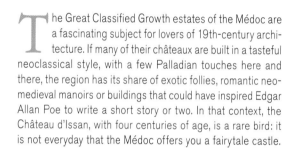

Mallard Duck
with Figs and Turnips

Michel TROISGROS

Troisgros - Roanne, France

SERVES 4

The duck

2 wild mallard ducks, about 2 pounds (900 g) each, plucked and ready for roasting, livers and hearts reserved

The garnishes

2¼ pounds (1 kg) young turnips, peeled and cut into the shape of garlic cloves

3 tablespoons olive oil

1¾ stick (200 g) unsalted butter

10 ripe black figs

⅛ pound (50 g) fresh foie gras

2⅛ cups (50 cl) Bordeaux red wine

3 tablespoons sherry vinegar

1 teaspoonn fresh ginger, finely chopped

1 cinnamon stick

2 star anise

2 whole cloves

½ cup (10 cl) veal demi-glace

fleur de sel

fine salt

freshly ground black pepper

For the duck and garnishes: Preheat the oven to 425°F (220°C). Season the ducks with salt and pepper. In a Dutch oven large enough to hold the ducks side by side, heat the olive oil, roll the ducks in it and cook until their legs are browned. When they are beginning to brown all over, put the pot in the preheated oven. Turn the ducks on their side, roast for 5 minutes on each thigh, 5 minutes on their backs, 15 minutes on the whole, basting them all the while so that their skin is nicely browned and crisped. Remove the ducks from the oven and let them rest on a rack, loosely covered with aluminum foil. Discard the fat but do not wipe the Dutch oven: you are going to make the jus in it.

While the ducks are roasting, lightly brown the turnips in butter in a sauté pan large enough to hold them in one layer. Add salt, cover with water, and simmer gently until tender. Test the doneness with the tip of a paring knife: when they seem tender, remove from the heat and set them aside.

Rinse the figs and cut off their stems. Cut 8 of the figs in a star shape at the top and insert a small knob of butter in the incision. Add a little fleur de sel and freshly ground black pepper, place them in a baking dish and bake them for 5 minutes after you have removed the ducks from the oven. Cut the 2 remaining figs into quarters and set them aside for the jus.

Pan-roast the duck livers and hearts with a little oil, keeping them pink at thecenter. Drain, purée and pass through a *tamis* (a fine-mesh sieve). Incorporate this mousse with the fresh foie gras and set aside.

For the jus: Deglaze the Dutch oven with the red wine and vinegar. Add the finely chopped ginger, cinnamon, star anise, cloves and quartered figs. Reduce, then add the demi-glace. Bring to a boil, add salt and pepper and stir in the foie mousse. Take the sauce off the heat and set aside for a few moments before straining. Keep the sauce warm.

For the presentation: Shortly before serving, carve the birds First remove the legs, separating the thighs from the drumsticks Then remove the wings, cutting along the breastbone. Reheat the ducks for 2 minutes in the oven with a little butter, making sure the meat remains pink. Slice the breast meat into long thin slices.

Arrange the duck on each plate, placing the hot turnips and figs around it. Serve the sauce on the side.

CHÂTEAU D'ISSAN BY ÉRIC BEAUMARD, SILVER MEDAL, BEST SOMMELIER OF THE WORLD, 1998

Cabernet Sauvignon retains its predominance here, supported by a complement of 30 percent Merlot. My recent tastings of the château's wines have shown them to be wonderfully delicious in their youth, while showing a definite potential for ageing and development. All these elements have been sought and brought to fruition by Emmanuel Cruse to accurately identify each vineyard parcel's character and better define the terroir at Issan.

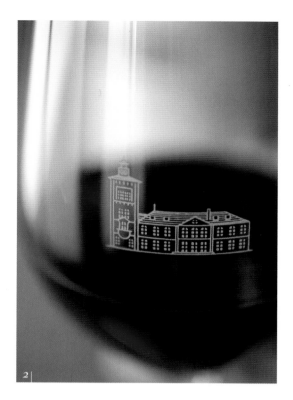

CHÂTEAU LAGRANGE

SAINT-JULIEN

VINEYARD SIZE	117 hectares
VINE DENSITY	10,000 stocks per hectare
SOILS AND SUBSOILS	two Günzian gravel hills
GRAPE VARIETIES	Cabernet Sauvignon 65% Merlot 28% Petit Verdot 7%

At the 1864 Paris Salon, a large oil on canvas by the naturalist painter Jules Breton bore the title *Les Vendanges à château Lagrange* (Grape Harvest in Château Lagrange). Now visible at the Joslyn Art Museum in Omaha (Nebraska), it shows a group of Médoc harvesters whose dignified, a trifle stiff attitudes reflect the late 19th-century ideal of peasant nobility that the naturalists held so high. Today's *Médoquines* no longer wear the white *quichenotte* head-dress that attracts the light at the centre of the painting, and harvest baskets and oxcarts are things of the past. When this painting was made, nine years after the 1855 Classification, the estate was going through its first golden age under the attentive care of Count Duchâtel, minister of Finances for King Louis-Philippe and a great lover of wines and art. The identity of the estate was visibly already quite structured to inspire and animate an artist's brush. At the time, Lagrange covered 280 hectares. However, the 20th century was a difficult period, resulting in severe surface loss. In 1983, when Château Lagrange was purchased by the Japanese spirits group Suntory, only 157 hectares remained. Lagrange nevertheless remained the most spacious of the Médoc Great Classified Growths.

Such a wide surface, in this region, necessarily implies diversified soils. Three main terroir types are found at Lagrange: heavy clayey gravel, good for Merlot; fine siliceous gravel enjoyed by Cabernet Sauvignon; and finally a local, rich in iron oxide red gravel, forming the end of a long strip that, starting at Ducru-Beaucaillou, runs through the Saint-Julien appellation. This particular soil, studded with large pebbles, has good draining and warming qualities, though its subsoil stays cool in high summer—all precious assets for the wines. Cabernet Sauvignon makes up 65 percent of the planting, followed by Merlot (28 percent) and Petit Verdot (7 percent). This last varietal was introduced in the late 1980s to increase the wine's intensity, and the proportion of Merlot was decreased.

"Right from the beginning," says Bruno Eynard, general manager of Château Lagrange, "Suntory has shown great respect for the place and serious long-term commitment. It takes two generations to work properly on a vineyard, a principle genuinely understood by the company's directors. As early as 1985, 60 hectares were planted, bringing us the opportunity to improve the plot selection. My objective is to keep the quality increase constant, leaning both on my respect for the terroir and on my attention to cutting-edge viticultural techniques." The estate also produces a second wine, Les Fiefs de Lagrange, and Les Arums de Lagrange, a delicate and aromatic white wine obtained from Sémillon, Sauvignon Blanc and Muscadelle grapes through a skilful ageing on lees.

The tannins of Château Lagrange are remarkably velvety and its aromatic precision is admirable. The wine is a seducer, offering plenty of red fruit, noble leather and precious wood. Recent vintages like 2006 and 2007 are wonderfully smooth, suave and palatable. "For a few years, climatic change has had a positive effect on Cabernet Sauvignon," Eynard explains. "It has improved the maturing qualities of this reputedly hard-to-mature grape varietal, while on the contrary Merlot indulges in its 'New World' tendencies more than ever." Given the fact that Cabernet Sauvignon is Médoc's landmark varietal, this is excellent news.

1. The great white stone château stands amid one of the largest wine estates in the Médoc.

2. Château Lagrange offers smooth, velvety tannins. The accent is placed on an accomplished cabernet Sauvignon typicity paired with the seductive style of great Saint-Julien wines.

3. A Médoc gravel hill. The extensive terroir of Lagrange necessarily includes a wide diversity of soils.

Lamb Croquettes

Yoshinori SHIBUYA
La Bécasse - Osaka, Japan

SERVES 6

The lamb

2¼ pounds (1 kg) boned lamb meat
(from the leg)

5 tablespoons (70 g) unsalted butter
(½ stick plus 1 tablespoon)

⅔ cup (100 g) chopped onion

2 garlic cloves, crushed

⅜ cup (60 g) finely diced carrot

1 cup (150 g) fresh tomatoes, peeled,
seeded and chopped

1 bouquet garni (thyme, bay leaf and
flat-leaf parsley)

3 tablespoons (50 g) tomato purée

1 soup plate of flour

2 beaten eggs

1 soup plate containing breadcrumbs

8 tablespoons (100 g) butter,
for frying the croquettes

salt and freshly ground black pepper

The sauce

1 red bell pepper,
peeled and finely diced

scant ½ cup (100 g) black olive paste

½ cup (10 cl) extra virgin olive oil

juice of ½ lemon

salt and freshly ground black pepper

For the lamb: Cube the meat. In a Dutch oven, brown the meat on all sides in hot butter. Remove the meat from the Dutch oven and set it aside on a plate.

In the Dutch oven, fry the onion, garlic and carrot until the onion is translucent. Add the lamb and its rendered juices, the tomato, the bouquet garni and a little water to make a quick sauce. Season with salt and pepper, cover and simmer for 1½ hours, or until the meat is tender. Let cool.

Purée the meat in a food processor. Mix it thoroughly with the tomato purée. Season with salt and pepper. Roll into a cylinder, wrap it in plastic wrap and refrigerate for at least 2 hours.

For the sauce: Mix the diced pepper, black olive paste and lemon juice. Season with salt and pepper.

For the croquettes: Take the meat cylinder out of the refrigerator and cut it into thickish slices. Coat them with flour, then with beaten eggs, then with breadcrumbs.

Melt the butter in a frying pan and brown the croquettes on both sides. Serve warm with the sauce on the side.

CHÂTEAU LAGRANGE BY FRANCK THOMAS,
BEST SOMMELIER OF THE WORLD, 2002

Château Lagrange is known for combining the austere power of Pauillac with the charm and elegance of Margaux. Gentle slopes descend gradually towards the Gironde, exposing the vineyard to the full and beneficial influence of the wide estuary. The growth is characterised by a high percentage of Merlot, which often gives it a more inviting style than wines from properties situated to the north near Pauillac.

CHÂTEAU LANGOA BARTON

SAINT-JULIEN

VINEYARD SIZE	18 hectares
VINE DENSITY	9,000 stocks per hectare
AVERAGE AGE OF VINEYARD	32 years
AVERAGE PRODUCTION	8,000 cases
SOILS AND SUBSOILS	gravelly soils, clayey subsoil
GRAPE VARIETIES	Cabernet Sauvignon 72% Merlot 20% Cabernet Franc 8%

In 1821, the Langoa estate, in Saint-Julien-Beychevelle, was the property of Pierre-Bernard de Pontet. Wishing to dedicate his attention to his other estate of Pontet-Canet, in Pauillac, he sold it to Hugh Barton, an Irish-born Bordeaux wine trader. Since that time, the Barton family has owned Langoa and its vineyard, as well as Léoville Barton, another Saint-Julien wine estate. In the 20th century, Ronald remained famous among the Bartons as the one most passionately devoted to winemaking. He also was one of the rare Bartons, after his ancestor Thomas (nicknamed "French Tom"), who decided to reside in France. During the difficult period that separated the two world wars, he managed to keep both of his estates whole and, after World War II, replanted his devastated vineyards. Since 1983, Château Langoa Barton has been managed by his nephew, Anthony Barton.

The château, of a very pure classic style, was built in 1758. Symmetrical in aspect, it has a slightly set-back central part, framed by two lateral wings housing the bedrooms. The shape and structure of the building are quite typical of the Bordeaux chartreuse pattern; the main floor, which receives plentiful light from many high windows, is slightly raised, above a half-basement that formerly housed the wine cellars and the kitchen. The magnificent park surrounding the château is planted with many rose and oak trees, sharing its surface between clean, orderly French-style flowerbeds and more informal English-style landscaped gardens.

"As soon as I arrived here," says Anthony Barton, "I saw that there was a lot of work to do. I first pondered over a possible renovation of the vathouse. We had these beautiful oak vats—which you still see. I wondered whether I should replace them with stainless-steel vats, but that was likely to be too expensive at the time. So I waited, and later, when the efficient modern thermoregulation system was devised, it could easily be adapted to the existing vats. That is how we were able to keep this lovely wooden vathouse while making it perfectly functional."

The Langoa Barton estate covers 18 hectares south of the Saint-Julien appellation, bordering Branaire-Ducru and Ducru-Beaucaillou. Its cool gravel soils on a clayey subsoil are planted with a large proportion of aged vines, to which a special winemaking team is devoted. The planting, a classic Médoc combination, is 72 percent Cabernet Sauvignon, 20 percent Merlot and 8 percent Cabernet Franc.

Anthony Barton considers good value an essential quality in wine. And Langoa Barton, one of the most affordable Great Classified Growths, is a wine after his own heart. A beautiful garnet colour, it offers delicate notes of dried rose, black currant and polished leather, with gamey accents. In the mouth, it is ample, velvety and elegant. It has a particular affinity with red meats and games, and is complex enough to harmonize with the fragrances of a ginger and mandarin peel–infused simmered beef stew.

"The days of 'tasting wines' are over," says Barton. "Finesse is back. I never changed my way of making my wines in order to adapt to modern tastes. These days, young people are led into believing that red wine should arouse stunning sensations, but melody and harmony are also precious! The dominance of woody taste was meant to conquer the Californian market, but those days, too, are over. Today's style consists of cultivating our style simply and honestly, and staying as close as possible to each terroir's personality."

1. *The style of the Bordeaux chartreuse finds one of its purest expressions through Château Langoa. The château is built on a half-buried cellar basement which raises the main level and brings more daylight inside.*

2. *During the primeur tastings, many rubber-stamped sample bottles are gathered on the table.*

3. *On a gravel soil resting on a clay basement, the vineyard of Langoa Barton has many aged vines and a large proportion of Cabernet Sauvignon.*

Tenderly Braised Beef Flank
and Tendon in Chinese Spices

Wai Kwan CHUI
Fook Lam Moon - Hong-Kong, China

SERVES 4

The meat

1⅓ pounds (600 g) beef flank

⅔ pound (300 g) beef tendon, cleaned

The stir-fry

2 to 3 ounces (80 g) fresh ginger, peeled and sliced

1 small piece of dried mandarin peel, soaked for 1 hour and shredded

1 peeled garlic clove, finely diced but not crushed

2 tablespoons (20 g) finely chopped shallot

2 tablespoons *chu hou* sauce (a fermented soybean paste with garlic, ginger and sesame oil)

1 scant cup (20 cl) Shaoxing rice wine

1 tablespoon soy sauce

1 tablespoon oyster sauce

For the meat: Briefly poach the meat and tendon in simmering water to clean them and defat them slightly. Drain.

Cut the meat into bite-size pieces. Poach the tendon for 1½ hours in simmering water, then trim and cut into 3-inch (7.5-cm) lengths.

For the stir-fry: Blanch the ginger briefly in boiling water, drain and pat dry. Fry it in a wok, in a good quantity of oil, until browned and crisp. Drain, discard the oil and heat the wok again. Add the ginger, shallot, mandarin peel and garlic. Stir-fry over high heat for 1 minute.

Add the meat, then the *chu hou* sauce, rice wine and oyster sauce. Mix well. Cover the wok and cook for 10 minutes to thicken the sauce. Add water to barely cover the meat.

Add the tendon, and cover with water accordingly. Cover the wok and braise for 2 hours on medium heat.

For the presentation: Remove the wok from the heat, and let cool completely before serving. When ready, reheat in a clay pot and serve burning hot.

CHÂTEAU LANGOA BARTON BY MARKUS DEL MONEGO, BEST SOMMELIER OF THE WORLD, 1998

This wine of great distinction is enticing when young, with its display of elegant fruit, yet age brings its own beautiful surprises. The recipe for this is deceptively simple: exceptional gravel terroir, hand harvesting, one-half new oak barrels and a lot of time. This may seem uncomplicated but it demands great dedication, meticulous work in both vineyard and cellar and attentive respect for the final result. This is at the heart of Château Langoa Barton's philosophy.

CHÂTEAU GISCOURS

MARGAUX

VINEYARD SIZE	83 hectares
VINE DENSITY	10,000 stocks per hectare
AVERAGE AGE OF VINEYARD	40 years
AVERAGE PRODUCTION	280,000 bottles
SOILS AND SUBSOILS	deep Margaux gravel
GRAPE VARIETIES	Cabernet Sauvignon 60% Merlot 32% Cabernet Franc 5% Petit Verdot 3%

The history of Château Giscours takes us far back in time. In the 14th century, a fortified dungeon, now disappeared, was already standing there. Some winemaking activity started there in 1552, under the impulse of Pierre de Lhomme, a rich Bordelais wine trader. From decade to decade, the wines of Giscours acquired an excellent reputation and King Louis XIV himself is said to have been a keen admirer of them. Many owners followed, until the early stage of the French Revolution, when the Marquis Claude-Anne de Saint-Simon, trying to get away from persecution, went into exile in Spain. His estate of Giscours was confiscated and sold as a Bien National. In 1847, Giscours was sold to Jean-Pierre Pescatore, a native of Luxembourg who had become an influent Parisian banker, as well as a consul of the Netherlands and a close friend of Emperor Napoléon III. In order to welcome the Empress Eugénie during her travels to and from Biarritz, he adorned the Château Giscours with all the necessary ceremonial grace, and the mansion gave way to a vast neo-renaissance palace.

In 1875, the wine trader Édouard Cruse took Giscours's destiny into his hands. His attention was devoted to the technical buildings, which were transformed to improve the production: a new cellar and vathouse were built under the direction of the architect Abel Duphot, as well as ultramodern facilities including the Ferme Suzanne—all inspired by rural Basque architecture, with ornamental crossed woodwork and prominent roofs. The massive park was designed by Eugène Bühler, a talented landscape architect who also conceived the Parc Bordelais.

After Cruse left Giscours, the estate went through a difficult period. In the early 1950s, when Nicolas Tari took it over, the 60 hectares of vineyards had shrunk to a few irregularly planted plots and the buildings were crumbling. The Taris worked hard to reinstate Château Giscours's rank of Third

Classified Growth. The 300 hectares of vineyards, meadows and woods were restructured and an artificial lake was created, as well as polo lawns between the château and the Ferme Suzanne. For 20 years, Château Giscours was famous for the sumptuous parties that were regularly held there.

However, in 1995, serious financial difficulties led the Tari family to yield the exploitation rights to the Dutch businessman Eric Jelgersma, who immediately set out to invest in the restructuring of the vineyard and the renovation of the buildings so that Château Giscours could recover its world-famous quality of Great Classified Growth. The optimal production level of the vineyard was recovered after a thorough reorganisation, which included a massive planting of 130,000 vine stocks. More investing was dedicated to the vathouse, which improved the plot selection by fermenting each lot separately.

Now the 83-hectare vineyard stretches on four gravel hills whose perfect draining qualities help the vines to penetrate deeply into the ground. The wine of Château Giscours is marked by a definite classic style, with a touch of seriousness. There is nothing small in this wine, whose expression is always ample and dignified, in perfect harmony with the majestic domain that produces it. Through its fine tannins, velvety elegance and extreme lengthiness, the slightly tense attack is followed by a growing gentleness and remarkable precision. Giscours is a mental wine, a wine of meditation, meant for masters of patience, whether in the glass or in the cellar.

1. The neo-renaissance style of the château was appreciated under the reign of Emperor Napoléon III. Giscours was built as a lodging for Empress Eugénie on her way to and from Biarritz.

2. Giscours' pure white gravel stones bear carefully tended vines. A building of service quarters stands at the edge of the park.

3. A barrel cellar at Château Giscours.

Squab with Black Truffles,
Candele Pasta Gratin and Sauce Périgourdine

Thomas KELLER

The French Laundry - Yountville (CA), United States

SERVES 4

The squab

4 squab breast halves

1 boneless duck breast,
about 6 ounces (180 g)

Kosher salt

1 large egg yolk

1/8 ounce (5 g) minced black truffle,
plus thin black truffle rounds
(to cover the squab breasts)

1½ teaspoons white truffle oil,
plus more for brushing

1/3 cup (75 g) crème fraîche

fleur de sel

The truffle sauce

½ cup (11 cl) veal stock

¼ ounce (6 g) black truffle,
finely minced

Champagne vinegar

2 teaspoons white truffle oil

Kosher salt and freshly ground white
pepper

The Brussels sprouts

4 small Brussels sprouts

beurre monté

The pasta

2 quarts (2 l) white veal stock

1 tablespoon canola oil

4½ tablespoons (57 g) unsalted butter

Kosher salt

1 1/8 pound (500 g) *candele* pasta,
handmade or store-bought

Mornay sauce

fleur de sel

For the squab: Cut the squab breasts from the bone. Remove the skin, fat and sinew from the squab and duck breasts. Lightly salt the skinned side of the squab and let sit for 20 minutes.

Cut the duck into pieces and put in a food processor. Add the egg yolk and purée. Pass the purée through a *tamis* (a fine-mesh sieve) into a bowl over an ice bath. Mix in the truffle and truffle oil. Add ¼ cup (50 g) of crème fraîche and stir vigourously until smooth and shiny.

Pat the squab breasts dry. Pipe the mousse into a dome on each squab breast, or, using a small palette knife, spread it over the squab in an even layer. Arrange overlapping truffle slices over the mousse on each breast to cover it.

Lay out 4 pieces of plastic wrap, each about 12 inches (30.5 cm) long, on the work surface with a short end toward you. Brush each piece lightly with truffle oil. Centre one breast across the bottom of one sheet of plastic wrap. Carefully roll up in the plastic so as not to disturb the layers. Gently twist one end of the plastic wrap a few times against the meat at both ends. Repeat with the remaining squab. Refrigerate until completely cold, then freeze the chilled breasts for 10 minutes. Place each wrapped squab breast in a bag. Vacuum-pack on medium-low. Cook in 140°F (61°C) water for 20 minutes, then remove and let rest for 10 minutes.

For the truffle sauce: Combine the veal stock, truffles and a drop or two of vinegar in a small saucepan; you should not taste the vinegar, just use it as you would use salt to enhance the other flavors. Bring to a simmer and cook for 3 to 4 minutes, until reduced to a sauce consistency; it should coat the back of a spoon.

For the Brussels sprouts: Remove 24 whole leaves from the sprouts and blanch them. Transfer the leaves to an ice bath, then drain and dry on paper towels. To finish, glaze the leaves in a little beurre monté in a sauté pan.

For the pasta: Bring the veal stock to a simmer. Heat the oil, butter, and a pinch of salt in a large roasting pan until the butter foams. Add the pasta and toss to coat. Cover the pasta with the veal stock and bring to a gentle boil. Cover with a sheet of parchment and cook until the pasta is *al dente*. Remove the pasta and lay side by side on a parchment paper–lined sheet pan. Gently press the pasta together.

Reduce the veal stock to a glaze and pour it over the pasta to bind the strands together. Let cool, then cut four 2- to 3-inch squares. Coat the surface of the 4 squares with Mornay sauce. Run under the broiler to brown just before serving.

For the presentation: Remove the squab from the bags and plastic wrap. Carefully turn the pieces and drain on paper towels. Trim away the two long edges of each breast. Cut each breast length-wise in half and arrange on the serving plates. Spoon the sauce around the breasts and arrange the Brussels sprout leaves around the squab. Place a square of pasta on each plate. Sprinkle the squab with fleur de sel.

CHÂTEAU GISCOURS BY YOICHI SATO,
BEST SOMMELIER OF JAPAN, 2005

Giscours has had varied fortunes but now once again enjoys an excellent reputation as a classic Margaux. The wine's classic aromas and a sensation of silky tannins, which are notable even when young, are its distinguishing characteristics.

Château Malescot Saint-Exupéry

MARGAUX

VINEYARD SIZE	28 hectares
VINE DENSITY	10,000 stocks per hectare
AVERAGE AGE OF VINEYARD	35 years
AVERAGE PRODUCTION	9,000 cases
SOILS AND SUBSOILS	Pyrenean gravel subsoil
GRAPE VARIETIES	Cabernet Sauvignon 50% Merlot 35% Cabernet Franc 10% Petit Verdot 5%

Set in the Margaux urban fabric, the Château Malescot Saint-Exupéry is a lovely surprise. The château, whose owner inhabits it permanently, looks like a haven of family peace and comfort. Here, you will find no dreamy panoramic view onto the vineyard but a wall-enclosed English-style garden with carefully tended lawn and flowers. The cellars and vathouse have a charm of their own; built around 1870, roughly at the same time as the château, they embody the estate's particular philosophy: remembering the values of the past while keeping track of modern technical innovations. The immediately noticeable soul of the place conveys great gentleness and the visible signs of a genuine dedication to wine.

The château bears the name of Simon Malescot, a royal councillor at the Bordeaux Parliament who, in 1697, purchased the vineyard from Louise Escoussès. His family made it thrive for the next century and a half, until 1827 when Count Jean-Baptiste de Saint-Exupéry (grandfather of Antoine, author of *The Little Prince*) acquired it. In 1855, it was under the owner-ship of one Mr. Fourcaude and his son-in-law Mr. de Boissac—who built the château and the winemaking buildings—that the wine was classified as Grand Cru. After 1880, the estate met the same fate as many others: mildew, phylloxera, frequent changes of owner, and finally World War II. During the 1950s, Paul Zuger, a Swiss-born winemaker who also owned the Château Marquis d'Alesme, decided to resurrect the vineyard with the help of his sons Jean-Claude and Roger. Later, he left Marquis d'Alesme to the former and Malescot Saint-Exupéry to the latter. Currently, Roger's son Jean-Luc, an expert and passionate winemaker, manages the estate, with the help of Gilles Pouget, technical manager, and Marie Kahn-Chabalier, cellar master.

The entrance into the vathouse produces a striking æsthetic impression: the ceiling is supported by an impressive timber framework made of Russian red fir—wood that was acquired in exchanged for many cases of wine—whose posts and beams frame the base of the stainless-steel vats. A delicate double-flighted staircase, made of the same Russian red fir, leads to the upper floor and harvest delivery zone, which houses the first gravitary fermenting system in the history of Médoc. The expression "cuvier de type Malescot" (Malescot-type vathouse) was even used in the late 19th century to describe such a system.

On 28 hectares of vineyard in the Margaux appellation, the planting is 50 percent Cabernet Sauvignon, 35 percent Merlot, 10 percent Cabernet Franc and 5 percent Petit Verdot. The vines, 35 years old on average, are in some places 50 years of age.

After the harvest, the grapes are left to rest for 24 hours in cold storage for a stage of pre-fermentation maceration without the addition of carbon dioxide. Then they are de-stemmed through a special spiked-roller device and conveyed to the sorting table. The idea is to work horizontally and manipulate the berries as little as possible. No exogenous yeasts are used for the alcoholic fermentation process and the wine is aged on lees, with batonnage, and bottled without any filtration. All these precautions combine to produce a rich texture in this Great Classified Growth, which has benefited from Michel Rolland's œnologic counselling since 1990.

The tasting is as striking an experience as the discovery of the vathouse: this Margaux shows a perfect balance of velvety texture and freshness, of character and deliciousness. Upon its highly distinguished tannic structure rest notes of dried red roses, mature cherry and geranium. Sometimes, the aromas evoke fresh green chillies, amaretto and Japanese cherry blossom: a truly original aromatic palette, another lovely surprise kept in store for you by this unique and elegant château.

1. Château Malescot Saint-Exupéry's bottle cellar keeps many magnums and large-volume bottles, which hint at the wine's ageing capacity.

2. While located in the heart of Margaux village, the château and garden enjoy a peaceful atmosphere.

3. The main gate opens directly onto the Route des Châteaux.

4. A lovely, delicate red Russian firwood staircase leads up from the vathouse's first level to the harvest reception space.

Beef Rib "De nos Monts"* à la Vigneronne

Gérard RABAEY

Le Pont de Brent - Brent, Switzerland

SERVES 2

The beef rib

1 beef rib "De nos Monts," about 2¼ pounds (1 kg), trimmed

¼ cup (5 cl) grape seed oil

3 tablespoons (40 g) unsalted butter

3 shallots

fleur de sel

salt and freshly ground black pepper

The red wine sauce

⅛ cup (20 g) finely chopped shallot

1½ tablespoons (20 g) butter

sprig of thyme

½ bay leaf

½ cup (10 cl) red wine

1 scant cup (20 cl) brown veal stock

salt

crushed black peppercorns

* "De nos Monts" ("From our Mountains") is a quality label from our region (the Vaud and Fribourg Préalpes).

Cut the roots of the shallots but do not peel them. Place them in a lightly oiled dish and roast in a low 250°F (120°C) oven for 1½ hours.

Trim the rib bones by tucking back the flesh. Cut out the fat and sinew, then set aside.

Thirty minutes before roasting the rib, take it out of the refrigerator to bring it to room temperature. Season with salt and freshly ground pepper. Preheat the oven to 510°F (266°F).

In a pan, brown the rib on both sides in the grape seed oil, and then stand it on the fatty part and brown for a while.

Roast for 12 minutes in the preheated oven, basting from time to time. Then lower the temperature to 400°F (200°C). Discard the fat from the pan and replace it with a knob of butter.

Roast for 18 more minutes, basting, then remove the rib from the oven, add a little more fleur de sel, cover with aluminum foil and let the rib rest for 20 to 25 minutes on a rack with a dish placed underneath to catch the juices; the rendered juice will be added to the sauce to finish it.

For the red wine sauce: Sweat the shallots in butter with a little crushed pepper, a small sprig of thyme and the ½ bay leaf. Add the red wine and reduce by two-thirds. Add the stock and the rendered juices and simmer gently until the sauce is thick, smooth and shiny. Strain and correct the seasoning.

For the presentation: Just before serving, place the beef rib on a platter with the roasted shallots. You may serve grapes and julienned country ham with it. Serve the sauce in a gravy boat.

CHÂTEAU MALESCOT SAINT-EXUPÉRY BY OLIVIER POUSSIER, BEST SOMMELIER OF THE WORLD, 2000

Owned by Roger Zuger, this property is comprised of around 20 hectares of very well-situated vines, with a classic composition of a majority of Cabernet Sauvignon accompanied by a high percentage of Merlot. For the past decade this exceptional terroir has shown the finesse and elegance for which Margaux is known, and the balance worthy of a Third Growth.

CHÂTEAU BOYD-CANTENAC

MARGAUX

VINEYARD SIZE	17 hectares
VINE DENSITY	10,000 stocks per hectare
AVERAGE AGE OF VINEYARD	44 years
AVERAGE PRODUCTION	5,000 cases
SOILS AND SUBSOILS	lean siliceous early Quaternary gravel
GRAPE VARIETIES	Cabernet Sauvignon 67% Merlot 24% Petit Verdot 9%

The perfect mastery of an art is not only a way to experience its finest nuances but also to multiply the amount of pleasure it provides. Wine is a perfect example of that principle. As you deepen your knowledge of its components—technology or tasting—the sensory palette that conveys that information gradually opens up to an infinite extent. Perfecting the analysis can only strengthen the capacity for synthesis; and pleasure is the synthesis of great wines, either through their organoleptic properties or the harmony of their pairing with food. The greatest wine experts, the most able and knowledgeable winemakers, never dissociate wine from the notion of pleasure.

You need to be face to face with Lucien Guillemet, owner of Château Boyd-Cantenac in Margaux, to hear him insisting, with intense solemnity, on the hedonistic dimension that should underlie any writing about wine. Promoting pleasure through seriousness? Absolutely. Pleasure is indeed a very serious affair. Lucien's words make it sound like a form of initiation: "Great Classified Growths are too often surrounded with an aura of esoterism, and considered somewhat out of reach. That is a mistake. Pleasure should be learned. And in matters of pleasure, you always learn on the job. Happiness is not at the end of the road, but along the road." Good wines, for Guillemet, are first and foremost the ones you want to drink again. And their field of application is the dining table, not the professional tasting.

Lucien Guillemet, from the first contact, radiates expertise and knowledge through his strong presence. "This château," he says, "is one of the few whose owner is completely in charge of the winemaking. We have no consultant œnologist. And I am quite happy with that."

The estate covers 17 hectares of deep siliceous gravel with good draining power, in the heart of the Margaux appellation. It owes its name to the Boyds, a family of cloth traders who had to leave Belfast when the prices of wool collapsed. They emigrated to the Bordeaux region and bought the vineyard in 1754. After being run for some time by John Lewis Brown, then by the Ginestets, it was purchased in 1932 by the Guillemet family, who now runs it alongside their other wine estate, Château Pouget. There is no château strictly speaking, but a former wine cellar converted into a house serves as a château for both Pouget and Boyd-Cantenac. The culture and winemaking methods are different for each wine. Boyd-Cantenac is made with 9 percent Petit Verdot, while at Pouget Cabernet Franc plays the part of the minority grape variety. Sixty-seven percent Cabernet Sauvignon and 24 percent Merlot complete the planting.

The wine of Château Boyd-Cantenac is often described as gentler than its companion, as well as richer in complex harmonies and enchanting aromas. After a clean and rich attack, its finish is quite generous, resting on noble and elegant tannins that ensure that the wine will keep for a long time. "I believe," says Lucien Guillemet, "that my wines are classical Margaux, endowed with a lot of finesse. Although they may seem a bit stern at an early age, time reveals their complexity. They are long and persistent, and not aggressive, dry or heavy. Merlot is a grape variety that tells everything at once. It has a tendency to slouch a bit, a slightly languid nature. Cabernet Sauvignon is quite the contrary: not as caressing as Merlot, but the charm of the Great Classified Growths of Médoc lies precisely in that exceptional aromatic persistence of Cabernet Sauvignon. The true essence of Margaux."

1. A detail of Château Boyd-Cantenac's stainless-steel vathouse.

2. The château is actually a former cellar converted into a house. It gets its peculiar grace from its wide facade with low side aisles, adorned with medallions.

3. The brand of the château is printed black on the red tin bottle cap.

4. The barrel cellar.

Vineyard Snails
and Mushroom Dariole

Hyo Nam PARK
Seasons - Seoul, South Korea

SERVES 4

The snails

1½ ounces (40 g) cooked snails

¼ cup (40 g) finely chopped onion

2 tablespoons finely chopped garlic

unsalted butter

⅓ cup (8 cl) Pernod

⅔ cup (16 cl) red wine

½ pound (200 g) mushrooms, finely chopped

¼ pound (120 g) fresh shiitake mushrooms

2 eggs, beaten

2 tablespoons dry breadcrumbs

1 teaspoon fresh thyme, chopped

2 tablespoons chopped parsley

4 bay leaves

salt

freshly ground black pepper

The thyme sauce

1 tablespoon (14 g) unsalted butter

1 tablespoon finely chopped onion

1 teaspoon finely chopped garlic

½ cup (12 cl) whole milk

pinch of chopped fresh thyme

2 tablespoons chopped parsley

salt

freshly ground black pepper

For the snails: Sauté the snails, chopped onions and minced garlic. Add the Pernod and red wine and cook for a few minutes.

In another pan, sauté the mushrooms in a little butter. When soft, take off the heat, and add to the snails. Add the chopped parsley, bread-crumbs, eggs and salt and pepper to taste.

For the darioles: Preheat the oven to 475°F (250°C). Quickly sauté the shiitake mushrooms in butter until slightly softened. Slice thinly.

Butter the inside of 4 round dariole moulds or small round ovenproof bowls. Arrange the thinly sliced shiitake mushrooms so that they line the inside, slightly overlapping. Fill with the snail and mushroom mixture. Then bake for 15 minutes, preferably in a bain-marie.

For the thyme sauce: Melt the butter in a saucepan and sweat the onion and garlic for 2 minutes. Add the milk and a pinch of thyme, and cook for 2 minutes. Boil down until thickened, then add the parsley, salt and pepper.

For the presentation: Pour the sauce onto the plates. Unmould the darioles in the middle of each plate, stick a bay leaf into each and serve.

CHÂTEAU BOYD-CANTENAC BY SERGE DUBS,
BEST SOMMELIER OF THE WORLD, 1989

I admire this property's firm and unwavering determination in clearly declaring fidelity to the authenticity and character of Margaux's terroir. Boyd-Cantenac seduces us by its refusal to yield to that technological concentration, which can often erase a terroir's finesse. This generous wine charms the senses and delicately caresses the taste buds; its fruity, spirited bouquet is tantalising, and a tender finish on a comfortingly soft note impresses the palate.

CHÂTEAU CANTENAC BROWN

VINEYARD SIZE	48 hectares
VINE DENSITY	8,500–10,000 stocks per hectare
AVERAGE AGE OF VINEYARD	35 years
AVERAGE PRODUCTION	20,000 cases
SOILS AND SUBSOILS	Günzian gravel
GRAPE VARIETIES	Cabernet Sauvignon 65% Merlot 30% Cabernet Franc 5%

In the midst of its landscaped garden, the imposing château can be seen from afar, standing out on a background of trees that line the Plateau de Cantenac to the east. Its unmistakeable British-mansion looks are easily explained by the Scottish origin of its first owner, John Lewis Brown, a wildlife artist who bought the vineyard in the 19th century and built the house in a remarkably pure neo-Tudor style that could also be described as "haunted house style." In spite of the visual grandeur of the place, though, there is no melancholy attached to it, and haunting it was probably not the easiest of tasks; if any ghosts ever had the intention of settling in at the time, they had to bear with the various celebrations, huge parties and memorable festivities organised by the lord of the château, a lover of fine wines and good living.

Regarding the wines, Mr. Brown had chosen his retreat wisely. The Plateau de Cantenac, which includes the plots of several prestigious Margaux wines, is famous for its deep soils of fine Günz gravel, a promise of elegant and complex wines.

The property, divided several times during its history, was restructured by AXA Millésimes, who purchased it in 1989. In 2006, when the English businessman Simon Halabi took charge of Cantenac Brown's destiny, he kept José Sanfins, who had managed it since 1989, at his position, paying hommage to the excellent job he had done for years and setting out to bring the wines to their highest level of quality. The Halabi family is currently buying back parts of the park and plots of vineyard; originally, the vines of Cantenac Brown covered 150 hectares. Now, 48 hectares are cultivated, mainly in Cabernet Sauvignon (65 percent), with 30 percent of Merlot and 5 percent in Cabernet Franc. The average age of the vines is 35 years.

The Great Classified Growth of Château Cantenac Brown is neither classical nor modern. It is, quite simply. It shows the characteristic finesse of the wines grown on this part of the plateau. In wine affairs, nothing happens by chance. You never see sad men making joyful wines, and vice versa. The passion and vigour that can be seen spinning in a glass of Cantenac Brown can also be heard in José Sanfins's voice and spread to the conversation itself. His wines are dense in the mouth, with a pure expression of the fruit, a solid structure, and fine, tight tannins. Wines for fun, for the table and for feasting.

Sanfins is also an advocate of sustainable wine-growing and winemaking methods, plant-based fertilisers, traditional soil maintenance techniques and gravitary fermentation. He loves to discuss and comment on the beauties of the land, from the rose trees that grace the end of each row of vines to the venerable trees growing in the park, which he likes for its lush, semi-wild appearance.

The ornamental forested park was created around 1870 by two renowned landscape architects, the Bühler brothers. They were, at the time, working in Gironde often, and among other landmarks they created the Parc Bordelais. They left their signature on the Château Cantenac Brown through distinctive features, some of them still visible more than a century and a half later—the serpentine watercourse; the great variety of tree species, both in the ornamental area and in the forested area; a circuit of footpaths designed in a bow-shape; garden sceneries showcasing the majesty of the plant varieties, either scattered or in dense bouquets; and, finally, the layout of the flowerbeds. This peaceful haven of a park, re-created in 2007 by the new owner, covers 15 hectares in one piece.

1. *A frontal view of the château and forested park in the background. This Tudor-style manor was built by wildlife painter John Lewis Brown.*

2. *In the high-ceilinged vathouse, fermentations are strictly watched in order to promote fruitiness and delicacy in the wines.*

3. *A barrel cellar in Château Cantenac Brown.*

Spit-roasted Veal Shank,
Garden Vegetables and Herbed Jus

Bernard & Guy RAVET
L'Ermitage - Vufflens-le-Château, Switzerland

SERVES 4

1 hind veal shank, 2⅛ pounds (1.3 kg);
have the butcher saw the bone
to an 8-inch (20-cm) length

1¼ cups (30 cl) white wine

2 cloves garlic

1 bouquet garni: bay leaf,
rosemary, thyme

4 tablespoons (50 g)
unsalted butter (½ stick)

1 scant cup (20 cl) veal jus

a choice of fresh garden vegetables

A day in advance, season the shank with salt and pepper, and marinate with the white wine, crushed garlic and herbs in a covered dish in the refrigerator.

The next day, place the shank on the spit (if you have one; otherwise, see below) and rub it with the half-stick of butter and some marinade. Begin roasting in a 450°F (230°C) oven until the shank begins to brown, then lower the temperature to 300 to 350°F (150 to 177°C) and roast for 2 hours, basting as often as possible.

If you do not have a spit, Preheat the oven to 400°F (200°C), brown the shank in a sauté pan with butter, then lay it in an ovenproof dish with more butter and roast for 30 minutes. Add the marinade, lower the oven temperature to 350°F (177°C), cover and roast in a covered dish for 1 hour, turning the shank over and basting it from time to time. Add the veal jus and roast for 30 minutes, uncovered, until nicely browned and glazed.

When the time is up, remove the shank from the oven. Cut it holding the knife perpendicular to the bone, then arrange the slices on a dish with the bone standing up. Strain the jus and serve it in a warmed gravy boat. Serve with the garden vegetables; you may add some diced beets, blanched rutabagas stewed in butter or a few artichoke hearts.

CHÂTEAU CANTENAC BROWN BY ANDREAS LARSSON, BEST SOMMELIER OF THE WORLD, 2007

Cantenac Brown is très Margaux to me, always built on a fine balance, between ripe dark berries, roasted coffee aromas and a medium-weight structure on the palate. It is a wine that in recent vintages has been fairly approachable in its youth with a nice purity of flavours and balanced tannins, even if it is a wine that is best drunk after five years and preferably more. An elegant and well-made Margaux!

CHÂTEAU PALMER

MARGAUX

VINEYARD SIZE	55 hectares
VINE DENSITY	10,000 stocks per hectare
AVERAGE AGE OF VINEYARD	38 years
AVERAGE PRODUCTION	7,000 cases
SOILS AND SUBSOILS	deep Pyrenean gravel
GRAPE VARIETIES	Cabernet Sauvignon 47% Merlot 47% Petit Verdot 6%

The wine of Château Palmer exerts a spell on those who make it. Upon discovering the ardent connection between this terroir and the team of winemakers who cultivates it, you are tempted to wonder which one communicates its passion to the other. One does not own a Great Classified Growth; one is owned by it. The terroir constantly brings to mind the essence that is inseparably attached to it; hence the enchanted atmosphere that greets anyone visiting those châteaux.

Château Palmer is a wine of ancient nobility. It was already celebrated in the early 18th century, when the estate was known as Château de Gasq. The terroir says it all: 55 hectares of Pyrenean gravel on a mineral-rich subsoil that "look onto the river." General Charles Palmer, who served in the English army under Wellington, acquired the estate in 1814 and gave it his name. Later, the Pereire brothers—famous bankers and urban planners who shaped much of Paris's appearance during the Haussmann era and founded the Arcachon seaside resort—bought Château Palmer and, in 1856, built the elegant neoclassical, turret-adorned castle. However, the winemaking facilities, built a few decades before under General Palmer's ownership, are no less beautiful in the simplicity of their bare stone facades, which have been recently restored. The cellars, with simple whitewashed walls, are also in harmony with the traditionally inspired winemaking spirit that reigns here.

Since 1937, Château Palmer has been owned by the descendants of the associated Sichel and Mähler-Besse families, with Thomas Duroux as technical manager. Some decades ago, the joint ownership included Louis Miailhe, a lover of Merlot. This explains why this grape variety shares the planting in equal proportion with Cabernet Sauvignon (47 percent each), Petit Verdot making up the remaining 6 percent. An atypical blend, which Duroux explains: "There is a general tendency to plant Merlot wherever you cannot plant Cabernet Sauvignon. That is precisely where Palmer's peculiarity lies: our Merlots are planted on Cabernet soils. This gives our Merlots an uncommon level of quality, a strong personality and distinguished finesse. On great soils, the grape variety disappears. Here, the terroir speaks, the vine follows."

Bursting with sensuality and passion, Château Palmer is one of the warmest Margaux Great Classified Growths. Fiery, crunchy and spicy, it has the power of awakening the senses and mind, creating the illusion of sunlight on a grey day. The refined typicity of this wine reflects a true dedication to terroir—fresh red and black fruit, a singing grace and a delicate fragrance of raindrops on warmed stones. Incidentally, it is interesting to note how close behind Alter Ego, a companion wine rather than a second wine, follows the Great Classified Growth. Alter Ego was conceived in 1998 from a new approach to selecting and blending. Its authors see it as the other version of the same terroir, in the way that a classic fugue may be played in a jazzy way or an 18th-century novel can be adapted to a 20th-century setting. The beautiful label is identical to that of Château Palmer with inverted colours—black on a gold background, whereas Palmer's label is gold on black—as a stylish expression of this brotherly relationship.

1. *A forested park, dominated by a tall stone pine, surrounds Château Palmer on the plateau de Margaux.*

2. *The château was built by the Pereire brothers in 1856.*

3. *The beautiful winemaking buildings, reflected in the cellar's French window pane, were built in the early 19th century.*

Smoked Eel on Burnt Toast,
Red Wine Sauce

Christian LE SQUER
Ledoyen - Paris, France

SERVES 4

The eel and potatoes

1 smoked eel, large enough to yield
8 filets, 2½ inches (6 cm) each;
1¾ ounce (50 g) per serving

8 roseval potatoes
(pink-skinned, firm-fleshed potatoes)

8 white bread rectangles cut the same
size as the eel filets;
⅔ ounce (20 g) per serving

sprig of dill

The fumet

head, bones and trimmings from the eel

4 finely sliced shallots

1¼ cups (30 cl) white wine

1¼ cups (30 cl) chicken stock

The red wine sauce

a bottle of Chinon

1 tablespoon sugar

heavy cream

1 tablespoon veal jus

The horseradish cream

1 scant cup (20 cl) crème fraîche

grated horseradish

juice of 1 lemon

salt and freshly ground black pepper

The herb butter

9 tablespoons (125 g) unsalted butter
(1 stick plus 1 tablespoon)

1½ tablespoons (10 g) chopped parsley

1 teaspoon garlic

¾ teaspoon pastis (Pernod will do)

salt and freshly ground black pepper

For the eel and potatoes: Filet the smoked eel, reserving the head, skin and bones. Use those to make a fumet with the sliced shallots, white wine and white chicken stock; strain the fumet and set aside. Cut the filets into 2½-inch (6-cm) rectangles, set aside. Keep the trimmings; dry them before grinding them into a fine powder that will be used to finish the dish.

Cut the potatoes into square shapes, about 1³⁄₁₆ inches (3 cm) in size and ½ inch (1.5 cm) thick. Carve them with a melon baller or a cutter. Once hollowed out, cook them in 2⅛ cups (50 cl) of eel fumet until tender.

For the sauce: Reduce the wine by half, and add the sugar. Add the cream and reduce until thick. Taste and correct the seasoning with sugar and salt. Keep the sauce warm.

CHÂTEAU PALMER BY VIRGINIA PHILIP, BEST SOMMELIER OF THE UNITED STATES, 2002

Château Palmer has an excellent reputation for its ability to age. Many consider Palmer to be one of the finest wines in Margaux and its second wine, «Alter Ego,» is almost as well known. Full-bodied with a combination of black and red fruits, the wine has a hint of spice and espresso on the nose. On the palate, dark fruits, spice and grip-y tannins make the wine complex and classic for its terroir.

CHÂTEAU LA LAGUNE

HAUT-MÉDOC

VINEYARD SIZE	80 hectares
VINE DENSITY	6,666 stocks per hectare
AVERAGE AGE OF VINEYARD	35 years
AVERAGE PRODUCTION	9,000 cases
SOILS AND SUBSOILS	gravel
GRAPE VARIETIES	Cabernet Sauvignon 60% Merlot 30% Petit Verdot 10%

The history of the southernmost Great Classified Growth of Médoc began in the 16th century, but the lovely chartreuse with its double-flighted stone staircase was built by the Baron Louis in 1730. Surrounded by the winemaking buildings and a vast park, the château crowned an estate whose wines were already celebrated for their elegance, harmony and feminine grace. The gravelly hill of La Lagune, stretching from South to North, is one of the finest in the Médoc. It is also the first one you encounter as you drive up from Bordeaux. Often referred to as a model of great Médoc terroir, it is remarkably homogenous—80 hectares of fine, deep, warm and draining gravel on a cool subsoil. Petit Verdot, as 10 percent of the blend, plays an unusually large part in the wine's typicity. This traditional grape varietal, known for it fragility but also for its ability to bring colour and a velvety texture, does very well on the La Lagune soil, where 60 percent Cabernet Sauvignon and 30 percent Merlot complete the planting.

Caroline Frey, trained as œnologist, has owned Château La Lagune since 2004. This clear-eyed young blonde woman, who initially intended to start a career in riding sports, traded her saddle and boots for a wine to which she now devotes her entire energy. In order to watch over the smallest details of the viticultural, winemaking and ageing processes, she lives on the property. Her team is led by Patrick Moulin, technical manager; Jérôme Juhé, cellar master; Pierre Vital, cultural director; and Denis Dubourdieu, consultant œnologist.

A visit to La Lagune is rich in contrasting experiences. The lovely, nicely renovated vaulted kitchen in the château's basement summons the memories of a classic lifestyle, as also do the two courtyards and the tree-planted park. However, this feeling of antique civilisation is sure to be counterbalanced by your discovery of the technical facilities, which will throw you into a Jules Verne– or Stanley Kubrick–like vision.

Immediately as you enter, 72 sparkling stainless-steel vats stand before you in a curve, laid out like huge chess pieces in a 2,000-square-metre fermenting room. Few vathouses in the region convey such an overwhelming visual sensation. The most interesting part, however, may be seen upstairs, on the steel platforms. The whole vathouse is designed for gravitary fermentation: once the grapes are brought up on two small elevators, they undergo three successive sortings before the final crushing. Then they are led into the selected vat through the use of two spectacular articulated stainless steel arms with a 5 percent slope. Each vat is treated individually, with respect to the plot selection, and the filling involves no pumping—a gentle style of winemaking whose results may be enjoyed in the glass. "The Bordeaux of today," says Juhé, "is not the one of 50 years ago, or even of 10 years ago. Which does not mean that the codes of traditional winemaking handed down by generations of Médocains have been lost."

"We strive to reach perfection", says Frey, "seeking to achieve optimal harmony between the soil and the vine, and fermenting gently, through successive phases of extraction, in order to preserve the berries' wholesomeness. Our ageing in barrels also shows this respect for the grapes: the proportion of new oak has dropped from 80 percent to 60 percent since 2004. That was also the year when we began to apply integrated pest control. Our next aim is to work entirely in biodynamic agriculture. That will take a bit of time, but our mind is firmly set."

1. The impressive stainless-steel vathouse of Château La Lagune is visible through large bay windows in the barrel cellar. The gravitary fermentation facilities are some of the most sophisticated in the region.

2. Shimmering garnet-coloured velvet and polished mahogany give the château's interior a luxurious, cosy classic atmosphere.

3. Protected by a finely wrought ironwork gate, the chartreuse is built in a charming 18th-century style.

Lamb Loin in Herb
and Preserved-Lemon Crust, Pineapple Maki

Arnaud BIGNON
Spondi - Athens, Greece

SERVES 2

The crust

¼ cup (20 g) chopped parsley

2 to 3 tablespoons chopped fresh cilantro leaves

⅔ ounce (20 g) preserved lemon

⅛ pound (50 g) fresh brioche

2 tablespoons olive oil

The relish

4 onions

olive oil

4 garlic cloves

sprig of thyme

1 teaspoon Madras curry powder

green curry paste

The maki

1 tablespoon chopped onion

olive oil

½ cup (80 g) basmati rice

coconut milk

chicken stock

1 pineapple

The lamb

2 lamb loins, about ¼ pound (130 g) each

⅓ ounce (10 g) jumbo raisins

lamb jus

gingerbread spice mix

shredded fresh coconut (for garnish)

fresh cilantro leaves (for garnish)

For the herb crust: Blend the ingredients for the crust and set them aside.

For the relish: Finely slice the onions and sweat them in olive oil with the garlic and the thyme sprig, covered. Uncover the pan towards the end of the cooking, and add the curry powder and a little green curry paste. Purée in a blender, strain and pour into a muslin towel or bag and let drip overnight until you achieve a thick paste.

For the maki: Sweat the chopped onion in olive oil, then add the basmati rice, two-thirds of the coconut milk and one-third of the chicken stock; the rice should be covered with three times its volume in liquid. Cook for 12 minutes over medium heat.

Finely slice the pineapple ⅛ inch (2 mm) thick on a slicing machine. Lay them, slightly overlapped, on a sheet of plastic wrap, then cover with the rice, roll up in the plastic wrap to form the maki and refrigerate.

When cold, cut the maki in slanted chunks of decreasing lengths, making 3 per serving. Steam for 1½ minutes.

For the lamb: Roast the lamb loins, and then cover them with the herb crust and brown for a few seconds under the grill (broiler). Trim the ends.

Plump the raisins in lamb jus with the gingerbread spices.

For the presentation: In two oval plates with rectangular cavities, place a spoon filled with the relish, then place 3 maki at the opposite side of each plate and top with a bit of shredded fresh coconut. Pour the jus in the middle of each plate and place a loin over it.

GRAND CRU CLASSÉ

CHÂTEAU LA LAGUNE
2005
HAUT-MÉDOC

CHÂTEAU LA LAGUNE BY ÉRIC BEAUMARD, SILVER MEDAL, BEST SOMMELIER OF THE WORLD, 1998

Major renovations have been made at the property, which allow this Third Growth to fully realise its potential. The château's wine is charming, with tannins that testify to the direct, attractive development of this growth. Of particular note is the wine's unusually high proportion (10 to 15 percent) of Petit Verdot. La Lagune has made a commitment to lower yields in order to produce a deep, tense wine of great quality.

CHÂTEAU DESMIRAIL

MARGAUX

VINEYARD SIZE	40 hectares
VINE DENSITY	7,000 stocks per hectare
AVERAGE AGE OF VINEYARD	25 years
AVERAGE PRODUCTION	10,000 cases
SOILS AND SUBSOILS	deep Quaternary gravel
GRAPE VARIETIES	Cabernet Sauvignon 69% Merlot 29% Petit Verdot 2%

The vineyard of Château Desmirail was originally part of Pierre de Rauzan's estates. In the late 17th century, a young lady of the Rauzan family brought some of that land as a dowry to her husband, the attorney Jean Desmirail. Their wines became so esteemed that they were classified as Third Growth in 1855. In the early 20th century, the Château Desmirail belonged to the Berlin banker Robert de Mendelssohn, a nephew of the famous composer. The property was confiscated by the French state during World War I and, in 1923, was auctioned to Martial Michel, a glove manufacturer from the North of France. He did not preserve the integrity of the estate, selling the château, the vineyard and the technical buildings in separate lots in 1938. Château Palmer got some of the plots, while the château went into the property of Château Marquis d'Alesme.

After World War II, Lucien Lurton, head of a famous family of Bordeaux winemakers, decided to resurrect Desmirail. Little by little, he bought the scattered plots and eventually laid down the last piece of the jigsaw puzzle by trading a few plots with Château Palmer in order to return the estate to its original name. The phoenix was rising again from its ashes, but the technical buildings were still missing. The cellar and vathouse of Port-Aubin, a former *palus* wine estate in Cantenac, were bought for that purpose, and a pretty neo-chartreuse was built right in front of the cellar. Lucien Lurton could rightly be proud of their work, all the more since the wines of the château were also undergoing a regeneration. The fact that all the elements at Desmirail fit together in perfect harmony makes its history particularly touching and admirable. Such is the meaning conveyed by the great pink Italian marble portal that Lucien Lurton erected at the entrance of Château Desmirail; it expresses the wish to create the individuality of the place after gathering spare parts into a coherent ensemble, in the same way that the ability to draw the boundary between inside and outside makes a front door the most sacred part of a house.

Since 1992, Denis Lurton has owned the Château Desmirail and pursued the work of his father, Lucien, with the help of Pierre Laffeuillade, *maître de chai* and vineyard manager, and the advice of the consultant œnologist Jacques Boissenot. The two-level wooden vathouse, with the harvest reception zone on the upper floor, has been preserved in its original state, underneath a splendid riveted-laminated wood roof. Another stainless-steel vathouse was added in 1997.

The vines cover 40 hectares on the communes of Cantenac, Arsac and Soussans. The current planting is 69 percent Cabernet Sauvignon, 29 percent Merlot and 2 percent Petit Verdot. However, says Denis Lurton, "the terroir leads and the grape varietal follows, not the other way around." No green harvest is necessary, the natural productivity of the vineyard being weak enough. Harvesting is done after careful tasting of the berries. "This remains the best way to judge maturity," he says. "The final decision is taken in the vineyard. Having scientific analysis to support us is always appreciated, but there is no way technology could ever replace human expertise."

The successful result of this delicate approach to winemaking is the rich fruity taste of Château Desmirail—red fruit and particularly red plum—and the soft feeling of its mature, velvety tannins with no trace of harshness. A rare, delicately spiced roasted piece of venison will be a perfect match for the elegant texture of this wine.

1. Behind the gate, the cellar buildings date from the last third of the 19th century.

2. The old Desmirail estate was patiently reconstructed by Lucien Lurton, who passed it onto his son Denis.

3. The harvest reception zone, where gravitary fermentation is carried on, lies under an original 19th-century riveted-laminated wood roof structure.

4. A classic, dark-coloured Margaux with rich fruity notes and a soft velvety texture.

Venison
with Scheiterhaufen

Heinz REITBAUER
Steirereck - Wien, Austria

SERVES 4

The venison

1¾ pound (800 g) venison loin
(off the bone and silver skin removed)
unsalted butter
streaky bacon
thyme
juniper berries
½ cup (12 cl) venison jus
salt

The glaze

1 cup (25 cl) Port
2 tablespoons red wine vinegar
2 tablespoons brown sugar
¼ cup (6.5 cl) maple syrup

The aromatic powder

2 teaspoons dried lavender
1 tablespoon dried cèpes
1 tablespoon chestnut powder

The scheiterhaufen
*Scheiterhaufen is a sort of
French toast prepared in
southern Germany and Austria.*

12 slices of zwieback
1 quince
1 cup (25 cl) apple juice
4 dates

The royal

1 cup (25 cl) heavy cream
2 teaspoons crème fraîche
2 eggs plus 2 egg yolks
cayenne pepper
berbere (an Ethiopian spice mix made
from pepper, cinnamon, coriander, chili,
cumin, cardamon, allspice and cloves)
sprig of rosemary, finely chopped
pinch of salt

For the glaze: Reduce the Port, vinegar and brown sugar until they reach a syrupy consistency. Allow the mixture to cool and then blend with the maple syrup. The recipe makes enough for approximately twenty portions but, correctly stored in a sealed container, it will keep indefinitely.

For the powder: Blend the cèpes and the lavender in a coffee grinder until fine, then mix with the chestnut powder.

For the scheiterhaufen: Cut four of the zwieback slices into circles so that they fit into the bottom of an ovenproof ramekin. Roughly dice the remaining slices. Peel, core and dice the quince and cook in the apple juice until soft, then strain. Finely chop the dates.

For the royal: Blend together the cream, crème fraîche, eggs and egg yolks and season with the cayenne, *berbere* and salt.

Spread the zwieback circles with the date mixture and place in the bottom of the ramekins, sprinkle with the chopped rosemary and drop a spoonful (10 ml) of the quince on each. Briefly marinade the diced zwieback in the royal and then use to cover the bases. Pour the remaining royal over the scheiterhaufen until the ramekin is three-quarters full. Bake in the oven at 400°F (200°C) for 15 minutes until the royal is set.

For the venison: Season the meat and sear it on both sides in the butter, bacon and juniper berries. Roast it for 6 minutes in a convection oven at 340°F (170°C), and then let it rest in the butter for 10 minutes more at around 150°F (65°C).

For the presentation: Brush the meat with the glaze and generously sprinkle with the powder. Serve with the scheiterhaufen and jus.

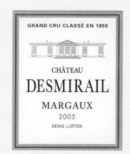

CHÂTEAU CALON SÉGUR

SAINT-ESTÈPHE

VINEYARD SIZE	55 hectares
VINE DENSITY	8,000 stocks per hectare
AVERAGE AGE OF VINEYARD	35 years
SOILS AND SUBSOILS	two different entities in the vineyard: sandy gravel with a layer of clay, and clayey-gravelly soil
GRAPE VARIETIES	Cabernet Sauvignon 50% Merlot 40% Cabernet Franc 10%

The great, sky-eaten landscapes of Saint-Estèphe, have no equivalent elsewhere. Amidst a voluptuous swell of gentle-sloped hills, châteaux appear like ships in the distance. Respectfully spaced apart, they meditate in their "sea of land" under an "ever-moving sky," as the painter Odilon Redon, a child of the Médoc, described this setting of oceanic majesty. This is where you will find Calon Ségur, one of the oldest vineyards in the Saint-Estèphe appellation. The château invites you in a melancholy way, with wide-open wings. Although it seems to promise mysterious pleasures, bear in mind that its vineyard is enclosed by walls. What lies at the core of its personal poetry? Is it enjoyment or solemnity, Molière or Racine? If you wish to know more, you should take a walk around the château, preferably on a cloudy mid-season afternoon, and discover it from all its different sides. Complete the exploration by seeking the truth that remains hidden in the bottle.

The name supposedly comes from Calonnes, an ancient denomination for Saint-Estèphe, and from the Marquis Nicolas-Alexandre de Ségur. The man who was nicknamed "The Wine Prince" at the beginning of the 18th century owned other estates. However, he used to say, "I make wine at Lafite and Latour, but my heart is at Calon." Hence the flattened heart-shaped lintel sculpted above a cellar door in the main court-yard and printed on the label, a promise of renewed international success each year at Valentine's Day. A definite touch of tenderness among those powerful, manly Saint-Estèphe wines, which are often described as stern and reserved.

Madame Capbern-Gasqueton is the soul of the estate, which the Capbern-Gasqueton family has owned since 1894. She devotes to it a special, aristocratic brand of love that is similar to the affection Monsieur de Ségur expressed three centuries ago. The place, indeed, has changed very little since the Marquis's days. The imposing chartreuse, dominated by two square corner towers, shows superb proportions. Simple and

elegant French-style gardens surround it. The technical buildings, both cellars and vathouse, remain discrete, not wishing to steal the show. The vineyards stretch, all in one piece, over 55 hectares of beautiful soft hills. All that is left is for the changeable Médoc sky to shed its light on this incredibly romantic site.

Two distinct entities may be discerned within the estate: the enclosure around the château consists of sandy gravel on a clay subsoil, while the Chapelle, a sandy-clayey zone, culminates around a lonely Romanesque building. These two different soils form the base of Calon Ségur's typicity; the wine is indeed both powerful and kind, hard to characterize as one or the other. Clad in a beautiful garnet robe and strongly marked by the freshness and seriousness of Cabernet Sauvignon in spite of 43 percent Merlot in the planting, it cannot be described as shy. Tenderness and severity merge seamlessly, almost miraculously, in this soulful wine. The tannic, masculine attack instantly gives way to rich and soft notes of blackcurrant and blackberry. Tannins melt in the mouth like a spoonful of snow, ending up in a sophisticated, organ-chord finale. Both male and female, a perfect marriage of opposites, Calon Ségur is a gorgeous classical wine, bare as a Jansenist and saucy as a 17th-century courtesan.

1. *On the highest hill of this vineyard, one of the oldest in Saint-Estèphe, this building called "La Chapelle" has given its name to the surrounding plot area.*

2. *The wine estate of Calon Ségur is partly enclosed in walls, which accentuates the dream-like, mysterious atmosphere that permeates it.*

3. *The vines, here seen shortly before their buds open, are tended in an traditional manner and tied to the canopy with wicker.*

Lamb Marinated in Miso

Nobu MATSUHISA & Mark EDWARDS
Nobu - London, United Kingdom

SERVES 4

The lamb

a large handful of dried gourd shavings

1 whole rack of lamb (8 ribs), frenched

1⅔ pounds (750 g) spicy miso sauce
(see below)

a little olive oil

The spicy lemon dressing

¼ cup (5 cl) lemon juice

1 tablespoon soy sauce plus 2 teaspoons

½ teaspoon finely grated garlic

¼ cup (5 cl) chilli-garlic sauce, strained

½ teaspoon salt

pinch of freshly ground black pepper

⅓ cup (8 cl) grape seed oil

The spicy miso sauce

½ cup (10 cl) sake

½ cup (10 cl) mirin

½ cup (10 cl) chilli-garlic sauce,
strained

⅔ pound (300 g) white miso paste

1⅓ cups (150 g) sugar

The vegetable garnish

4 white asparagus spears

4 heads of baby bok choy

4 garlic shoots

4 tablespoons spicy lemon dressing
(see above)

sea salt

freshly ground black pepper

Lamb is rarely used in Japanese cooking, but in this recipe the miso marinade transforms the lamb into something quite different and truly delicious.

For the spicy lemon dressing: Mix all the ingredients except the oil. When the salt has dissolved, add the oil.

For the spicy miso sauce: At least 6 hours ahead, make the sauce by mixing together all the ingredients.

For the lamb: Bring a pan of water to a boil. Rub salt into the gourd shavings, rinse with cold water and plunge into the boiling water for 2 minutes. Drain well.

Trim off any excess fat from the lamb and wrap the exposed bones with the dried gourd. Place the rack of lamb in the spicy miso, making sure the wrapped bones stick out of the clear liquid. Leave to marinate for 6 hours.

To cook the lamb: Preheat the oven to 400°F (200°C). Heat an ovenproof frying pan with some olive oil in it. Remove the lamb from the marinade and quickly brown it all over in the oil over high heat for 2 minutes, then transfer to the oven for 12 minutes to finish cooking (2 to 3 minutes longer, if you prefer it medium to well-done.) Remove the lamb from the oven and transfer it to a warm plate to rest for 2 minutes.

For the vegetable garnish: Preheat a broiler or a barbecue grill. Meanwhile, bring another pan of water to the boil. Brush the asparagus stalks with olive oil and season with salt and pepper. Cook under the broiler or on the barbecue grill until just tender. Blanch the bok choy quickly in the boiling salted water for 1 minute, and the garlic shoots for 30 seconds, then drain.

For the presentation: Cut the rack into 6 chops and arrange on a serving dish. Place the grilled asparagus, bok choy and garlic shoots neatly around the lamb and dress with the spicy lemon dressing. Wrapping the bones with the dried gourd, as well as giving a Japanese look, allow your guests to eat the chops with their fingers.

CHÂTEAU CALON SÉGUR BY MARKUS DEL MONEGO, BEST SOMMELIER OF THE WORLD, 1998

It is easy to fall in love with this splendid and abundant wine, whose label is adorned with a heart. The property's three gravel hills bring together the perfect conditions for a great wine: a unique terroir, tense work in the vineyard and a rigourous selection of the harvest. These three elements are the foundation for a Great Classified Growth that is vinified with true savoir-faire. The wine offers complex aromas and a rich, opulent taste in which freshness is key.

CHÂTEAU FERRIÈRE

MARGAUX

VINEYARD SIZE	10 hectares
VINE DENSITY	10,000 stocks per hectare
AVERAGE AGE OF VINEYARD	40 years
SOILS AND SUBSOILS	Günzian gravel and coarse sand
GRAPE VARIETIES	Cabernet Sauvignon 70% Merlot 25% Petit Verdot 5%

The New World? What New World? If wine is the topic, the New World should indeed be sought here, in Médoc. It is as much a matter of people as of soil. The new world of wine is this young generation of passionate winemakers who have successfully reacted to the competition of non-French wines, not by positioning themselves on their level but by asserting their own personality and paying more attention to the terroir than ever before. "What you are criticized for," Jean Cocteau wrote, "is your style. Cultivate it." Being true to oneself, as a major rule of life, is valid in any circumstance. It never disappoints.

Charm and energy are in command at Château Ferrière by the grace of its owner, Claire Villars-Lurton. Eight hectares make up the smallest Great Classified Growth in the Médoc. Back in 1855, Ferrière was already the smallest terroir, but what a terroir! "I was lucky," says Villars-Lurton, "to inherit a vineyard where the right vines were already planted at the right places." It consists of 70 percent Cabernet Sauvignon, 25 percent Merlot and 5 percent Petit Verdot, all in four pure gravel plots, one on the Plateau de Cantenac and three next to the Château Margaux.

Claire Villars-Lurton is a beautiful example of this new world of wine. She makes the rebirth of a Great Classified Growth fully visible, which is not a total surprise, for cases of this sort are not rare in the region. While her approach to winemaking is quite modern, Claire insists that she does not make modern wines. The paradox is apparent. "We have realized here that nothing beats our ancestral winemaking methods," she says. "For us Médoc winemakers, this is one of our main assets." She focuses on the elegance and the tannic quality of the wines, incidentally praising Cabernet Sauvignon as the superstar of grape varietals. Villars-Lurton is very aware of

being part of a revival movement and enjoys the mutual feeling of solidarity that runs through the Margaux winemakers. "Many of them are young. We all started in our mid-thirties. We all try to promote the personality and style of our wines while interfering as little as possible on the natural cycles. The New World? We no longer fear the competition. We gave up foreign methods some time ago and took a new look at ourselves," she says.

For a long time, though, this beautiful terroir could not exist in its own right. From the 1950s to the 1990s, Château Ferrière was exploited in tenant farming by Alexis Lichine. The wine was known as the second wine of Château Prieuré-Lichine or sometimes went into the blending of Château Lascombes. Sorry to see such a fine terroir underexploited, Bernadette Villars, the owner of Château Chasse-Spleen, bought Ferrière in 1988 and terminated the farming contract in 1992. Since her daughter Claire has taken control, a creative and courageous viticultural research has been led at Château Ferrière, resulting in a highly personal style.

To describe this "Claire touch," a wonderful persistence in the mouth should first be mentioned, held up by a delicate sensation of melted tannins and mature, slightly liquorice, black fruit notes. These are finely chiselled, intelligent wines, wines that think, subtly interacting with the dishes that are served with them. They slowly unfold in the glass, in an ascending curve, and never fall back. More than a feminine wine, Château Ferrière is a wine of femininity; refined and resolute, it recalls the memory of great ladies of the past, whose intimacy was guarded by a long phase of courtship and chivalrous friendship before they offered access to their treasures.

1. 1930s Art Deco is the dominant style inside the château, from the picturesque trompe-l'œil murals to the light-coloured fruitwood furniture.

2. The chartreuse de Ferrière.

3. A delightful feminine touch is characteristic of Claire Villars-Lurton's style; it may be seen in the way she decorates her house as it may be tasted in the wine she produces on her small Margaux vineyard.

West Flanders Beef Sirloin, Maroilles Cheese Flamiche Tartlet, Potato Mousseline

Kobe DESRAMAULTS
In De Wulf - Dranouter, Belgium

SERVES 4

The steak

4 pavés (tile-shaped pieces) of sirloin
steak, 2½ inches (6 cm) thick

clarified unsalted butter

Guérande fleur de sel

freshly ground black pepper

The flamiche

1⅜ ounces (40 g) fresh yeast,
diluted in a scant cup (20 cl) warm milk

5 tablespoons (70 g) softened
unsalted butter

3¼ cups (400 g) flour

1 teaspoon salt

1 teaspoon sugar

2 eggs

The Maroilles cream

¾ cup plus 1½ tablespoons (20 cl)
heavy cream

⅛ pound (400 g) well-aged Maroilles,
edges and corners cut off

1 finely sliced onion, cut on a mandoline

The potato mousseline

a few cooked and peeled chestnuts

1⅛ pounds (500 g) baking potatoes,
such as Idaho

whole milk

14 tablespoons (200 g) softened
unsalted butter

Guérande fleur de sel

freshly ground black pepper

For the flamiche: Mix together the yeast and
butter for the crust. Mix them into the flour
with the remaining ingredients, until you get
a smooth dough. Roll it out to a thickness of
⅛ inch (2 mm). Cut it into disks, then bake at
350°F (177°C) for 15 minutes between two
baking sheets.

For the Maroilles cream: All ingredients
for the cream should be at room temperature.
Blend them into a smooth paste. Lay the
onions over the baked and cooled tartlet crusts,

add the Maroilles cream, and bake for 10
minutes at 400°F (200°C), until golden.

For the potato mousseline: Cook the potatoes
in milk over low heat. When tender, drain and
let cool 180°F (82°C). Push through a potato
ricer, add the butter and some of the cooking
milk, and season with sea salt and pepper.

For the chestnut garnish: Run the chestnuts
over hot embers until they puff out, then
quickly mix in some Guérande salt.

For the steak: Season the *pavés* with salt and
pepper, and 15 minutes before serving, brown
in clarified butter. Let them rest for 10 minutes
until their internal temperature is 120°F
(50°C). Slice and serve.

For the presentation: On serving plates, arrange
the sliced beef, the Maroilles flamiche and the
chestnut-studded potato mousseline.

CHÂTEAU FERRIÈRE BY YOICHI SATO, BEST SOMMELIER OF JAPAN, 2005

*Not too long ago, this was a small, rather discreet château; today it produces very good
wines with power and concentration. Although it can appear timid compared to wines
more concentrated in style—it needs time in the glass to open up—I find that it has
an attractive personality and a lot of character.*

CHÂTEAU MARQUIS D'ALESME

VINEYARD SIZE	15 hectares
VINE DENSITY	9,000 stocks per hectare
AVERAGE AGE OF VINEYARD	40 years
AVERAGE PRODUCTION	5,000 cases
SOILS AND SUBSOILS	40% siliceous gravel, 40% marly gravel, and 20% clay-limestone
GRAPE VARIETIES	Cabernet Sauvignon 65% Merlot 30% Petit Verdot 5%

How do you revive a great wine? The team of wine-makers at Château Marquis d'Alesme is currently answering that question, making it a case of the utmost interest for whoever tries to understand the current evolution of the Médoc's Great Classified Growths. The processes of qualitative recovery, which in other châteaux took place roughly between 1995 and 2005, can be witnessed in real time. Restructuring the vineyard, developing the terroir, refining the plot selection, the attentive study of the vine plant, soil analysis, intensified "green" work and environmental concern: all of that is currently in an early stage of application, which helps to compare past and present and to fully grasp the extent of the improvement.

This vineyard, among the oldest in Margaux, was created by the Marquis d'Alesme in 1585. Its emblem, the horseshoe, hints at the title of squire held by some members of the d'Alesme family. The name "Becker" was added until very recently, a Germanised form of Bekker, Jan Bekker being a Dutch wine trader who owned the château when it was classified as Third Growth in 1855. The post-Classification history of the estate is extremely complex, marked by many divisions and ownership-related highs and lows. In 1996, Hubert Perrodo, already the owner of the Margaux châteaux Labégorce and Labégorce-Zédé, bought the vineyard minus the château, which remained with its owners. No effort, then, was spared to bring this wine back to its Third Classified Growth-quality level. However, in the very year of this purchase, Perrodo died in an accident. He was buried in Margaux, a place that was dear to his heart although he was not a native of it. Now, the recovery of the vineyard continues under the direction of Philippe de Laguarigue, an agricultural engineer who formerly worked at Château Montrose and Château Lynch-Bages.

On a surface of 15 hectares including three different pedologic entities, the vineyard shows a remarkable diversity of soils, with 20 percent clay-limestone aside siliceous and marly zones. The blend varies according to the vintage, but Cabernet Sauvignon always dominates with a proportion of about 65 percent, Merlot following with 30 percent and Petit Verdot 5 percent, giving the wine its dark colour and characteristic black tones.

"The Marquis's wines, until we arrived, were a bit on the tough side," explains Philippe de Laguarigue. "We are now in the midst of a re-creation process and cannot lean on a long series of vintages." But the 2006, 2007 and 2008 vintages are more than enough to provide, on three arpeggio notes, the material proof of that rebirth. From one vintage to the next, the message is clearer, the personality is more assertive—2006 with a clean, round, fruity and generous mouth; 2007 exploding into notes of soft ripe cherry, red rose, peony and orchid; and 2008, still young but soon ready to confirm the typicity of the previous vintages. "We are confident," says de Laguarigue. "The terroir is here to stay, even if the vine remembers its recent fate. We have analysed the situation carefully and we are perfectly aware that there is a very great wine waiting to be made here. We had to prove our worth. But our business potential lies in our history and in our style. Changing our style every other week would amount to sawing the branch we are sitting on."

1. Beneath a beautiful solid wood roof structure, the wine sleeps in the barrels. Vine leaves naturally come as a decorative element in the design of the cellar gates.

2. Until recently, the wine was still named Château Marquis d'Alesme-Becker. This Margaux vineyard is going through a phase of qualitative resurrection.

3. The temperature-controlled concrete vats are used for alcoholic fermentation; this material is mostly appreciated for its thermal inertia.

"Forgotten" Vegetables in a Clay Crust, Lightly Buttered and Emulsified Truffle Juice

Marc VEYRAT

La Maison de Marc Veyrat - Veyrier-du-Lac, France

SERVES 6

The parsnips and kohlrabi

⅔ pound (300 g) parsnips

½ pound (200 g) kohlrabi

The Jerusalem artichokes

2 quarts (2 l) water

½ cup (10 cl) olive oil

1 teaspoon (5 g) salt

½ teaspoon (2 g) sugar

juice of 1 lemon

½ pound (200 g) Jerusalem artichokes, peeled

The spruce bark

¾ to 1 pound (400 g) spruce bark

The crust

2⅛ pounds (1 kg) clay

16 slices of fresh black truffle, frozen sous-vide

1 teaspoon (4 g) Guérande fleur de sel

1⅜ ounces (40 g) chestnuts, cooked sous-vide

The truffle juice

1 scant cup (20 cl) truffle juice

4 tablespoons (50 g) unsalted butter (½ stick)

For the parsnips and kohlrabi: Peel and cut the parsnips and kohlrabi into ½-inch (1-cm) slices. Using a 1½-inch (4-cm) round cutter, make 4 parsnip disks and 8 kohlrabi disks. Place them ona slotted sheet and cook them in a dry steam oven with salt: 30 seconds for the parsnip and 2½ minutes for the kohlrabi. Set aside.

For the Jerusalem artichokes: Pour the water and olive oil into a saucepan, and add the salt, sugar and lemon juice. Place over medium-high heat. As soon as it simmers, add the peeled Jerusalem artichokes, and once the liquid starts to boil, reduce the heat to low and cook them for 15 minutes. Drain, then cut them into 8 disks of 1½ x ½ inch (4 x 1 cm) using the round cutter.

For the spruce bark: Steam the spruce bark for 30 minutes in a steam oven to soften it. Cut it into four 2½-inch (6-cm) pieces to be rolled up into cylinders 2½ inches (6 cm) in diameter. Keep them in shape by placing them in round cutters or rings of the same diameter. Make 4 disks of the same diameter to serve as lids.

For the crust: Roll out the clay ¼ inch (5 mm) thick. Cut out 4 disks, 12 inches (30 cm) in diameter. Cut 4 disks, 2 inches (5 cm) in diameter, out of parchment paper. Lay each one in the centre of each parchment-lined clay disk.

Season each truffle slice with salt. On each clay disk, layer some parsnips, kohlrabi, truffle, Jerusalem artichoke, more kohlrabi and some sliced chestnuts. Circle each stack of layered vegetables with one spruce cylinder, and top with a lid. Wrap hermetically in the clay and bake at 400°F (200°C) for 10 minutes.

For the presentation: Warm the truffle juice, add the butter and emulsify with a hand mixer.

Remove the clay disks from the oven, break the clay crust and discard the spruce bark. Place a stack of vegetables on each plate and serve with some emulsified truffle juice on the side.

CHÂTEAU MARQUIS D'ALESME BY OLIVIER POUSSIER, BEST SOMMELIER OF THE WORLD, 2000

This small property, purchased by the Perrodo family in 2006, appears to have risen from the ashes. Dormant for too long, a major renovation of everything from the vineyard to the barrels promises a brilliant future on an equally brilliant terroir. The assemblage focuses on Cabernet Sauvignon while incorporating a significant amount of Merlot to produce a semi-powerful style. Its greater depth and maturity will allow this wine to be deserving of its status as a Third Growth again.

CHÂTEAU SAINT-PIERRE

SAINT-JULIEN

VINEYARD SIZE	17 hectares
VINE DENSITY	10,000 stocks per hectare
AVERAGE AGE OF VINEYARD	50 years
AVERAGE PRODUCTION	5,000 cases
SOILS AND SUBSOILS	Günzian Garonne gravel on clayey-sandy gravel
GRAPE VARIETIES	Cabernet Sauvignon 75% Merlot 15% Cabernet Franc 10%

Jean-Louis Triaud is willing to admit that the history of Château Saint-Pierre is a little tangled. "We know at least," he says, "that it goes back to the 16th century, that the land was originally bought from Étienne de Brassieux, Lord of Beychevelle, and that the estate covered about 40 hectares at the time. To make a long story short: in 1693, records show the existence of the wine estate of Sérançan, which belonged to the Marquis de Cheverny. In 1767, the Baron de Saint-Pierre decided to acquire it and gave it his name." Mr. Triaud adds that the keys shown on the label are supposedly those of Heaven, which this fervent Catholic eagerly hoped would open wide before him. In 1832, as he was negotiating the entry with his patron saint, his two daughters were sharing the inheritance. "Through marriage," Mr. Triaud goes on, "one half stayed at Saint-Pierre and the other half went to La Tour Carnet. It was bought back later on. Château Saint-Pierre was classified as Fourth Growth in 1855, but that did not make the story any simpler, for it was divided into two growths, each one managed by a different family: Saint-Pierre Sevaistre and Saint-Pierre Bontemps du Barry. Over time, plot by plot, the Bontemps du Barry sold their property to Sevaistre, who gradually reunified the estate, until the 1950s when only Saint-Pierre Sevaistre remained. The Bontemps du Barry kept the lovely, though somewhat run-down, early 19th-century white stone chartreuse, some meadows and a few hectares of Saint-Julien vineyards, which they exploited under the name Château Bontemps du Barry, no longer a Great Classified Growth. And when their last descendants, two old spinsters, died in 1981, Françoise Triaud bought back the château, meadows and vineyards. In 1982, Henri Martin, father of Françoise, bought Saint-Pierre-Sevaistre. It so happened that since 1922, Château Saint-Pierre's winemaking facilities were all at Château Gloria. Therefore we were able to reunite the scattered elements of Château Saint-Pierre bit by bit, design a simpler label and update the vineyard and technical facilities."

After this historical rollercoaster, it is time to re-enter the present. Triaud pushes an iron door that opens out onto a vast winemaking warehouse. Both the vathouse and the barrel cellars are built in a modernist high-tech fashion, based on raw metal and wide spaces, with extreme æsthetic and functional elegance, a style that is rather rarely seen in Médoc. "Fake 18th-century style leaves me cold," he says, adding that he does not believe modernism and tradition should be considered antagonistic. "Technology," he says, "is nothing but tradition in motion."

The vineyard, 17 hectares of sandy-clayey Günzian gravel, is planted with 75 percent Cabernet Sauvignon, 15 percent Merlot and 10 percent Cabernet Franc. The respectable age of the vines—50 years on average—guarantees a fine minerality and complex taste. Château Saint-Pierre is a fleshy, fragrant and ample Saint-Julien, whose suave and luscious notes include cedar wood, liquorice and black fruit. Straightforward and totally unaffected, this wine asserts itself with perfect honesty, without a touch of haziness. These precious qualities are consistently present in every vintage. "Some time ago," says Triaud, "great vintages were climatic accidents because the variables were not known. It is now possible to handle deficiency and imbalance. Nothing is subject to chance anymore. And since we have learned to master the phenolic maturity of the grapes, all our wines are good to drink young and good for ageing."

1. The central corridor of Château Saint-Pierre, with a French window at either end. Such a room, serving as a "light tunnel," is frequently seen in Bordeaux chartreuses.

2. Cupids at the wine press: this 17th-century tapestry, kept at the Château Saint-Pierre, expectably celebrates wine.

3. The winemaking buildings, both barrel cellars and vathouse, were built in a deliberately modern and functional high-tech style.

4. A distinctive Saint-Julien, produced from a diversified soil and reflecting the delicate complexity of the vineyard's plot structure—but is never fails to be ample and straightforward.

Stuffed Porcini Mushrooms, *Piedmont Style*

Luisa MARELLI VALAZZA

Al Sorriso - Sorriso, Italy

SERVES 4

4 medium-size firm porcini mushrooms

1 garlic clove

1 shallot

extra virgin olive oil

1 bunch parsley plus 1 tablespoon chopped flat-leaf parsley leaves

1 bunch chervil

2 chive blades

½ cup (10 cl) vegetable oil

salt and freshly ground black pepper

For the porcini: Preheat the oven to 350°F (177°C).

Clean the porcini and trim their stalks. Hollow out the stalks and chop the flesh with the finely chopped garlic and shallots to make a fine stuffing.

In a Dutch oven, lightly heat some olive oil, add the stuffing and cook it quickly for 1 minute. Season with salt and pepper, then add the chopped parsley. Stuff each porcini stalk with the stuffing.

Pour a little olive oil into an ovenproof dish. Place the porcini in it and season with salt and pepper. Add a drop of olive oil on each one of the caps and then bake the porcini in the preheated oven for 10 minutes.

For the sauce: While the porcini are baking, blend the leaves from the parsley and chervil bunches with the chives and vegetable oil.

For the presentation: When the porcini are cooked, serve them on warmed plates and spoon the sauce over them.

GRAND CRU CLASSÉ EN 1855

CHATEAU SAINT-PIERRE
SAINT-JULIEN
2005
DOMAINES MARTIN

CHÂTEAU SAINT-PIERRE BY SERGE DUBS, BEST SOMMELIER OF THE WORLD, 1989

Saint-Pierre has a beautiful halo, but the expression of this wine's miraculous character becomes evident with tasting. Unerringly good decisions in both vineyard and vathouse allow Château Saint-Pierre to shine and express the best of Saint-Julien's great terroir. This full-bodied, aromatically expressive wine immediately offers a complex and tempting bouquet. Its excellent structure and harmoniously full body are qualities of the subtle tannins that make this a wine for long keeping.

Château Talbot

VINEYARD SIZE	102 hectares
VINE DENSITY	7,700 stocks per hectare
AVERAGE AGE OF VINEYARD	40 years
AVERAGE PRODUCTION	25,000 cases
SOILS AND SUBSOILS	Médoc gravel
GRAPE VARIETIES	Cabernet Sauvignon 67% Merlot 27% Petit Verdot 5% Cabernet Franc 1%

Château Talbot, on the central gravel hill of Saint-Julien, is graced with its own very special, peaceful atmosphere. It may have to do with the ocean of vines that surrounds it, or with the classic, simple beauty of the ivy-clad chartreuse in its park. Everything here conveys a feeling of calm, controlled intelligence and serene confidence. The whole estate, close to the Landes forest, breathes deeply and makes you breathe in unison; and the winemakers have their share of this gentleness, shown in every human gesture. From the vineyard to the bottling through the 24 beautiful oak-fermenting vats, the journey from grape to wine is a labour of love.

This ambient sensation of peace is confirmed by the château's interior, permeated by the comforting scent and loving aura of old family houses and a mysterious feeling of intimacy. The generations that followed one another at the table of the beautiful wood-panelled dining room left the warmth of their presence there, as well as a lovely, lavish early 19th-century china set from the Johnston Bordeaux factory, whose decorative pattern of pale blue flowers spreads around the room like handfuls of forget-me-nots thrown onto the mahogany background and up to the ceiling.

The large estate is named after the Connétable Talbot, the former governor of Guyenne, who was defeated in 1453 at the battle of Castillon. For a long time, the château belonged to the family of the Marquis d'Aux de Lescout, until it was bought in 1917 by Désiré Cordier, a Lorraine-born Bordeaux winemaker and wine trader. In 1940, he left the château to his son, Georges, who in turn left it to his son, Jean, in 1947. The estate is currently managed by Jean's daughters, Lorraine Cordier and Nancy Bignon-Cordier, assisted by Jean-Pierre Marty, general manager since September 2006.

Of the 150 hectares, all in one piece, covered by the estate, 108 are devoted to winemaking, with 67 percent Cabernet Sauvignon, 27 percent Merlot, 1 percent Cabernet Franc and Petit Verdot taking up the remaining 5 percent. The exceptional terroir is composed of fine gravel on a core of fossil-rich limestone. The estate produces a second wine, Connétable Talbot, and a Sauvignon-based white wine with a touch of Sémillon named Caillou Blanc, aged on lees in its own particular cellar—one of the oldest white wines ever made in a Great Classified Growth Médoc château.

Saint-Julien wines age in a carefree way, and Talbot, widely known as a longevity champion, is no exception. The extensive storage cellar speaks for itself and the sleep of the bottles is eloquent. From the 1930s, 1920s, 1910s, and far into the 19th century, this wine is unaffected by time. "We advise our customers not to drink Château Talbot too young," points out Jean-Pierre Marty. "Our wines develop so much seduction over the years that it would be a shame not to give them a chance to do so. Now, in 2009, whatever follows 2001 should still be left to wait, but whatever was bottled before will be remarkably open and luscious."

Château Talbot has beautiful velvety tannins and a crispy, sensuous mouthfeel. With a deep, dark colour, eternally young fruit notes and plenty of enduring freshness, it is smooth and harmonious, often celebrated for its notes of Havana cigar and liquorice. Each bottle keeps its pleasure potential intact through the decades with perfect confidence. Always cheerful, never severe, Château Talbot is a wine for happy occasions and celebrations of the heart.

1. The interior of the Cordier family home has kept its charm intact through generations. The house, like the wine, ages well.

2. The Château Talbot vineyard and exceptional terroir: 102 hectares of fine gravel on a limestone subsoil.

3. The ageing cellar: once bottled, these wines will sleep for a long time.

Jasmine-smoked Wagyu Beef Cheek, *Cèpe Vermicelli*

Alvin LEUNG DESMON
Bo Innovation - Hong-Kong, China

SERVE 4

The broth

2¼ pounds (1 kg) wagyu beef cheeks

1⅛ pound (500 g) oxtail

¼ pound (100 g) Chinese scallions

3 garlic cloves

3 parsley stalks

¼ pound (100 g) carrots

⅛ pound (50 g) dried scallops

⅛ pound (50 g) dried shrimp

sea salt

To smoke the cheeks

brown sugar

loose green jasmine tea

raw rice

The cèpe vermicelli

1 quart (1 l) cold cèpe stock, made with
¼ pound (100 g) dried cèpe mushrooms

8 ounces (200 g) bean thread vermicelli

4 tablespoons (50 g)
unsalted butter (½ stick)

salt and freshly ground black pepper

The garnish

fresh coriander

4 Chinese scallions

1¾ ounces (50 g) black truffle
(about 1½ truffles)

For the broth: Put all the ingredients for the broth in a large saucepan, cover generously with water, bring to the boil and simmer for 3 hours. Remove from the heat and drain and reserve the beef cheeks. Strain and clarify the broth.

For smoking the beef cheeks: Season the cheeks with sea salt and hot-smoke them for about 4 minutes in a wok with the sugar, rice and jasmine tea leaves.

For the cèpe vermicelli: Soak the vermicelli in the cèpe stock overnight, then cook them gently in the stock until tender. Drain, add butter and season with salt and pepper.

Grill the scallions until soft and golden-brown. Set aside for garnish.

For the presentation: Cut the cheeks in slices 4 inches (10 cm) thick. Arrange them on the plates on a bed of the cèpe vermicelli. Garnish with fresh coriander and grilled scallion.

Add sliced black truffle to the beef broth and serve in a glass alongside.

CHÂTEAU TALBOT BY ANDREAS LARSSON,
BEST SOMMELIER OF THE WORLD, 2007

This wine manages to combine dense and bright dark fruit, with fine spices, damp tobacco and a texture that, despite its density, always gives a notion of freshness and refinement. Château Talbot belongs to the forerunners of the appellation Saint-Julien and has over the years been showing consistently great wines, showing the typicity of the appellation but spiced up by its own personal touch. Like many of its peers, this is a wine that is rather smooth and enjoyable after four to five years but some of the great old vintages easily convince you to be patient.

CHÂTEAU BRANAIRE-DUCRU

SAINT-JULIEN

VINEYARD SIZE	50 hectares
VINE DENSITY	10,000 stocks per hectare
AVERAGE AGE OF VINEYARD	35 years
AVERAGE PRODUCTION	20,000 cases
SOILS AND SUBSOILS	Quaternary gravel
GRAPE VARIETIES	Cabernet Sauvignon 70% Merlot 22% Petit Verdot 5% Cabernet Franc 3%

B etween Arcins and Saint-Julien, Beychevelle, is one of the Médoc's most astonishing sights as you drive up north. Without warning, the landscape seems to swell up like a big wave as the D2 road makes a sharp turn around the château before going on straight towards Pauillac. This turn, on the softly meandering Route des Châteaux, is the most likely to induce a stiff neck; if you admire Branaire-Ducru on the left, you might miss Beychevelle on the right, and the other way around. If you haven't missed Branaire-Ducru, you have just seen one of the loveliest chartreuse facades of all Médoc. Many places on Earth are graced with that kind of civilised melancholy and pure classical beauty, but few greet you as this one does, with a slap in the face that leaves you a bit dizzy as you drive up towards Léoville.

In 1666, when Bernard de La Valette, Duke of Épernon and Lord of Beychevelle, passed away, he left so many unpaid bills behind that his entire properties were confiscated by the crown of France. A certain Jean-Baptiste Braneyre acquired one part of the estate, which was to become Branaire-Ducru. His descendants, the Duluc family, founded the estate during the 1720s, went through the Revolutionary period without much trouble, built the beautiful chartreuse in 1824 and were quietly ageing their excellent wines when the 1855 Classification honoured them with the distinction of Fourth Growth. Soon afterwards, Louis Duluc sold the property to his cousin Gustave Ducru, who later passed it on to two distant cousins, Viscount du Périer de Larsan and Count Jacques de La Tour. On the wine label, four angular crowns pay tribute to these four gentlemen. Since 1988, Château Branaire-Ducru has been the property of a family group directed by Patrick Maroteaux.

The castle stands on a long strip of coarse Günz gravel, which stretches in a crescent shape between Ducru-Beaucaillou and Gruaud Larose, encompassing a remarkable collection of great Saint-Juliens. Branaire-Ducru covers 50 hectares planted with 70 percent Cabernet Sauvignon, 22 percent Merlot, 4 percent each Cabernet Franc and Petit Verdot and an undetermined percentage of roses. From the garden to the vineyard, beautiful rose trees rising from thick, ancient stumps scatter their grace over the whole estate. There is even a rose tree named Branaire-Ducru.

The fine Saint-Julien typicity shown by Château Branaire-Ducru, according to Patrick Maroteaux, is based on three main principles. First, gentle, respectful winemaking. The harvest is received on the upper floor of the vathouse to undergo gravitary fermentation. Second, the vathouse is finely detailed in order to ferment the must in distinctly separated lots according to the age of the vines, the grape varieties and the plot selection.

The third principle is product philosophy. For Patrick Maroteaux, the notion of style is of utmost importance. Geological and climatic variations help create style, unlike uniform climatic conditions and vast surfaces of even soil. Variations make up the terroir, and the terroir is everything. The more contrast in the variations, the more personality in the style. "This is," says Maroteaux, "precisely what makes old Europe inimitable. Of all things, our task consists of promoting that style. Château Branaire-Ducru should be recognizable among thousands of other wines." And what is Branaire-Ducru's style? "A graceful relationship between terroir and taste, a fine expression of fruitiness, and freshness. What we seek, above all, is elegance."

1. The tasting room, overlooking the vathouse. The crowns allude to the four noblemen who successively managed the estate after the 1855 Classification.

2. The classic, bright interior of the château.

3. Château Branaire-Ducru amidst its vines— one of the most strikingly beautiful Médoc chartreuses.

4. Working on the barrels.

Duck, Beets and Fried Rice

Michel RICHARD

Michel Richard Citronelle - Washington, United States

SERVES 2 TO 4

The duck

6-to 7-pound (3- to 3.5-kg) Muscovy duck breasts

fine sea salt

freshly ground black pepper

The fried rice

3 cups (600 g) potatoes, cut on a mandoline

5 tablespoons unsalted butter

2 garlic cloves, peeled

1 cup (about 200 g) yellow onions, cut into ⅛-inch dice

1 small carrot, peeled and diced (¼-inch)

¼ cup (about 50 g) red bell pepper, peeled and diced (½-inch)

1 tablespoon soy sauce, or to taste

1 teaspoon peeled, grated fresh ginger

2 large eggs, beaten

⅓ cup (25 g) snow peas, cut on the diagonal into ⅛-inch slices

fine sea salt

freshly ground black pepper

The sauce

2 teaspoons extra virgin olive oil

½ cup diced shallots (about 4)

2 garlic cloves, crushed

1½ cups beets, peeled and diced (¼-inch)

1 teaspoon sugar

2 cinnamon sticks

1 teaspoon coriander seeds, crushed

1 teaspoon balsamic vinegar

3 cups (75 cl) dry red wine

¼ teaspoon ground cinnamon

1 tablespoon cold unsalted butter, cut up

fleur de sel

For the fried rice: Rinse the diced potatoes in cold water 3 times and leave them in cold water for up to a day, refrigerated. Drain and pat dry on a kitchen towel.

Melt 4 tablespoons of the butter in a large non-stick skillet over medium-high heat. Once the bubbles subside, spread the potatoes out in an even layer in the pan. Do not stir for about 1 minute, then stir the potatoes from time to time as they brown evenly. After 2 minutes, season to taste with salt. When the potatoes are golden brown and tender, transfer them to a large plate lined with a paper towel.

Return the skillet to the heat and add the remaining tablespoon of butter. Add the onions and sauté for 1 minute. Add the diced carrot and bell pepper. Grate the garlic directly into the pan and cook for 1 minute. Stir in the soy sauce and ginger. Add the potatoes and stir gently with a spatula. Stir the eggs into the potatoes until they are cooked. Stir in the snow peas and heat through. Season with pepper, and if necessary, additional soy sauce.

For the duck and sauce: Turn the duck breast skin side down. With a sharp knife, make a cut down the length of the centre bone, just to break it. Smack the blade across the bones just to break them slightly; do not cut through the meat. Season the duck breast with salt and pepper and 1 teaspoon of sugar.

In a large sauté pan, heat 1 teaspoon of the olive oil over medium high heat. Reduce the heat to medium. Place the breast in the pan, skin side down, and cook slowly for about 10 minutes, or until golden brown. When browned, place on a cutting board. Separate the breast meat from the bone. Chop the carcass into small pieces.

Add the chopped bones to the oil remaining in the pan, increase the heat and sauté until the bones are richly browned. Add the shallots and sauté until translucent. Add the garlic, beets, sugar, cinnamon, coriander and balsamic vinegar. Pour the red wine into the pan and bring to a simmer, scraping the bottom. Simmer over low heat for 20 minutes. Season with salt and pepper. Remove from the heat and strain.

Sprinkle the breasts with the ground cinnamon. Heat the remaining 1 teaspoon olive oil over medium heat in a sauté pan just big enough to hold the breast. Place the breast skin side down in pan, weigh it down and cook for about 4 minutes to crisp the skin. Remove from the heat.

Just before serving, swirl the cold butter into the sauce.

For the presentation: Cut the duck breast in half. Cut each breast half into 2 pieces. Place the duck on the serving plates; spoon the sauce to the side, and sprinkle the duck with fleur de sel and black pepper. Place a portion of the fried rice on each plate, and serve with beaucoup de LOVE.

CHÂTEAU BRANAIRE-DUCRU BY VIRGINIA PHILIP, BEST SOMMELIER OF THE UNITED STATES, 2002

The wines show jammy, fruit-forward notes, with a hint of a floral component, followed by cigar, tobacco and earth. The palate is well-balanced with the black fruit profile carrying over with mineral and florality. Well-balanced tannins with a bit of grip allow the wines to be drunk somewhat young—three to five years—with the potential to age for 25-plus years.

CHÂTEAU DUHART-MILON

VINEYARD SIZE	73 hectares
VINE DENSITY	9,000 stocks per hectare
AVERAGE AGE OF VINEYARD	30 years
AVERAGE PRODUCTION	30,000 cases
SOILS AND SUBSOILS	fine gravel mixed with aeolian sands on a Tertiary subsoil
GRAPE VARIETIES	Cabernet Sauvignon 67% Merlot 33%

The vines of Château Duhart-Milon stretch west of Lafite-Rothschild, but the château's cellar and vathouse are located in the heart of Pauillac. A château used to stand on the Pauillac docks. Mr. Duhart, an ex-corsair of Louis XV, had built that house for his retirement after a lifetime of loyal service to his king. The Pirate's House, as it used to be known, was still standing in the 1950s, but it now remains only on the wine's label. Between the two world wars, the owners of the vineyard planned to build a new château on the Duhart-Milon estate. This project never materialised, but on the very same spot the cooperage of Lafite was built, where most of the barrels used by Domaines Barons de Rothschild are made. The trees that still shade the cooperage today were planted as part of the first project.

In the 18th century, the wine of the château that was then known as Mandavy-Milon served as additional income for Lafite's owner, Nicolas Alexandre de Ségur, and became Château Lafite's second wine, which shows how highly esteemed they already were. In 1815, when the courtier Guillaume Lawton classified the wines of Médoc, he referred to Duhart-Milon as a Pauillac Fourth Growth in the making. And in 1855, when the wine was indeed classified as Fourth Growth, the château was a property of the Castéja family. In 1962, it was purchased by the Rothschilds of Lafite. The vineyard was entirely restructured. The soils were drained, old vines were pulled out, new ones were replanted, and neighbouring plots were added to the estate.

A cellar and vathouse were also installed in Pauillac. These beautiful and functional buildings were extended and entirely renovated in 2003. They include the longest *chai* in the Médoc (110 metres) and a vathouse composed of epoxy-lined concrete vats painted blue and yellow, and stainless steel vats. The harvest reception zone is mobile, and the ageing of the wine lasts from 12 to 14 months in 50 percent new French oak

barrels, all made at the Domaines Barons de Rothschild (Lafite) Cooperage.

The wine of Duhart-Milon could be described as a textbook case, an archetypal Pauillac endowed with all the characteristics of the appellation. The planting of its 70 hectares—70 percent Cabernet Sauvignon and 27 percent Merlot, the average ratio of 70/30 changing slightly for each vintage—also makes it a typical example of the reputedly masculine Pauillac style. Its dark colour, its supple elegance, the remarkable depth and subtlety it develops with time have earned Château Duhart-Milon its nickname, "Lafite's little brother." A second wine, Le Moulin de Duhart, is also produced.

Although Château Duhart-Milon is a classic wine, it is nevertheless surprising through its intensity and liveliness—a quality, by the way, it shares with Lafite—and the freshness of its tannins. It offers not only the vanilla and concentrated black fruit notes that are expected from the appellation, but also *flavours* in the strong sense of the word: black olives, fruity olive oil, Mediterranean pairings. This wine would adore being served with a big anchoïade—a Languedocian first course of raw vegetables and anchovy sauce—followed by ribeye steak broiled on vine shoot embers. But it has other assets and mixes well with strong-tasting vegetables like parsnip, parsley root, celeriac and mushrooms. A wide, eclectic, aromatic palette waiting for a sensible chef to make the most of this beautiful wine.

1. The wine produced by the vines of Duhart-Milon, on vast gravel hills bordering Lafite, has a typical "North Pauillac" character.

2. A preparation to tasting.

3. The ageing cellar of Château Duhart-Milon, located in Pauillac town, is the longest in the Médoc.

Veal Sweetbreads
with Saffron, Rutabaga, Parsley Root Mousseline

Anne-Sophie PIC
Maison Pic - Valence, France

SERVES 4

The sweetbreads

⅔ pound (300 g) veal sweetbreads

pinch of saffron threads

flour for dredging

¼ cup (50 g) clarified unsalted butter

oil

The veal jus

½ pound (250 g) veal trimmings

2 tablespoons (30 g) unsalted butter

2 quarts (2 l) veal stock

The vegetable garnish

1 rutabaga (Swede)

1¾ ounces (50 g)
black trumpet mushrooms

salt

freshly ground black pepper

The parsley root mousseline

1⅛ pounds (500 g) parsley roots

heavy cream

3⅛ cups (75 cl) whole milk

a little peanut oil

For the sweetbreads: Blanch the sweetbreads for 3 minutes in boiling water. Peel and trim them, then cut them into 4 equal portions, 2 to 3 ounces (75 g) each. Add 3 saffron threads to each.

For the veal jus: Brown the veal trimmings in foamy butter. Discard the fat and add the veal stock. Cook for 2 hours, strain and set aside.

For the vegetable garnish: Peel the rutabaga, wrap it in parchment paper after adding a little butter and some salt, and bake in a 350°F (180°C) oven for about 1 hour depending on the size. Cut into ½-inch (1-cm) slices, and then into cubes, using a square cutter.

Wash the mushrooms in water several times, then shred them coarsely. Cook them briefly in a little oil, until just softened.

For the mousseline: Cook the parsley roots in the milk until tender. Drain and blend until smooth. Season with salt and pepper, adding a little cream and milk, as needed, until you reach the right consistency. Add a little peanut oil for sheen. Taste and correct seasoning and pour into a siphon.

For the sweetbreads and garnish: Flour the sweetbreads, shake them lightly to remove excess flour and fry them in clarified butter.

Glaze the rutabaga cubes in a little butter, then do the same with the mushrooms.

For the presentation: On 4 serving plates, arrange the rutabagas and the mushrooms, add some jus and then the sweetbreads. Serve immediately with the parsley root mousseline on the side.

CHÂTEAU DUHART-MILON BY ÉRIC BEAUMARD, SILVER MEDAL, BEST SOMMELIER OF THE WORLD, 1998

This château enjoys a privileged location next to Lafite, with north- and west-facing exposures that are extensions of its neighbour's terroir. Its vineyard composition saw an important increase in its proportion of Cabernet Sauvignon. Today, these new plantations have reached maturity. The wine's quality on the nose and palate is deeply anchored in the very characteristics typical of a Pauillac, whose structure is based on firm tannins and an ever-present balance of finesse. Duhart's style is evolving towards one of greater refinement.

CHÂTEAU POUGET

MARGAUX

VINEYARD SIZE	10 hectares
VINE DENSITY	10,000 stocks per hectare
AVERAGE AGE OF VINEYARD	42 years
AVERAGE PRODUCTION	3,000 cases
SOILS AND SUBSOILS	lean siliceous gravel of the early Quaternary
GRAPE VARIETIES	Cabernet Sauvignon 60% Merlot 30% Cabernet Franc 10%

The château got its name in 1748, when François Antoine Pouget inherited it. In 1771, his daughter Claire married Pierre François de Chavaille, an attorney and general secretary for the City of Bordeaux. For a century and a half, the Pouget de Chavaille managed the estate, which was confiscated during the French Revolution. They recovered it shortly afterwards, except for a portion of the land which remained *Bien National*. At the time of the 1855 Classification, Chavaille was mentioned as owner of the growth.

"Châteaux Pouget and Boyd-Cantenac have been in my family since the early 20th century," explains Lucien Guillemet, owner of Château Pouget. "Pouget since 1906 and Boyd-Cantenac since 1932. There is no château, properly speaking, at Boyd-Cantenac; for both properties the château is at Pouget, and it is actually a barrel cellar that was converted into a house towards the end of the 19th century."

A pretty and unusual house, besides, and quite different from the Bordeaux chartreuse style: its wide triangular facade, supported by two side aisles, is an obvious reminder of its former function. Below the rooftop, two marbled medallions are engraved with the mention of pre-1855 classifications. Indeed the success of Château Pouget is not a recent one. In the 18th century, it provided the Maréchal-Duc de Richelieu with the inspiration for some ardent verse:

L'amour sur ton cœur étendra sa puissance
Ton verbe sera clair comme le chant du Coq,
À l'égal du Lion tu ne craindras le choc,
Si de cestuy nectar tu te remplis la panse

Love upon your heart will exert its power
Your words will be as clear as the Rooster's crow,
You'll equal the Lion in withstanding all shock,
If you fill your belly with this very nectar

… adding to this tribute the offering of a coat of arms which is still shown on the wine label, one of the most striking in all Médoc for its graphic simplicity. This streamlined elegance echoes the soul of the wine, its delicacy and classic charm to perfection.

The 10-hectare vineyard, located in the heart of the Margaux appellation on lean soils with good draining power, is planted with 60 percent Cabernet Sauvignon, 30 percent Merlot and 10 percent Cabernet Franc. Guillemet prefers to refer to his two wines in terms of Yin and Yang rather than of radical differences. "First and foremost," he says, "all the Médoc Great Classified Growths play in the same league. Each has a distinct personality, that cannot be denied; but they are not dramatically different from each other." And to demonstrate his views, this remarkable artisan of wine takes his educational concern to the point of setting up a genuine assemblage tasting, unveiling the treasures of one sample after the other, comparing grape varietals, evaluating the tannins in a press wine and commenting upon the vintages with you. A wonderful first-hand initiation and a unique experience that impresses the memory far more than any theoretical teaching would. "Château Pouget," says Guillemet, "has great ageing qualities. When young, its colour is dark, tinged with blue. With age, it gradually takes on warmer tones until it reaches a bright ruby, then a slightly browner shade after a few decades. The nose also develops throughout the years, with a mellower attack, an ample and velvety cycle in the mouth until the lengthy finish. Pouget has plenty of freshness and harmony, which is the distinctive mark of traditional Margaux wines." To those great historical growths, Guillemet patiently devotes his considerable winemaking wisdom. Château Pouget is hand-chiselled like precious jewellery.

1. Seen from the barrel cellar, the tasting room where wines are blended with meticulous care.

2. Cabernet Sauvignon: the Médoc's emblematic grape variety, from which delicate, long-keeping wines are made.

3. The bottle, dressed in its elegantly designed label, contains the treasure of a distinguished Margaux.

Manzo Perduto

Nicola & Pierluigi PORTINARI
La Peca - Lonigo, Italy

SERVES 10

The bollito misto

1 ox tongue

1 piece of beef short rib

1 beef cheek, trimmed

1 calf's head, boned and rolled up

1 beef and pork cotechino sausage

1 chicken leg

3 carrots

3 onions

3 celery stalks

¼ cup (30 cl) stock made with beef bones and trimmings and a few vegetables (onions, celery, carrots, etc.)

coarse salt

The radish and tomato sauce

¼ pound (100 g) grey radish

7 ounces (200 g) sun-dried tomatoes, soaked for a few hours

½ pound (250 g) cooked ox tongue

1 to 1¼ cups (25 to 30 cl) extra virgin olive oil

salt

The green sauce

1 generous cup (80 g) flat-leaf parsley

3 tablespoons (50 g) capers packed in salt, rinsed

1 garlic clove

about 4 (15 g) salted anchovies

4 hard-boiled egg yolks

½ pound (235 g) bread, soaked in vinegar and squeezed dry

2 small fresh chilli peppers

¼ cup (20 g) grated Parmigiano Reggiano

3 tablespoons dry white wine

The pearà sauce

⅛ pound (50 g) beef marrow

1 tablespoons extra virgin olive oil

2 cups (250 g) dried breadcrumbs

1 quart (1 l) beef stock

⅓ cup (30 g) grated Grana Padano

salt

Sarawak black pepper of the Kuching variety (to taste, keeping in mind that the recipe should be heavily peppered)

The vegetable garnish

10 small carrots

about 1 pound (400 g) cauliflower or broccoli, boiled

about 1 pound (400 g) potatoes, boiled

about 1 pound (400 g) mixed vegetables, pickled in vinegar

For the bollito misto: Marinate all the meats with coarse salt and the vegetables for about 6 hours. Then rinse both the meats and vegetables and pat dry. Put each different meat into a sous-vide bag, add a few spoonfuls of vegetables into each bag, then seal it well and cook for 48 hours in 150°F (65°C) water.

For the radish and tomato sauce: Blend all ingredients together except the oil, then run them through a fine-mesh sieve and whisk in the olive oil. Season with salt.

For the green sauce: Blend all ingredients together until smooth.

For the pearà sauce: Melt the beef marrow in a casserole with the oil. Add the breadcrumbs and let them brown slightly. Add the stock and stir until completely absorbed. Keep cooking on low heat for about 2 hours, stirring from time to time. Add the Grana Padano, cook for 10 more minutes and season with salt. Add a generous dose of pepper just before serving.

For the presentation: Remove all meats from the sous-vide bags and drain them. Slice them and arrange them on a serving dish, alternating from the most delicate to the strongest-tasting. Garnish with the boiled vegetables: The carrots should be julienned, the potatoes trimmed into "pearl" shapes using a paring knife and the little cauliflower or broccoli florets should be scattered all around.

Place the sauces around the meats, and finish with the pickled vegetables. Serve with 1 glass of hot stock from the sous-vide bag per person.

CHÂTEAU POUGET BY FRANCK THOMAS, BEST SOMMELIER OF EUROPE, 2000

From every angle, Château Pouget and its wines represent an expression of the classic, authentic Médoc spirit, joined with the rather feminine style of its appellation. In youth, Pouget's wines display aromas that are often austere and slightly severe, but as with all Médoc wines, once the vigour of early age passes, the terroir finally comes through in all its tranquil softness.

CHÂTEAU LA TOUR CARNET

VINEYARD SIZE	68 hectares
VINE DENSITY	8,333 stocks per hectare
AVERAGE AGE OF VINEYARD	30 years
AVERAGE PRODUCTION	17,500 cases
SOILS AND SUBSOILS	gravelly clay-limestone
GRAPE VARIETIES	Merlot 50% Cabernet Sauvignon 45% Cabernet Franc 3% Petit Verdot 2%

Here is another one of those sites of vines and stones that the Médoc does so well. The undulating lines of the wide, soft hills impart a lovely grandeur to the landscape. A low sky of moving clouds saturates the turquoise colour of the tags set on the newly planted vines. Beyond a monumental gate, a square dungeon meets your eye with impressive majesty, the whiteness of its facade emphasised by the lead-coloured storm clouds. For one thing, it is not neo-medieval: this is a genuine fortified castle standing in its ditch, one of the oldest Medocan monuments.

Leaning on a round 12th-century turret, the dungeon was built in the 13th century. Towards the end of the Hundred Years War, when it was still named Saint-Laurent, it was the setting of a long siege held by Carnet, squire of the Count Jean de Foix, who continued the fight in fidelity to the Crown of England. Carnet was overcome by Dunois, one of Joan of Arc's companions, but the château retained his name as a tribute to his bravery.

At the time, a fine wine estate already laid around the fortress. In 1407, a hogshead (240 litres) of its wine sold for 36 écus instead of 6 écus for a Graves wine. When Château La Tour Carnet entered the 1855 Classification, it had been appreciated for some time.

Under the French Revolution, the château belonged to Charles de Luetkens, a Swedish wine trader whose descendants kept it until the late 19th century. The phylloxera plague struck a hard blow to a plurisecular winemaking tradition and the 20th century was a period of highs and lows. During the 1960s, the estate perked up again thanks to his new owner, Louis Lipschitz, a ship owner who took care of the vineyard until 1978, after which his daughter Marie-Claire Pèlegrin continued the work. In 2000, the estate was purchased by Bernard Magrez, and since then a vast replanting and renovation program has been carried out.

The estate, which for the most part sits on Günzian gravel, offers a pedologic idiosyncrasy: the Butte de La Tour Carnet, a clay-limestone hill that is the only one of its kind in Médoc. On this cool-soiled 68-hectare vineyard, maturity usually comes late. The planting follows that characteristic, with a large proportion of Merlot (50 percent) to Cabernet Sauvignon (45 percent).

"Since 2000," says estate director Anne Le Naour, "we have been trying to eliminate astringency in the wines. That can be achieved through working on maturity and on the best possible sorting of the harvest, an operation we carry out with utmost care. Destemming is followed by the picking out of every single remaining green bit on a 25-metre long sorting table operated by 20 to 30 workers. The fermentation is entirely gravitary, carried in wood or stainless steel vats of varying capacities. This long process—about 30 days—is preceded by three to five days of cold pre-fermentation maceration. We prefer manual cap immersion to pumping over, and we perform that with long stainless-steel poles held down to immerse the cap into the must. All our wines are aged in oak, with 50 to 70 percent new barrels each year."

As a result of expert, careful winemaking, Château La Tour Carnet offers great harmony in the mouth and a generous aromatic bouquet. A classic, balanced wine with a rich fruity texture, it is both complex and accessible. A wine for friends, long-awaited reunions, fireplace corners, Bordelais rib steaks broiled on incandescent vine shoots or tasty squab roasted rare.

1. The dungeon of La Tour Carnet, built in the 12th and 13th centuries, is one of the oldest monuments in the Médoc.

2. The winemaking process is carried out very gently. A feature of red Médoc wines, cap immersion is performed during fermentation.

3. The interior decoration of the dungeon is done in a colourful neo-medieval style.

Landais Squab Breast, Cabbage Cannelloni, Juniper

Jannis BREVET

Manoir Restaurant Inter Scaldes - Kruiningen, the Netherlands

SERVES 4

2 squab
2 tablespoons (25 g) unsalted butter

The cabbage cannelloni
1 young cabbage
2 tablespoons (25 g) unsalted butter
¼ cup (50 g) chicken stock
5 to 6 tablespoons (50 g) persillade
(finely chopped garlic and parsley)
salt

The carrot garnish
16 young carrots
1 scant cup (20 cl) young carrot juice
1 scant cup (20 cl) chicken stock
2½ tablespoons (35 g) unsalted butter
parsley

The ginger and lime sauce
2½ cups (60 cl) pigeon stock
zest of 2 limes
⅔ ounce (20 g) fresh ginger
2 tablespoons (25 g) unsalted butter
soy sauce
a few drops lime juice

The juniper crumbs
5 tablespoons (15 g) fresh orange peel
3 tablespoons (20 g) juniper berries
(about ⅔ ounce)

For the cabbage cannelloni: Wash and blanch the outer leaves of the cabbage. You will need 4 large leaves for 4 cannelloni; cut the remaining cabbage into ½-inch-round (1-cm) slices and stew them in butter and chicken stock. Season with salt and add the persillade. Pat the 4 cabbage leaves dry, roll them up and stuff them with stewed cabbage.

For the carrot garnish: Gently cook the young carrots in carrot juice and chicken stock. Drain the carrots. Reduce the cooking liquid and bind it with butter, then return the carrots to the jus and season with salt and parsley.

For the ginger and lime sauce: Reduce the pigeon stock with the lime zest and ginger to about 1¼ cups (30 cl). Strain through a fine-mesh sieve, bind with butter and correct the seasoning with soy sauce and a little lime juice.

For the juniper crumbs: Chop the orange peel into fine brunoise, chop the juniper berries finely and mix both together.

For the squab: Remove the breast filets from the squab. In a frying pan, pan-sear the squab in butter, keeping them pink.

For the presentation: Sprinkle the plates with a few juniper crumbs, then arrange the cabbage cannelloni, the young carrots and one slice of squab. Serve the sauce on the side.

CHÂTEAU LA TOUR CARNET BY MARKUS DEL MONEGO,
BEST SOMMELIER OF THE WORLD, 1998

A 19-metre-high hill forms this magnificent terroir with its enormous reserves of potential. Through the savoir-faire of Bernard Magrez this potential has emerged, and today this great growth is renowned for the excellence of its wines. In youth they offer aromas of black fruit, with hints of toast and spice; when fully mature the wines reveal a supple, velvety character with complex and fine aromas.

Château Lafon-Rochet

SAINT-ESTÈPHE

VINEYARD SIZE	45 hectares
VINE DENSITY	9,000 stocks per hectare
AVERAGE AGE OF VINEYARD	45 years
SOILS AND SUBSOILS	early Quaternary gravel on a clay-limestone subsoil
GRAPE VARIETIES	Cabernet Sauvignon 55% Merlot 40% Cabernet Franc 3% Petit Verdot 2%

H e has probably been asked the question many times, but Michel Tesseron always answers with the utmost courtesy. "Why is my château yellow? Because, for 40 years, I suffered from the greyness of concrete. When my father, Guy Tesseron, bought the estate in 1960, we tore down the ruined building that we found there, and built the château between 1964 and 1974. As it was not clearly visible from the road, we decided to brighten it up a little. First, we tried a Venetian green—a complete failure. Amidst the vine leaves and the trees, it was no longer visible at all. In 2000, we settled our minds on this shade of yellow. It is a carefully studied colour, bright and cheerful but not overpowering."

The colour affinity of the Château Lafon-Rochet with the Médoc daylight, which so closely resembles Venetian light, cannot be denied. This yellow, also found on the wine label and the cellar walls, is in perfect harmony with the vast moving skies of Saint-Estèphe and the green colour of the vines, getting more intense between springtime and autumn. It cannot be denied that Michel Tesseron likes colours: he may greet you in a green sweater and lilac shirt, brown hat and red parka. Or wearing green clogs. For him, life is too short for dull hues, and he finds the local nickname of his house, "le château de la Poste" (hinting at the French postal service's corporate yellow), highly amusing.

But do not let that mislead you. Tesseron takes seriously the few things in life that require it—wine, for instance—and greets everything else with a poetic mind. But who would dare say that the poetic approach is devoid of seriousness? The warm atmosphere of the château speaks eloquently. This is a real home, with all the necessary items: soft couches, an admirable assortment of wine decanters and an antique sabre collection. The two cats, Mistauffe and Mistouffe, sniff curiously at you. One of them will escort you during your visit and will follow you up to the chai, rubbing her fur on the windowpane during the tasting and trying to purr her way in. She will not, though,

carry her audacity to the point of hopping into the car with you for a tour of the vineyard—40 hectares all in one piece, of which Tesseron describes every single plot, finally stopping in front of a magnificent lone tree: "There," he says. "This is my tree."

Tesseron recently built a spectacular cellar building for first-year barrels, in a rotund shape with a splendid wooden roof. Inside, the dark red harmonies and chiaroscuro effects create a dramatic atmosphere. Water drips at regular intervals down the shafts of thick Minoan-style pillars, regulating the hygrometry. The ingenuity shown through this device reminds one of the same quality in Michel's brother, Alfred Tesseron of Pontet-Canet, himself in permanent search of uncommon technical innovation.

The wine of Château Lafon-Rochet is powerful, rich and concentrated—a true Saint-Estèphe. When young, it may go through a period of inhibition, but year after year it develops into a suave fullness. Cabernet Sauvignon makes up 55 percent of its planting, Merlot 40 percent, and 5 percent of Cabernet Franc enrich the bouquet. This is a wine for game, for hearty and warm foods, the ones Jules Romains referred to as "profound cooking." For instance, the food served at the Lion d'Or, an Arcins restaurant where, Tesseron recalls, in the early days meals were served on upturned barrels standing on a dirt floor. If ever one needed to uncork a good bottle by a big fireplace with a generous cut of meat roasting on the embers, Château Lafon-Rochet would be the ideal choice.

1. *The walls of Château Lafon-Rochet are painted a rich ochre yellow, a carefully chosen colour which helps the building to fit into the vineyard landscape.*

2. *The cellar door opens out onto a chiaroscuro scenery, a mysterious theatre where dark red tones dominate the atmosphere.*

3. *In a Bordeaux chartreuse, the vineyard should be visible from as many windows as possible. This architectural feature plays a part in the region's soulful poetry.*

Milk-fed Veal Chop in a Sauté Pan,
Salsify with Parmesan Cream and Jabugo Ham

Alain PÉGOURET
Le Laurent - Paris, France

SERVES 6

The veal chops

3 veal chops for 2 servings each

⅛ cup (3 cl) grape seed oil

2 tablespoons (30 g) unsalted butter

salt and freshly ground black pepper

The garnish

6 even-size salsify, peeled, washed, and cooked in à blanc (water, flour and lemon juice)

1 cup plus 1 tablespoon (250 g) heavy cream

¼ pound (100 g) aged Parmesan cheese, finely chopped

1 teaspoon agar-agar

6 thin slices Jabugo ham

⅛ cup (3 cl) parsley juice

For the garnishes: Line the bottom and sides of a rectangular dish with plastic wrap.

Boil the heavy cream, whisk in the Parmesan and then the agar-agar. Cook for 1 minute, then pour into the dish in a ½-inch (1-cm) layer. Refrigerate.

Cut the salsify into ½-inch (4-cm) lengths.

For the veal chops: Season the veal chops with salt and pepper. In a sauté pan, melt the butter in the grape seed oil until it foams, then add the chops to the pan. Cook them over low heat for 10 minutes on each side, basting them regularly with the butter. Then set them aside to rest on a rack for 15 minutes.

For the presentation: Cut the Parmesan jelly into 6 portions, 1¼ inch (3 cm) thick, using a 1½ x 5-inch (4 x 12-cm) rectangular cutter.

Reheat the chops, the veal jus, the salsify and the parsley juice.

Arrange the garnishes on six plates, and arrange the Jabugo ham like a veil over the salsify.

Cut the veal chops into thick slices, arrange them on the plates, and season with veal jus and parsley juice.

CHÂTEAU LAFON-ROCHET BY YOICHI SATO,
BEST SOMMELIER OF JAPAN, 2005

In its youth the wine seems to have trouble controlling its physical force; with age, it softens, becomes rounder and begins to show the characteristic forest-floor, dried-bark aromas that are much appreciated in Japan. Personally, I like to drink this in winter, offering myself the luxury of having the wine with furred or feathered game—venison, squab or duck.

CHÂTEAU BEYCHEVELLE

SAINT-JULIEN

VINEYARD SIZE	78 hectares
VINE DENSITY	10,000 stocks per hectare
AVERAGE AGE OF VINEYARD	30 years
AVERAGE PRODUCTION	23,000 cases
SOILS AND SUBSOILS	deep Garonne gravel for the most part
GRAPE VARIETIES	Cabernet Sauvignon 62% Merlot 31% Cabernet Franc 5% Petit Verdot 2%

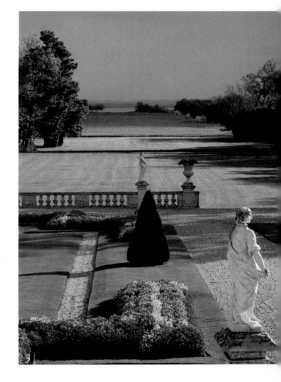

The Château Beychevelle, home of the Dukes of Épernon since the days of the Valois, already had it all: a terroir of exceptional quality, a Classified Growth, a château known as the Versailles of Médoc, a rich history and a setting of majestic beauty. But it holds another asset: the whole place seems to be cut out of the fabric of dreams.

The bizarre perspective that it creates with the Château Branaire-Ducru on either side of a turn of the D2 road is but one element of this dream-like effect. You can already sense it a half-mile ahead, coming from the south, driving along a large stretch of poplar trees that may well be flooded if you pass by in late winter, especially during a high full-moon tide. You immediately know this is a place where water, earth and sky merge poetically. A sharp right turn will take you to the port of Beychevelle, a peaceful haven where the soft lapping of the waters invite you to a moment of meditation.

On your way back, you will discover cool green meadows between the river and the château. They, too, may be flooded, or rather covered with a thin watery mirror that reflects the strange, swift-moving sky of the Médoc. From the terrace of the château, you will see the same water mirror trying to eat up the whole green surface, on the soft-sloped patch of land stretching between the white solitary statues adorning the garden and the Gironde. The limits separating the garden, the meadows and the river, appear nowhere; there are no clear lines. Describing the beauty and strangeness of this landscape is not easy; it seems more immaterial, more permeable than any other, a connecting point to another world. You thought that only painters and gods could create this sort of place, but it appears, surprisingly, within the means of human beings. The emblem on the bottle label also hints at that navigation between worlds: a griffin, the creature Dionysus, god of wine, harnessed to his chariot, is featured at the front of a ship in the act of lowering its sail. This is said to be the origin of the name Beychevelle, derived from "baisse voile" (drop sail), an action ship crews never failed to do as a sign of allegiance to the duke when in sight of the castle.

Built in the 17th century, the château was modified in the 18th century and enlarged in the 19th. Recently restored, it now belongs to Grands Millésimes de France (GMF and Suntory groups). The estate covers 250 hectares, including 90 hectares of vines. Seventy-eight hectares, located in the Saint-Julien appellation, produce the Classified Growth and the second wine Amiral de Beychevelle. The remainder is in the Haut-Médoc appellation and produces another wine, Les Brûlières de Beychevelle. The planting is based on 62 percent Cabernet Sauvignon, 31 percent Merlot, 5 percent Cabernet Franc and 2 percent Petit Verdot. Three great entities constitute the vineyard, where 14 different types of soil may be identified. The central part is located on a sandy-gravelly plateau shared with Château Ducru-Beaucaillou. Clay is rare, except along the jalles, the small rivers where Merlot is planted. A diversity of soils is closely reflected by the vatroom, equipped with small-capacity vats in order to fine-tune the plot selection. The wines are aged between 16 and 18 months in oak barrels in a large underground cellar.

Château Beychevelle is a rich wine with a silky, ample mouthfeel. Its attack is soft and pleasant, with a very tactile satiny touch and lengthy finish. Notes of tobacco, liquorice, black currant and red berries express the maturity of the crop. This lively, masculine Saint-Julien gently leaps into the glass with a silvery flash as if to break the spell of this dreamy, fairytale setting. Quite in vain, obviously, for the wine itself is part of the spell.

1. The port of Beychevelle at night. The moonlight, the soft lapping of the Gironde water: a distinctive, strange and romantic atmosphere.

2. The château Beychevelle, former home of the Duke of Épernon, is nicknamed "the Versailles of Médoc".

3. The vast lawns of the château descend in soft slopes to the river. At a distance, they merge with the meadows, and in times of flood the meadows merge with the river.

Saddle of Lamb
in a Potato Crust "Bocuse d'or"

Léa LINSTER
Léa Linster - Frisange, Luxembourg

SERVES 4

The potato crust

1¾ pound (800 g) potatoes, about 4 large ones

⅛ cup (4 cl) oil

2 tablespoons chopped parsley

The lamb

1 to 1⅛ pounds (400 to 500 g) boned saddle of lamb

¾ cup (50 g) dry breadcrumbs

fine sea salt

freshly ground black pepper

The sauce

2 cups (50 cl) lamb jus

1 sprig rosemary

3½ tablespoons (50 g) cold unsalted butter

fine sea salt

For the potato crust: Peel the potatoes, grate them into fine julienne using a mandoline and squeeze them between your hands to dry them. Heat 2 tablespoons of the oil in a large non-stick pan, spread half the potatoes into the pan in a thin layer in order to make a large pancake, 9½ inches (24 cm) in diameter. Brown it on one side, slide it onto a clean towel without turning it over. Sprinkle it with half the parsley. Repeat with remaining grated potatoes.

For the lamb: Preheat the oven to 425°F (220°C). Cut the saddle into two equal pieces, about 8 inches (20 cm) long. Dry them with paper towels, and season with salt and pepper. Coat them lightly with breadcrumbs. Place each piece of lamb onto a potato pancake and roll up the pancake with the aid of the towel. Seal the edges of the pancake and place both rolls onto a baking sheet. Bake in the preheated oven for 15 minutes.

For the sauce: Add the rosemary to the lamb jus, reduce by half, and remove the rosemary. Bind the sauce with the cold butter, adding it in small pieces and rotating the pan with a slight gesture of the hand. Taste, and correct the seasoning.

For the presentation: Remove the saddles of lamb from the oven and cut each one into four pieces. Arrange two pieces on each warmed plate, and serve the sauce on the side.

CHÂTEAU BEYCHEVELLE BY OLIVIER POUSSIER, BEST SOMMELIER OF THE WORLD, 2000

This magnificent and majestic estate with 90 hectares of vines in the Saint-Julien appellation produces one of the great values for wine lovers among the Médoc's Fourth Growths. The director, Philippe Blanc, has fashioned wines of great balance and flavour, emphasising elegance over extraction.

CHÂTEAU PRIEURÉ-LICHINE

MARGAUX

VINEYARD SIZE	70 hectares
VINE DENSITY	10,000 stocks per hectare
AVERAGE AGE OF VINEYARD	28 years
AVERAGE PRODUCTION	15,000 cases
SOILS AND SUBSOILS	Günzian and Pyrenean gravel
GRAPE VARIETIES	Cabernet Sauvignon 50% Merlot 45% Petit Verdot 5%

First, you discover an astonishing modern round-shaped barrel cellar, topped with a former helipad. Further on, as you admire the classic style of the chartreuse, you may think that the collection of black chimney back plates set into chalky white walls makes the courtyard look like a Balkan monastery. A closer look will reveal small faucets at the bottom of the walls: the precious back plates actually decorate hidden concrete fermenting vats, used for the second wine. The first wine ferments in its own concrete vathouse, also painted a vivid white outlined with royal blue, the estate's colours. This peculiar combination of decorative and functional features helps you to understand that nothing here is done quite as it is elsewhere. As a matter of fact, the charismatic personality of Alexis Lichine, who owned the place between 1951 and 1989, is still vividly present within those walls.

As the name hints, the property has ecclesiastical origins. In the 12th century, the Benedictine canons of the Vertheuil Abbey created the Priory of Cantenac around a now-vanished Romanesque church. Church vineyards, which may be seen as precursors of the Great Classified Growths, started their development in Médoc at that time. Historical sources mention the wines of Priory of Cantenac for the first time in 1444, and in the early 18th century they were considered equal to those of Issan and Gasq (later to become Château Palmer). Under the reign of King Louis XV, the Médoc peninsula underwent a radical change through the discovery of the positive influence of gravel soils on wine quality; the "planting frenzy" that burst out at the time did not spare the Priory, where polyculture was abandoned to the benefit of vineyards, which were given the whole land surface to cover.

Left untouched by the French Revolution, the Priory of Cantenac became the property of Bordeaux wine traders during the Napoleonic era. After the 1855 Classification, its destiny fluctuated somewhat, until 1951, when Alexis Lichine bought the estate. The new owner, a former journalist who had switched to international wine trading, set out to thoroughly restructure the vineyard and gave it his name two years later. He completed this activity with the writing of two reference books, *Wines of France* (1951) and *Alexis Lichine's Encyclopedia of Wines and Spirits* (1967).

In 1999, after ten years of management by Sacha Lichine, son of Alexis, Château Prieuré-Lichine was purchased by the Ballande Group, based in New Caledonia. The growth's beautiful potential did not stay unnoticed either from Louis Ballande, CEO of the group, or from Justin Onclin, managing director. Since their arrival, a quality-improvement policy has been applied to the estate's 70 hectares of Günzian and Pyrenean gravel: yield control, raising of the canopy, integrated pest control, refining of the plot selection and a 15-year replanting program. In the barrel cellar, methods such as ageing on lees and micro-oxygenation are used with the help of consultant œnologist Stéphane Derenoncourt. Since 1990, the château has also been producing a delicate white wine, Le Blanc de Prieuré-Lichine.

The refinement and balance of the wines of Prieuré-Lichine are rightly celebrated. Their ageing on lees imparts to them a velvety smoothness, a silky and generous texture, held up by a moderately woody framework. This great wine succeeds in achieving a harmony of intensity, substance and an airy lightness reminiscent of spirituality. Perhaps a reminder of the clerical origins of the growth; at any rate, an unmistakable proof of the talent and efficiency of the winemaking team.

1. The chartreuse of Prieuré-Lichine was built in the 18th century, but the wine estate is much older. Its history is rooted in the Church vineyards of the Medieval era.

2. This classic Margaux, since it was bought in 1999 by the Ballande group, has been undergoing a quality improvement policy, which includes ageing on lees.

3. The estate's 70 hectares of gravel soils are cultivated with integrated pest control and much attention to the plot selection.

Potato and Black Truffle
en Papillote

Michel TRAMA

Les Loges de l'Aubergade - Puymirol, France

SERVES 4

The truffled potatoes

4 potatoes, unpeeled and scrubbed

8 large Swiss chard leaves

2 to 3 ounces (80 g) black truffles
(3 to 4 truffles)

salt and freshly ground black pepper

The truffle sauce

1 cup (25 cl) chicken or vegetable stock

½ cup (12 cl) truffle juice

1⅓ ounce (50 g) black truffles
(1 to 2 truffles)

9 tablespoons (130 g) unsalted butter
(1 stick plus 1 tablespoon)

salt and freshly ground black pepper

For the truffled potatoes: Cook the potatoes in boiling salted water, using 1 large tablespoon of salt per quart (1 l) of water, for about 30 to 40 minutes. They should be melting, but quite firm. Let cool, then peel the potatoes.

Wash the Swiss chard, using only the green part. Blanch it in boiling water, then cool in ice water. Drain on a kitchen towel.

Cut the truffle into 32 thin slices using a mandoline. Cut each potato into 8 slices, season with salt and pepper and reconstruct the potato, inserting 1 truffle slice between 2 potato slices.

Spread a 12 x 12-inch (30 x 30-cm) square of plastic wrap on a work surface, lay the chard leaves on the plastic wrap. Roll the potatoes in the plastic wrap tightly to make the papillotes.

For the truffle sauce: Reduce the stock by one-third. In a saucepan, soak the truffle in 2 tablespoons (30 g) melted butter at 140°F (60°C) for 5 minutes. Add the reduced stock and truffle juice, transfer to a blender and blend with the remaining butter. Correct the seasoning.

For the presentation: Steam the papillotes for 12 minutes until quite hot, unwrap them and serve them in warmed soup plates. Pour the warm sauce over them.

CHÂTEAU PRIEURÉ-LICHINE BY SERGE DUBS,
BEST SOMMELIER OF THE WORLD, 1989

A historic château that is part of the quality and cultural heritage of Bordeaux's Great Classified Growths. This wine authentically expresses its Margaux terroir with exactness and precision. Prieuré-Lichine's identity is based on an exceptional expression of finesse, delicacy, elegance and refinement. The wine is consistently pleasant and tender, velvety and silky, with charming flavours that never fail to delight the palate and the spirit.

CHÂTEAU MARQUIS DE TERME

MARGAUX

VINEYARD SIZE	38 hectares
VINE DENSITY	10,000 stocks per hectare
AVERAGE AGE OF VINEYARD	35 years
AVERAGE PRODUCTION	12,000 cases
SOILS AND SUBSOILS	gravel hills
GRAPE VARIETIES	Cabernet Sauvignon 55% Merlot 35% Petit Verdot 7% Cabernet Franc 3%

The sight of the château's courtyard soothes the eye, the horizontal lines of the winemaking buildings framing a vast white courtyard shaded by huge beautiful plane trees. If this grand, orderly layout is a good example of French formal aristocratic grace, you get more of a Spanish Golden Age feeling as you enter the cellar buildings, whose antique furniture and ironwork were imported from Spain. In the tasting room, an early Baroque tapestry hanging on the wall completes this decorative program, which was devised in the 1940s by the father of the current owners, Pierre Sénéclauze, to evoke the presence of a noble man.

"Je suis le Marquis de Terme," says this Margaux through the title of a small 1999 monograph devoted to the wine and its history. It also says it in the glass, draped in a stately dark velvet dress whose folds glisten at every move. A long-keeping wine of great character, a true figure of the tradition, Château Marquis de Terme has a demure bearing which fails to conceal a profound, philosophical sense of joyfulness. Ludovic David pours three vintages into decanters and ponders over the tasting as meditatively as you do as his visitor. As the new general manager of the estate, this young man from Libourne, trained into the wine business, has only spent a few months at the château at the writing of these lines. The former technical manager, Jean-Pierre Hugon, spent 36 years on the property; therefore David is in the process of getting to grips with the place and studying the available data. His challenge is to keep up with the Médoc tradition while bringing the wine into modernity, without betraying its own style. "This is a very traditional Margaux, surrounded by a classic aura. The idea is not to modify its nature but to breathe a little openness and novelty into it, so that all lovers of great wines may enjoy it."

David reviews all the current elements he could work on. "The vathouse is classic but functional, temperature-controlled and already equipped with vats of various capacities which closely reflect the plot layout. The cellar was built in 1984 and is very healthy, with perfect ventilation and hygrometry." So how will David launch the Marquis into the third millennium? "The planting, on 38 hectares of diversified soils, is 55 percent Cabernet Sauvignon, 35 percent Merlot, 7 percent Petit Verdot and 3 percent Cabernet Franc. My intention is to adopt a more gentle style of winemaking. I have the grapes painstakingly sorted in the vineyard and sorted once more after de-stemming, on a sorting table. I also intend to reduce the handling and transportation of the grapes in order to keep the fruit as whole as possible. We rely on five different cooperages for our barrels; I would like to rely on ten in order to have a wider 'toast' range and impart a more open taste to the wine."

In the cellar, a new steam-cleaning system has been set up to cleanse the inside of the barrels thoroughly and insure that the fruity character of the wines is perfectly preserved. "Through that sort of detail," says David, "I mean to introduce a touch of modernity into our winemaking. To sum up the matter, I will do everything in my power to promote fruitiness. The typicity will only be reinforced—and typicity, at any rate, is safeguarded by the terroir. My task consists in giving the terroir the best chance to express itself fully."

1. Heavy antique Spanish doors open out onto the barrel cellar. Improved winemaking methods are being applied to this Great Classified Growth in order to breath some extra life into its noble, classic style.

2. On 38 hectares of a diversified plot layout in the Margaux appellation, the planting is very balanced. 7% Petit Verdot give the wine a dark, deep colour.

3, 4. The large courtyard of château Marquis de Terme, shaded by majestic plane trees.

Hare Chasseur
on Celeriac Mousse and Wild Mushrooms

André CHIANG
Jaan par André - Singapore

SERVES 4

2 young hares or wild rabbits

The stock

4⅜ pound (2 kg) hare bones

3 sticks plus 4½ tablespoons
(400 g) unsalted butter

2¼ cups (300 g) shallots, peeled and sliced

2 tablespoons (25 g) garlic, peeled and sliced

5 bay leaves

2 tablespoons (10 g) thyme leaves

white chicken stock

fleur de sel

about 1 cup (25 cl) truffle juice

the chopped hare or rabbit trimmings

mirepoix (diced carrot and onion)

7 egg whites (about 210 g)

The hare confit

2⅛ cups (50 cl) fat from the hare stock

the hares' legs

The risotto

1⅛ pounds (500 g) bulgur wheat

⅓ pound (150 g) hares' front-leg flesh, chopped

1¼ cups (30 cl) heavy cream

⅛ cup (20 cl) dry white wine

1¾ ounces (50 g) chopped *cuisse-de-poulet*
shallots plus 1½ teaspoons (5 g) chopped shallot

chopped chives

salt and freshly ground black pepper

The fried hare

1⅜ ounces (40 g) curly endive

1 teaspoon whole-grain mustard

juice of ¼ lemon

4 hare chests, halved, trimmed into rib racks

oil

micro cress

The poached hare

1 finely sliced black truffle

2 hare loins

2 tablespoons (20 cl) truffle juice

wild mushrooms

celeriac mousse

For the stock: Cut each hare into 2 legs, boned loins, 2 chest halves and carcass including front legs. Clean the carcass and chop finely. Brown well in butter in a sauté pan, add the garlic and shallot and sweat until the aromatics are translucent. Add the thyme, bay leaf and fleur de sel, and keep sautéing until golden brown. Add the butter and cook for 5 minutes until it sizzles. Strain all the fat; set aside for the confit.

Deglaze the sauté pan with chicken stock to just cover the ingredients. Simmer for 5 hours over very low heat. After 5 hours, sieve and reduce by half. Pick the leg meat off the carcasses, shred it by hand and set it aside for the risotto.

For each quart (1 l) of hare stock, add a scant cup (20 cl) truffle juice. Mix well and clarify by cooking the preparation with the mirepoix, chopped trimmings and egg whites.

For the confit: Place the hare legs and the oil from the sauté pan in sous-vide bags. Seal and cook for 9 hours at 130°F (55°C).

For the risotto: Cook the bulgur al dente for 6 minutes in boiling salted water. Cool it in ice water, drain and set aside. Finish by drying for 4 minutes over low heat with cream, white wine and the *cuisse-de-poulet* shallots. Just before serving, add the chives, shallot, reserved leg meat and salt and pepper.

Season the curly endive with a vinaigrette of olive oil, lemon juice, and mustard and arrange it on the plates. Just before serving, sear the hare racks in oil and place them on the salad.

For the hare: Tie the loins with butchers' twine, put them into a sous-vide bag with the truffle juice and the sliced fresh truffle. Cook for about 15 minutes at 130°F (55°C).

For the presentation: Sauté all the mushrooms until golden. Add the shallot and chopped parsley. Just before serving, sprinkle with a little hare stock and arrange them in the middle of each plate. Remove the leg confit from the sous-vide bags, broil under the grill and put each leg piece on the mushrooms.

On one side of the plate, place the risotto, one potato chip, the salad (decorated with microcress) and the fried hare rack. Finally, add the poached and sliced hare loin onto the celeriac mousse. Serve some boiling hare broth on the side in a small pitcher.

CHATEAU
MARQUIS DE TERME

MARGAUX
2005
GRAND CRU CLASSÉ EN 1855

LE CHÂTEAU MARQUIS DE TERME BY MARKUS DEL MONEGO,
BEST SOMMELIER OF THE WORLD, 1998

Elegance and delicacy are among the most enchanting features of great Margaux wines. Château Marquis de Terme never fails to produce that emotion at tasting. In this vineyard, the density of 10,000 vine stocks per hectare forces the roots to plunge deeply into the ground, allowing the grape varieties—Cabernet Sauvignon, Merlot, Petit Verdot and Cabernet Franc—to show their best. And the wine's aromatic complexity and smooth tannins express the minerality of the terroir—sandy or clayey gravel—to perfection.

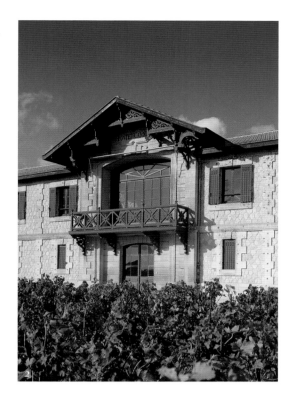

CHÂTEAU PONTET-CANET

PAUILLAC

VINEYARD SIZE	81 hectares
VINE DENSITY	9.800 stocks per hectare
AVERAGE AGE OF VINEYARD	35 years
AVERAGE PRODUCTION	250,000–300,000 cases
SOILS AND SUBSOILS	Quaternary gravel
GRAPE VARIETIES	Cabernet Sauvignon 62% Merlot 32% Cabernet Franc 4% Petit Verdot 2%

"Knowing where I want to go and taking my time to get there." Alfred Tesseron's calm voice does not belie the wisdom in the sentence he just uttered. Everything the master of Pontet-Canet does is surrounded by the same aura of peaceful confidence. Theory interests him only to the extent that it may lead to a concrete result. Right now, he is thinking about a technical ventilation device that might cause air to run naturally through the barrel cellar without creating unwelcome drafts. Maybe he can achieve that with the help of chimney shafts and high windows. He has not found it yet, but it has to exist, so he will find it. Tesseron's practical imagination at the service of winemaking knows no limits: biodynamic viticulture; 7-kilogram harvest trays specially designed by him to carry the grapes to the sorting tables untouched; minimal handling of berries; and three horses, three handsome *postiers bretons*, for vineyard tasks. "*Postiers bretons* are small as plough horses go," he says, stroking a tousled light blond mane. "They go through the vineyard more easily." A few sulkies are parked in the courtyard. Tesseron had them specially fitted for ploughing, spraying, uprooting. He is planning to design more of those. "Horses," he says, "do not tamp down the ground. Unlike machines, they never damage anything. And, besides, they are soothing to the mind." The virtue of calmness plays an important part at Pontet-Canet; everything seems to originate from it.

A melancholy, poetic atmosphere permeates this vast and beautiful estate bordering Mouton and Armailhac. After belonging successively to its founder Jean-François Pontet in the early 18th century, then to Hermann Cruse, it was acquired in 1975 by Guy Tesseron, a Cognac brandy trader. His sons, Alfred and Michel, inherited his two estates—Pontet-Canet for Alfred and Lafon-Rochet for Michel. The place has a special magic; it fills you with the wish to settle down and give yourself some time to understand. Your mind wanders over well-drained gravel hills that bear the typical Médoc

grape planting: 62 percent Cabernet Sauvignon, 32 percent Merlot, 4 percent Cabernet Franc and 2 percent Petit Verdot. You then admire the dignified 18th-century chartreuse, which contains an astonishing monumental staircase, before going to the beautiful tasting room, built in cut stone by the Compagnons du Devoir. Then you step down into the three-aisle underground barrel cellar, where the *Penicillium* fungus has covered the walls with a thick layer of grey cotton wool. Finally, you hover over the vast winemaking facilities for a few moments of meditation: high-walled barrel cellars, two-storey wooden vathouse built in the late 19th century by Skavinski with a noticeable Gustave Eiffel influence. The lovely iron ribs lining the whole framework echo the rails laid upstairs for carrying the harvest. The untrussed roof leans on an interesting structure of thin iron beams and cables. The latest addition is a spectacular double row of unpainted tronconical concrete vats whose shape facilitates the circulation of the lees and helps in giving the wine body and texture.

Has the mystery been revealed? Have you understood what goes on in the deep heart of Pontet-Canet? Certainly not. The sum total of these painstakingly delicate methods, the constant questioning of technique, help to understand the power of this dense, profound and masculine wine, but never completely. They fail to explicit this lovely, velvety black fruit mouthfeel, the light vanilla and liquorice touch, the treasures that appear after long ageing. One thing is certain: Château Pontet-Canet will pair beautifully with turtledove, a well-known Médoc feathered game much liked by Tesseron.

1. *A Breton post horse is drawing one of the sulkies that were specially designed by the team of Château Pontet-Canet for vineyard tasks. The estate is entirely cultivated in biodynamy.*

2. *The winemaking facilities date from the late 19th century, when the Cruse family owned the estate. Under the deceptive surface of the Basque-Landais style, their architecture was distinctly ahead of its time.*

3. *Pontet-Canet's wooden vathouse, designed by Skavinski. The influence of Gustave Eiffel is quite visible in the beautiful iron framework.*

Turtledoves with Chocolate Air,
Touches of Pedro Ximénez, Tarragon and Coffee

Ferran ADRIÀ

El Bulli - Roses, Spain

SERVES 4

The turtledoves

4 turtledoves, ⅛ poound (130 g) each

olive oil

salt

The sauce

wings, legs and bones of trimmed turtledoves

olive oil

¼ cup (50 g) finely chopped onion

3 tablespoons (25 g) finely chopped carrot

¼ cup (25 g) finely sliced leek (white part only)

1 tablespoon sherry vinegar

⅔ cup (15 cl) red wine

½ sprig fresh rosemary

½ sprig fresh thyme

1 juniper berry

½ cinnamon stick

zest of ¼ orange

zest of ¼ lemon

muscovado sugar

¼ pound (125 g) fresh duck foie gras

½ cup (12 cl) boiling water

1 cup (25 cl) Pedro Ximénez

3½ ounces (100g) fresh tarragon leaves

½ cup (10 cl) water

pinch of agar-agar

¼ of 2-g gelatine leaf, rehydrated in cold water

4 teaspoons black olive purée

2⅛ cup (50 cl) warm espresso coffee

The chocolate air

1 scant cup (100 g) chopped chocolate

⅛ ounce (25 g) cocoa paste

2⅛ cups (50 cl) water

1 rounded teaspoon (3 g) soybean lecithin

For the turtledoves: Remove the breasts, leaving them on the bone. Cut off the legs and the wings. Reserve all trimmings for the jus.

For the sauce: In a sauté pan, brown the trimmings, wings and legs in oil. Add the vegetables. Deglaze the pan with the vinegar and add the red wine. Reduce, then add water to cover and simmer for 3 hours over low heat. Strain and reduce to taste. Pour into a small saucepan and add the herbs, juniper, cinnamon, zests, and muscovado sugar. Strain in a Super-bag (superfine straining bag) and set aside.

Put the coarsely chopped foie gras in a Thermomix bowl. Add the boiling water and process in the Thermomix on medium for 3 minutes at 250°F (120°C). Pass through a fine-mesh sieve, then refrigerate for 12 hours.

After 12 hours, bring the foie gras to a simmer to the cream separate from the fat. Let rest off the heat for 15 minutes, then pass through a sieve. Pour into a tall, narrow vessel and keep refrigerated until the fat solidifies at the top. Separate the fat from the liquid and reserve it.

Season ½ cup (7.5 cl) of the turtledove jus to taste and bind with cornmeal, if necessary. Mix with 2 tablespoons of foie gras fat and set aside.

Reduce the Pedro Ximénez in a small saucepan. When it becomes syrupy and has the texture of light caramel, remove from the heat and let cool to room temperature. Check the consistency, then pour into a plastic bottle with a nozzle.

For the chocolate air: Heat the water to 250°F (120°C) and pour it over the chocolate and cocoa paste in a small bowl. Whisk well until mixed, then whisk in the lecithin.

In a small saucepan, bring 2 tablespoons water, tarragon and the agar-agar to a boil, stirring. Remove from heat and skim the surface. Add the drained gelatine and the remaining water and mix well. Pour into a rectangular container to a depth of about ¼ inch (6 mm). Refrigerate 3 hours to set. Cut into ⅛-inch (3-mm) cubes.

For the presentation: Season the dove breasts with salt and sear them over medium heat, skin side down, for 10 seconds. Turn them over and sear for 40 seconds. Remove from the pan and wrap in aluminum foil. Rest for 1 minute.

In large shallow plates, alternate 4 dice of jelly, 4 drops of reduction and 4 drops of black olive purée to cover the plate. Warm the plates under the grill (broiler). Bone the breasts and warm them up in the sauce.

With a handheld mixer, emulsify the coffee until foamy. Let rest for 5 minutes until the foam settles. Run the mixer on the surface of the chocolate preparation to create the "air."

Arrange 2 turtledove breasts in the centre of each plate, and pour some sauce over them. Beside each breast, place a spoonful of chocolate air. Finish with a touch of coffee foam on the upper side of the plate.

CHÂTEAU PONTET-CANET BY VIRGINIA PHILIP, BEST SOMMELIER OF THE UNITED STATES, 2002

The wines of this château are fantastic and many would argue this Fifth Growth can easily compete with its higher-ranking neighbours. The nose is deep with cassis, blackberry, blueberry and a hint of black pepper, as well as tobacco and earth. A hint of smoke and toast alludes to the judicious use of approximately 60 percent new French oak. Full-bodied on the palate, the dark fruits carry over with well-balanced tannins with a bit of grip on the back palate. Spice-box notes linger on the palate, with that hint of underbrush and a powerful, long finish.

CHÂTEAU BATAILLEY

PAUILLAC

VINEYARD SIZE	58 hectares
VINE DENSITY	10,000 stocks per hectare
AVERAGE AGE OF VINEYARD	35 years
SOILS AND SUBSOILS	gravel
GRAPE VARIETIES	Cabernet Sauvignon 70% Merlot 25% Cabernet Franc 3% Petit Verdot 2%

The Château Batailley supposedly got its name from the last battle that was fought before the English troops abandoned the Médoc. A likely hypothesis, for the area was the scene of harsh fighting towards the end of the Hundred Years War. Such was also the case at Château Latour, a few miles away. Nevertheless, the history of this château merges with that of its neighbour, Château Haut-Batailley, since both formed one large estate from the 18th century to the early 20th century.

In 1791, the vineyard belonged to the Saint-Martin family. Two of its three heirs, Marianne and Marthe, sold their shares to a certain Jean-Guillaume Pécholier. Batailley was then divided into two parts, although not according to the present pattern. The successive stages of transformation that followed until the 20th century are quite complicated; suffice it to say that in 1932, the Batailley estate, then a comfortable 55 hectares, was purchased by the brothers François and Marcel Borie, to be divided into two properties 10 years later. To François Borie, who later acquired Château Ducru-Beaucaillou, remained the smaller part of the estate. Shortly afterwards, he added a few plots he purchased from Château Duhart-Milon and thus put together Haut-Batailley as we know it today. Marcel, who owned Château Batailley, had his share of vineyards plus the château and its garden. In 1961, Château Batailley was added to the properties of the Castéja family, who already owned Château Lynch-Moussas in Pauillac, Château Beau-Site in Saint-Estèphe and Château Trottevieille in Saint-Émilion. Today, Mr. Philippe Castéja runs and operates the Château Batailley vineyard.

The chartreuse, a beautiful, classical building of the early 19th century, may offer a slightly stern face as seen from the road. But the gorgeous, shady garden stretching in the back, carpeted with purple cyclamens in late summer, expresses a much lighter, hedonistic feeling. A graceful melancholy permeates the whole place.

Château Batailley covers 58 hectares of sandy-clayey gravel, planted with vines of an average age of 30 years. The planting is dominated by Cabernet Sauvignon (70 percent), Merlot following with 25 percent and completed with 3 percent of Cabernet Franc and 2 percent of Petit Verdot. The vatroom is an ideal reflection of the vineyard layout, with 58 vats corresponding to the exact number of plots. The wine is aged up to 16 months in French oak, with 60 percent of new casks each year. After being clarified with egg whites, the wine is bottled without any filtration. Only Château Batailley is made in the dark, majestic cellars. There is no second wine.

Pauillac wines are often described as manly, and indeed Château Batailley fits the description. But its masculinity is of a refined nature. Rather than a hussar or a pirate, Batailley is an old-fashioned young man with a taste for poetry. Well-mannered and well-groomed, he needs time and the progress of intimacy to release his inner nature and reveal his emotions. The wine has a remarkable freshness of taste, a very personal nose of red flowers, a frank expression of red fruit and a clean, precise mouthfeel. As years go by, it mellows out and gives out distinguished notes of black pepper, tobacco, and a slight touch of lead mine. It will then be successfully served alongside grilled or roasted beef with plenty of black pepper, or perhaps a rare-cooked duck seasoned with ginger and liquorice. Either way, a red, juicy meat dish will make this young gentleman hum with pleasure through the protective coat of his apparent shyness.

1. If the generous ageing capacities of this Pauillac wine needed to be recalled, a single visit to the bottle cellar would be enough to get the message home.

2. The chartreuse of Batailley, surrounded by a magnificent park.

3. The château has the cosy atmosphere of an old family house. Here, the impressive library, next to the entrance hall.

Blue Mallard Duck,
Purple Potatoes

Juan Mari ARZAK

Arzak - San Sebastian, Spain

SERVES 4

The duck

2 mallard ducks, plucked
and ready for roasting

The blue mix

1 blanched onion

1 purple potato, cooked and peeled

2 slices of bread, fried

1 ounce (25 g) blue cheese

¼ cup (5 cl) vermouth

2 teaspoons extra virgin olive oil

salt and freshly ground black pepper

The sauce

1 scant cup (20 cl) olive oil

3 medium onions

4 leeks

1 cooked purple potato

1 bouquet garni

pinch of ground ginger

chopped sweet onions and oil to brown
the duck bones

salt and freshly ground black pepper

12 violet-flavored candies

The blue potato crisps

4 purple potatoes

½ cup (10 cl) olive oil

pinch of ground ginger

salt and freshly ground black pepper

borage flowers

For the duck: Cut off the duck breasts from the bone, season them lightly with salt and pepper. Reserve all the bones and trimmings for the sauce. Spread a thin layer of the blue mix onto the duck breasts and grill them *à la plancha*. Set aside.

For the sauce: Cut the bones into pieces and brown them in a Dutch oven with a little oil. Chop the vegetables and brown them slightly in the remaining olive oil. Pour off excess oil, and reserve. Add the vegetables and bouquet garni to the browned bones, sweat for a few minutes, then cover with water and reduce slightly. Strain, and add salt, pepper and ginger.

For the blue oil and violet crystals: Using the remaining blue mix and the reserved oil from browning the vegetables, make blue oil. This oil will be added at the last minute to the sauce, along with a few slices of sweet onion.

Put the violet candies between two sheets of parchment paper. Melt them in the oven, let cool, then crush them with a rolling pin in order to produce thin crystals. Set aside.

For the blue crisps: Wrap the potatoes in plastic wrap and microwave them. Peel, mash, add salt, pepper and a pinch of ginger. Spread a thin layer of this purée on squares of parchment paper (3½ x 3½ inches (8 x 8 cm), cover them and let them dry in a 140°F (60°C) oven. Once the crisps are dried, carefully peel off the paper and fry the crisps in 240°F (115°C) oil, without letting them brown.

For the presentation: Arrange the duck breasts on the plates, covering them with a little sauce. Scatter the violet candy crystals and a few borage flowers over the plate. Make 4 quenelles of the blue mash and place one oneach plate, sticking a blue crisp into each quenelle.

CHÂTEAU BATAILLEY BY ÉRIC BEAUMARD, SILVER MEDAL, BEST SOMMELIER OF THE WORLD, 1998

This property, belonging to Philippe Castéja, is situated on some of the finest gravel outcrops in Pauillac. Batailley's wines are delicious and fresh, worlds apart from the trend towards over-concentration. Rare in the Médoc, Batailley has a unique wine library that allows one to follow the evolution of the château's wines for more than a century. One just has to taste the 1962 to understand the remarkable potential of this terroir.

CHÂTEAU HAUT-BATAILLEY

PAUILLAC

VINEYARD SIZE	22 hectares
VINE DENSITY	10,000 stocks per hectare
AVERAGE AGE OF VINEYARD	40 years
AVERAGE PRODUCTION	9,000 cases
SOILS AND SUBSOILS	gravel
GRAPE VARIETIES	Cabernet Sauvignon 70% Merlot 25% Cabernet Franc 5%

Southwest of the Pauillac appellation, the vineyard of Haut-Batailley includes two distinct entities, one next to the estate of Batailley and the other one on the Plateau de Bages. The impressive winemaking buildings that dominate the vineyard date from the last third of the 19th century. Their "basco-landais" building style, inspired by French southwestern farmhouse architecture, was much appreciated at that time in the Bordeaux region and is often noticed in the technical wine buildings of the period throughout the Médoc: sharp protruding roofs held by wooden structures, wooden staircases and balconies outside the facades, stone walls enhanced by ornamental red brick. In this case, remarkable work has been done on the masonry, judging by the large, tightly assembled stone blocks that reinforce the lower part of the technical buildings, giving them a sturdy monumental beauty. That is, however, not the only architectural curiosity of the place; the Tour L'Aspic, also erected in the late 19th century, stands prominently amidst the vines. This narrow two-storey construction is topped by a statue of the Holy Virgin crushing the serpent of Evil with her foot—an unusual monument, which probably arose from a wish to get even with the deity after the painful collective curse of phylloxera. At any rate, it inspired the name and label of the château's second wine.

Since 2003, François-Xavier Borie, after manageing the vineyards of the Borie family at Ducru-Beaucaillou, has been taking care of his Pauillac estates, Château Haut-Batailley and Château Grand-Puy-Lacoste. After 2005, he restructured and modernised all the buildings and built the cellar, vathouse, harvest reception zone and the bottling room. Back in the 1970s, his father installed the concrete vats. Borie's lively sensuality and respect for the natural state of things are displayed through everything he creates, and notably through his fitting-out of the vast barrel cellar—a harmonious, well-lit

space, under a beautiful poplar-wood roof structure and a plain turf floor for barrels to rest on. The walls of this chai, of the vathouse and of the harvest reception zone are painted with Borie's favourite colour, the same deep, wine-y ruby red that that can also be seen at his other estate of Grand-Puy Lacoste.

The 22-hectare vineyard is planted in a typically Pauillac fashion, with 70 percent Cabernet Sauvignon, 25 percent Merlot and 5 percent Cabernet Franc. The vines are of an average age of 40 years and 55 percent new oak barrels are used each year for ageing. "We have light, easy-to-cultivate soils," says Borie. "They have a very 'south Pauillac' character, based on less dramatically hilly landscapes, shallower gravel layers and a sandier soil than north of the appellation. The wines are rounder and smoother here."

These are appropriate words for describing the wines of Haut-Batailley, whose charm and generosity also offer an opportunity to praise Borie's admirable success. Dense and bright in colour, giving out very pure fruity fragrances and clear notes of raspberry and fresh cherries, these wines are particularly melodious in certain vintages (2006), with a crisp mouthfeel. The 2004 vintage offers smoky, earthier tones. Either way, these Pauillacs are tailor-made for roast lamb—slow-roasted milk-fed lamb or garlic-studded gigot.

1. *In the barrel cellar and vathouse, the walls are painted with François-Xavier Borie's pet colour: a winey, sensuous, deep dark red.*

2. *A careful attention devoted to the slightest details of the winemaking facilities is a characteristic of Mr. Borie's style.*

3. *The cellars were built in the late 19th century in a Basque-Landais style often seen in the region. Here, the familiar style is associated with admirable cut-stone work.*

4. *Generous and straightforward, the wines of Haut-Batailley have the vivid pleasantness of South Pauillac wines.*

Lamb Saddle in a Salt Crust, *Vine Shoots*

Éric PRAS

Lameloise - Chagny-en-Bourgogne, France

SERVES 10

The lamb saddle

1 lamb saddle, about 3⅓ pounds (1.5 kg)

dry vine shoots

The salt crust

½ pound (150 g) coarse sea salt
plus ¼ pound (125 g) for the wash

⅔ pound (300 g) flour

1½ teaspoons fresh rosemary

1 teaspoon fresh thyme

½ cup (10 cl) water

1 large or extra-large egg white (37 g)

freshly ground black pepper

The wash

1 whole beaten egg (75 g)

2 egg yolks (about 50 g)

½ teaspoon salt

½ teaspoon sugar

The lamb jus

½ pound (250 g) lamb trimmings

1 small onion

1 small carrot

1 garlic clove

1½ teaspoons soy sauce

1 cup (25 cl) white chicken stock

1½ tablespoons olive oil

1½ tablespoons (21 g) unsalted butter

a sprig of thyme

The stuffing

¼ pound (100 g) white bread, crust removed

1 ounce (25 g) flat-leaf parsley

1½ teaspoons fresh thyme

1 to 2 tablespoons fresh basil

3½ tablespoons (50 g) unsalted butter

1½ tablespoons oil

salt and freshly ground black pepper

For the lamb saddle: Cut off the lamb filets, keeping the belly flaps on. Trim the filets. Chop the bones and the trimmings and brown them in a sauté pan with olive oil and a little butter. Add the aromatics for the jus and brown some more. Deglaze with the soy sauce. Add stock to barely cover, and simmer for 45 minutes. Pour through a fine sieve, reduce by half and set aside.

For the salt crust: Mix the flour and salt, add the rosemary and chopped thyme. Mix in the egg whites and the water, let the dough rest for

2 hours in a cold place, then roll it out 1/8 to ¼ inch (4 mm) thick. Cover with parchment paper and refrigerate.

For the stuffing: Blend the bread and herbs in a food processor, season and add olive oil.

To stuff the meat: Season the lamb with salt and pepper. Spread the stuffing over the meat and roll it up, wrapping it hermetically in the belly flaps. Tie with kitchen twine, and brown the meat on the filet side. Place some dry vine shoots onto the salt crust, place the lamb on them and wrap hermetically into the salt crust.

Put the lamb on a baking sheet, mix the egg wash ingredients and brush the salt crust all over with it. Sprinkle with coarse salt, and brush again.

Bake in a 470°F (243°C) oven for 16 minutes. Remove the lamb from the oven and let rest at an 85°F (30°C) temperature for about 30 minutes, until the core temperature reaches 187°F (86°C).

For the presentation: Arrange vine shoots on a serving dish and place the lamb over them. Serve.

CHÂTEAU HAUT-BATAILLEY BY FRANCK THOMAS, BEST SOMMELIER OF EUROPE, 2000

The wines of Haut-Batailley achieve a fine balance of power, length and a great capacity for ageing. Several years are needed to express the potential of the estate's gravel soils. Imagine a shaded terrace, a breeze blowing thorough the reeds of the Gironde estuary at harvest's end, and finally a delicious woodcock napped with a truffle-studded demi-glace sauce. Haut-Batailley, proudly displaying its evolved colours and its rural trappings, fully expresses a similarly satisfying, well-truffled character.

CHÂTEAU GRAND-PUY-LACOSTE

PAUILLAC

VINEYARD SIZE	55 hectares
VINE DENSITY	10,000 stocks per hectare
AVERAGE AGE OF VINEYARD	38 years
AVERAGE PRODUCTION	15,000 cases
SOILS AND SUBSOILS	deep, coarse gravel
GRAPE VARIETIES	Cabernet Sauvignon 75% Merlot 20% Cabernet Franc 5%

The quaternary Médoc hills covered with the pebbly soil known as Günzian gravel are an ideal ground for the Cabernet Sauvignon grape, which needs this well-drained type of terroir to reach its full maturity; hence the dominating presence of this varietal in the Pauillac appellation, where this soil is present on many hills. And it is no surprise that the wines produced on the hill of Grand-Puy-Lacoste, on the Plateau de Bages, are fully representative of the Pauillac character.

The local term puy means "ground elevation." And this particular puy, since the 18th century, has been a large estate of 90 hectares on which 55 are planted with vines. Since the 1855 Classification, its plot layout has retained the same configuration.

At the time of the classification, the estate was a property of the Lacoste family, who left us the lovely neoclassical chartreuse. It had several successive owners until 1932, when it fell into the hands of Raymond Dupin, a colourful character, who was remembered by many as a lover of the high life. When the time came to think about the property's future, he insisted on choosing his heirs. The lucky ones were the Bories, a Correzian-born family of wine traders and winemakers. The transaction, held shortly before Mr. Dupin passed away, was of the utmost simplicity: two lunches where the practical details of the contract were discussed and a signature in September 1978, immediately before the harvest.

Grand-Puy-Lacoste, covering 55 hectares in one piece, is planted with vines of an average age of 50 years. Cabernet Sauvignon makes up 75 percent of it, Merlot 20 percent and Cabernet Franc 5 percent. The wines are bouncing, fleshy and full of character. They call for meat—flesh, ripe and generous fare—and should be associated with high-quality foods to match the satisfaction level on either side. François-Xavier Borie, owner of Grand-Puy-Lacoste and Haut-Batailley,

another Pauillac Great Classified Growth, puts his own personal mix of technical skill and intuition into his wines. When questioned about plot selection, he replies, "Being able to make choices and decisions is important. I gather the grapes from different plots according to my experience of this terroir. Thus, I can identify distinct plot 'families,' and the harvest is done according to grape variety, age of the vines, type of soil and maturity. There is nothing wrong with fermenting grapes from different plots together when they show the same characteristics." This intuitive approach led by a keen sense of reality probably helps to explain the coherence and unity of taste that can be found in Borie's wines.

The history of the Borie family and of its influence in the Médoc would require an English-style saga in several volumes. Let it only be said that François-Xavier embodies the family qualities with an imposing, lively presence, sensible winemaking skills, an acute sense of beauty and a love for good living. His wines look like him in the same way that they look like the land that yields them, for terroirs and men never meet by chance. The whole place radiates a strong feeling of vitality, a masculine power that seems to rise from the earth itself. As an illustration of this particular earthy energy, François-Xavier painted the inside walls of the cellars with a beautiful winey colour, a bright, warm carmine red, which seems to convey a message. It is the blood-like sparkle of the young wine oozing onto the wood of the barrel, the stuff of life itself.

1. The wine chartreuses of the Médoc are often surrounded with lush, peaceful parks. At Grand-Puy-Lacoste, the park is set on a hillier ground than average.

2. This Pauillac terroir, planted with venerable aged vines, produces fleshy, tannic wines with good minerality.

3. A corridor of the château Grand-Puy-Lacoste.

Farm-raised Guineafowl with Goose Foie Gras, White Cabbage and Potato Croustilles

Émile JUNG
Au Crocodile - Strasbourg, France

SERVES 4

4 sticks of raw goose foie gras, about
1 ounce (30 g) each
2 to 3 tablespoons (20 g) flour
⅛ cup (3 cl) oil
4 farm-raised guinea-fowl breasts,
about ¼ pound (120 g) each
salt and freshly ground black pepper

The potato croustilles
½ pound (120 g) peeled potatoes
⅛ cup (3 cl) oil

The white cabbage
¼ pound (100 g) peeled onions
1 garlic clove
6½ cups (500 g) raw white cabbage
1⅔ cups (40 cl) whole milk
1¼ cups (30 cl heavy cream
salt

The jus
6 tablespoons (60 g) finely diced carrot
¼ cup (40 g) minced shallots
1¼ cups (30 cl) Pauillac red wine
pinch of crushed black pepper
⅔ cup (15 cl) brown chicken stock

For the guinea fowl: Season each foie gras stick with salt and pepper, then flour and fry in a little oil. Let cool. Cut the guinea-fowl breasts open, stuff them with the foie gras. Heat a little oil in a frying pan and lightly brown the guinea-fowl breasts on both sides over low heat. Finish the cooking for 8 minutes in a 400°F (200°C) oven.

For the potato croustilles: Grate the potatoes, and squeeze out all the excess moisture. Add a little salt and shape into one flat cake per serving. Brown each cake in oil on both sides in a small frying pan.

For the white cabbage: Finely slice the onion, the garlic and the cabbage. Cook in the milk and cream with a little salt for 40 minutes.

For the jus: Reduce all the ingredients (except the chicken stock) to ¼ cup (5 cl). Add the stock, bring to the boil, then strain.

For the presentation: On each plate, place a potato croustille, a guinea-fowl wing and a little cabbage. Serve the jus on the side.

CHÂTEAU GRAND-PUY-LACOSTE BY MARKUS DEL MONEGO,
BEST SOMMELIER OF THE WORLD, 1998

A vineyard planted solely with Cabernet Sauvignon and Merlot, and an ideal location on a small hill—two important aspects of a terroir that produces one of Pauillac's great, classic wines. With its great tannic structure and its dense and opulent body, this wine requires a little patience for its evolution. This patience is rewarded by complex aromas of dried fruit, Havana tobacco and cedar wood; velvety tannins; and an exceptional aromatic length.

CHÂTEAU GRAND-PUY DUCASSE

PAUILLAC

VINEYARD SIZE	40 hectares
VINE DENSITY	9,000 stocks per hectare
AVERAGE AGE OF VINEYARD	25 years
SOILS AND SUBSOILS	Garonne gravel
GRAPE VARIETIES	Cabernet Sauvignon 60% Merlot 40%

The story began in the mid-16th century when the Ducasse family purchased a small house in Pauillac, on the banks of the Gironde. In the 18th century, Pierre Ducasse, an attorney with a passion for winemaking, bought a few vineyard plots in Pauillac, Saint-Lambert and Saint-Sauveur. From purchase to purchase, the family soon found itself at the head of a large estate then named Ducasse-Grand-Puy-Artigues-Arnaud, covering 60 hectares including two thirds in vineyards. Around 1820, the small house had been replaced by a large mansion built in a beautifully unadorned neoclassical style, one of the very few Médoc wine châteaux that are set in the urban fabric and away from the vineyards. Here, you will see none of the classic panoramic views on the Médoc vine rows, but the château compensates by offering from every one of its rooms a no less romantic view over the Gironde, with the ever-changing colours of its skies reflected in the waters. The winemaking buildings, where the harvest is brought in from the various plots, are located around the courtyard at the back of the château.

In 1855, the wine was classified under the name of Artigues-Arnaud, and did not become Grand-Puy Ducasse until 1932. Since 2004 the estate, managed by Thierry Budin, has been a property of CA Grands Crus, a subsidiary of the Crédit Agricole which also owns the Château de Rayne-Vigneau in Sauternes and the Château Meyney in Saint-Estèphe. Through April 2009, an enhancement of the whole vineyard was led by the late Bernard Monteau, the technical manager, with Denis Dubourdieu as consultant œnologist.

"As is the case with all CA Grands Crus properties," says Budin, "the vineyard of Grand-Puy Ducasse has been treated in 'lutte raisonnée' (integrated pest management) since 2007. Some tests that we led during the previous years have proven

the validity of those methods, whose application requires a certain amount of initial risk-taking."

The plot layout of Grand-Puy Ducasse is one of the most scattered in the appellation. Its 40 hectares are spread over three large zones of Garonne gravel, bordering Pontet-Canet, Mouton and Lafite at the north. Another one may be seen as you exit from Pauillac towards Saint-Estèphe, shortly before you reach Pédesclaux. The planting is 60 percent Cabernet Sauvignon and 40 percent Merlot. The harvest is tried at the vineyard first, then again at the vathouse. After a thorough de-stemming and a slight crushing, the berries are conveyed into thermoregulated stainless-steel vats, some of them divided in half for a better plot selection. After blending, the ageing in casks varies between 18 to 24 months, depending on the vintage.

The wine of Grand-Puy Ducasse resembles its château: a classical, masculine Pauillac, resting on a harmonious structure. Easy to recognize by its freshness and aromatic persistence, it presents itself as a well-mannered young man who loosens up after a few minutes in a decanter or glass. Then it releases some spicy, delicately woody notes, with the odd touch of caramel.

The freshness and the solidity of the tannic framework, usually typical of Cabernet Sauvignon, may surprise in a wine with such a large proportion of Merlot. "This is because the terroir rules," says Olivier Bergia, the cellar master. "Our Merlots are well wrought, with a rich but acidic and structured character. Also, we try to harvest at full maturity, but not beyond. This gives us opulent, fruity wines, which remain tightly woven, with wonderful ageing capacities."

1. Built in a tasteful modern style, the cellars of Grand-Puy Ducasse are located in the heart of Pauillac.

2. In 1855, the wine of Grand-Puy Ducasse was classified under the name Artigues-Arnand. It got its current name in 1932.

3. Here and there, a few discreet sculpted ornaments punctuate the château's sober neoclassical architecture.

4. Inside the château.

Roast Squab, *Blueberry Vinaigrette*

Normand LAPRISE
Restaurant Toqué! - Montréal, Canada

SERVES 4

The beans

1 2/3 cup (38 cl) classic mirepoix (finely diced onion, carrot, and garlic)

¾ cup (2 1/8 ounces) (60 g) bacon, cut into sticks

2/3 pound (300 g) fresh white haricot beans, shelled

The squab

4 squab, about 1 pound (375 g) each

oil and unsalted butter as needed

The garnishes

1/3 pound (210 g) fresh chanterelle mushrooms

¼ pound (90 g) fresh blueberries

4 tablespoons tarragon-scented oil

4 tablespoons balsamic vinegar, reduced by half

1 tablespoon beurre noisette (browned butter)

salt and freshly ground black pepper

caramelised pickling onions, optional

a few leaves of sea orache, optional

puréed blueberries, optional

For the beans: Sweat the mirepoix with the bacon, add the beans, add water to barely cover, bring to the boil and simmer for about 45 minutes. Discard the mirepoix, keeping the beans in their cooking stock.

For the squab: Preheat the oven to 375°F (191°C). Season the squab with salt and pepper. Heat a little butter and oil in a pan, brown the squab on all sides, then roast them for 6 minutes in the oven. Remove them from the oven and let them rest, loosely covered, for 10 minutes.

For the garnishes: Meanwhile, sear the chanterelles in a little butter and oil. Warm the blueberries in the tarragon oil, then add the reduced balsamic vinegar.

For the presentation: Add 1 tablespoonful of *beurre noisette* to the squab jus.

Reheat the squab for 1 minute in a 450°F (232°C) oven, then bone them.

On each plate, place a generous spoonful of beans and mushrooms. Place the squab meat on top and coat with the jus. Just before serving, add a few drops of blueberry vinaigrette. You may also add some caramelised pickling onions, a few leaves of sea orache, and puréed blueberries, if desired.

CHÂTEAU GRAND-PUY DUCASSE BY YOICHI SATO, BEST SOMMELIER OF JAPAN, 2005

This is a serious, reserved wine, towards the head of its class. Although it can take a bit of time to open up and shows noticeable differences from one vintage to another, it remains consistent in character. This last characteristic makes it a valuable wine for a restaurateur. I suggest that you enjoy it following a lengthy decanting period, or even give it extra time in your glass.

CHÂTEAU LYNCH-BAGES

PAUILLAC

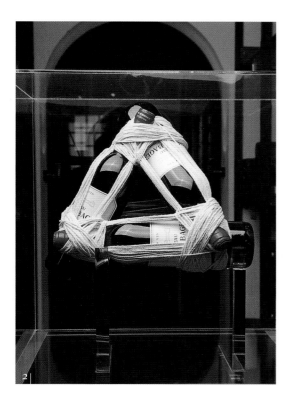

VINEYARD SIZE	96 hectares
VINE DENSITY	8 700 stocks per hectare
AVERAGE AGE OF VINEYARD	35 years
AVERAGE PRODUCTION	400 000 bottles
SOILS AND SUBSOILS	Garonne gravel
GRAPE VARIETIES	Cabernet Sauvignon 75% Merlot 17% Cabernet Franc 6% Petit Verdot 2%

Bages is of a type that is rarely seen in Médoc: a village perched atop a vine-planted hill. More frequently, that type of pedestal supports a château. Even more frequently, it supports nothing at all; the vast, soft sloping heights that give such a moving charm to the peninsula wave away without any other ornament than their vines. A few years ago, Bages was threatening to become a ghost village. The buildings were empty and run down, the streets were riddled with potholes. Jean-Michel Cazes spent three years nursing the village, resurrecting it and giving it the pleasant and smiling look it has today, gathered around the Château Lynch-Bages: "I wanted Bages to be a real village again, not just a tourist destination. I have seen so many little Médoc villages disappear! And I did not want Bages to suffer the same fate."

Jean-Michel Cazes, president of the supervisory board of the family-run château, succeeds many generations of owners. As early as 1749, the old estate of Bages, of which traces may be found as early as the 16th century, was the property of the Lynch family. Their ancestor was John Lynch, an Irishman who immigrated to Bordeaux in 1690. In 1824, Michel Lynch sold the property to the Geneva trader Sébastien Jurine. Under the care of the Jurine Family, the wine of the château was classified as Fifth Growth in 1855. Soon afterward, the Jurines sold the estate to Jérôme Cayrou, and finally Jean-Charles Cazes took it over in 1934. The excellent reputation of the wines of Lynch-Bages owes a lot to this great winemaker. In 1972, at the age of 95, Jean-Charles Cazes passed away. Following his death, the property was managed by his son André, mayor of Pauillac from 1947 to 1991, then by his grandson Jean-Michel. Recently, Jean-Michel passed on the reins to his son, Jean-Charles, and his sister, Sylvie Cazes.

Located on the Plateau de Bages, the 96 hectares of the vineyard are planted with 75 percent Cabernet Sauvignon, 17 percent Merlot, 6 percent Cabernet Franc and 2 percent Petit Verdot. The ageing is carried in 70 percent new oak

barrels. A second wine, Château Haut-Bages Averous, is obtained from the selections. Powerful and balanced, Château Lynch-Bages rests on a finely chiselled tannic structure. It unfolds in longs notes like an arpeggio, giving out plenty of opulent, mature red fruit. This strong personality partly explains the worldwide success of this wine and its regular rating above its category in the classification.

Jean-Michel Cazes, half-jokingly, cites other reasons. "Lynch-Bages," he says, "does well in countries where its name is easy to pronounce. In China, for instance, where *Lin Zhi Ba* is much appreciated. More seriously, our loyalty policy to our customers is also instrumental. We always strive to be sincere, equally through our wines and through our discourse, and to know and respect our buyers. We make a point of meeting our clientele personally by travelling a lot. We welcome them, too. Twenty thousand people are greeted at Lynch-Bages each year."

Since 1989, in the château's Holy of Holies—the well-preserved old chais and beautiful 19th-century wooden vathouse, with its upstairs rail system for the harvest reception, vertical press and crusher—Jean-Michel has been regularly exhibiting the works of internationally renowned artists. Pierre Alechinsky in 2001, Antony Tàpies in 2002, Hervé Di Rosa in 2008 and, recently, Ryan Mendoza's works have been shown at Lynch-Bages. This is a way, for Jean-Michel Cazes, of celebrating the beauty of life through a choral reunion—art, the village of Bages reborn from its ashes, and a wine bursting with vitality.

1. Château Lynch-Bages' long barrel cellar.

2. Under the impulse of Jean-Michel Cazes and his family, contemporary art has been invited into the winemaking spaces of the château, which offer a generous exhibition surface. Art is of course allowed to draw its inspiration from wine to its heart's content.

3. The château is set on top of a hill at the edge of the plateau de Bages.

4. The former harvest reception space and the old wooden vathouse that lies below it have been preserved in their original state, thus giving the visitor a clear notion of winemaking in the 19th century.

Ready-to-eat Pig's Trotters
and Cèpes

Thierry MARX

Château Cordeillan-Bages - Pauillac, France

SERVES 6

18 fresh or frozen whole cèpes (porcini),
defrosted if needed, and blanched

6 pig's trotters, precooked, refrigerated,
then brought to room temperature

unsalted butter

a little flambéed red wine

a little beef broth

1 garlic clove, chopped

chopped parsley

a few dollops of whipped cream

1 bunch fresh herbs

The bordelaise sauce

5½ pound (2.5 kg) beef ribs

2 bottles red wine

10 shallots

1½ lumps of sugar

1 tablespoon (14 g) unsalted butter

cornstarch or potato starch

cold butter to bind the sauce

salt

The cèpe stuffing

1 pound (375 g) raw boned chicken

1½ cups (35 cl) heavy cream

½ pound (200 g) diced cèpes,
fried in a little butter

salt and freshly ground black pepper

For the bordelaise sauce: Brown the beef ribs in a hot oven; when well browned add 1 bottle of wine. Flambé the wine, put the ribs and wine into a stockpot and reduce the wine to a glaze. Add water and simmer for 4 hours.

Meanwhile finely chop the shallots. Make a caramel with the sugar and the butter, add the shallots and some salt. Sweat and let brown slightly, then add 1 bottle of red wine, flambé and reduce until almost dry.

When the beef stock is ready, pour it through a fine sieve, add some of the reduced shallots, reduce by three-quarters, purée the sauce and if necessary bind it with a little starch. Bind and mount the sauce with cold butter, taste and correct the seasoning and strain without pressing.

For the cèpe stuffing: Chop the chicken meat finely then purée in a food processor. Season it with salt and pepper, and add the cream. Blend again, then sieve. Correct the seasoning, and add the diced cooked cèpes.

For the pig's trotters: The pig's trotters should be at room temperature. Bone them entirely, open them out, add a generous tablespoonful of cèpe stuffing, roll them in plastic wrap, then into aluminum foil. Poach for 15 minutes at 175°F (80°C) then set aside.

For the cèpes: Separate the cèpe heads from the stalks. Brown the blanched cèpe heads, round side first. When almost done add the flambéed red wine, and reduce until almost dry. Add a little butter and beef stock, reduce until syrupy, then drain and coat with bordelaise sauce.

Sauté the diced cèpe stalks in butter with the garlic clove. Drain.

For the presentation: Shortly before serving, reheat the wrapped pig's trotters for 1 minute in a microwave oven, unwrap and cut each trotter into 3 thick chunks.

Just before serving, reheat the cèpes in butter, add the parsley and drain again. Divide them among the serving dishes, add emulsified cream, salt and pepper.

For the presentation: Place 3 chunks of trotters in a large white plate, and top them with the cèpe heads. Add a bunch of fresh herbs on the middle trotter. Add a dash of sauce on either side of the trotters, then a smaller one on the right side of the plate. Serve with the cèpe stalks on the side, dotted with a little whipped cream.

CHÂTEAU LYNCH-MOUSSAS

PAUILLAC

VINEYARD SIZE	60 hectares
VINE DENSITY	8,500 stocks per hectare
AVERAGE AGE OF VINEYARD	27 years
SOILS AND SUBSOILS	Günzian gravel with a few clay veins
GRAPE VARIETIES	Cabernet Sauvignon 70% Merlot 30%

This beautiful property borders a forest originally belonged to the Count Lynch, an Irish soldier who settled in Bordeaux as a cloth and leather trader at the end of the 17th century. Both his family and the Castéja family each gave a mayor to the city of Bordeaux. The Lynches owned several wine estates in Médoc, most notably Lynch-Moussas in Pauillac. The 18th-century château nestles in the woods, some distance away from the road, which gives it a slightly wild atmosphere that is not without charm. It remained whole until the 19th century, when it was divided into two different entities, Moussas and Bages, which resulted in the creation of the Lynch-Bages estate.

A vast property where woods and vineyards share the surface, Lynch-Moussas covered 150 hectares at the time of the 1855 Classification. Today, it is concentrated on about 60 hectares of its best soils. The woods and the land are still intact, with woodcock and mushroom hunting still favourite local occupations. In 1919, Jean Castéja, whose family owned the Château Duhart-Milon, acquired Lynch-Moussas for himself. Thus the Castéja family has owned wine properties in Pauillac for more than three hundred years.

About 50 years later, in 1970, Émile Castéja purchased Lynch-Moussas from his family. He then set out to apply an ambitious reconstruction and replanting policy to this dormant property. In the course of 30 years, he gave it back a name, a quality and a soul. Since 2001, Philippe Castéja has managed the estate and pursued the same quality policy.

On a typically Pauillac soil of fine Günzian gravel, the vineyard of Lynch-Moussas is located on the famous Moussas plateau, where its plots border those of Batailley, Grand-Puy-Lacoste, Lynch-Bages and Pichon. Cabernet Sauvignon dominates the planting with 70 percent, Merlot making up the remaining 30 percent. Philippe Castéja carries the winemaking, with Denis Dubourdieu as consultant œnologist, as precisely and carefully as he does at his other estate of Batailley. The winemaking is carried out in a stainless-steel vathouse of various capacities, reflecting the plot structure of the vineyard and allowing for very precise fermentations. The wine ages in 60 percent new oak casks from 18 to 24 months, with no filtration until the bottling at the château.

"Since the 1960s," says Castéja, "there have been several successive viticultural revolutions in the region. First, the mechanisation of vineyard tasks brought a notable increase in the depth of the ploughing. This made the vine plants more robust and less vulnerable to disease, which is always a concern in this oceanic type of climate. In the late 1970s, œnology became predominant and a better control of the winemaking data was achieved, but the importance of controlling the yield was not fully understood until the 1980s, when green harvest, thinning, leaf stripping and improved pruning techniques were adopted. These efforts towards quality and carefully thought-out treatments that are applied to our 1855 Great Classified Growths are unequalled the world over. They produce a unique freshness in the wines, which remains a common feature throughout the diversity of all the growths and imparts to them their wonderful ageing qualities."

1. The beautiful white chartreuse of Lynch-Moussas stands remote from all turmoil, in a lush forested park. The young vines in the foreground are part of the replanting project currently carried out on the estate.

2. French-style flowerbeds adorn the main courtyard.

3. The central aisle of the barrel cellar.

Red Tuna Carpaccio,
Three-Mustard Sauce

Kiyomi MIKUNI
Mikuni - Tokyo, Japan

SERVES 4

The tuna

¾ pound (280 g) trimmed red tuna

½ cup (65 g) finely diced carrot

½ cup (65 g) finely diced onion

½ cup (65 g) finely diced cucumber

4 stoned, chopped black olives

4 stoned, chopped green olives

4 tablespoons chopped chives

4 tablespoons chopped chervil

red mustard
(mustard mixed with ketchup)

green mustard
(mustard mixed with chopped parsley)

yellow Dijon mustard

The sauce

½ cup (10 cl) olive oil

2 tablespoons balsamic vinegar

4 tablespoons soy sauce

a little lemon juice

salt and freshly ground black pepper

For the tuna: Thinly slice the red tuna with a very sharp knife in order to make very thin and round slices. Arrange them on the plates.

Mix the chopped vegetables.

Mix the sauce ingredients.

For the presentation: Around this tuna arrangement, place the finely chopped vegetable brunoise and season with salt and pepper.

Dress the whole plate with the three mustards in a nice design, then add the chopped olives, the sauce, chives and chervil.

GRAND CRU CLASSÉ EN 1855

CHATEAU
LYNCH-MOUSSAS

2005

PAUILLAC

CASTÉJA   MIS EN BOUTEILLE AU CHÂTEAU

CHÂTEAU LYNCH-MOUSSAS BY SERGE DUBS,
BEST SOMMELIER OF THE WORLD, 1989

We have witnessed a true renaissance at this Bordeaux Great Growth, whose cultural and historical roots go deep into Médoc soil. Today, the prestige and splendour of Lynch-Moussas makes it one of Pauillac's flagship properties. A proud and lively temperament characterises this spirited wine, whose tannic richness gives it full body and good structure, density and depth. This is true class.

CHÂTEAU DAUZAC

MARGAUX

VINEYARD SIZE	42 hectares
VINE DENSITY	10,000 stocks per hectare
AVERAGE AGE OF VINEYARD	35 years
SOILS AND SUBSOILS	deep gravel
GRAPE VARIETIES	Cabernet Sauvignon 55% Merlot 45%

Among the Great Classified Growths of Margaux, the Château Dauzac is both the easternmost and the closest to the Gironde. Although records show that there were vineyards here as early as the 12th century, the creation of a true wine estate at Dauzac did not happen until the 17th century, when wine trader Pierre Drouillard built a vathouse, a cellar and wine presses that were considered quite innovative at the time. The *palus* vines were dug up from the marshy lands near the river and the new planting was gathered on the beautiful gravel soils of the estate, particularly on the Croupe de Dauzac, a majestic hill that rises before the château.

In 1740, Count Thomas Michel Lynch married into the owners' family, inheriting the estate and making Dauzac one of his main places of residence. Later, the château was sold to Thomas Diedrich Wiebrook, then to the Johnston family, who kept it until 1920. However, since the late 19th century, Dauzac was already considered a model vineyard and the birthplace of much viticultural innovation, thanks to Nathaniel Johnston's sensible and efficient management. During the 1880s, Dauzac's estate manager, Ernest David—with the counselling of Alexis Millardet and the Science Faculty of Bordeaux—invented the Bordeaux mixture, a mix of copper sulphate and hydrated lime, which saved all European vineyards from downy mildew.

Following the death of Nathaniel Johnston in 1914, the Château Dauzac went through a difficult period, which lasted until 1978, when the ownership group Félix Chatellier et Fils took command of the vineyard and decided to restructure it, building a new chai and a stainless-steel vathouse. In 1988, the estate was bought by the MAIF, a mutual insurance company for French schoolteachers. In 1992, André Lurton became président du directoire and gave all his expertise to the service of the Château Dauzac, in order to develop the wine's quality and the château's image. Today, the estate is run by a board of directors led by André's daughter, Christine Lurton de Caix, assisted by Éric Boissenot as consultant œnologist.

The terroir of Dauzac covers 45 hectares all in one piece on a deep gravel soil, stretching to the southwest between Labarde and Macau. The technical buildings stand facing the vineyard, while the lovely 18th-century chartreuse stands at a slight distance in the vast park, behind a small lake.

"Our best wine," says Lurton de Caix, "comes from the Croupe de Dauzac, facing the château. Our vines, of an average age of 35 years, are 55 percent Cabernet Sauvignon and 45 percent Merlot. We do a lot of work on the soils, especially those of the croupe, and on the buds, leaves and green clusters, raising the canopy by 10 centimetres for a better leaf surface. We try to interfere as little as possible with the vine's natural cycle. In 2004, we restructured the stainless-steel vathouse and adapted it to gravitary fermentation, splitting the vats to improve the plot selection."

The wine of Château Dauzac, made with passion and dedication, shows all the characters of a classic Margaux, with a deep and velvety garnet colour, a lot of freshness and nicely melted tannins. It often shows empyreumatic notes—smoke, mocha, cocoa—as well as rich, concentrated fruit tastes like blackberry, prune and black cherry. Such a balance reflects the earnest, painstaking work of Christine Lurton, with much attention to the whims of nature. "Everything," she says, "can change in the course of 48 hours. We are so tiny on a planet scale! Just consider how many different wines can be made on a small surface. The character or the quality of a wine can change with a few metres or a few days, even hours. Little details make the difference."

1. Elongated and horizontal in shape, the chartreuse of Dauzac is set into the vast lawn of the park and is separated from the vineyard by a large pond.

2. The main entrance to the winemaking and office facilities. Right here, at Château Dauzac, experiments led to the creation of the Bordeaux mixture in the late 19th century.

3. The inside of the high stainless steel vats in Médoc wineries is often divided into two to help with the plot selection. Steel bridges at the top allow to control the gravitary filling of the vats.

Guinea Fowl
and Lamb's Lettuce Salad, Black Truffle Oil

Jean-Pierre MOULLÉ
Chez Panisse - Berkeley (CA), United States

SERVES 4

1 guinea fowl, about 3 pounds
(1.2 to 1.5 kg)

The vinaigrette

2 medium shallots, diced
2 tablespoons Banyuls wine vinegar
1 tablespoon balsamic vinegar
¼ cup (6 cl) extra virgin olive oil

The salad

4 handfuls lamb's lettuce (mâche),
or mesclun salad
¼ pound (125 g) yellow or grey
chanterelles, cleaned
1 garlic clove , finely chopped
1 black truffle, about 1 ounce
(30 g), peeled
¼ cup (6 cl) grape seed oil
salt and freshly ground black pepper

For the guinea fowl: The guinea fowl should be at room temperature before roasting: take it out of the refrigerator 1 hour in advance of cooking.

Preheat the oven to 450°F (232°C). Truss the guinea- fowl and season it with salt and pepper. Place it into an ovenproof dish, breast side up, and roast for 20 minutes. Lower the temperature to 400°F (200°C), turn the fowl on its side and roast for 20 minutes. Turn it on the other side and roast for 20 more minutes. All the while, baste it frequently with the roasting juices.

When the guinea fowl is cooked, let it rest for 10 minutes out of the oven, breast side down, loosely covered with aluminum foil, before carving.

For the vinaigrette: Marinate the chopped shallots for 10 minutes in the mixed vinegars and a little salt. Whisk in the olive oil and add freshly ground black pepper to taste.

For the salad: Rinse and dry the lamb's lettuce.

In a very hot skillet, heat a little olive oil and sauté the chanterelles in it with a little salt. When they are tender, add the chopped garlic and cook for 2 minutes over low heat. Set aside.

Crush the truffle in a bowl with the tines of a fork. Mix it with the grape seed oil and a pinch of salt, and heat gently over low heat. Set aside.

Discard the fat from the baking dish, and deglaze the pan with ½ cup (12 cl) water. Pour this jus into a small bowl.

Season the salad with the vinaigrette and half the guinea-fowl jus.

Cut off the legs and breast meat of the guinea fowl. Carve the breast meat diagonally and halve the legs.

For the presentation: Divide the salad among 4 large plates. Place the breast meat onto the salad and add 1 piece of leg. Scatter the whole surface of the plate with chanterelles, spoon the remaining jus over the plate and add the warm truffle oil.

CHÂTEAU DAUZAC BY ANDREAS LARSSON,
BEST SOMMELIER OF THE WORLD, 2007

This is a remarkably good Margaux that, during the last years, has been increasing in quality and gaining complexity, density and concentration, without losing its benchmark Margaux character. A wine that would be difficult to call either traditional or modern, its youth shows a magnificent nose of dark berries, roasted coffee and gently roasted oak with some floral violet notes offers maybe more of a "modern" notion; however as it ages, it starts to display a subtle perfume, a silky structure and marked minerality that most of us would call very classic. A truly good wine that still is accessible in every sense, both drinking-wise and price- wise. A Margaux with a bright future.

Château d'Armailhac

PAUILLAC

VINEYARD SIZE	54 hectares
VINE DENSITY	8,500 stocks per hectare
AVERAGE AGE OF VINEYARD	50 years
AVERAGE PRODUCTION	220,000 bottles
SOILS AND SUBSOILS	80% gravel and 20% clay-limestone
GRAPE VARIETIES	Cabernet Sauvignon 54% Merlot 31% Cabernet Franc 12% Petit Verdot 2% Carmenère 1%

Since its foundation in the first half of the 18th century by the brothers Dominique and Guilhem Armailhacq, after they bought it from the famous "Wine Prince" Nicolas Alexandre de Ségur, the Château d'Armailhac has borne different names—and the names different spellings—throughout history. Around 1750, the property known as Mouton d'Armailhacq covered 52 hectares between Brane-Mouton (which was to become Mouton Rothschild) and Pibran. In 1844, it was bought by Mrs. Darmailhacq, the estranged wife of Mr. Joseph Odet Darmailhacq the Elder.

In 1855, when the château's wine was classified as Fifth Growth, its owner, Armand (by then known as d'Armailhac) wrote and published a book that has remained a classic, *De la culture des vignes, de la vinification et des vins dans le Médoc*. The improvement, in this period, of the quality of wines owes a lot to Armand, as do the grape-planting methods, particularly the promotion of Cabernet Sauvignon as the dominant grape variety in the Médoc against other varieties such as Cabernet Franc, Malbec or Petit Verdot. He also brought on many innovations in vine growing, fermentation and ageing.

After the death of Armand d'Armailhac, the estate was run by his brother-in-law, Count Adrien de Ferrand. The wine, to which Armand had given a positive impulse, kept thriving until the phylloxeric storms of the late 19th century and the difficulties of the following decades. In 1931, Roger de Ferrand, Adrien's descendant, sought external funding to support the estate. The young Baron Philippe de Rothschild became the main shareholder and finally bought the remaining shares through a life annuity sale. The destinies of Château Mouton d'Armailhac and Château Mouton Rothschild were joined. The vast facilities of Château d'Armailhac sheltered the technical and agricultural equipment of both châteaux and the house itself was used by the general manager of the properties from 1947 to 1966. From 1956 to 1988, the name of the wine changed to Mouton Baron Philippe, then to Mouton Baronne

Philippe. In 1989, its new owner, Baroness Philippine de Rothschild, restored its original d'Armailhac identity and had the label illustrated with a small spun-glass dancing Bacchus, a delicate 18th-century masterpiece that can be admired at the Museum of Wine in Art at the Château Mouton Rothschild. Through a play of graphic similarity, Château d'Armailhac is the matching piece of a diptych formed with Château Clerc Milon, another Classified Growth owned by Baroness Rothschild.

The Château d'Armailhac is run by Philippe Dhalluin and Hervé Berland, respectively technical and commercial general managers (châteaux) of the family-owned Baron Philippe de Rothschild SA Company. The vines cover 54 hectares north of Pauillac, on three distinct pedologic zones: the Plateau des Levantines et de l'Obélisque, with light gravel for Cabernets; the Plateau de Pibran, gravel on clay-limestone subsoil; and the Croupe de Béhéré, with very deep gravel. The planting is 54 percent Cabernet Sauvignon, 31 percent Merlot, 12 percent Cabernet Franc and 2 percent Petit Verdot. The ageing is led for 15 to 16 months in 25 percent new oak barrels.

A large proportion of Cabernet Franc gives Château d'Armailhac a very personal touch. Spicy, meaty and melodious, it somehow escapes from the Pauillac typicity, hovering towards pomerol, while remaining based on a typically Médoc straightforward structure. Juicy cherries, ripe raspberries and a beautiful dense colour are lit up by quick sparkles and notes of caramel, vanilla and cedarwood. Château d'Armailhac is a cheerful, fleshy, sensuous wine. The happy Bacchus who decorates its label is fully entitled to dance with joy; the wine shows itself worthy of its ruling deity.

1. In the 19th century, the estate belonged to Armand d'Armailhac, who wrote a famous treaty on Médoc winemaking.

2. The grape planting of Armailhac, rather unusual for Pauillac, contains a good proportion of Cabernet Franc.

3. The château and vineyard in Winter.

Seared Lamb Rossini, Beets,
Roasted Mushrooms, Cassis and Black Truffles

Anthony SICIGNANO
The Breakers - Palm Beach (FL), United States

SERVES 4

The lamb and foie gras

4 double lamb rib chops

1 teaspoon *fines herbes*

1 tablespoon olive oil

four 2-ounce medallions
of well-cleaned foie gras

salt and freshly ground black pepper

The beets

16 baby beets (no more than 1 inch
in diameter), assorted and peeled

2 tablespoons unsalted butter

salt and freshly ground black pepper

The mushrooms

½ cup chanterelle mushrooms,
cleaned and quartered

½ cup (about 100 g) morel mushrooms,
cleaned and quartered

½ cup (about 100 g) black trumpet
mushrooms, cleaned and quartered

6 tablespoons (90 g)
unsalted butter (¾ stick)

1 tablespoon extra virgin olive oil

salt and freshly ground black pepper

The croutons

four 2-inch rounds country white bread

4 tablespoons (60 g) unsalted butter
(½ stick), melted

The sauce

2 tablespoons (28 g) unsalted butter

3 shallots, peeled and finely sliced

1 small garlic clove, roughly sliced

8 whole peppercorns

1 bay leaf

½ sprig rosemary

½ sprig thyme

1 tablespoon flour

½ cup mushroom stems, cleaned and
roughly chopped

½ cup (12 cl) dry red wine

½ cup *liqueur de cassis*

1 cup (25 cl) lamb jus

3 tablespoons (42 g) cold unsalted
butter, cut into small pieces

salt and freshly ground black pepper

For the beets: Cook the beets in boiling salted water (be sure to cook different-coloured beets in separate pans). Remove the beets from the boiling water and toss with the butter.

For the mushrooms: Put the butter and olive oil in a smoking hot sauté pan. Add the mushrooms in one even layer. Cook over high heat until mushrooms are crisp on one side. Turn the mushrooms and repeat process. Season with salt and black pepper to taste.

For the croutons: Brush each side of each bread round with melted butter. Bake in a 375°F (190°C) oven until browned on both sides.

For the lamb: Rub each chop with olive oil and *fines herbes*. Season well with salt and black pepper. Sear on both sides in a hot skillet until desired doneness, medium-rare recommended.

For the sauce: In the same pan used to sear the lamb, remove any excess oil and then add the butter, shallots, garlic, peppercorns, bay leaf, rosemary and thyme. Sauté until lightly caramelised. Sprinkle with flour, add the mushrooms and cook until dry. Add the red wine and reduce by half. Add the cassis and reduce by half. Add the lamb jus and reduce until you almost reach a sauce consistency. Strain, finish with butter, salt and black pepper to taste and a touch of cassis.

For the foie gras: Season the foie gras well. Sauté in a hot skillet until each side is lightly caramelised and foie gras is cooked medium.

For the presentation: Arrange a neat pile of the mushrooms and beets in the centre of each plate. Assemble the lamb by placing two croutons on each plate next to the beets and mushrooms. Top each crouton with a double lamb chop, seared foie gras and shaved truffles. Drizzle each plate with a bit of the sauce.

CHÂTEAU D'ARMAILHAC BY VIRGINIA PHILIP,
BEST SOMMELIER OF THE UNITED STATES, 2002

D'Armailhac shares similar terroir to its famous neighbours—Mouton Rothschild, for instance—with gravel-clay over limestone and sand. Approximately 20,000 cases are produced yearly and the wines see partial new oak and used oak from barrels previously used by Château Mouton Rothschild. Considered more feminine and lighter than Mouton and Clerc Milon, the wine has overtones of blackberry, cherry and black plum with a hint of spice. The tannins are softer and very elegant on the finish.

CHÂTEAU DU TERTRE

VINEYARD SIZE	52 hectares
VINE DENSITY	8,500 stocks per hectare
AVERAGE AGE OF VINEYARD	45 years
AVERAGE PRODUCTION	16,000 cases
SOILS AND SUBSOILS	gravelly-sandy terroir made up of gravel of the early Günzian era. Subsoil includes 8% to 15% clay
GRAPE VARIETIES	Cabernet Sauvignon 36% Merlot 33% Cabernet Franc 26% Petit Verdot 5%

If our nightly dreams should create, behind our closed eyelids, the archetypal Médoc chartreuse, they would certainly pick no other than Le Tertre. All its elements converge to confirm that typicity: the classical beauty of the building, the delicate blonde hue of the stone, the regular pattern of vine rows underlining the architecture like corduroy ribs. In a dominating position, the château seems to attract and absorb the light that surrounds it from every side.

Such a fairytale vision is the work of the architect Bussière, who built the château in 1740 for an Irish trader, Pierre Mitchell, the founder of the first glass-bottle factory in Bordeaux. Throughout the centuries, owners followed each other on the "beautiful hill of Arsac," de Brezets, de Vallandé, Koenigswarter, De Wilde and Capbern-Gasqueton. All of them loved it in their own way, but the château remained a sleeping princess for a long time. The prince's kiss dates from 1997, when the Dutch businessman Eric Albada Jelgersma, having realized that all the basic elements for making a dream wine were gathered there, decided to resurrect Le Tertre.

He found the visual harmony of the chartreuse destabilised by the absence of a wing collapsed long ago, the only part of the building that was not resting on a foundation. The wing was rebuilt according to the original plans, while a large garden, a pond and an orangery were built nearby. If the French Régence style of the exterior is clear, the interior is unique among the Médoc châteaux; here there is none of the slightly overburdened graces of the French house, but a decor inspired by the sober elegance of the north with a touch of Tuscan sensuality. Comfy corners, wide and relaxing spaces make up a perfect home for living and meditating.

The technical buildings are laid around two courtyards—three cellars, including two underground, and three vathouses of wood, concrete and stainless steel. The château is surrounded by 52 hectares of vineyards in one piece, where one-fifth Cabernet Franc gives the wines a rich, spicy character, while the large Günzian pebbles give the grapes at night the warmth they absorbed during the day. All criteria promise a mature and generous wine.

Exceptional conditions translate into exceptional wines as long as the technology goes along with them and does not compete. Such is the approach of Albada and his team. "A perfect product," says Alexander Van Beek, the general manager, "is the one that allows nature's full expression without overdoing anything." Gentle winemaking methods are used. Entirely gravitary fermentation in the beautiful oak vats produces a silkier mouthfeel, thus expressing the true Margaux typicity. The concrete vats are no less remarkable; ten of them are tronconical and one is egg-shaped. This shape, which reproduces the physical conditions of antique amphoras, induces a slow rotation of the must, keeping the lees in suspension and, through a technique akin to batonnage, gives smoothness to the wines. If you add to that the warm round-ness brought on by the terroir and the subtle balance of the planting, the harmony between the radiant nature of the place and the wines that are made there becomes obvious. "Fulfill-ment" is the word that comes to mind.

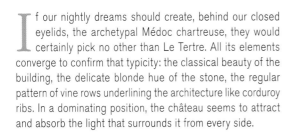

1. The barrel cellars of Château du Tertre are built on two levels, including one of the Médoc's few underground chais.

2. The château's owner has suceeded in creating dream-like, cosy spaces inside the house. Here, an antique pharmacy was reconstructed and converted into a small salon.

3. The chartreuse, built in a very pure French Regency style, is a striking sight atop its lovely gravel hill. A missing lateral wing was rebuilt from scratch to restore the visual harmony.

Cod, Smoked Mashed Potato,
Pickled Mushrooms, Red Pepper Oil

Wylie DUFRESNE

WD-50 - New York City, United States

SERVES 4

The cod

four 7-ounce pieces of cod
(halibut can be substituted)

salt

cayenne pepper

clarified unsalted butter, for frying

The smoked mashed potato

3 Idaho potatoes, peeled

3 Yukon Gold potatoes, peeled

1 cup (25 cl) heavy cream

4 tablespoons (50 g)
unsalted butter (½ stick)

salt and freshly ground black pepper

The pickled mushrooms

1 quart champagne vinegar

½ cup plus 1½ tablespoons (120 g)
sugar

1 tablespoon cumin seeds, toasted

1 tablespoon fennel seeds, toasted

1 tablespoon coriander seeds, toasted

¼ teaspoon crushed red pepper flakes

1 tablespoon salt

4 shiso leaves

1 quart (1 l) water

½ cup (50 g) julienned
shiitake mushrooms

½ cup (50 g) honshimeji mushrooms

½ cup (50 g) enoki mushrooms

The red pepper oil

4 red bell peppers

grape seed oil

For the smoked mashed potatoes: Simmer the potatoes until tender and drain. Place in a hot smoker, using one cup of wood chips, and smoke until the chips are used up. Rice the potatoes and fold in the cream and butter. Season to taste.

For the fish skin: Peel off the cod skin. Clean it of any scales and flesh. Place on a cooling rack overnight to air-dry. The next day, place the skin between two silicone mats on sheet pans and bake at 275°F (135°C) for 50 minutes to 1 hour. Once cooled, cut into triangles and reserve.

For the pickled mushrooms:, Caramelise sugar and add spices, water, vinegar, salt and red pepper flakes and bring to a boil. Steep for 15 to 20 minutes, strain over the mushrooms, and add the shiso leaves. Let marinate at least 24 hours.

For the red pepper oil: Seed and stem the peppers, and roughly chop. Dehydrate for three days at 125°F (52°C), until thoroughly dry. Grind to a powder and place in a blender. Drizzle in grape seed oil until a thick consistency is achieved (about 1 cup of oil, but the viscosity is up to the individual). Strain through a conical sieve, pressing firmly. Reserve.

For the presentation: Season the cod with salt and cayenne. Sauté gently in clarified butter. Warm the mushroom mixture. Place some of the smoked mashed potato on the serving plates with mushrooms to the side. Sprinkle the crispy fish skin and chopped tarragon over the mushrooms. Place the fish on top of potatoes and drizzle the red pepper oil around.

CHÂTEAU DU TERTRE BY ÉRIC BEAUMARD, SILVER MEDAL,
BEST SOMMELIER OF THE WORLD, 1998

This property's 52 hectares of vines are planted on one of the highest points in the Médoc, enhancing the vineyard's maritime character. So important is this gravelly mound in Arsac that it gives this Classified Growth its name. Since 1997, Eric Albada Jelgersma, a Dutch businessman, has committed to returning this historic château to all its former glory. Under the direction of Alexander Van Beek, the estate's manager, the wine has come to be defined by an elegance, which can be fully enjoyed in its youth, without any hint of rusticity.

CHÂTEAU HAUT-BAGES LIBÉRAL

PAUILLAC

VINEYARD SIZE	30 hectares
VINE DENSITY	10,000 stocks per hectare
AVERAGE AGE OF VINEYARD	40 years
SOILS AND SUBSOILS	Garonne gravel on limestone bedrock
GRAPE VARIETIES	Cabernet Sauvignon 75% Merlot 25%

"Haut-Bages" because the vineyard stretches over the higher part of the Plateau de Bages. "Libéral" from the name of the family who founded the estate back in the 18th century. But what this airy and melodious name does not describe is the beauty of the hill it sits on, 30 hectares of Garonne gravel protected by the powerful thermal regulation offered by two daily tides. Thus saved from sudden climatic contrasts, the soil stays cool in summer and hardly ever sees frost in winter. The pedologic core of the property, 15 hectares bordering Château Latour, consists of quaternary limestone gravel of a rather rare type, with limestone breathing a masculine vigour into the wine. The remaining plots, scattered beyond Pichon-Longueville and on the Plateau de Bages, sit on a pure gravel soil. The typicity of Château Haut-Bages Libéral is conditioned by these two components.

The vineyard, which was entirely replanted in the 1960s, is 75 percent Cabernet Sauvignon, 25 percent Merlot. It was purchased in 1983 by Bernadette Villars, also the owner of several Médoc châteaux, including Chasse-Spleen in Moulis and La Gurgue in Margaux. Her daughters, Claire and Céline, were still students at the time. When their parents died in 1992, each one of them got a share of the properties. Céline Villars-Foubet got Chasse-Spleen and later bought Camensac in Haut-Médoc with her husband Jean-Pierre, while Claire Villars-Lurton took over Ferrière, La Gurgue and Haut-Bages Libéral. Her husband, Gonzague Lurton, owns the Château Durfort-Vivens in Margaux.

Villars-Lurton imparts an intensely personal style to all her wines, giving them a sunny, passionate impetus, which paradoxically leans on reasonable decisions. Having learned winemaking with much dedication, she was helped by her uncle Jean Merlaut, owner of Château Gruaud Larose, to perfect her knowledge and handle the two châteaux suc-

cessfully. At Haut-Bages, she first rebuilt the cellars and did not decide to restructure the stainless-steel-and-concrete vathouse until 2001, when she had developed enough familiarity with her terroir to be able to adapt the vathouse to the vineyard, and not the other way around.

Ninety percent of the work is done in the vineyard by a well-trained technical team who controls the quality on a permanent basis. The malolactic fermentation is carried in vats for the most part, producing a more classical typicity. Villars-Lurton believes that carrying "malo" in barrels yields over-flattering notes. The ageing lasts between 16 and 20 months in 40 percent new oak from six different cooperages. In an unusual touch, 5 percent of the barrels are made of Estonian oak, which is slightly more coarse-grained than French oak but has its own superior qualities. The château produces second wines under two labels, La Chapelle de Bages and La Fleur de Haut-Bages Libéral.

As is the case with Ferrière, her other Great Classified Growth château, the "Claire Villars touch" is unmistakable as soon as you taste her very elegant wines. She calls them classic, but they also burst with originality and aromatic complexity. Château Haut-Bages Libéral even has a little asset of its own, notes of Alba white truffle. As you discover such a rich and rare aroma, you think twice and check again, but the white truffle is actually present throughout the vintages, even as a residual fragrance in the empty glass. Add to that some enticing notes of jalapeño chilli and fresh flowers, particularly iris, and you will understand why this is a precious wine, one that deserves to be better known.

1. An exceptional terroir on the plateau de Bages: around the château, the gravel-limestone soil, of a type rarely seen in the region, gives the wine a vivid, assertive style.

2. The front steps of the château.

3. Claire Villars-Lurton makes extremely elegant wine, with a distinctive aromatic palette. This one is known to give out interesting notes of white truffle.

Warm Foie Gras
with Shellfish, Saffron and Lemon

Michel PORTOS
Le Saint-James - Bouliac, France

SERVES 4

The shellfish

2 squid

4 dog-cockles

12 whelks

¼ pound (100 g) cockles

¼ pound (100 g) mussels

½ pound (200 g) carpet-shell clams

The garnish

1 hard-boiled egg

1 preserved lemon

1/8 ounce fresh dill

12 green asparagus

saffron threads

olive oil

The foie gras

4 slices frozen foie gras

juice of 1 lemon

salt

For the shellfish: Clean the squid, roll them up and freeze them hard.

Steam the shellfish open.

For the garnish: Finely dice the white of the hard-boiled egg. Finely chop the skin of the preserved lemon, discard the dill stalks, keeping the leaves. Cook the asparagus.

To finish: Cut the frozen squid into rounds and deep-fry them in oil at 350°F (177°C) until crispy.

In a small bowl, dilute the saffron in a little warm water. Let steep, then strain. Add salt and olive oil.

Pan-sear the foie gras.

For the presentation: In a salad bowl, mix the fried squid, the shellfish, the diced egg white, the preserved lemon peel, the lemon juice and the dill. Place 1 foie gras slice on each plate, and pour the saffron infusion over it.

CHÂTEAU HAUT-BAGES LIBÉRAL BY FRANCK THOMAS, BEST SOMMELIER OF EUROPE, 2000

In pure Pauillac style, the wines of Château Haut-Bages Libéral are firm and powerful, with a masculine structure that calls for tranquil patience to fully develop. Not long ago, a rich, balanced, recent vintage of Haut-Bages Libéral matched with a morsel of guanaja chocolate was a revelation. The strong character of the bitter chocolate balanced and complemented the power and rigidity of this young Pauillac wine. With its proud and impetuous sprit, the young virtuoso succumbed to the cocoa bean's sweet call.

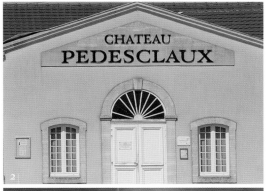

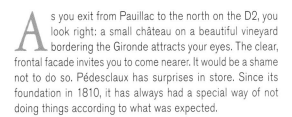

Château Pédesclaux

PAUILLAC

VINEYARD SIZE	26 hectares
VINE DENSITY	8,300 stocks per hectare
AVERAGE AGE OF VINEYARD	35 years
AVERAGE PRODUCTION	8,500 cases
SOILS AND SUBSOILS	gravel; clay-limestone gravel
GRAPE VARIETIES	Cabernet Sauvignon 50% Merlot 45% Cabernet Franc 5%

As you exit from Pauillac to the north on the D2, you look right: a small château on a beautiful vineyard bordering the Gironde attracts your eyes. The clear, frontal facade invites you to come nearer. It would be a shame not to do so. Pédesclaux has surprises in store. Since its foundation in 1810, it has always had a special way of not doing things according to what was expected.

In 1855, when the wine of the estate, founded by Urbain Pédesclaux, was classified as Fifth Growth, it was already known as a rather austere wine. It kept that reputation under the rule of its successive owners, from the Comte de Gastebois after 1891 to Lucien Jugla, who in 1950 acquired the estate he had been manageing for some time. The year 1996 was a turning point: the management was taken over by Brigitte and Denis Jugla, Lucien's daughter-in-law and grandson, respectively. From then on, everything changed. The wines were the first to improve, and the château followed in 2004. Drillings and soil analysis, plot selection, green harvest and leaf pruning as soon as 1999, and many efforts aimed at producing rounder, fuller-bodied and more delicate wines, Château Pédesclaux embraced a new life of voluptuousness. This was no revolt, this was a revolution. Before the chartreuse underwent complete refurbishing and regained its original grace, the seductive power of the wines had increased considerably.

Old Médoc cultural clichés hardly need to be recalled—dignified and solemn Saint-Estèphe, velvety and structured Saint-Julien, feminine and delicate Margaux, warm and tender Haut-Médoc. Pauillac is the masculine, even a tad macho, wine. Pédesclaux deliberately breaks that reputation. Its wines, built more on a male-female harmony than on the domination of one over the other, are androgynous. They evoke the union of opposites, the rotating yin-yang symbol. If there is femininity at work, it is based on assertive energy. Great ladies are a local specialty: after all, this is the place where Mrs. Pédesclaux, having barely buried her beloved Urbain, hopped onto a horse cart and set out to reach Paris, carrying her wines for Emperor Napoléon III to taste.

Cabernet Sauvignon and Merlot in almost equal parts, and 5 percent Cabernet Franc—the balance of elements is also found there. The two main grape varieties help and support each other, Merlot resting its opulent roundness on the elegant framework provided by Cabernet Sauvignon, a marriage that yields melodious, shimmering, intensely lively wines. The colour is a bright ruby, and the extremely long mouthfeel keeps swaying between fresh pomegranate and smoky green chilli, then back to red fruit before giving out a splendid violet finish. This delicious richness makes Château Pédesclaux one of the most appreciated Great Classified Growths among Belgians. The second wine, Sens de Pédesclaux, and the Haut-Médoc La Rose de Pédesclaux follow their sister close by.

Everything at Château Pédesclaux is designed for hospitality and meeting the world. The wine is a complete sensory experience; for this reason, the Juglas prolonged that experience by creating five beautiful guest rooms in the château. Through fragrances, colours and textures, their decor revolves around the five-senses theme. The largest of the five, dedicated to the sense of sight, opens out onto a vast stretch of vineyard, suggesting an old tradition of the Médoc chartreuses. The vines' parallel rows follow the gentle curves of the ground, almost giving out subtle sounds, a visual melody that makes them an endless object of contemplation.

1. The chartreuse of Pédesclaux recently underwent a thorough beauty treatment. Five lovely guest rooms, whose decor revolves around the Five Senses theme, may now be booked there.

2, 3. In the cellars, a rich and delicious wine with a distinctive feminine touch is elaborated.

4. The slightly ajar front door of a château whose family history has often been influenced by strong feminine characters.

Slow-roasted Lamb Shoulder,
Orange Zests and Juniper Berries

Marc MENEAU

L'Espérance - Saint-Père-en-Vézelay, France

SERVES 4

2 milk-fed lamb shoulders,
about 1⅓ pounds (600 g) each

2 sprigs thyme

grated zest of 2 oranges

2 teaspoons juniper berries, crushed

½ cup (10 cl) peanut oil

½ pound (200 g) shallots plus 1 shallot

2⅛ cups (50 cl) lamb jus

⅓ ounce (10 g), about ½ cup loosely
pack young spinach

juice of 2 oranges

a dough made with flour, starch
and water, to seal the lid

For the lamb: Bone the lamb shoulders, leaving a chunk of bone in the narrow part of each one. Season with salt and pepper, then rub the meat with thyme, a bit of orange zest, and half of the crushed juniper berries. Refrigerate for 12 hours.

In a large pan, heat the oil and brown the shoulders on each side. Put them in a sous-vide bag and cook for 11 hours in a 130°F (55°C) water-bath.

For the jus: Meanwhile, mince the shallots and sweat them with more orange zest and the remaining crushed juniper berries. Reduce, add the lamb jus and reduce again until you reach the desired consistency. Strain the jus and set aside.

Purée the remaining shallot and rub it on the cooked meat. Blanch the spinach and wrap the lamb shoulders in it. Place the warm shoulders in a Dutch oven, add the orange juice and the juniper lamb jus, cover and seal the lid with the dough. Bring to a boil, then take off the heat.

For the presentation: Bring the Dutch oven to the table and carve the lamb just before serving. You may serve with steamed vegetables.

CHÂTEAU PÉDESCLAUX BY MARKUS DEL MONEGO,
BEST SOMMELIER OF THE WORLD, 1998

This Great Growth originates from a gravel plateau overlooking the commune of Pauillac. From this terroir and the classic grape varietals of Cabernet Sauvignon, Merlot and Cabernet Franc, Château Pédesclaux creates a pleasing and charming expression of Pauillac. Its delicate bouquet, elegant structure and fine length in the mouth make this a truly traditional Fifth Growth.

CHÂTEAU BELGRAVE

HAUT-MÉDOC

VINEYARD SIZE	61 hectares
VINE DENSITY	10,000 stocks per hectare
AVERAGE AGE OF VINEYARD	20 years
AVERAGE PRODUCTION	16,000 cases
SOILS AND SUBSOILS	deep gravel on a clayey subsoil
GRAPE VARIETIES	Cabernet Sauvignon 44% Merlot 48% Cabernet Franc 4% Petit Verdot 4%

A dense blueberry-tinged colour and a soft, velvety texture. A subtle taste of liquorice harmonizes the fresh, opulent nose of cedarwood and frankincense with notes of ripe, freshly crushed black fruit. A well-structured wine with a silky mouthfeel and rich gamey tones, Château Belgrave has everything you might expect from a Great Classified Growth. "Our wines are proof that harvesting at full maturity is a good idea," says Antoine Gonzalez, maître de chai, while a 2004 Belgrave spins in his glass and his passion for his job shows through every sentence he speaks. He nurses his six oak vats with a loving eye. "Into these go the very best grapes from all our plots," he adds. Gonzalez is a strong advocate of ageing wine on lees, without any racking. Likewise, a pigeage (punching of the cap) is performed in the vats during fermentation. Both methods ensure that the wines are elegantly rounded and generous.

Little is known about the history of the estate. A hunting lodge was originally built there, as shown by the ferret in the Belgrave coat of arms. When the growth was classified in 1855, it belonged to a Mr. Coutanceau. The Belgrave name was given shortly after, when Mr. Bruno Devez built the château. It is not clear whether that name was inspired by the *belles graves* (fine gravelly soil) of the vineyard or by the London borough of Belgravia, evidently loved by the anglophile owner.

Château Belgrave, a Haut-Médoc, could have been a Saint-Julien without a small stream separating it from that other appellation zone. This is indeed of little importance. There is more than one way of crossing the Rubicon. A big step forward was taken in 1979, when the Dourthe wine company took Belgrave for tenant farming. Despite historical difficulties, Belgrave still retained its original size, 61 hectares of vineyards on 70 hectares of total surface. The change of management was to prove highly beneficial.

"When we arrived at Belgrave," says Dourthe CEO Patrick Jestin, "the place had just lived through its worst period. The property was in a poor state, with the vineyard at the end of its tether. The equipment was obsolete and the wine was sold at a low price in Northern Europe. We did our best to restore the quality of this Great Classified Growth; we restructured the vineyard, raised the canopy in order to expand the foliage surface, densified the planting and completely renovated the technical buildings, the vathouse and the cellars. By 1986, we were satisfied with the results, but satisfaction was not enough. Winemaking has to be a work of endless progress. Around 1995, we decided to raise Belgrave to newer heights, building a new vathouse in 2004 and a new cellar in 2007. Meanwhile, we ordered an in-depth study of the soils, and improved the work on the vineyard as well as the plot selection."

When asked about the contribution of consultant œnologist Michel Rolland to the wines of Château Belgrave, Patrick Jestin takes the opportunity to explain a type of intervention that is too often misunderstood by the general public. Indeed, what does an œnologist bring to a château where competent and committed winemakers already do their best? Above all, he gives them a chance to stand back and have a more global view of what they do. He does not "make" the wine but uses his experience to communicate a broader, more serene vision, while supporting them and helping them out on tricky decisions. But isn't a consultant likely to standardise the wines? Mr. Jestin answers, "Of course not. The terroir always has the last word."

1. *This view of the stainless steel vats of Château Belgrave shows the spiral-shaped temperature control system below the metal surface. The vathouse was installed soon after the Dourthe wine company purchased the estate. A few wooden vats are still used.*

2. *A barrel cellar at Château Belgrave.*

3. *A delicate, opulent wine, offering notes of black fruit—particularly blackberry.*

4. *The name of Belgrave is contemporary to the building of the château. It is assumed to be inspired by the London borough of Belgravia.*

Keftedhes, Wedding Rice

Vangelis KOUMBIADIS
Ta Kioupia - Rhodes, Greece

SERVES 4

The meatballs

⅔ pound (300 g)
fresh sourdough bread

1¼ cups (30 cl) water

1⅛ pounds (500 g) ground beef

½ pound (200 g) fresh tomatoes,
peeled, seeded and chopped

¾ cup (150 g) chopped red onion

2 tablespoons Greek olive oil

1 cup plus 1 tablespoon (25 g) flat-leaf
parsley, chopped

1 cup plus 2 tablespoons (25 g) fresh
mint leaves, chopped

salt and freshly ground black pepper

2 eggs

2 tablespoons pine nuts

1⅛ pounds (500 g) self-rising flour

oil for deep-frying

The rice

2½ cups (500 g) long-grain rice

11 tablespoons (150 g) unsalted butter
(1 stick plus 3 tablespoons)

½ cup (80 g) blanched whole almonds

½ cup (80 g) pine nuts

½ cup plus 1 tablespoon (80 g) sultanas

2⅛ cups (50 cl) freshly squeezed
orange juice

2⅛ cups (50 cl) water

1½ tablespoons (25 g) salt

2 teaspoons freshly ground black pepper

For the rice: Prepare the rice before frying the meatballs.

Cover the rice with lukewarm water in a large bowl, stirring all the while. Drain and repeat two or three times until the water runs clear.

In a medium-sized Dutch oven, fry the almonds in the butter until they are golden. Add the pine nuts and raisins. Fry for 1 or 2 minutes over low to medium heat. Add the orange juice, bring to the boil, add water. Bring the liquids to a boil again, then add the rice, salt, and pepper. Do not stir; cover and simmer on the lowest possible heat for 10 minutes. Remove from the heat, cover the Dutch oven with a towel and let rest for 15 to 20 minutes until the water is completely absorbed and rice is tender.

To make the meatballs: In a large bowl, crumble the bread, add the water and set aside. When the bread is soaked, squeeze it dry, add the other ingredients and knead by hand without making the forcemeat too compact.

Sprinkle with a teaspoon of the flour and knead some more. Pour the rest of the flour into another bowl, and sprinkle some onto your work surface. Take a walnut-size portion of forcemeat, roll it into a ball and coat it with flour. Set aside on a piece of aluminum foil. Repeat until all ingredients are used up, spacing the meatballs apart as you place them on the foil.

Heat the oil in a deep fryer or a large pot, and fry the meatballs. When they are golden-brown, remove them with a slotted spoon and drain them on paper towels.

For the presentation: Stir the rice with a fork, and serve with the meatballs and some fresh vegetables.

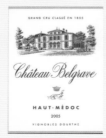

CHÂTEAU BELGRAVE BY YOICHI SATO, BEST SOMMELIER OF JAPAN, 2005

With its rather soft and round flavours, this wine goes well with Chinese or oriental cooking. In fact, it's a natural for any type of cuisine, never losing that classic Bordeaux style that is so appreciated by many wine drinkers.

Château de Camensac

VINEYARD SIZE	70 hectares
VINE DENSITY	10,000 stocks per hectare
AVERAGE AGE OF VINEYARD	35 years
AVERAGE PRODUCTION	20,000 cases
SOILS AND SUBSOILS	fine, deep gravel
GRAPE VARIETIES	Cabernet Sauvignon 60% Merlot 40%

After having been managed for 40 years by the Forner brothers, owners of the Spanish wine trademark Marqués de Cacéres, the Château de Camensac was bought in 2005 by Céline and Jean-Pierre Foubet, also the owners of Château Chasse-Spleen in Moulis. Céline Villars-Foubet, who was trained as an architect, inherited her passion for winemaking from her family. Her sister, Claire Villars-Lurton, runs the Châteaux Ferrière and Haut-Bages Libéral (page 235) and their uncle is Jean Merlaut, owner of the Château Gruaud Larose (page 67) and an expert winemaker. When Villars-Foubet first took hold of Camensac, he provided her with help and advice for improving the quality of the estate's wines.

Taking advantage of the characteristic style of their lovely château, the Foubets go into a vivid description of the main typical features of the Bordelaise chartreuse, the local name for a wine château. The form was set sometime between the late 18th and the mid-19th centuries and was conditioned by the winemaking purpose of the building. The sense of sight played a decisive part: a full, wide view of the vineyard from the house was always sought. Hence the double east–west exposure, with a large corridor running from one facade to the other, a bay window at the end or at either side in order to let as much Médoc daylight in and open out onto the vineyard from many directions. Another distinctive feature is the slight raising of the first level, the cellar below acting as both a crawl space and a platform to promote the panoramic effect. This elevated position requires the building of a stone staircase, partly double-flighted, to access the house.

The Château de Camensac is a perfect example of that style: the vineyard may be contemplated from the main room beyond a large garden adorned with a magnificent stone pine. Both the interior and the exterior of the house show the owners'

refined taste. The furniture and the decor's late Art Deco style have recently inspired the wine's new label: a thin lattice pattern on a lavender background, reminiscent of the graphic arts of the 1930s and 1940s. Even the wine's haunting fragrance—black tulip, chypre, dried roses and sandalwood—evokes the scent of antique powder boxes.

The vineyard, which can be admired as an extension of the inner decoration, covers 70 hectares, planted with 60 percent Cabernet Sauvignon and 40 percent Merlot. Before the Foubets acquired the place, the wines of Camensac were a little stern and took a long time to soften down. "I am surprised by how little time it took us to improve those wines", says Jean-Pierre Foubet. "Only three years. What we did was let our tastes speak through, instead of making standardised competition wines."

"Merlot indeed," adds Céline, "but subtle and well-wrought Merlot. Not in the way of hot, show-offy wines designed for the tastings, but in the way of finesse." These efforts are beautifully rewarded: the wines of Château de Camensac are delicate, round and velvety. Endowed with a tasteful aromatic density and singing tannins, they are extremely seductive with opulent, smoky notes: havana, cedar wood, powdered red roses, peony, black currant, gingerbread and cinnamon. Wines that are well worth discovering.

"The difference lies partly in the fact that the maturing process of grapes is better known now than it was 10 or 15 years ago," says Céline. "The wines of today are pleasant in their youth and they also age well. During the last decade, the trend was 'œnologists' wines.' Now, the trend is simply vine wines."

1. A small park, dominated by a large stone pine, opens out directly onto the vines. Through the château's windows, no one ever tires of seeing them.

2. The pretty classic chartreuse of Camensac with its interesting double-arched front steps.

3. By means of the massive care devoted to the vineyard by the new owners, each one of the last three vintages of Camensac has only been getting better. Now, the terroir and vines get all the attention.

Daehajjim: King Prawn, Beef and Cucumber Salad with Pine Nut Sauce

Bock-Ryo HAN
Goongeyon - Seoul, South Korea

SERVES 4

The prawns

16 king prawns

1/3 ounce (10 g) ginger, finely sliced

½ teaspoon kosher salt

The beef shank

¾ pound (280 g) beef shank

5 cups (1.2 l) water

The vegetables

½ English cucumber

½ teaspoon kosher salt

½ teaspoon canola oil

¼ pound (100 g) bamboo shoots

½ teaspoon kosher salt

½ teaspoon canola oil

pinch of freshly ground white pepper

The pine nut sauce

¼ cup (31 g) pine nuts

3 tablespoons king prawn stock

1 teaspoon kosher salt

2 teaspoons sesame oil

pinch of freshly ground white pepper

For the prawns: De-vein the king prawns with a bamboo skewer but do not shell them. Season them generously with salt in a bowl. Sprinkle ginger slices on top of the prawns. Steam for 7 to 8 minutes.

Remove the prawns' heads and shells. Boil them in a little salted water until you achieve a fragrant prawn stock. Slice the prawns into 1³⁄₁₆-inch (3-cm) chunks.

For the beef: Pour the cold water into a pot and add the beef shank. Place it over medium heat and boil for 1 hour. Slice the shank into 1³⁄₁₆-inch (3-cm) slices.

For the garnishes: Halve the cucumber length-wise and cut it diagonally into crescent shapes. Sprinkle with salt and let stand.

Squeeze out the excess water from the salted cucumbers, sauté lightly in a little oil and let cool.

Halve the bamboo shoots length-wise and cut diagonally. Sauté lightly in a little oil, season with salt and pepper and let cool.

On a paper towel spread on a cutting board, chop the pine nuts finely.

For the presentation: In each of four bowls, combine the chopped pine nuts, some king prawn stock, salt and sesame oil. Grind white pepper over the bowls and add the remaining ingredients. Mix well.

CHÂTEAU DE CAMENSAC BY OLIVIER POUSSIER, BEST SOMMELIER OF THE WORLD, 2000

On the border with Saint-Julien and neighbouring La Tour Carnet, this château is managed by the team from Château Chasse-Spleen. Since 2005, this property has successfully regained a well-deserved renown. Its main wine is now the object of the greatest care and shows increased body, with a profile and density that will certainly make this one of the Médoc Fifth Growths that any wine lover can count on.

CHÂTEAU COS LABORY

SAINT-ESTÈPHE

VINEYARD SIZE	18 hectares
VINE DENSITY	8,700 stocks per hectare
AVERAGE AGE OF VINEYARD	35 years
AVERAGE PRODUCTION	6,500 cases
SOILS AND SUBSOILS	Günzian gravel on a marly limestone subsoil
GRAPE VARIETIES	Cabernet Sauvignon 55% Merlot 35% Cabernet Franc 10%

A few steps away from the unabashedly neo-Chinese folly of Cos d'Estournel, the lovely château Cos Labory modestly nestles among the trees of its garden. The two buildings, separated by a narrow road, share their gravel hill like two old friends giggling about the trick they are playing on the visitor. Indeed the visual contrast offered by the two properties side by side is not devoid of irony and fun, wisdom next to excess, humility next to expansiveness, the small classical 19th-century chartreuse almost wall-to-wall with a grand building of undecided style and unclassifiable inspiration.

The origins of the estate take us back to the 1770s. At the time, it was known by the name of Cos-Gaston. It got its present name later, through the marriage of Marie-Sany Gaston and François-Armand Labory. In 1847, Louis-Gaspard d'Estournel acquired the château through an auction, thus materializing the closeness, even the intimacy, joining the two properties. Shortly after that, in 1852, he sold the estate to the Englishman Charles Cecil Martyns. Cos Labory passed through several hands until 1922, when it was bought by the Weber family from Argentina, who later sold it to Mrs. Cécile Audoy, a distant cousin of theirs, in 1959. The château is now managed by one of her sons, Bernard Audoy.

Audoy, who defines himself as a "hands-on" man, insists on being always physically present on the property. Not a believer in the latest trendy methods, he takes painstaking care of his vineyard in an old-fashioned way and makes his wine accordingly. He is not a fanatic of green harvest either, being of the mind that this practice actually strengthens the vine stock and stimulates it into producing more grapes. He prefers a good pruning and a wise use of thinning. A keen observer of grape varieties, he claims not to follow the Merlot trend that characterizes a certain type of fashionable winemaking. Instead of increasing the proportion of this "smoothing" varietal, he leans passionately towards Cabernet Sauvignon, the pride of the Médoc, and a guarantee of intense, structured wines with great ageing capacity. In fact, 55 percent of his vineyard's Günz gravel on a clay-limestone subsoil is planted with Cabernet Sauvignon, while 35 percent remain in Merlot and 10 percent in Cabernet Franc, which provides colour and opulence. The exact match between each plot and the variety it bears is, to him, a crucial quality factor.

For a long time, the wines of Cos Labory were characterized with the severity that is generally associated with their appellation. Since the end of the 1980s, Bernard Audoy has been taking special care to develop their fruitiness and finesse, without impairing their classic Saint-Estèphe quality. They are elegant, dignified wines of very good value. They owe their personal style to the exceptional terroir of the Croupe de Cos, on which they are produced. The name Cos comes from caux, which means "hill" in the Gascon dialect. This is an arid, beautifully drained soil, separated from the hills of Lafite by the small Jalle du Breuil river. The depth of the gravel layer forces the vine to send its roots very deep into the ground, which gives the wines concentrated aromas. Noble, balanced and tannic, yet smooth and fruity, the pleasurable wines of Cos Labory can be drunk in their early years, although the rich notes of smoke, spices and velvety black fruit they develop with time are indisputably worth waiting for.

1. The simple and tasteful château atop its precious gravel hill. Cos means "height" in the Gascon dialect.

2. A detail of the courtyard.

3. Working in the barrel cellar.

Lamb Bandoneon

Emilio GARIP
Oviedo - Buenos Aires, Argentina

SERVES 4

The chops
4 spring loin lamb chops
fresh sprigs of thyme and rosemary
1 crushed garlic clove
3½ tablespoons (5 cl) arbequina olive oil
salt and crushed black (*mignonette*) pepper

The saddle
1 boned, trimmed lamb saddle
fresh sprigs of thyme and rosemary
1 crushed garlic clove
3½ tablespoons (5 cl) olive oil
½ pound (200 g) leek greens, blanched
salt and crushed black (*mignonette*) pepper

The pea purée
¾ cup (100 g) blanched green peas
1 garlic clove, boiled for ½ hour in milk
⅛ cup (25 g) heavy cream
⅛ cup (25 g) vegetable stock
⅓ ounce (10 g) fresh spinach
1 teaspoon sugar
1½ teaspoons olive oil

The pea stew
1 shallot, very finely diced
1½ teaspoons olive oil
¼ cup (20 g) smoked bacon, finely diced
pinch of dried thyme
¾ cup (100 g) peas, blanched and peeled

The potatoes
4 potatoes, 1½ x 3-inch (4 x 7-cm) disks
1 shallot, cut into thin half-moons
olive oil (enough to cover)
sprig of fresh thyme

The romesco powder
10 tablespoons (50 g) almonds, ground
1¾ ounces (50 g) white bread,
lightly toasted and finely grated

3 garlic cloves, peeled, degermed, finely sliced
1 teaspoon pimentón dulce de la Vera
1 teaspoon cayenne pepper
salt

The sauce
1⅛ pounds (500 g) finely chopped lamb bones
unsalted butter and olive oil
3 shallots
2⅛ cups (½ l) red wine
sprig of fresh rosemary
1 tablespoon brown sugar
2 quarts (2 l) brown lamb stock
beurre manié (butter and flour kneaded together)

For the chops: Trim off the fat. Sprinkle with the herbs, garlic, pepper and olive oil. Cover with plastic wrap and refrigerate at 35°F (2°C) for 8 hours. Leave at room temperature for a few minutes, then brown on both sides. Season with salt and pepper. Bake in a 350°F (180°C) oven for 3 minutes. Let rest out of the oven, covered with aluminum foil, for 5 minutes. Bake for 2 minutes. Let rest, then carve. The inside temperature should be 110°F (45°C).

For the saddle: Sprinkle with the herbs, pepper, garlic and olive oil. Cover with plastic wrap and refrigerate at 35°F (2°C) for 8 hours. Leave at room temperature for a few minutes. Brown on both sides. Season with salt and pepper. Remove from heat. Cut the leek greens in half and lay on plastic wrap 4½ inches (12 cm) larger than the saddle all around. Lay the meat on the leeks and roll into a cylinder. Bake at 350°F (180°C) for 3 to 4 minutes. Let rest for a few minutes. Carve.

For the pea purée: Put the peas, garlic, cream, stock and spinach in a Thermomix. Add salt and pepper, sugar and olive oil. Blend at high speed for 5 minutes at 150°F (65°C). Set aside.

For the pea stew: Sweat the shallot in a sauté pan with olive oil. When it is softened, add the bacon, thyme, and peas. Season and serve.

For the potatoes: Put the disks on a baking sheet, add salt, pepper, thyme and shallots and cover with olive oil. Cover and bake for 40 minutes in a 300°F (150°C) oven. Let cool and drain. Cut the ends of each potato disk diagonally and the centre crosswise. Bake again in a 400°F (200°C) oven for 5 minutes. Roll in the romesco powder.

For the sauce: Brown the bones in a saucepan with butter and olive oil. Drain, add fresh butter and oil, then brown the shallots. Deglaze with red wine and reduce by half. Add the rosemary, stock and a little sugar. Cook for 3 hours. Strain, reduce, and add salt, pepper and some *beurre manié* if necessary.

For the presentation: Drop some pea purée at one end of the plate and stretch it into a drop shape. In the middle, place a chop and a slice of saddle. On the other side, add the pea stew and potatoes, and decorate with a few drops of lamb sauce. Add thyme and rosemary blossoms.

CHÂTEAU COS LABORY BY SERGE DUBS, BEST SOMMELIER OF THE WORLD, 1989

I have a lot of affection for this very fine wine, which by temperament and taste I rank among the Bordeaux I'd like to have in my cellar every year. Its great consistency of quality and genuine style give this wine its true Bordeaux character. Always flavourful, its content, appearance and soft, elegant structure reveal a spirit that can charm the most demanding palates. The wine is always a good value and ages well over several decades.

Baronne Philippine de Rothschild g.f.a.
PROPRIETAIRE
PRODUCE OF FRANCE
Bouffons dansants en or émail et perles
XVIIe s. Musée de Mouton
CHATEAU
CLERC MILON
2004
PAUILLAC
APPELLATION PAUILLAC CONTRÔLÉE
Grand Cru Classé
MIS EN BOUTEILLE AU CHATEAU
75 cl
13% vol.

CHÂTEAU CLERC MILON

PAUILLAC

VINEYARD SIZE	45 hectares
VINE DENSITY	8,500 stocks per hectare
AVERAGE AGE OF VINEYARD	50 years
AVERAGE PRODUCTION	160,000 bottles
SOILS AND SUBSOILS	60% gravel and 40% clay-limestone
GRAPE VARIETIES	Cabernet Sauvignon 50% Merlot 36% Cabernet Franc 11% Petit Verdot 2% Carmenère 1%

The history of Château Clerc Milon takes us back to the early 19th century and to the small village of Milon, northwest of Pauillac. The land around it included, aside from the vineyards that were to become those of the Château Duhart-Milon, another vineyard set between Lafite-Rothschild and Mouton Rothschild. When the wine of this small estate was classified as Fifth Growth in 1855, the owner was Mr. Jean-Baptiste Clerc. Before he died in 1863, he sold part of the land to a Mr. Lamena, leaving the remainder to his widow. Later, Lamena sold the vineyard to Jacques Mondon, who asked for the right to continue to exploit it under the name of Clerc Milon, although the size of the land had decreased. Thus the Château Clerc Milon-Mondon, as it came to be named, went through the hands of several successive owners, under whose direction it did not particularly thrive. It was in a poor state in 1970, when it was purchased by Baron Philippe de Rothschild.

Major investments were made during the next decade. The vineyard was entirely restructured, the cellars underwent complete restoration and a new vathouse with thermoregulated stainless-steel vats was installed. In the early 1980s, the efforts of Rothschild were fully rewarded with wines of great personality and high quality. The next stage of improvement will soon be achieved; the château and its technical facilities will be fully restored in order to showcase the renewed reputation and generous potential of this wine, now a property of Baroness Philippine de Rothschild and her children.

The vineyards of Clerc Milon, with an average age of 50 years, cover 45 hectares on the hills of Milon and Mousset. The terroir is composed largely of cool clay-limestone soils, which explains the relatively large proportion of Merlot in the planting, almost 40 percent for 50 percent Cabernet Sauvignon, 11 percent Cabernet Franc, 2 percent Petit Verdot and 1 percent Carménère, an old Médoc varietal that has virtually

disappeared elsewhere. A most original planting, through which Clerc Milon may appear atypical amongst the classical wines of the Pauillac appellation. That does not make it less of a Médoc classic and the intense, and very personal, expression of a great Pauillac.

To quote a wine critic Château Clerc Milon "punches high above its weight." It is placed under the responsibility of Philippe Dhalluin and Hervé Berland, respectively technical and commercial general managers (châteaux) of the family-owned Baron Philippe de Rothschild SA Company. A brotherly relationship is reflected by the similarity of the labels in Château Clerc Milon and Château d'Armailhac, another jewel of the Rothschild estates; both are illustrated with figurines, which can be seen at the Museum of Wine in Art at the Château Mouton Rothschild. The Clerc Milon label represents a small couple of Bacchic dancers made of precious gems by a German goldsmith in the 16th century. What better way to express vitality and joy waiting to express themselves in the glass?

Aged between 16 and 18 months in 30 percent new French oak barrels, Château Clerc Milon is a sensual, ample and intense wine, with rich toasty and smoky notes mixed with touches of flowers and dark berries. With a tender expression, a crisp and fresh mouthfeel and plenty of exotic spice throughout its aromatic palette, it is naturally cut for spicy pairings—rich Indian curries and tandooris, South American grilled meats and rich paprika stews of Eastern Europe, not to exclude the much-loved classic expression of French gastronomy. This is a wine to serve on every continent, for any kind of celebration.

1. The bottle label shows two dancing figures, drawn after a small jewelry artefact kept at the Museum of Wine in Art at Château Mouton Rothschild.

2. Mostly produced from aged vines on clay-limestone soil, Château Clerc Milon shows some atypicity amidst the great Pauillac growths.

3. The grapes, always harvested by hand, are gathered into crates.

Chicken Offal Pâté
with Mushroom Caviar

Alexander ZAITSEV
Pushkin - Moscow, Russia

SERVES 4

The herbed jelly

¼ to ⅓ ounce (8 g) leaf gelatine

2½ cups (60 g) fresh basil leaves

4 cups (100 g) spinach leaves, loosely packed

1¾ ponces (40 g) fresh tarragon

½ cup (50 cl) water

1½ teaspoons (8 g) salt

The mushroom caviar

¼ pound (120 g) oyster mushrooms

⅛ pound (80 g) mushrooms of mixed varieties

⅛ pound (80 g) cèpe mushrooms

1½ teaspoons oil

⅛ pound (80 g) roasted onions

¾ teaspoon (2 g) minced garlic

½ teaspoon truffle oil

2⅛ ounces (60 g) mushroom jelly mixed with mayonnaise

a few olives

a few pieces of carrot or bell pepper

¼ ounce (8 g) mushrooms marinated in oil

salt and freshly ground black pepper

The pâté

¾ pound (280 g) chicken gizzards

¼ pound (120 g) chicken hearts

¼ pound (120 g) cockscombs

⅛ pound (40 g) onions

⅛ pound (40 g) carrots

1⅔ cup (40 cl) water

1 teaspoon ground coriander seed

¾ teaspoon minced garlic

½ teaspoon salt

⅓ cup (8 cl) cooking stock (see recipe)

½ pound (200 g) chicken breasts

¼ ounce (8 g) salmon roe (red caviar)

⅛ pound (40 g) plums

pimiento-stuffed green olives

fresh fennel sprigs

For the herbed jelly: Soak the gelatine in cold water for 10 minutes. Blanch the basil, spinach, and tarragon leaves in boiling lightly salted water. Drain them and squeeze gently. Blend them with ½ cup (10 cl) of their blanching water until smooth.

Add the drained, squeezed gelatine. Pour the preparation into a dish into a thin layer, and let cool before cutting the jelly into drop shapes or feather shapes.

For the mushroom caviar: Sauté all the mushrooms in a pan with the oil, then add salt, pepper and the roasted onions. Blend until you get a caviar-like texture. Warm this over low heat for a few minutes, then add the garlic, truffle oil and a little black pepper. Spoon the mushroom caviar into an oval-shaped, stainless steel ring and let cool.

Once cold, cover with a thin layer of mushroom jelly mayonnaise, decorate with olives and vegetables (carrots or bell peppers), and cover with another layer of mushroom jelly. When the terrine is quite cold, remove the ring and decorate the sides with marinated mushrooms.

For the pâté: Cut the offal into large chunks and cook them in a pressure cooker with the onions, carrots and water for 40 minutes. When cooked, discard the vegetables. Mix 2⅓ ounces (65 g) of the offal with ⅓ cup (8 cl) of the cooking stock. Add the coriander, garlic and salt.

Finely slice the chicken breasts and spread the preparation over them, then roll them into a cylinder. Wrap in plastic wrap and steam at 155°F (68°C) for 40 minutes. Let cool completely, then slice.

For the presentation: Place a little mushroom caviar in the middle of each plate, and surround with thin slices of chicken pâté, a little herbed jelly in a feather pattern, then dot with salmon roe. Decorate the outer edge with thinly sliced plums, a few pimiento-stuffed olives and fresh fennel sprigs.

CHÂTEAU CLERC MILON BY ANDREAS LARSSON, BEST SOMMELIER OF THE WORLD, 2007

A Pauillac that offers a lot of the attributes I first read about when Hugh Johnson was talking about great Pauillac—leather, cigar box, cassis, graphite and that great austerity. Even though the Merlot is present in a higher content than at its siblings Mouton or d'Armailhac, the wine nonetheless displays a very rigid structure, à la Cabernet. With age it will soften and round out some of those tannic edges and that elusive perfume will increase and give a lot of pleasure. This is a superb introduction to the great wines of Pauillac. The recent vintages of Clerc Milon have been very promising and it seems to have gained in both finesse and refinement.

CHÂTEAU CROIZET-BAGES

PAUILLAC

VINEYARD SIZE	30 hectares
VINE DENSITY	8,500 stocks per hectare
AVERAGE AGE OF VINEYARD	40 years
SOILS AND SUBSOILS	deep gravel and gravelly sands
GRAPE VARIETIES	Cabernet Sauvignon 60% Merlot 30% Cabernet Franc 10%

In the first half of the 18th century, two lawyers, the Croizet brothers, bought a few small vine plots on the Bages plateau in Pauillac, with the intention of constituting a vineyard. In the early 19th century, their property was acquired by the Gascon Jean de Puytarac, and later, in 1853, by the Bordelais Julien Calvé. The château, from then on called Calvé-Croizet, bore the name of Croizet-Bages when the 1885 Classification took place. The château that had been originally built, not on the vineyard but on the Pauillac docks, was later removed from the property and therefore from the wine's label, which now shows the award medals from various fairs, framed by two branches of laurel.

After the First World War, Château Croizet-Bages was purchased by Jean-Baptiste Monnot, an American citizen—despite the French name—who was known for importing the Klaxon car horn to France. In 1942, it became the property of Paul Quié, a Bordeaux-born Paris wine trader. After 1968, the vineyard was directed by his son, Jean-Michel, with the help of his two children, Anne-Françoise and Jean-Philippe. The Quié family also owns the châteaux Rauzan-Gassies in Margauxand Bel-Orme-Tronquoy-de-Lalande in Haut-Médoc.

As these lines are written, the technical buildings at Croizet-Bages are about to undergo a complete remodelling. The old concrete vathouse will be replaced, as well as a few other installations. Only the stainless-steel vathouse, built 21 years ago, will stay untouched, and a brand new cellar will be added. "We are lucky to run a family business," says Jean-Philippe Quié. "It is essential for us is to reach beyond the technical aspects. Our basic principle is classicism, for which we stand fully responsible. On the one hand we are aware of the necessity to keep up to date with the latest technical innovations, but our customers also expect this typicity from us, this fidelity to the Pauillac tradition.

"Here, we are graced with one of the finest soils of the appellation, a thick layer of gravel on a ferruginous sandy subsoil, a specific feature of the Bages plateau. Our 30 hectares are planted with 60 percent Cabernet Sauvignon, 30 percent Merlot and 10 percent Cabernet Franc. There used to be a time when the proportion of Merlot was larger, but Cabernet Sauvignon does thrive on this type of soil, so it plays a larger part in the composition. Our vines are of an average age of 40 years, we plough the rows and we use a compost made of ground pine bark and grape seeds."

One of the aims of the Quié family is to obtain a good tannic structure in the wines and to develop the intensity of the mid-palate sensation. These characteristics make Château Croizet-Bages a high-personality wine with a sturdy backbone and a rich masculine texture, warm without being heavy. It has elegant fruity notes (blackberry jelly, blackcurrant) and heady flower aromas (rose, peony, violet), tinged with a hint of hyssop and angelica. The affinity with herbs and spices is obvious. These tannins, indeed, will beautifully match the tasty marinades of Mughlai and other Indian traditional grilled meats, a luscious tandoor-roasted kebab for instance. The array of spices involved—garam masala, black cumin, ginger, chilli and cardamom—is not likely to intimidate Croizet-Bages.

1. In the quiet secrecy of the barrel cellar, a traditional Pauillac wine slowly matures.

2. Château Croizet-Bages' spicy notes make it a perfect companion for hearty cuisines.

3. Gravel on ferruginous sand: the vineyard is located near the village, on the Plateau de Bages.

Barrah Kebab

Manjit SINGH GILL
Bukhara - New-Delhi, India

SERVES 4

The lamb

8 cubes of lamb leg on the bone,
⅛ to ¼ pound (70 g) each

8 double lamb chops (with 2 bones),
⅛ to ¼ pound (70 g) each

4 baby lamb shanks,
⅛ to ¼ pound (70 g) each

salt

2 teaspoons cayenne pepper

2 tablespoons malt vinegar

2 tablespoons ginger paste

1 tablespoon cooking oil

4 tablespoons garlic paste

8 teaspoons green papaya paste
(acts as a tenderizer)

8 teaspoons natural plain yogurt

1 teaspoons garam masala
(spice mixsee below)

½ teaspoons black cumin

1 teaspoon kebab masala spice mix
(see below)

2 tablespoons melted butter

1 tablespoon lemon juice

The garam masala
(makes about 1 ounce, or 30 g)

½ teaspoon toasted bay leaf powder

2 teaspoons toasted peppercorn powder

½ teaspoon ground cloves

½ teaspoon black cardamom powder

½ teaspoon green cardamom powder

¼ teaspoon ground nutmeg

½ teaspoon ground mace

¼ teaspoon ground cinnamon

The kebab masala
(makes 1¾ ounces, or 50 g)

5 teaspoons chaat masala powder

2 teaspoons fenugreek powder

1 teaspoon black salt

1 teaspoon cayenne pepper

1 teaspoon garam masala (see above)

For the spice mixes: Mix the spices for the garam masala and then for the kebab masala. Set each aside.

For the lamb: Place the lamb cubes, chops and shanks in a large mixing bowl, pat dry with paper towels. Sprinkle with the salt, cayenne and garam masala, and mix well. Add the malt vinegar and oil and rub well for 7 to 10 minutes. Add the ginger paste, garlic paste and green papaya paste. Rub each piece thoroughly until evenly coated. Add the whisked yogurt and blend in well.

Marinate for at least 3 to 4 hours at room temperature to tenderize the lamb (10 to 12 hours refrigerated, do not forget to bring to room temperature before cooking).

Arrange the lamb onto skewers. Place the skewers into a low to medium-hot clay tandoor or spit grill for 10 to 12 minutes, turning occasionally.

After cooking, remove the skewers and allow to cool in a drip tray.

Cook the kebab for 8 to 10 minutes in a medium-hot tandoor, turning often. When done, baste with half of the melted butter.

For the presentation: Arrange the meats on a platter, sprinkle with kebab masala, lemon juice and the remaining melted butter. Serve with a salad.

CHÂTEAU CROIZET-BAGES BY VIRGINIA PHILIP,
BEST SOMMELIER OF THE UNITED STATES, 2002

The Bages Plateau is known for its gravel and white sub-soil base. Croizet-Bages is a lighter style Pauillac with a perfumed nose of black fruits and dark flowers on the nose. On the palate the wine has overtones of blackberry, blueberry and cherry with a hint of earth and spice. The tannins are light-bodied, allowing the wine to be drunk in a more youthful time frame.

CHÂTEAU CANTEMERLE

HAUT-MÉDOC

VINEYARD SIZE	90 hectares
VINE DENSITY	8,300 stocks per hectare
AVERAGE AGE OF VINEYARD	30 years
AVERAGE PRODUCTION	33,000 cases
SOILS AND SUBSOILS	Quaternary siliceous gravel
GRAPE VARIETIES	Cabernet Sauvignon 58% Merlot 33% Petit Verdot 6% Cabernet Franc 3%

"First you get a white shock, and then everyone falls in love." So Philippe Dambrine, the general manager, describes the arrival at Château Cantemerle. The man and the place were evidently meant for each other: both radiate the same aura of kind serenity. The majestic courtyard, planted with huge trees, is framed by impressive neoclassical buildings. Their whiteness, indeed, produces a slight shock. Were it not for the 19th-century neo-renaissance mansion, you could imagine yourself in a monastery. The wide facade of the cellar house is pierced with curved windows and circular oculi. A stone cross tops the flared roof, as a distant memory of a disappeared medieval abbey. Beyond, the vast park of 28 hectares, redrawn in the 19th century by botanist Louis-Bernard Fischer, is one of the most beautiful arboretums in the region.

No description does justice to that magical atmosphere. Dambrine speaks of "deafening silence" and spirituality. "Cantemerle is a place for meditation, not for confrontation. It is a haven. Thousands of springs flow below our feet. Four thousand years of human presence are here to contemplate us; a feeling of comfort, protection and security permeates this place."

The first historical record of the lords of Cantemerle dates back to 1147, when the cartulary of the Abbaye de la Sauve-Majeure mentions Pons de Cantemerle. In 1340, one of his descendants paid his taxes with a barrel of claret. Wine was already made there. But winemaking as a main activity really took off in the 16th century. In 1858, the estate was directed by Caroline de Villeneuve-Durfort and covered 91 hectares of vineyards, increased to 110 hectares in 1866. In 1892, it was purchased by the Dubos family, who kept it until 1981. Currently, the Château Cantemerle belongs to an insurance company, the Mutuelles d'Assurance du Bâtiment et des Travaux Publics.

Dambrine, who has been directing the estate since 1993, likes to use traditional winemaking methods in association with the newest innovative techniques. His deep admiration for ancient knowledge and for the long tradition of winemaking skills passed on through generations of maîtres de chai shows through his poised, sensible words. Cantemerle, which now covers 170 hectares including the woods and the park, has retained the very best plots from the mid-19th century period—90 hectares of siliceous gravel with 58 percent Cabernet Sauvignon, 33 percent Merlot, and equal parts Cabernet Franc and Petit Verdot to complete the planting. The grapes are painstakingly sorted at harvest so that not the tiniest bit of stem goes into the wine. The cellar buildings house three thermoregulated vatrooms, one with wooden vats for the old vines, restored in 1990; one with stainless-steel vats for young vines, built in 1981; and concrete vats for blending.

"On a great terroir, the grape variety disappears," says Dambrine. "Such is the message we wish to get through. The character of the soil always rules. The wines we make here are delicate and delicious. If I had to describe them in a few words, I would say aromatic potency, delicate structure resting on a lengthy finale and no tannic sensation whatsoever. They are generous, deeply satisfying, spiritual, soulful, benevolent and made for pleasure. Have you noticed that feeling of peace that seizes you as soon as Château Cantemerle enters your mouth? The attack is not an attack: it relaxes you and releases your tensions. The very same feeling of peace that you feel when you enter the place! Each year, when the wine leaves the property, I silently speak to all its future buyers, 'We are sending you a piece of Cantemerle.'"

1. First-time visitors are always strongly impressed by their discovery of Château Cantemerle. The atmosphere of peace is palpable.

2. A staircase in the 19th-century château.

3. Your first mouthful of Château Cantemerle contains the surprise of a both mental and physical soothing sensation.

Mock Langoustine Millefeuille

Peter KÖRNER

Les Roses - Mondorf-les-Bains, Luxembourg

SERVES 4

The millefeuille

4 sheets rice paper

1½ tablespoons (20 g)
unsalted butter, melted

2 tablespoons (20 g)
black sesame seeds

The langoustines and sauce

16 large langoustines

⅛ cup (4 cl) olive oil

4 shallots

1 tablespoon pink peppercorns

⅓ cup (8 cl) dry white wine

⅛ ounce (4 g) saffron thread

⅓ cup (8 cl) Mandarine Impériale

1 scant cup (20 cl) heavy cream

6 tablespoons (80 g) cold diced
unsalted butter (¾ stick)

salt and pepper

The vegetables

2⅛ ounces (60 g) fresh ginger
(a 4-to 5-inch piece)

⅛ pound (60 g) carrot

⅛ pound (60 g) celery root

⅛ pound (60 g) leek

⅛ pound (60 g) pak choy

⅛ pound (60 g) mung bean sprouts

⅛ cup (4 cl) lemon juice

unsalted butter

salt and freshly ground black pepper

For the millefeuille: Cut the rice paper sheets in half on the diagonal to get 2 triangles. Brush both sides with melted butter and place on a lined baking sheet. Sprinkle one side with sesame seeds. Bake in a 400°F (200°C) oven for 3 to 4 minutes.

For the sauce: Shell and de-vein the langoustines, and refrigerate.

Sweat the shells in olive oil with the chopped shallot, the pink peppercorns, the white wine, the saffron, half of the Mandarine Impériale, and the cream. Simmer for 30 minutes, then remove from the heat an let infuse for 30 more minutes. Strain through a conical sieve, pressing on the solids in order to extract as much liquid as possible.

For the vegetables: Cut into thin strips or julienne, and cook al dente.

In a sauté pan, melt a little butter, add ginger first and the vegetables a few moments after. Sauté for 2 minutes, and deglaze with the lemon juice. Season with salt and pepper. Set aside.

For the langoustines: Sear the langoustines in a little olive oil, just on the back side, for no more than 2 or 3 minutes. Season with salt and pepper, then deglaze with remaining Mandarine Impériale.

For the presentation: Just before serving, bring the sauce to a boil, taste and correct the seasoning, then bind the sauce with the cold butter.

Place one part of the vegetables on the plates, cover with 2 langoustines, 1 rice sheet, more vegetables 2 more langoustines and then the last rice sheet. The whole dish should look like the tower of Pisa. Decorate with some herb salad or a few blades of chives.

CHÂTEAU CANTEMERLE BY ÉRIC BEAUMARD, SILVER MEDAL, BEST SOMMELIER OF THE WORLD, 1998

With a vineyard covering 90 hectares and one of the most beautiful parklands in the Médoc, this château produces tender wines that are predominately Merlot-based. These wines are pleasing, flavourful and made to be enjoyed in their youth, with the capacity to give great pleasure when mature. The 2000 vintage, for example, is drinking very well right now, showing notes of ripe black fruit and supple tannins.

SAUTERNES

CHÂTEAU D'YQUEM

SAUTERNES

VINEYARD SIZE	100 hectares
VINE DENSITY	6,700 stocks per hectare
AVERAGE AGE OF VINEYARD	30 years
AVERAGE PRODUCTION	9,000 cases
SOILS AND SUBSOILS	clayey sand and gravel; clay-gravel subsoil; permeable limestone bedrock
GRAPE VARIETIES	Sémillon 80% Sauvignon Blanc 20%

Our imagination tends to surround the First Growth châteaux of the 1855 Classification with intimidation. The idea of entering them for the first time feels like entering the Holy of Holies. Sometimes, as in Lafite, the dark romanticism of the setting somewhat confirms that feeling. But as you approach the Château d'Yquem, you are greeted by quite a different impression. The Sun in person throws himself at your face, melting away all shyness or inhibition. Yquem is mainly known through this simple name for good reason: this great prince likes to push all solemnity aside; and etiquette, here, is only a cream-coloured square of paper, cut at the corners and printed with gold letters.

Naturally, the effect will be more obvious if you encounter Yquem on a bright sunny day. But even on a foggy morning, the inner light of the place will still welcome you. Set on a hilltop, the château reminds you of an Andalucian citadel, towers and crenulated walls showing through the huge stone pines and tall oak trees concealing lush gardens. There are gardens indeed—in the glass.

Originally, the château was a 16th-century fortified farm, which was enlarged and transformed throughout the centuries. First a property of the dukes of Aquitaine, it was bought in 1711 by the Sauvage family. In 1785, through the marriage of Françoise-Joséphine de Sauvage d'Yquem to Count Louis-Amédée de Lur-Saluces, the estate entered that famous family, who kept it until 1999. Since that year, Yquem has been the property of the LVMH/Moët-Hennessy-Louis Vuitton company. Pierre Lurton, from a famous lineage of Bordeaux winemakers, has been running Yquem since 2004 as CEO.

The château sits on 125 hectares of vineyards; only 100 produce Château d'Yquem, from 80 percent Sémillon and 20% white Sauvignon. A dry white wine, simply named "Y," is made, but the Great Classified Growth has no second wine: it is Yquem or nothing—Yquem most of the time and sometimes nothing, about one year out of ten. The 1992 vintage is absent, as are eight others of the 20th century.

"Yquem," says Pierre Lurton, "is timeless. An elegant way of travelling through time. Making a great wine is like reinventing history on a permanent basis. Sauternes wines are uncommon and inimitable, for they are based on the elegance of human gestures. Money has its limits, and technique is within anyone's reach. But great wines are based on taking risks with nature, not on technique. And experience compensates the risk. The Sauternais tradition is not chaptalisation or cryoextraction; it is indeed noble rot, concentration, man's effort and hand-sewn craftsmanship. Yquem is built through the fine-tuning of minute details, like cutting the thousand facets of a diamond."

Château d'Yquem's uncanny complexity made it a mythical wine, the quintessence of Sauternes. Within the 1855 Classification, the rank of Superior First Classified Growth was created solely for it. Its château floats over the Sauternes landscape rather than dominates it. In the same way, Yquem is princely, but never haughty or out of reach. Its lengthy, voluptuous golden bouquet of apricots, fresh figs and ripe grapes is held up by a fresh, acidic frame of unique richness, tinged with a fine note of resin, which magically summons the smell of wind-caressed pines, tempering the summer heat. However, any attempt to describe this wine falls short of conveying the sensation. Yquem is much more than a wine; it is an experience in meditation that will bewitch your memory forever.

1. Delicate decorative details abound inside the Château d'Yquem. Fireplaces are painted with gracious motifs and enigmatic smiles.

2. A night view of the château.

3. A Baroque streak runs throughout the estate and château, up to the cellars and the wine's golden colour.

Next pages: In the daytime, Yquem looks a fortress sitting on the highest hill of the Sauternais. At night, it seems to be part of a legendary kingdom.

Passionfruit
and Tahitian Vanilla Soufflé

Dominique ANSEL & Daniel BOULUD
Daniel - New York City, United States

SERVES 6

The pastry cream

½ cup (13 cl) milk

½ Tahitian vanilla pod

⅛ pound (40 g) egg yolks, about 2

1 cup (130 g) sugar 1 rounded teaspoon flour

½ teaspoon cornstarch

1¼ cups (280 g) egg whites, about 9

The passionfruit jelly

¼ cup (30 g) sugar

¾ teaspoon apple pectin

¼ cup (6 cl) passionfruit juice

For the pastry cream: Scrape the seeds of the half vanilla pod into the milk, add the pod and bring to the boil. Take off the heat and let rest. Beat the egg yolks with about 2 tablespoons (20 g) sugar until pale and creamy, then add the sifted flour and cornstarch. Pour some of the warm milk onto the yolks, beating all the while. Return to the saucepan and cook over low heat, stirring, for 3 to 4 minutes. Pour into a bowl.

Beat the egg whites to soft peaks, adding the remaining sugar towards the end of the beating. They should not be too firm.

Fold one third of the egg whites into the pastry cream using a whisk, then add the remaining egg whites gradually with a spatula.

For the passionfruit jelly: Preheat the oven to 340°F (171°C). Mix the sugar and pectin. Bring the passionfruit juice to the boil, and add the sugar and pectin. Cook for 4 to 5 minutes, stirring constantly.

Butter 6 small soufflé dishes and sprinkle them lightly with sugar. Put 1 tablespoonful of passionfruit jelly into each dish, then add the pastry cream, lightened with egg whites. Smooth the surface, then bake for 6 or 7 minutes. Serve immediately upon removing from the oven.

Château d'Yquem

Sauternes

— 2005 —

CHÂTEAU D'YQUEM BY MARKUS DEL MONEGO, BEST SOMMELIER OF THE WORLD, 1998

This celebrated property imposes itself on the landscape from afar, sitting atop the highest hill in Sauternes. This Great Growth not only represents the appellation's heart but also the finest expression of great sweet wine. The vineyard's deep gravel and traces of clay guarantee grapes of great complexity and aromatic richness; concentration by Botrytis cinerea *transforms their juice into liquid gold. Power and aromatic persistence on the nose and palate is underscored by a freshness, an elegance and a fine thread of acidity which assures an almost eternal longevity.*

CHÂTEAU LA TOUR BLANCHE

VINEYARD SIZE	37 hectares
VINE DENSITY	6,500 stocks per hectare
AVERAGE AGE OF VINEYARD	30 years
AVERAGE PRODUCTION	4,000 cases
SOILS AND SUBSOILS	gravel on a clay-limestone subsoil
GRAPE VARIETIES	Sémillon 80% Sauvignon 15% Muscadelle 5%

In the late 18th century, Jean Saint-Marc du Latour Blanche, a councillor at the Bordeaux Parliament, created this wine estate on a hilltop near Bommes. After 1815, the German winemaker Frederic Focke took hold of the château's destiny and brought the quality of its wines to such a height that the 1885 Classification placed them immediately behind Yquem, the Superior First Growth, which positions La Tour Blanche as the first of firsts among the Classified Growths of Sauternes.

However, the château as we know it today results from transformations that took place in the early 20th century. After 1876, La Tour Blanche belonged to Daniel Iffla, better known as Osiris, a Bordeaux-born banker-cum-philanthropist from a Jewish-Moroccan family. He left a strong mark, sharing a passion for *tzedakah* (the Jewish notion of charity) and for the French Republican ideal. He left to the world an early example of a floating soup kitchen (a charity barge that stayed moored to the Bordeaux docks from 1913 to 1940). He also left a fortune to the Institut Pasteur, the whole Château de La Malmaison to the French state and many subsidies to public facilities, and erected several synagogues, along with public statues of Joan of Arc and William Tell. Osiris was also a distinguished œnologist, who donated the Château La Tour Blanche to the French state on the condition that a tuition-free viticulture and œnology school be established on the premises. This public secondary school is still very active today and is managed jointly with the vineyard. As tribute to the great man, the phrase "Donation Osiris" is still printed on the wine's label.

Both the school and the vineyard are owned by the French Ministry of Agriculture and managed by Corinne Reulet. The sparkling white buildings, which include the school, the viticultural facilities and the château, are disposed around a vast garden courtyard. The vineyard spreads onto a clay-gravel hill overlooking the Ciron. Thirty-seven hectares are devoted to the Great Classified Growth. The vines, aged 30 years on average, are comprised of 80 percent Sémillon, 15 percent Sauvignon and 5 percent Muscadelle, and are tended with integrated pest control. In spring and summer, only one row of every two is ploughed, in order to let the grass act as a fertiliser and growth regulator. Sauvignons and Muscadelles are blended before fermentation in vats. Sémillon alone ferments in oak. The wine is aged for 16 to 18 months in 100 percent new oak barrels.

Nothing can satisfactorily explain a great wine. The most you can do is identify a few factors that contribute to its excellence. The extraordinary aromatic richness of La Tour Blanche is owed to its balanced blend, to the rigorous tending of the vineyard, to new wood and also to the quality of the terroir. The concentrated nose of white and yellow flowers—lime blossom, acacia, yellow gorse, jasmine—is always astonishingly powerful. The attack reveals opulent tropical fruit—mango, ripe pineapple and lychee. Some vintages, like 2002, play on vanilla, pine honey, a very slight toasty note, a touch of lemongrass and a resinous tang in the upper palate. The 2006 vintage has more of an acidic bite, with green mango, passion fruit and star fruit. Château La Tour Blanche will benefit from being served with some creamy cheeses—aged banon, saint-marcellin, creamy ewe's-milk cheeses from the French Southwest or vacherin mont-d'or—or with milky oysters, raw carpet-shell clams or, better yet, some raw white fish. But it should also be drunk on its own without hesitation, for it is a delicacy in its own right.

1. Around the small château, the winemaking facilities, then the agricultural school were successively built. The whole compound, of a chalky white colour, sits atop its own hill.

2. In the entrance hall leading to the vathouse, an ornamental mosaic of bottles displays the bright golden palette of Sauternes wines.

3. A tasting table stands in the same hall.

Celery Ice, Poire William Granita,
Frozen Mango, Beet and Fruit Jam

Martín BERASATEGUI
Martín Berasategui - Lasarte-Oria, Spain

SERVES 6

The frozen mango

¼ cup plus 3 tablespoons (175 g)
mango purée

one 1-g sheet of leaf gelatine

3½ tablespoons (75 g) glucose

⅛ cup (4 cl) water

⅓ teaspoon agar-agar

The Poire William granita

2 1/8 cup (50 cl) water

½ cup (100 g) sugar

3 tablespoons (62.5 g) inverted sugar

½ cup (12 cl) Poire William

The celery ice

4 leaves gelatine (2 g each)

2⅛ cups (50 cl) water

¾ cup (125 g) sugar

½ cup (100 g) glucose

juice of ½ lemon

1 cup (250 g) celery juice obtained by
blending and then sieving fresh celery

2 tablespoons (40 g) inverted sugar

The beet and fruit jam

½ pound (200 g)
Golden Delicious apples

½ pound (200 g) pineapple,
peeled and cored

scant ½ cup (80 g) sugar

1 cooked baby beet,
about 1 inch in diameter (7.5 g)

For the frozen mango: Soak the gelatine in ice water for 10 minutes, then drain it. Mix half of the mango purée with the glucose, water and agar-agar. Bring to the boil, add the gelatine and the remaning mango purée. Pass through a fine-mesh strainer and spread the mix on a baking sheet, no more than ¼ inch (5 mm) thick. As soon as the jelly begins to set, freeze the sheet. Just before serving, cut the mango jelly into slivers.

For the granita: Make a syrup with water, sugar, and inverted sugar. Add the Poire William and spread onto a sheet. Freeze solid, then scrape into crystals immediately before serving.

For the celery ice: Soak the gelatine for 10 minutes in ice water, then drain it. Mix together the water, sugar and glucose. Heat until the glucose has melted, then add the celery juice, inverted sugar, lemon juice and finally the gelatine. Freeze in an ice cream maker according to the manufacturer's directions.

For the beet and fruit jam: Cut the apples into quarters and peel and core them. Sprinkle them all over with the sugar and place them on a baking sheet. Cut the pineapple flesh into ¾-inch (2-cm) cubes, sprinkle them with 3 tablespoons (40 g) of the sugar, and place them on a baking sheet. Bake both fruits for 45 minutes at 300°F (150°C).

Pour off excess juice from the fruit, then blend in a Thermomix with the beet. Pass through a perforated strainer and refrigerate.

For the presentation: Paint each plate diagonally with a small quantity of jam. In the centre, arrange a sliver of frozen mango, and then a quenelle of celery ice, topped with a little granita. Decorate with celery shoots and leaves.

CHÂTEAU LA TOUR BLANCHE BY MARKUS DEL MONEGO,
BEST SOMMELIER OF THE WORLD, 1998

Even classic winemaking regions have discoveries in store, like Château La Tour Blanche. Endowed with modern and efficient equipment, this property has nonetheless preserved a traditional, hands-on style of winemaking. The result is a rich and refined expression of a great terroir, which seduces the nose and palate with aromas of exotic fruit, white flowers or citrus notes, according to the vintage and age of the wine.

Château Lafaurie-Peyraguey

SAUTERNES

VINEYARD SIZE	36 hectares
VINE DENSITY	7,000 stocks per hectare
AVERAGE AGE OF VINEYARD	40 years
AVERAGE PRODUCTION	5,000 cases
SOILS AND SUBSOILS	Quaternary gravel, gravelly clay and clayey sand
GRAPE VARIETIES	Sémillon 90% Sauvignon 8% Muscadelle 2%

If the beautiful Sauternes region seems at times to remind you remotely of Spain, Yquem and Lafaurie-Peyraguey are partly responsible for that. To each one their style: within the royal zone of the Sauternes appellation, the famous upper terrace which primarily breeds Premiers Grands Crus, Yquem sails atop of the highest wave like an Andalusian citadel; La Tour Blanche is reminiscent of a stark-white Mediterranean village clutching the edge of its cliff, Rayne Vigneau of a romantic château painted in ink by Victor Hugo, and Lafaurie-Peyraguey displays the Spanish-Moorish allure of its massive crenelated fortress.

The most ancient parts of the building—beginning with the entrance porch—date back to the 13th century, making the château one of the oldest in the Bordeaux region. The first owner on record was Raymond Peyraguey, who was settled in Bommes in 1618. His estate covered the whole hill, starting from the top, now the vineyard of Clos Haut-Peyraguey, to a little beyond the current limits of Lafaurie-Peyraguey. In 1742, Pierre de Pichard, Baron de Saucats, bought the vineyard and created the wine estate. Unfortunately, he lost his head in the French Revolution, and the estate was taken over by one Mr. Lafaurie. The new owner took the quality of the wines to a high point; it is said that King Alfonso XII of Spain loved them more than any other. In 1865, when Lafaurie's widow sold the property to Count Duchâtel, Lafaurie-Peyraguey covered 27 hectares.

Between 1860 and 1870, under Duchâtel's impulse, a vast construction program gave the château its present appearance. Then the château entered a period of decline until 1917, when the Bordeaux wine trader Désiré Cordier, also the owner of Châteaux Talbot and Gruaud Larose in Saint-Julien, set out to resurrect this magnificent property. For more than 80 years, his company exploited the estate and distributed the wines. In 1984, the entire Cordier group was sold to the

Suez group, which renovated all the buildings and facilities between 1998 and 2004. Currently, GDF-Suez owns the property, which is managed by Éric Larramona, a young œnologist whose joie de vivre and sunny sense of humour are in perfect harmony with the fresh and lively spirit that dances in the wine.

The vineyard, all 36 hectares of Pyrenean gravel, enjoys a beautiful diversity of soils. Sémillon takes up 90 percent of the planting, Sauvignon 8 percent and Muscadelle 2 percent. The harvest tries are quite painstaking and can be repeated up to seven times. In some years, some plots may be sacrificed in order to promote the ones that show a better quality potential. The handmade nature of Sauternes winemaking shows itself through the use of four beautiful antique vertical wine presses, still going strong in spite of the simultaneous use of a pneumatic press, and guaranteeing slow, regular pressure. After blending, the ageing is carried out for 18 to 20 months.

Aromatic, creamy, delicately fruity, Château Lafaurie-Peyraguey is a sublime wine—paradoxical too, like all great Sauternes. At no point do its richness and sweetness ever conceal the continuous fresh and acidic note, revealing a citrus framework in the finish. Accents of peach, nectarine and spices—notably Bourbon vanilla—rest on a finely caramelised, buttery and toasty structure. Lafaurie-Peyraguey's ageing potential, which can reach 100 years, is extraordinary; no less so are its pure deliciousness and gastronomic versatility.

1. Rooted in his terroir of Pyrenean gravel, the château is protected by a 13th-century fortified wall and hidden from view by high trees.

2. Four antique vertical presses are still fully functional at Château Lafaurie-Peyraguey.

3. Clarity, aromatic persistence, balance, ethereal fruity notes on a Bourbon vanilla framework—the distinguished, sensuous beauty of a Sauternes First Great Classified Growth.

Bresse Chicken Roasted in a Salt Crust

Georges BLANC
restaurant Georges Blanc - Vonnas, France

SERVES 4 TO 6

The chicken

one 4- to 5-pound (2-kg) Bresse
chicken, singed and gutted,
but not trussed

½ head of garlic cut in half crosswise

½ large onion, peeled

1 bouquet garni

1 beaten egg

salt and freshly ground black pepper

The salt crust

2⅝ pounds (1.2 kg) coarse salt

2¼ pounds (1 kg) flour

2 eggs plus 4 egg yolks

⅔ cup (15 cl) water

The day before: Using a small sharp knife, remove the tendons from the chicken's legs: make a 2-inch (5-cm) cut on the inside of each leg, just above the spur. Using tweezers, pull out the tendons that run down to the feet and tear them off. Place the halved head of garlic, the half-onion and the bouquet garni inside the cavity of the chicken. Do not truss the chicken. Refrigerate overnight.

For the salt crust: Pour the flour and salt into the bowl of an electric mixer. Add the eggs, the egg yolks and the water. Mix until smooth. Refrigerate overnight.

The next day: Preheat the oven to 350°F (175°C). Roll out the salt crust to less than ½ inch (1 cm) thick. Season the inside and the outside of the chicken with salt and pepper, then wrap it hermetically in the salt crust. Be careful not to tear the crust even slightly. The remaining salt crust can be used to make decorative flowers and leaves that you can paste onto the salt crust–wrapped chicken.

Brush the crust with beaten egg mixed with a few drops of water, and then bake the chicken for 1 hour and 15 minutes. The crust should be golden brown. Turn off the oven and let the chicken rest for 30 minutes in the oven.

For the presentation: Just before serving, break the salt crust with a heavy knife and carve the chicken. You may serve it with creamed morels and the season's best vegetables.

CHÂTEAU LAFAURIE-PEYRAGUEY BY YOICHI SATO, BEST SOMMELIER OF JAPAN, 2005

Personally, I love to savour the delicious unctuosity of this wine unaccompanied by food; nonetheless, I can suggest drinking it with a fine Roquefort. The attractive sensation at the back of the palate, the balance between sweetness and a light acidity—evident when chilled or at ambient temperature—are characteristic aspects of this wine.

Clos Haut-Peyraguey

SAUTERNES

VINEYARD SIZE	12 hectares
VINE DENSITY	6,600 stocks per hectare
AVERAGE AGE OF VINEYARD	35–40 years
AVERAGE PRODUCTION	1,500 cases
SOILS AND SUBSOILS	sandy-gravelly on a clayey subsoil
GRAPE VARIETIES	Sémillon 92%
	Sauvignon 8%

The history of Clos Haut-Peyraguey, on the top of the Plateau de Bommes, goes back to the ancient baqrony of Peyraguey, whose wines were classified in 1855 under the name of Château Peyraguey. King Alfonso XII of Spain was such a passionate lover of those wines that he purchased a cask of the 1858 vintage for 6,000 gold francs. In 1879, the Peyraguey estate was split in two. The highest part was named Clos Haut-Peyraguey, while the remaining plots became the vineyard of Château Lafaurie-Peyraguey.

In 1914, Eugene Garbay, already the owner of Château Haut-Bommes, bought the estate. In 1969, both Haut-Bommes and Clos Haut-Peyraguey were entrusted to Jacques Pauly, a true winemaker at heart. His daughter, Martine Langlais-Pauly, has been running them since 2003.

"Clos Haut-Peyraguey," says Langlais-Pauly, "has been managed by our family for five generations. I am the first woman to be in charge. Before I came here, I had taken a different professional path, directing a psychiatric clinic for 20 years. At the beginning, I was spending part of my vacation time at the Bordeaux Œnology Faculty until I passed the DUAD (degree of proficiency in wine tasting). Then I got training in viticulture and particularly on the making of liqueur wines, while being at the head of the DUAD Graduates Club for five years. When, in 2003, my father handed me the estate, I realized how deeply fond I was of this land I had known since I was a child.

"I was holding the firm conviction that there was a wonderful terroir lying there, with fresh and lively wines waiting to come out of it—12 hectares on the hilltop for Clos Haut-Peyraguey, at an altitude of 50 to 80 metres, in the very heart of the Sauternes First Classified Growths zone, facing Château d'Yquem. That is Clos Haut-Peyraguey. And 5 hectares for Château Haut-Bommes. Sandy gravel on a clay subsoil, and the slopes facing north and northeast. Ninety-two percent Sémillon, a varietal that gives the wines power and structure and 8 percent Sauvignon and the wonderful freshness of taste that comes from the terroir.

"I was then 51 years old, with no time to waste. I decided to go out of my way to bring out the best in this classified growth. How? By being present in the vineyard throughout the year and particularly during harvest time. Starting from the 2004 and 2006 vintages, I dedicated all my time and energy to that. I introduced a strict method of selection. A lot of grapes remained on the ground. The picking was particularly uneasy during those years. Several different types of rot could be found on the same cluster. The tries were difficult. As a rule, Sauternes wines today are no longer made like they used to be 20 years ago. The picking and sorting are more painstaking and the harvest comes out purer than ever. That is how you get a better expression of botrytis.

"We began to reap the fruit of our hard work in 2008. The press was enthusiastic. Michel Bettane assured that our wines were brisker, neater, more streamlined than ever before. Jacques Dupont mentioned their 'insistent fruitiness' and finely tuned structure. Jancis Robinson described them as punchy and went as far as using the word 'miracle.' The balance, soft texture, minerality and sharpness of the wines were praised. From 2006 to 2008, they were celebrated for their notes of fresh fruit, jasmine and wisteria. All that praise is to us no more than an incentive to keep up the good work. Sauternes winemakers are too dependent on weather conditions and on the unpredictable whims of botrytis to be big-headed. Each vintage brings us a new challenge. There is no way we can rest on our laurels."

1. The pale gold colour of Clos Haut-Peyraguey takes on lemony hues with time and its aromatic range shows a remarkable balance of fruity and flowery.

2. Clos Haut-Peyraguey stands on the highest point of the plateau de Bommes, an exceptional terroir which gives the wines their delicacy and fresh taste.

3. A detail of Clos Haut-Peyraguey.

Dublin Bay Prawns,
Warm Melon and Sauternes

Alain DUTOURNIER
Carré des Feuillants - Paris, France

SERVES 4 TO 6

The prawns

24 very large Dublin Bay prawns

1 cup (25 cl) Sauternes

½ cup (12 cl) heavy cream

scant ½ cup (10 cl) water

pinch of curry powder

pinch of Espelette pepper

large pinch of saffron threads

The garnish

¼ pound (65 g) fresh red currants

1 large cantaloupe,
about 1¾ pounds (800 g)

½ bunch fresh cilantro

salt

For the prawns: Remove the heads from the prawns, shell the tails, split the prawns in two length-wise and refrigerate. Boil down the Sauternes in three stages, so as to layer its fragrances and obtain a syrupy, exotic, acidic ½ cup (8 cl) of nectar.

In a small enamelled cast-iron Dutch oven, crush the prawn heads and claws using a pestle. Add the reduced Sauternes, cream, and water. Add the curry powder, Espelette pepper and a pinch of salt. Simmer for 10 minutes (be careful: if the heat is too high or the simmering too lengthy, an ammonia smell might appear, even if you used live prawns).

Strain the preparation into a large sauté pan; it should be nice and creamy. Add the saffron, lightly crushed. Keep warm without boiling.

For the garnish and presentation: Rinse and stem the red currants. Peel the melon as you would peel an apple, cut it in two and remove the seeds, then cut it into ⅛-inch (3-mm)

slices. Put the melon slices into the warm sauté pan with the prawn cream; let warm up without boiling. After 3 or 4 minutes, add the prawn tails and the red currants. Simmer for 3 more minutes.

Rinse and drain the cilantro, and cut the leaves finely.

Divide the shrimp and melon slices among individual serving bowls. Scatter with the currants and sprinkle with fresh cilantro leaves.

CLOS HAUT-PEYRAGUEY BY OLIVIER POUSSIER, BEST SOMMELIER OF THE WORLD, 2000

Managed by Martine Langlais-Pauly since 2003, this 17-hectare property is situated on one of the finest terroirs in the heights of Bommes. The château makes a moderately oaked wine with a notably fine constitution, marrying power and richness, and a remarkable ability to age. We should also mention that among lovers of great sweet wines, Clos Haut-Peyraguey is considered one of the most affordable of the First Growths.

CHÂTEAU DE RAYNE VIGNEAU

SAUTERNES

VINEYARD SIZE	85 hectares
VINE DENSITY	5,600 stocks per hectare
AVERAGE AGE OF VINEYARD	30 years
SOILS AND SUBSOILS	sandy-gravelly, clayey subsoil and semiprecious stones (agates, amethysts, onyx, etc.)
GRAPE VARIETIES	Sémillon 74% Sauvignon 24% Muscadelle 2%

As a child, you certainly read fairytales where fantastic, pointy-towered castles were surrounded with dream-like, unpredictable landscapes. As the story went, it was not easy to get near the building (for instance to free a princess) without being greeted by strange surprises.

The Château de Rayne Vigneau looks like it just came out of an old etching. This romantic troubadour fantasy exists more as a silhouette than as a monument. It was designed to be part of a landscape; seen close up, it loses some of its romanticism, appearing as one of many neo-medieval architectural fantasies the 19th century was so fond of. But seen from far away, emerging from its cluster of trees, it shines with remarkable grace and fits into the setting as if it had always been there. It should indeed be admired at a distance, the best view being from the top of the Rabaud-Promis hill, particularly on a misty morning. And at the bottom of the croupe, where the vineyard meets the small road, the two posts of a stone gateway stand alone, without walls, railing or path, stuck in the grass and opening onto nothing. Opening, therefore, onto everything—a parallel world, a supernatural kingdom. If by any chance you weren't quite convinced that there were fairies here, now you won't doubt it anymore. And if you taste the wine, then you are sure.

Rayne Vigneau is a perfect château in an extraordinary setting. Nothing else could sit at the top of this hill, on the famous upper terrace of Sauternes, studded with prestigious First Growth châteaux and dominated by the Yquem fortress. Set on exceptional subsoil where amethysts, sapphires and onyx mingle with the Pyrenean gravel, Rayne Vigneau is considered one of the finest terroirs in the region. Interesting pieces of quartz and chalcedony may be picked up in the vineyard. A mineralogy collection is kept at the château. It is closed to the public, but Patrick Eymery, the estate's manager, keeps

a few of those wonderful stones in a glass box. Their beauty inspired him to have them polished, thus revealing the fantastic hues of orbicular jasper, golden quartzite and finely striped agate.

The most precious treasure of this exceptional soil is, of course, the wine. Made here since the 17th century, it was always rated second to Yquem, but it was weakened by ill-inspired plantings during the second half of the 20th century. Since 2004 and the purchase of the estate by CA Grands Crus, a subsidiary of the Crédit Agricole, a restructuration policy has been applied to the vineyard, with the help of œnologist Denis Dubourdieu, to develop the wine's character and delicacy. "Our current objective," says Thierry Budin, manageing director of CA Grands Crus, "is to promote the freshness and the aroma rather than the sweetness, in order to widen the range of food pairings."

The croupe of Rayne Vigneau, on 85 hectares of vineyard surface, is planted with 74 percent Sémillon, 24 percent Sauvignon—which gives the wine its characteristic freshness of taste—and 2 percent Muscadelle. Château de Rayne Vigneau smells, simply, of summer, with a noble and distinguished fragrance of fruits and flowers pouring down in cascades—sweet lemon, mandarin orange, wisteria, honeysuckle and a touch of beeswax. Although it is produced on an ancient terroir, this Sauternes proves very contemporary and remarkably versatile. It is equally happy alongside spicy, sophisticated modern cooking or rustic, more traditional fare like aged Roquefort cheese and roasted game birds—for indeed, nobility is a matter of both delicacy and strength.

1. *The château that crowns this beautiful Pyrenean gravel hill seems to have come out of a Romantic-era etching. The terroir was always considered second in value to Yquem.*

2. *Great Sauternes wines, after decades, turn to a darker colour—from a fiery red to mahogany brow—but their clarity is never dimmed.*

3. *One of the two vertical presses displayed in the white tasting room.*

Priprioca-scented Milk Custard
with Lime and Banana Ouro Ravioli

Alex ATALA
D.O.M. - São Paulo, Brazil

SERVES 10

The caramel

3¼ cups (320 g) confectioners' sugar

⅓ cup (8 cl) water

⅛ cup (2 cl) priprioca essence

The custard

1 cup (25 cl) whole milk

1 cup (25 cl) heavy cream

4 egg yolks (80 g)

⅓ cup (60 g) confectioners' sugar

2 gelatine leaves (2 g each)

The crème patissière

2 egg yolks (40 g)

3 tablespoons sugar (40 g)

8 g flour

1 scant cup (20 cl) whole milk

The ravioli

1½ cups (175 g) sugar

¾ cup (17.5 cl) water

½ cup (10 cl) lemon juice

1 teaspoon agar-agar

⅔ ounce leaf gelatine

(20 g) banana ouro, finely sliced

The lime zest syrup

4½ cups (500 g) sugar

2⅛ cups (50 cl) water

zest of 1 lime, cut in fine julienne

The kikurague mushroom

1 white *kikurague* mushroom

2⅛ cups (50 cl) water

4 cups plus 2 tablespoons (500 g) sugar

gold leaf powder

For the caramel: Make a caramel with the sugar at approximately 288°F (142°C). Add the water and the priprioca essence.

For the custard: Simmer the milk and cream together. Do not let them boil.

Whisk the yolks with the sugar until they are pale yellow. Soak the sheets of gelatine in cold water for 10 minutes, drain and dissolve them in the hot milk. Gently whisk the milk into the yolks and strain the custard. Cover the bottom of a ⅛-cup (3-cl) spherical silicone moulds with caramel. Pour the custard over the caramel and bake in a steam oven, at 200°F (90°C), for 10 to 12 minutes, until set.

For the crème patissière: Whisk the egg yolks, sugar and flour in a bowl. Scald the milk, add it to the yolks slowly while stirring, to temper the eggs. Strain the mixture and cook it over low heat, stirring constantly, for about 5 minutes. Transfer it to a bowl and place the bowl in another bowl of ice water to, then cover with plastic wrap, pressed directly against the surface so it will not form a skin.

For the ravioli: Boil all the ingredients, with the exception of the gelatine and banana. Soak the gelatine in cold water for 10 minutes, then drain it. Add it to the syrup. Pour the jelly onto a tray, less than ⅛ inch (2 mm) thick. Let set, then cut the jelly into disks with a 2-inch

(5-cm) round cutter. Mount the raviolis as follows: a layer of gelatine, a drop of crème patissière, 3 thin slices of banana, another layer of gelatine.

For the lime zest syrup: Boil the sugar and water. Blanch the lime zests 3 times in boiling water, cooling them each time in ice water. Add them to the boiling syrup.

For the *kikurague* mushroom: Rehydrate the *kikurague* for one day in cold water. Cook it in 2⅛ cups (50 cl) water, then add the sugar.

For the presentation: Using a piping bag, pipe a little crème pâtissière on top of each ravioli and dot with a few strands of candied lime zests. Brush a little gold leaf powder onto the pieces of *kikurague* mushroom.

Place the flan on the left side of a 4 x 10-inch (10 x 25-cm) rectangular, preferably slate, plate. Put the ravioli in the middle, and a piece of *kikurague* on the other side. Sprinkle with a little priprioca caramel.

Château de Rayne Vigneau by Serge Dubs, Best Sommelier of the World, 1989

Curiously, this Sauternes jewel is not widely known, but it is nonetheless praised and sought out by connoisseurs of sweet wines. It is a quintessential example of subtlety, refinement and elegance. In youth the wine can appear slender and somewhat timid, but its pleasant bouquet of fruity, overripe grapes and floral notes is always charming, tempting and entrancing. Suave and tender, supple and sweet, its subtle freshness allows it to age well and fully express all its nuanced quality when mature.

CHÂTEAU SUDUIRAUT

SAUTERNES

VINEYARD SIZE	92 hectares
VINE DENSITY	7,000 stocks per hectare
AVERAGE AGE OF VINEYARD	25 years
AVERAGE PRODUCTION	depending on the vintage
SOILS AND SUBSOILS	mainly composed of sandy-clayey gravel
GRAPE VARIETIES	Sémillon 90% Sauvignon 10%

When Château Suduiraut was built in the mid-17th century, it replaced a fortress that had been previously torn down by the Duke of Épernon, lord of Beychevelle. A simple and tasteful interior gives this otherwise lofty building a welcoming atmosphere. A general feeling of rustic peace surrounds the place; a handful of geese and duck make the most of a small green meadow in front of château, planted with venerable trees and graced with a long rectangular pond—a kingdom over which no one even thinks of challenging them. On the other side of the château, Le Nôtre designed the garden. King Louis XIV was known to appreciate the wines of Suduiraut to the point of subsidising their production.

Bordering Yquem and Rieussec, on the commune of Preignac, the Suduiraut estate covers 200 hectares, including 92 hectares of vineyard. Its poor, draining hills of white sandy Pyrenean gravel rise at an altitude of 55 metres. The planting is 90 percent Sémillon and 10 percent Sauvignon. "Sauvignon is there for the spice," explains technical manager Pierre Montégut. "We never age it in new oak, not wanting to harm its fruitiness. Sémillon provides the framework and is the key to good ageing."

After going through a difficult period in the 1930s, Suduiraut was bought and revitalised by Leopold-Francois Fonquernie with the help of Pierre Pascaud, an attorney with a passion for liqueur wines. AXA-Millésimes bought the estate in the late 1980s. General manager Christian Seely devotes a special affection to this wine. "In order to get an improvement in terms of quality," he says, "we had to sacrifice a lot in terms of quantity. We gave up making crèmes de tête so that the Classified Growth could get more attention. Harvest selection is of course very strict. Each bucket is carefully inspected in the vineyard before the berries go directly to the press, without any further sorting. If we cannot have the best, we just do nothing. Thus, in 1991, 1992 and 1993, we did nothing.

In 2004, we left three-quarters of the grapes on the ground. And it proved to be one of our best vintages, on which we made no profit. We used to make 10,000 cases in the 1990s—in 2004, we made 2,000 cases."

The well-known longevity of Suduiraut is remarkable. "These wines are lovely when young," says Montégut, "but I recommend an ageing of 10 years. That sounds reasonable; suggesting a wait of 40 years would be slightly excessive!"

With an admiring look, as if they were seeing it for the first time ever, Montégut and Seely watch the golden nectar of a small vertical tasting flow into the glasses. The wine is sunshine at different hours of the day: a morning daylight for the 2003, with notes of preserved pineapple calling for a contrasting pairing—blue Stilton or young Roquefort. A copper-coloured sun for the more distinctive and fresher-tasting 2002, whose slightly musky notes call for good roasted chicken. With the 1999, the light turns to amber and deepens into twilight, but what an illumination inside! A light, elegant rancio taste outlines notes of spices, lemon verbena and lime blossom. At this point, Montégut reveals Suduiraut's royal gastronomic affinity: Chinese cuisines, namely those of Guangdong and Fujian, which form celestial harmonies with the wine—ginger, fresh vegetables, mushrooms, seafood, slightly fermented condiments. And finally, when Pierre uncorks a 1975, the experience reaches a spectacular dimension: fireworks of bitter orange, marmalade, cinchona, honey; a polished, delicately saffron-y rancio, and gentle, creamy blond tobacco notes. It is time to bring out the spice-roasted duck, the sweet and delicious char siu pork belly, the oyster omelette and the vanilla-flavoured lobster.

1. The château, built in the mid-17th century, replaced a medieval fortress that was torn down by the Duke of Épernon.

2. The wines of Château Suduiraut were among King Louis XIV's favorite.

3. A mahogany chimneypiece inside the château.

Dover Sole Filets Breaded
with Cocoa, Saffron-Chocolate Cream Sauce

Annie FÉOLDE
Enoteca Pinchiorri - Firenze, Italy

SERVES 4

The fish

**1 large sole,
divided into 4 individual filets
oil for frying**

The saffron sauce

**a few saffron threads
a little olive oil
2 tablespoons heavy cream**

The polenta

3 tablespoons fine polenta

**1 egg white
½ cup (50 g) breadcrumbs
⅛ cup (20 g) crushed cocoa beans
grated chocolate
salt and freshly ground black pepper**

For the sole: Fillet the sole and keep the bones and trimmings. Refrigerate the 4 filets.

Chop the fish bones and trimmings finely and soak them in cold water to remove any blood. Meanwhile, soak the saffron in a little warm water.

For the saffron sauce: In a saucepan, sauté the sole trimmings in a little oil for a few minutes. Cover with water and bring to a boil. Simmer for 30 minutes, then strain the fumet through a fine sieve. Measure out ⅓ cup (10 cl) of the sole fumet and put it in a saucepan. Add the cream and the saffron and its soaking water. Cook for 15 minutes, correct the seasoning and set aside.

For the polenta: Cook the polenta in ⅓ cup (10 cl) lightly salted boiling water for 40 minutes, correct seasoning and set aside.

To fry the sole: Dip the sole filets into slightly beaten egg white, then into a mix of breadcrumbs and crushed cocoa beans. Fry them in a good quantity of hot oil. Drain and season with a little salt.

For the presentation: Spread the polenta in a disk shape on each plate, arrange a sole filet over it, pour a little warm saffron sauce over the dish and garnish with some grated chocolate and a few drops of olive oil.

CHÂTEAU SUDUIRAUT BY ANDREAS LARSSON,
BEST SOMMELIER OF THE WORLD, 2007

Suduiraut really does belong in the top league and it's difficult to adequately express the versatility and complexity of the golden drops. With an enormous intensity of perfume, yellow fruits, acacia honey, minerals and a taste that is not only lusciously sweet but beautifully balanced and harmonious, offering an invigourating freshness, layers of complex flavours and a never-ceasing aftertaste. Splendidly drinkable from day one, but after around five to six years, the complexity dramatically increases and continues to do so for decades.

CHÂTEAU COUTET

BARSAC

VINEYARD SIZE	38.5 hectares
VINE DENSITY	5,500 stocks per hectare
AVERAGE AGE OF VINEYARD	38 years
AVERAGE PRODUCTION	3,300 cases
SOILS AND SUBSOILS	clay-limestone
GRAPE VARIETIES	Sémillon 75% Sauvignon 23% Muscadelle 2%

"There is a good feeling about this place," says Aline Baly, alluding to the serene atmosphere of the château. If winemaking at Coutet can be traced to the 17th century, its remarkable medieval monuments make it one of the oldest Barsac properties. The crenulated tower overlooking the courtyard dates back to the 13th century, and the chapel was built in the 14th. In the vineyard, the interesting Round House was a lodging for pilgrims on their way to Santiago de Compostela. Close by, La Salace is a 15th-century fortified house. Other parts of the château date back from the 16th to the 18th centuries.

In 1695, Château Coutet's owner, Charles Le Guérin, sold the estate to his nephew Jean Le Pichard. In 1788, the Le Pichards sold it back to a cousin, Barthélemy de Filhot, president of the Bordeaux Parliament and owner of the Château Filhot in Sauternes. His grandson, Romain Bertrand de Lur-Saluces, made Coutet a family property, which it remained until 1922. Coutet was then purchased by Louis Guy Mital, a wine-press manufacturer, who handed it down to his daughter. In 1977, Marcel Baly and his two sons, Philippe and Dominique, acquired Château Coutet and undertook an ambitious renovation program, with the help of Mr. Constantin, maître de chai, and recently, Aline Baly. First the vineyards were restructured, then the cellar and vathouse were renovated, the growing methods were modernized and finally the château was restored. Since 1994, a technical partnership has been established with Baroness Philippine de Rothschild and her company, Baron Philippe de Rothschild SA, who own Château Coutet's exclusive distribution rights.

The estate covers 42 hectares in one piece, including 38.5 hectares of vineyards—75 percent Sémillon, 23 percent Sauvignon and 2 percent Muscadelle—planted on a terroir of fine gravel left by the nearby Garonne or, for some plots, of Aeolian sands, all on a clay-limestone subsoil. The average age of the vines is 35 years. The plot layout closely follows the pedologic structure, which makes cultivation and harvesting easier. At Château Coutet, people are the most highly valued; teamwork is of utmost importance.

The wines are aged between 16 and 18 months in oak barrels. The cellar, 110 metres long, is the longest in the Barsac-Sauternes region and was formerly the stables of the Lur-Saluces family. There are even rumours of an underground tunnel between Coutet and Yquem.

It is believed that the name Coutet could be derived from couteau, which means knife—a reference to the sharp and assertive character of the wine, its confident acidic and aromatic structure. Château Coutet is full of finesse and intensity, with notes of fruit cheeses, preserved citrus and apricot, and a rich and creamy mouthfeel. It expresses the château's soul, as if the Balys had managed to bottle the gentle and serene mood of the place. Its bright, fiery yellow-orange colour quickly darkens with time into cinnamon hues. That is particularly the case with the Cuvée Madame, a choice vintage that was created in 1922 for the owner's wife. Obtained from late-season pickings on vine stocks of 40 years of age or more and aged for three years in casks, it is the quintessence of the estate.

As for pairings, these powerful wines call for foods worthy of their intense nature—foie gras with toasted sourdough bread, lobster prepared with spices and potent sauces, chicken with whole garlic cloves. With a young Château Coutet, desserts and delicate dishes will be good matches, but the old vintages were meant for black truffles, aged blue cheeses and choice cigars.

1. This estate, one of the oldest in Barsac, has a long history of winemaking. The "Cuvée Madame" produced from carefully selected grapes is deservedly famous.

2. The winemaking facilities include the longest barrel cellar in the Sauternais—actually the former horse stables of the Lur-Saluces.

3. The tower dates from the 13th century, and other medieval buildings may be seen on the estate, standing among the vines.

Vanilla Crémeux with Caramel,
Meringue Roses, Dulce de Leche Ice Cream

Sergio HERMAN
Oud Sluis - Sluis, the Netherlands

SERVES 10

The crémeux

⅛ ounce (6 g) leaf gelatine

1⅓ cups (33 cl) heavy cream

1 vanilla pod, split length-wise

4 egg yolks (80 g)

¾ cup (60 g) superfine granulated sugar

The praline jelly

1 rounded tablespoons plain sugar

¾ cup (18 cl) water

¼ pound (100 g) praline

½ teaspoon agar-agar

The meringue roses

¼ cup (6 cl) water

½ teaspoon beetroot juice

1½ tablespoons dried egg powder

1 teaspoon rose water

⅓ to ½ teaspoon
superfine granulated sugar

The ice cream

1 cup (25 cl) whole milk

1 egg yolk (20 g)

3 tablespoons confectioners' sugar

¾ ounce (21 g) ice cream stabiliser

2 ounces (55 g) dulce de leche powder

The croustillant

1 scant cup (20 cl) water

3½ ounces (100 g) dulce de leche powder

3 tablespoons sugar

¼ cup (50 g) confectioners' sugar

1½ teaspoons glucose

2 teaspoons xanthan gum

rose jelly

walnut cream

vanilla sabayon

For the crémeux: Soak the gelatine for 10 minutes in cold water. Simmer the cream with the vanilla pod for a few minutes. Mix the egg yolks with the sugar, strain the cream and dissolve the drained gelatine in it. Mix both preparations together.

For the praline jelly: Bring the water to a boil with the sugar and the praliné. Add the agar-agar, boil for 1 minute and blend.

Strain and pour onto a baking sheet.

For the meringue roses: Blend all the ingredients in a standing mixer except the sugar. Add the sugar and blend until thick. Spray onto a silicone mat and bake at 195°F (90°C) for 45 minutes.

For the ice cream: Whip the egg yolk in a standing mixer until it forms a ribbon. Mix the milk, stabilizer, and dulce powder; boil until everything is dissolved. Add to the egg yolk little by little, pour into Pacojet bowls and process in the Pacojet machine.

For the croustillant: Mix all the ingredients for 13 minutes in the Thermomix at (160°F) 70°C. Spread out thinly and bake in a 195°F (90°C) oven for 2 hours. Break into pieces.

Before serving, lay on each late a little crémeux, some praline jelly, 1 meringue rose and some dulce ice cream. Stick a piece of croustillant into the ice cream. You may add some vanilla sabayon, walnut cream and rose jelly.

CHÂTEAU COUTET BY MARKUS DEL MONEGO,
BEST SOMMELIER OF THE WORLD, 1998

Benefiting from an exceptional terroir, this First Growth is a quintessential Barsac. Persistence, elegance and freshness are typical characteristics of its great wine (as well as its celebrated "Cuvée Madame"); complex aromas of exotic fruit and a succulent taste with a mineral touch on the finish are typical. Château Coutet proves that the human element is part of the terroir, bringing out its optimal expression thanks to meticulous work in the vineyard and the vathouse.

CHÂTEAU CLIMENS

BARSAC

VINEYARD SIZE	30 hectares
VINE DENSITY	6,600 stocks per hectare
AVERAGE AGE OF VINEYARD	30 years
AVERAGE PRODUCTION	2,000 cases
SOILS AND SUBSOILS	red sand on fissurated limestone bedrock
GRAPE VARIETIES	Sémillon 100%

"I smell mimosa." Everyone looks at the flower vase placed at the centre of the table. The vase is discarded and the tasting is resumed. The vase isn't the culprit; mimosa still hovers in the glass. "This wine is very spring-like," adds Bérénice Lurton. Indeed, amidst this celestial harmony, notes of narcissus, freesia and a delicate marine scent soon unfold. On the occasion of this mid-March tasting, this 2002 Climens has donned a light coat of white and yellow flowers to harmonize with the clear, radiant weather.

The wines of Château Climens are like a spring day: they have their own kind of sprightly, bouncy energy, like the tight strings of a musical instrument. "Wines are just like us," says Lurton. "Their mood changes with the weather. A heavy atmosphere may break their olfactory palette, whereas a day like this one makes them cheerful and optimistic." The second wine, Cyprès de Climens, shows the same delicate characteristics as the first growth, leaning towards white fruit like pear nectar, green guava and slightly under-ripe banana.

The chartreuse of Climens was built in the 17th century, the two towers that adorn it dating from a century later. Its simple, peaceful lines and elongated shape make it easy to spot in the Barsac landscape. Wine has been made there since the 16th century and has always been celebrated for its constant quality. Sémillon, as the only grape varietal planted on the estate, finds a remarkable expression on these clayey-ferruginous red sands for which the Barsac region is famous, with good natural draining provided by the finely cracked limestone subsoil that shows through the sand in some parts of the vineyard. The 30 hectares of vines, all in one piece, stretch around the château. They were bought in 1971 by Lucien Lurton, Bérénice's father, a passionate winemaker who fell in love with Climens after tasting a few of its old vintages.

The purity of botrytis is a major goal for Bérénice Lurton and her technical manager, Frédéric Nivelle. All the work done at this Barsac estate seems to serve one purpose: an intense commitment to perfection shown by an experienced and dedicated team through ancestral winemaking methods such as the use of endogenous yeasts and fermentation in barrels. The painstaking process of Sauternes grape-picking makes it easy to picture what Lurton means by "devilish harvesting." But the infernal metaphor stops there; the exceptional purity of the wines, their finesse and aerial magic seem to buy them a seat in the most angelic spheres. Lurton insists on the meticulous skills required in the vineyard; she also mentions the need for careful blending when 1 percent of physical difference (i.e. one barrel out of a hundred) is likely to produce 20 percent of aromatic difference.

Lurton does not devote herself only to Climens. She also manages the Château Doisy-Dubroca and fights for a noble cause: the gastronomical dimension of Sauternes wines, whose pairing possibilities are indeed endless—spices, fresh or dried fruit, fresh and smoked fish, shellfish and other seafoods, white meats and poultry—and are waiting to be explored. So many associations to experience! Among those, the most interesting are not the ones based on harmony, but on contrast or subtle kinship, as is the case with many Asian cuisines, Thai dishes playing on the taste balance of lime juice, fish sauce and palm sugar; the sweet spices and coconut creaminess of Malay and Indonesian cooking; or, closer to us, a delicate union of colours and tastes, blue Breton lobster and pink grapefruit.

1. *At Château Climens, wine has been made since the 16th century. The château was built in the 18th century and enlarged in the 19th. The sculpted emblem hints at an ancient custom: when bargemen navigating the Ciron had paid their crossing fees, a cypress sprig was given to them as a token.*

2. *The square towers of the Climens chartreuse are easily spotted in the Barsac countryside. The vineyard, enclosed with ancient walls, is planted with 100% Sémillon vines.*

3. *The aerial magic of Climens wines rests, among other things, on painstakingly meticulous blending. One barrel out of a hundred may suffice to change the wine's taste dramatically.*

Blue Lobster, Pink Grapefruit
and Château Climens Butter

Pierre GAGNAIRE
Pierre Gagnaire - Paris, France

SERVES 4

4 blue lobsters,
1 to 1⅛ pounds (500 g) each

The vegetable garnish
1 to 1⅛ pounds (500 g)
fresh small broad beans

16 small white spring onions

⅔ pound (300 g) fresh green beans

The purée
3¾ cup (500 g) fresh peas

whole milk

1 bottle Château Climens

The syrup
2 pink grapefruits

1 teaspoon potato starch

The butter
11 tablespoons (150 g) cold diced
unsalted butter (1 stick
plus 3 tablespoons)

olive oil

salt and freshly ground black pepper

For the lobsters: Blanch the live lobsters in boiling salted water for 3 minutes, drain them, pull off the claws, and boil them for 2 more minutes. Meanwhile, cool the lobster bodies in ice water, and add the claws when cooked. Shell both the tails and claws. Set aside.

For the vegetable garnish: Shell the broad beans, blanch them in boiling salted water for 1 minute, drain and plunge into iced water. Peel the beans and set them aside. Clean and trim the onions, keeping 1 to 1½ inches (3 to 4 cm) of green parts, slice them thinly, and steam them for 2 minutes. Set aside. Trim the green beans and cut them onto ¾-inch (2-cm) pieces. Boil them briefly in salted water, until tender-crisp, then cool them in ice water and set aside.

For the purée: Shell the peas and cook them in briskly boiling salted water. Cool them in ice water, drain and purée in a blender. Strain the purée, thin it with a little milk, add a little Château Climens. Taste and correct the seasoning. The purée should be light and airy with a lovely bright green colour. Set aside.

For the syrup: Squeeze the grapefruits and reduce the juice by half. Mix the potato starch with a little cold water and pour it, drop by drop, into the boiling grapefruit juice, whisking all the while, until you get a thick syrup. When the texture pleases you, stop adding starch. Set aside.

For the butter: Bring ⅓ cup (8 cl) of the wine to a boil, lower the heat and gradually whisk in the cold diced butter. When the butter sauce is silky and thick, add a little salt and keep warm in a bain-marie.

For the presentation: Slice the lobster tails in half length-wise and reheat them in the Climens butter without boiling. Reheat the vegetables in the grapefruit syrup. Pour the pea purée into 4 small bowls, place the lobster claws on top, seasoning them with a little Château Climens. In 4 large soup plates, arrange the vegetables and the lobster tails. Serve the Climens butter on the side.

GRAND VIN DE SAUTERNES
2005
Château Climens
1ᵉʳ CRU
BARSAC
BÉRÉNICE LURTON
MIS EN BOUTEILLE AU CHATEAU

CHÂTEAU CLIMENS BY ÉRIC BEAUMARD, SILVER MEDAL, BEST SOMMELIER OF THE WORLD, 1998

Completely planted with Sémillon, this "Lord of Barsac" has made wines since the 16th century that are characterised by a rare refinement and delicacy. The dynamic Bérénice Lurton continues to make wines with the unique purity and magic that is the standard here. Among the illustrious vintages of the past century that have produced great and distinctive wines, let us mention 1959, 1983 and 1986; these remain classic examples of what this property is capable of.

CHÂTEAU GUIRAUD

SAUTERNES

VINEYARD SIZE	100 hectares
VINE DENSITY	6,500 stocks per hectare
AVERAGE AGE OF VINEYARD	30 years
AVERAGE PRODUCTION	10,000 cases
SOILS AND SUBSOILS	80% clayey gravel and 20% clayey sand
GRAPE VARIETIES	Sémillon 65% Sauvignon 35%

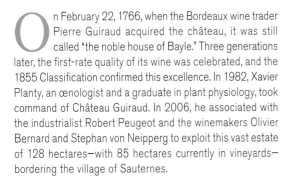

On February 22, 1766, when the Bordeaux wine trader Pierre Guiraud acquired the château, it was still called "the noble house of Bayle." Three generations later, the first-rate quality of its wine was celebrated, and the 1855 Classification confirmed this excellence. In 1982, Xavier Planty, an œnologist and a graduate in plant physiology, took command of Château Guiraud. In 2006, he associated with the industrialist Robert Peugeot and the winemakers Olivier Bernard and Stephan von Neipperg to exploit this vast estate of 128 hectares—with 85 hectares currently in vineyards—bordering the village of Sauternes.

The spacious, magnificent site offers a classic view that soothes the eye. Although the countryside of Sauternais and Médoc are not similar, both irresistibly summon memories of landscape paintings of the past centuries. Neither the Industrial Revolution nor 20th-century agrarian models have substantially altered these landscapes. Guiraud is a good example of this geographical persistence. The plane trees lining the long alley leading to the château, the restrained style in the architecture, the quiet perspective of the whole estate, take you back into the Romantic era.

However, Xavier Planty will not give you a lesson in history. Ecology is what runs in his veins. His work relies on a deep and subtle reflection on soils, vegetation and winemaking. If the château's website is lavishly illustrated with pictures of wild flowers, bees grazing on overripe grape berries, or spiders weaving their web between vine shoots, it is not just for decoration but because Planty prizes ecosystem harmony above all else. He will explain to you why some of the plane trees lining the alley are shorter beyond a 100-foot distance: "This is a spot where underground water accumulates, trapped by clay beds, and prevents the deep rooting of trees." He will also mention, with the same precise eagerness, the thorough

restructuring he performed on the vineyard as soon as he got here, uprooting many stocks of Tannat, Mourvèdre and Cinsault, all ill-adapted southern varietals left by the previous owner—and replaced them with the more region-friendly Sémillon (65 percent) and Sauvignon (35 percent). The vineyard is tended with integrated pest control, with special attention devoted to the wild flora and the management of spring water. On top of that, chaptalisation and cryoextraction are strictly avoided. All conditions produce a wine that blossoms out into an aromatic palette of great purity.

Planty is a keen observer of the biology and organoleptic properties of botrytis. "This fungus," he says, "exponentially multiplies the grape's aromatic powers. Our work consists of promoting its development." For Planty, therein lies one of the great principles of Sauternes winemaking—cultivating the sapidity, not the sugariness. And indeed, the wine's spicy, roasted notes and sapid quality are seductive; umami, the famous "fifth taste" stressed by the Japanese cooking theory, is even present. The first sip provokes hunger, bringing buttered sole meunière and roast chicken to the mind. "A professor at the Leuven University even located Maillard reactions in Sauternes wines!" Planty exclaims, referring to the so-called caramelisation process that enhances the taste of grilled or roasted foods. But he has another reason to be proud of his work: when he recovered the Guiraud vintage collection dating from 1863 to 1929, he invited a former Yquem trader to an investigative vertical tasting. It was discovered that the wine now made at Guiraud was closest in taste and aromas to the one made in 1914, a reputedly superlative vintage. If that is not being on the right track, nothing is.

1. A long, stately alley of plane trees leads from the road to Château Guiraud.

2. 128 hectares, including 100 hectares of vineyard: Château Guiraud is one of the largest wine estates in the Sauternais.

3. The 19th-century château was built in a sober style, following the wish of the family of Protestant wine traders who owned the estate at the time.

Foie Gras Brulé,
Kumquat Confiture and Orange Liqueur Gelée

Jean-Georges VONGERICHTEN
Jean-Georges - New York City, United States

SERVES 4

The foie gras

1 duck foie gras

1 brioche, sliced and toasted

unsalted butter

raw cane sugar, such as
Sugar-in-the-Raw™

fleur de sel

freshly ground pink peppercorns

The confiture

1 quart (1 l) kumquats,
quartered and seeded

1½ cups freshly squeezed orange juice

1 cup pineapple pureé

1½ cups ginger syrup

2 teaspoons salt

The gelée

4 gelatine leaves, ⅛ ounce (2 g) each

3 cups (75 cl) Cointreau

For the foie gras: Clean, marinate and cook the foie gras in the classic Jean-Georges style. Lay out on plastic-lined half-sheet pans and let cool.

For the confiture: Combine all the ingredients in a pot, bring to a boil, reduce to simmer and continue to cook until the liquid has reduced to a thick coating consistency. Remove from heat and cool in an ice bath.

For the gelée: Soak the gelatine in cold water for 15 minutes. Reduce 2½ cups of the Cointreau to 1½ cups. Add the remaining raw alcohol to the reduction.

Stir in the drained gelatine and dissolve. Let set. When set, break up with a hand blender.

For the presentation: Cut the brioche into slices ½-inch (1.5-cm) thick, fry them in butter on both sides and drain them on absorbent paper.

When the foie gras is set, cut it out into rectangles. Place each one on top of a piece of toasted brioche. Dust with some raw cane sugar, and caramelise with a torch. Season with fleur de sel and top with a liberal dusting of ground pink peppercorns. Serve with the confiture and the Cointreau jelly.

CHÂTEAU GUIRAUD BY FRANCK THOMAS, BEST
SOMMELIER OF EUROPE, 2000

Château Guiraud is one of those ageless wines, capable of defying the passage of decades—indeed, of centuries! Mature vintages are unique and sensational, an invitation to travel through time and experience ever-growing emotions evoked by a venerable flask with several centuries of age. Here is an aromatic symphony of sensual pleasure and harmony to satisfy your expectations and reward your patience! Open a bottle in impatient haste and you will experience but a part of the qualities that Guiraud has to offer, without ever enjoying its full, brisk intelligence. It is an aromatic concerto that creates a unique moment of gastronomic bliss.

CHÂTEAU RIEUSSEC

SAUTERNES

VINEYARD SIZE	92 hectares
VINE DENSITY	6,000–8,000 stocks per hectare
AVERAGE AGE OF VINEYARD	35-40 years
AVERAGE PRODUCTION	10,000 cases
SOILS AND SUBSOILS	gravel soils with some clay loam
GRAPE VARIETIES	Sémillon 90% Sauvignon 7% Muscadelle 3%

If you approach the Sauternais starting from Langon, the hills of Rieussec are the first part of the Upper Terrace of Sauternes that you will discover. The elegance and grace of their ample curves is a perfect introduction to this unique region. Even if no wine was made there, you would very probably stay—whatever the season—to contemplate these lovely undulating lines and soft overlapping shapes in the wide-open landscape. Such a radiant beauty, all you want to do is immerse yourself in that splendour. And the spell does not vanish when a lover of this terroir helps you to read its language. Charles Chevallier, property manager for the Domaines Barons de Rothschild (Lafite), does not make a mystery of his passion for Château Rieussec: "Before 1789 and the French Revolution, the property belonged to the Carmelite monks of Langon. When Baron Éric de Rothschild took over the estate in 1985, he asked me to come here and take a look. I fell in love with the place. I believe that Rieussec was the Rothschild's first step abroad because this place is like no other. It is Astérix the Gaul's little village, holding out against the invaders. For indeed it does take a good dose of guts to make Sauternes. . . .

"The magic of great wines and of their terroirs may be experienced anywhere, but here, there is something special—a poker game against nature. Making red wines implies that you fight botrytis. But here, you have to encourage it, promote it, cultivate it in every sense of the word. This constant questioning of our very actions, on every harvest day, is like an erotic fight. In a system where any normal, sensible winemaker harvests its grapes when ripe, we wait for over-ripeness and, plainly, rot. We increase risk to the maximum. For botrytis means never being sure. And from the very moment it settles in, you have to follow it to the end of its process. You no longer have a choice. In 1993, it did not stop raining until December. The grapes were washed of their entire substance. I gave up; the harvesters were sad when they left. Such is the Sauternes culture, that irresistible passion.

"In 1988, we did seven tries in the vineyard. On November 4th, Éric de Rothschild, who was travelling, called me on the phone. I told him the harvest was ending. But later on, I noticed that botrytis was showing timid signs of progress. . . . So I called the Baron back and told him we were resuming the harvest. And so we did, from the fourth of November to the last tries, on the 16th, 17th and 18th. A successful gamble. At Lafite and Duhart-Milon, taking the harvest in takes me less than 10 days. Here, the harvesters do not work more than four hours a day. Another idiosyncrasy of winemaking in Sauternes is the strong synergy uniting the vineyard manager and the maître de chai. If you make red wine, they can be dissociated. But here, the two entities have to work closely together."

The Rieussec vineyard stretches over 92 hectares of clayey gravel, all in one piece around the château, on a total surface of 120 hectares, with a north–south exposure. The vines are 35 to 40 years old on average and include 90 percent Sémillon, 7 percent Sauvignon Blanc and 3 percent Muscadelle. The entire fermentation process is carried in barrels, and ageing is carried on for 16 to 26 months in about 80 percent new oak barrels from the Lafite cooperage.

The wine of Château Rieussec gives out a pure, vivid sensation. A light-coloured, very floral wine through its fragrance and attack, it yields notes of acacia blossom, garden marigold, daisies in the sun and yellow or white fruit (ripe pear, apple, mirabelle plum). Its fruity taste and crisp mouthfeel call for the company of a vanilla-flavoured fruit tart or any apple dessert devised by an inspired chef.

1. *In Château Rieussec's bottle cellar, venerable vintages sleep for many decades.*

2. *The property is located on the site of an ancient monastic wine estate, formerly owned and tended by the Langon Carmelite monks.*

3. *During the four daily hours of harvest, selecting grapes with a perfect amount of noblel rot demands extreme attention—and generously staffed teams.*

Caramelised Apple Croustillant
with Calvados, Rum-raisin Ice Cream

Hiroyuki HIRAMATSU
Hiramatsu - Tokyo, Japan

SERVES 6

The apple croustillant

½ cup (100 g) sugar plus a little for sprinkling

2 tablespoons (25 g) unsalted butter

6 apples

⅔ cup (15 cl) heavy cream Calvados

toasted pine nuts

clarified butter

filo pastry rectangles

The apple coulis

3 green apples

2⅛ cups (50 cl) water

1 scant cup (115 g) sugar

juice of 1 lemon

The nougat

2 cups (150 g) sliced almonds

¾ cup plus 1 tablespoon (100 g) sugar

1 tablespoon (15 g) unsalted butter

rum-raisin ice cream

a few mint leaves

confectioners' sugar

For the apple croustillant: Caramelise the sugar in a saucepan, adding butter towards the end of caramelisation to perfect it.

Put the peeled and diced apples in another saucepan, and cook for a few minutes Add the apples to the caramel, add the cream and cook for a few more minutes. Add a little Calvados and continue cooking. Remove the apples and reduce the cooking liquid until syrupy, then return the apples to the syrup and let cool at room temperature. Measure out about 1 to 2 ounces (50 g) of cooled caramelised apples. Mix them with the toasted pine nuts. Brush the filo rectangles with clarified butter, cover with the apple-pine nut mix and roll up into cylinders. Sprinkle with sugar. Bake for 8 to 10 minutes in a 400°F (200°C) oven, until the surface is well browned and the inside is quite warm.

For the apple coulis: Peel, core and quarter the green apples. Put them in a saucepan with the water, sugar and lemon juice. Caramelise the apples, then let them cool. When cool, place in a blender and purée. Strain the purée.

For the nougat: Toast the almonds. Pour the sugar into a saucepan and caramelise it until lightly coloured. Add the butter and toasted almonds. Spread this paste out about ⅛ inch (3 or 4 mm) thick on a sheetpan lined with parchment paper. Cover with another sheet of parchment paper. Cut the nougat into 1¼ by 1½-inch (3.5 x 4-cm) squares while still hot.

For the presentation: On the middle of a large square plate, draw a line of apple coulis. Add a square of nougat, then a quenelle of rum-raisin ice cream. In front of the coulis, lay a roll of apple croustillant. Decorate with a mint leaf and sprinkle with confectioners' sugar.

CHÂTEAU RIEUSSEC BY MARKUS DEL MONEGO, BEST SOMMELIER OF THE WORLD, 1998

Richness and opulence are the keys to this great wine's charm, which exuberance does not preclude finesse. Aromas of ripe apricots and juicy peaches, as well as citrus and jammy fruit seduce the nose and the palate. Already excellent in its youth, its true rewards await those who are patient: the wine's complexity and aromatic richness increase with each passing year.

CHÂTEAU RABAUD-PROMIS

VINEYARD SIZE	33 hectares
VINE DENSITY	6 600 stocks per hectare
AVERAGE AGE OF VINEYARD	40 years
AVERAGE PRODUCTION	3,000 cases
SOILS AND SUBSOILS	gravelly soils, clayey-gravelly subsoil
GRAPE VARIETIES	Sémillon 80% Sauvignon 20%

The beautifully exposed Rabaud hill is located at the northwestern edge of the famous Upper Terrace of the Sauternes appellation. As you drive upon the small winding road that leads to many First Great Classified Growth châteaux, Rabaud attracts the eye in the same peculiar way that it catches and absorbs the daylight. However, the Rabaud-Promis chartreuse, sitting on the hilltop, will be easier to see from the D116 road which circles around the hill on the north side: there, its elegant shape appears in its entirety. The rather extensive château was built in the late 18th century, in a deceptively simple architectural style, by Victor Louis, architect of the Grand Théâtre de Bordeaux.

The chartreuse is asleep. Awaiting restoration, it opens out in late summer and early autumn to welcome the feasting harvesters in the main salon, between tall chiselled mirrors, marble fireplaces and time-darkened paintings of shady groves and streams. In the quiet courtyard, a small cat and a huge dog are playing in the flower beds, all claws withdrawn and fangs tempered. Nothing here is ostentatious or showy, but you would be mistaken in believing that the peaceful family scenes you may spot here and there mean that a one-dimensional wine is made at this château. Quite the contrary. Rabaud-Promis has a lot to say.

On the 40 hectares covered by the whole estate, 33 hectares are planted in vines and show two different pedologic entities: clayey Pyrenean gravel on the south slope, facing Rayne Vigneau, and sandier gravel to the northwest, towards the Ciron River. This beautiful terroir is planted with 80 percent Sémillon, 20 percent Sauvignon. The property is a result of the division of the former Rabaud estate, which used to cover the entire hill. Its owner, Gaston Drouilhet de Sigalas, believed his land was too heterogeneous. In 1903, he divided it into two parts and sold one to Adrien Promis, who added to his share the Peixoto estate, whose exact location is still not clearly known. Promis kept Rabaud until the mid-20th century, when Pierre Ginestet owned it for a brief period before selling it to Raymond-Louis Lanneluc. Today, the château is still managed by Lanneluc's grandchildren, Michèle and Philippe Déjean.

The barrel and bottle cellar, attached to the château, was built by Philippe Déjean in 1998. After the usual sorting at the vineyard, the harvest is checked on a sorting table, closely watched by the whole family, and then goes into two pneumatic presses. The fermentation is carried by lots, the size of each vat matching the amount of grapes harvested in one day. The must ferments in vats, then the wine is aged in barrels for 12 to 24 months. The second wine, Domaine de l'Estramade, is not made every year. An interesting white wine, Allegria de Rabaud-Promis, is also made in a confidential amount.

Château Rabaud-Promis is an intense and structured Sauternes whose reputation is growing in proportion with the painstaking care its authors devote to it. Ageing extends its aromatic complexity to a spectacular dimension. When young, it has a buttercup yellow colour and lovely notes of gorse and lime blossom. Delicate mushroomy flavours develop with time, maturing into characteristic black truffle aromas. The food pairings are easy to imagine: foie gras, feuilleté of veal sweetbreads or game pies, roasted fowl. This latter affinity is no news to the Déjean family: "Whenever there was roast chicken for dinner," says Philippe, "my father would fetch a bottle of liqueur wine from the cellar !"

1. On the beautiful slopes of the Rabaud-Promis hill, the vines get plenty of sunlight. The château, built by Victor Louis in the late 18th century, used to crown the whole Rabaud estate, now divided into two.

2. The wine is aged from 12 to 14 months in oak barrels.

3. A Sauternes with a remarkable aromatic potency and enough structure to pair up with many different styles of cooking.

Blue Cheese Bavarois
with Sauternes Jelly

Tetsuya WAKUDA
Tetsuya's Restaurant - Sydney, Australia

SERVES 16

The bavarois

2⅛ cups (50 cl) plus 2 cups (45 cl) whole milk

1 vanilla bean

about 4 egg yolks (75 g)

¼ cup plus 2 tablespoons (75 g) sugar

Gorgonzola dolce cheese to taste, about 1⅜ ounces (40 g)

¼ ounce (17 g) leaf gelatine, soaked in cold water for 10 minutes

1 scant cup (20 cl) heavy cream

The Sauternes jelly

3¾ cup (19 cl) Sauternes

⅛ ounce (3.5 g) leaf gelatine, soaked

1 Asian nashi pear, finely diced

For the bavarois: Pour the 2⅛ cups milk into a pot, add the vanilla bean and bring to the boil. Whisk together the egg yolks and sugar until completely combined and light in colour. Add half of the boiled milk to the egg and sugar mixture while whisking. Pour this back into the milk in the pot and cook until the mixture coats the back of a spoon.

Crumble the cheese and add to the custard mixture while still hot, tasting to check how strong the mixture becomes. Add the soaked gelatine and stir until dissolved. Add the remaining 1⅞ cup (45 cl) milk.

Strain the mixture into a bowl and place over another bowl of ice, stirring until the mixture thickens slightly. Add the cream while still stirring over ice, then pour the mixture into the moulds and let set overnight.

For the Sauternes jelly: Slowly bring the Sauternes to the boil in a large saucepan to burn off the alcohol. Set aside to cool a little. Squeeze out the excess water from the gelatine and stir into the Sauternes until dissolved.

Pour the mixture through a fine-mesh sieve. Cover and refrigerate 3 to 4 hours, or until set. Gently mix with diced pear.

For the presentation: Peel the pear and cut it in small pieces. Mix with the Sauternes jelly. Turn out the bavarois and serve with the jelly.

CHÂTEAU
Rabaud-Promis
— 2005 —
Premier Grand Cru Classé
SAUTERNES

CHÂTEAU RABAUD-PROMIS BY YOICHI SATO,
BEST SOMMELIER OF JAPAN, 2005

With its incredible power in the mouth, this wine has the necessary structure to take the lead in a classic French winter meal. It will work equally well with an apricot tart or with my favourite dessert, an orange soufflé just out of the oven. Under any circumstances, I'm certain that this wine will bring a lot to a meal.

CHÂTEAU SIGALAS-RABAUD

SAUTERNES

VINEYARD SIZE	14 hectares
VINE DENSITY	6,600 stocks per hectare
AVERAGE AGE OF VINEYARD	40 years
AVERAGE PRODUCTION	2,000 cases
SOILS AND SUBSOILS	siliceous gravel on a clay subsoil
GRAPE VARIETIES	Sémillon 80% Sauvignon 20%

"The vine is the worst of all mistresses, as my father used to say. The costly, whimsical type. But everyone knows that the worst mistresses are also the best, the ones that give you the greatest pleasures." The Marquis de Lambert des Granges could not sum up his relationship with his land any better. He mentions it tenderly, speaks of the vine as of a person. And, recalling that overripe grape harvesting is the particularity of Sauternes, he adds, "That makes us a crazy lot."

The original château was at Rabaud-Promis, a short distance uphill. Back in the 18th century, it sat on top of the large Rabaud estate, which included both properties. In 1863, Rabaud was acquired by Henri Drouilhet de Sigalas, great-great-grandfather of René de Lambert des Granges. Widowed at the birth of his one son, he left the child to a wet nurse in the Landes forest. At the age of 15, when the younger Mr. de Sigalas returned home, he was a wild man who did not speak any French and could not care less about the vineyard. Ten years later, his French had improved considerably, but his devotion to the vineyard had not. In 1903, as he found the estate too heterogeneous, he sold the northern part of Rabaud as well as Peixoto, a sandy estate located downhill, to the Promis family, keeping for himself his favourite part of the land, the gravelly south slope, "the jewel of Sigalas."

In the late 1920s, a well-meaning friend suggested to de Sigalas that he should associate with the Promis family. But the reconstruction of the estate put him in a weak position; he died three months later and his share of the estate was absorbed by Promis. The label still displayed the Sigalas coat of arms, but it bore the name "Château Rabaud" until 1948. The 1949 and 1959 vintages were labelled "Sigalas-Rabaud and Rabaud-Promis Reunited." But in the meantime, the bad harvests of the 1930s and '40s, the turmoil of history and a few family problems had lowered the quality and reputation of the wine.

In 1950, Fernand Ginestet, then the tenant farmer of Rabaud, planned to buy Château Margaux. As the sole owner of the original Promis shares, he offered them to Mrs. de Lambert des Granges, born Sigalas. The Sigalas-Rabaud estate recovered its pre-1930s state, one-third of the ancient Rabaud—but some third, with 14 hectares of beautiful Pyrenean gravel and a homogeneous vineyard, perfectly fit to produce a great wine.

The grapes are harvested at a stage called "shrivelled-up hairy," when the juice smells of blooming lime trees. The painstakingly sorted berries go into a pneumatic press for a slow pressing, and then undergo further pressing in antique vertical presses. Then the must spends two or three days in debourbage vats kept at a temperature of 8°C–10°C, before being warmed to 20°C. As soon as fermentation begins, the must is led into barrels where it stays from four to six weeks at low temperature. The ageing is carried on for 20 months in an air-conditioned cellar. When young, the wine of Sigalas-Rabaud still smells of lime blossom. A feminine and elegant wine, it has been nicknamed "the Barsac of Sauternes" for its freshness and delicacy.

The Marquis explains that Sauternes wines go through three main stages in their lifetime. During their first three to five years, they are fresh and pleasant, fruity and flowery. They are then good to drink before meals. After that stage, they dry up a little bit and alcohol is more dominant. This may be referred to as adolescence, or even as the awkward stage. It is not possible to know in advance how long this crossing of the desert may last—three months, two years, perhaps five years. And then? "Oh, then," says the Marquis, "sixty years of bliss."

1. The château stands on the "jewel of Sigalas," a beautiful terroir of Pyrenean gravel.

2. A detail of one of the paintings that decorate the barrel cellar.

3. Wisteria adorns the walls, but the floral aroma of Château Sigalas-Rabaud leans more towards lime blossom in the early years of ageing.

Warm Gillardeau Oyster Cannelloni, *Foie Gras and Watercress Vermicelli*

Christian SINICROPI
La Palme d'Or - Cannes, France

SERVES 4

The pasta dough

⅔ cup (80 g) flour

2 egg yolks

1 tablespoon olive oil

salt

The garnish

⅛ pound (50 g) foie gras per serving

8 n°2 oysters (medium oysters)

1 teaspoon plus 2 teaspoons (5 g plus 10 g) unsalted butter

1⅜ ounces (40 g) vermicelli

2 teaspoons dry white wine

1 cup (25 cl) water

1 tablespoon (10 g) grated Parmesan

salt and freshly ground black pepper

aged red wine vinegar reduced with a little honey

1 grey shallot, about ⅔ ounce (20 g)

a few crushed peppercorns

4 bunches of watercress, picked and washed

juice of 1 lemon

1 tablespoon olive oil

salt

For the pasta dough: Pile the flour into a volcano shape and add the 2 egg yolks, oil and salt in the crater. First stir with one finger, mixing gently. Then knead until you get a smooth dough. Put it in a bowl, cover with plastic wrap and let it rest for 30 minutes.

In a saucepan, bring some salted water to the boil. Roll out the dough paper-thin (4 mm thick) on a lightly floured board. Cut it into 4 x 4-inch (11 x 11-cm) squares. Cook these for 40 seconds in the boiling water, then throw them into cold water. Drain well. Then lay them onto a dish in an overlapped manner, cover them with plastic wrap and keep refrigerated.

For the garnish: Season the foie gras with salt and pepper, sear in a non-stick pan. Set aside on a plate. Do not refrigerate.

Shuck the oysters. Keep them refrigerated.

Melt 1 teaspoon (5 g) butter in a saucepan. Add the vermicelli and fry it until lightly coloured. Deglaze with the white wine. Add the water and boil until reduced. Stir in the remaining butter and the Parmesan cheese. Taste and correct the seasoning, and set aside.

For the presentation: Halve each square of dough. Place a slice of foie gras on each one.

Cover the foie gras with vermicelli, add 2 drained oysters, then roll up the dough into cannelloni.

In a non-stick pan, lightly brown the surface of the cannelloni. Then place them on a dish.

Brush each cannelloni with a thin layer of reduced vinegar, then garnish with the chopped shallot and a pinch of crushed pepper. Cut each cannelloni in two crosswise. Place the cannelloni onto warmed plates, add some watercress and season with salt, lemon juice and olive oil.

CHÂTEAU SIGALAS-RABAUD BY OLIVIER POUSSIER, BEST SOMMELIER OF THE WORLD, 2000

Freshness, finesse and balance—these are the aims of the Lambert des Granges family, who watches over the fortunes of this First Growth. These goals are achieved with great talent, thanks to meticulous work in developing a Haut-Sauternes terroir so well suited for the growth of the precious Botrytis cinerea. A sure value for lovers of Sauternes.

CHÂTEAU DE MYRAT

VINEYARD SIZE	22 hectares
VINE DENSITY	6,800 stocks per hectare
AVERAGE AGE OF VINEYARD	21 years
AVERAGE PRODUCTION	2,500 cases
SOILS AND SUBSOILS	clay-limestone on fissurated limestone bedrock
GRAPE VARIETIES	Sémillon 88% Sauvignon 8% Muscadelle 4%

A fragile grace seems to permeate the whole place, from the beautiful chartreuse built in a pure 18th-century style to the bounty of powdery yellow mimosa and magnolia blossoms in the garden, not to forget the wine—delicate, lacy, aromatic, fresh and delicious, with a nose of wisteria and freshly baked brioche. With a nostalgic smile, Xavier de Pontac remembers the 1950s: "In those days, when local priests traded wines, a bottle of Barsac was worth three bottles of Château Cheval-Blanc. The exchange rate has changed." This descendant of Arnaud de Pontac—the man who created château wines in the 17th century—greets you simply and courteously at Château Myrat, which, he points out, is "two days away from Bordeaux on horseback. You have to remember that the Bordeaux chartreuse got its name from the Carthusian monasteries—it was meant as a retirement place from the hectic pace of city life."

The estate covers 30 hectares, 8 for the park and 22 for the vineyard, planted with 88 percent Sémillon, 8 percent Sauvignon Blanc and 4 percent Muscadelle. From the antiquity of the viticultural facilities—the footbath for the horses' feet; the large vertical presses under the huge, twisted beams of a venerable roof structure—you could believe that wine has been made here for centuries. Actually, Château de Myrat is spiritually young, as its vineyard is the result of a resurrection process.

"We just celebrated the 20th anniversary of the vineyard," says de Pontac. My father bought this estate in 1936, stripped the chartreuse bare of all the creeping ivy and bramble, and finally replanted the vineyard. Sauternes wines, at the time, reached high prices. Then came the mediocre from 1960 to 1969. Winemaking being no longer profitable, my father shocked everybody in town by pulling out every single vine he had planted before. When he died, in April 1988, my brother Jacques and I realized that if, within the next few months, the vineyard was still bare, our planting rights would not be renewed. So, between the Pentecost and the 1st of August, we replanted all the vines. We had difficult beginnings, for then came the excellent 1988, 1989 and 1990 vintages, and all we could do was watch our neighbours making their wines." But de Pontac has his share of the winemaking skills that have run in the family since the 17th century. Château de Myrat, beneath its lovely engraved label, unites sweetness and freshness in a miraculous alchemy. The wine is aerial, honeyed and lemony, beautifully chiselled by its author. "It is crucial," he says, "not to contradict the terroir and to obtain the best botrytis possible. Botrytis gives the smoky, spicy touch. The more there is, the finer the sweetness and the fruit will be. And the wood of the barrel plays the part of salt and pepper."

On the subject of food, de Pontac remembers a meal he had at Alain Senderens' restaurant in Paris, 15 years ago, and his conversation with the chef and his sommeliers. "It was so absorbing that I missed my plane. Senderens cried out, 'Two thirds of my menu may be served with Sauternes!' When you mention Sauternes food pairings, though, most sommeliers look appalled. They do not often stray from classic, unimaginative pairings like foie gras and desserts. As a result, Sauternes are not popular enough, in spite of their wonderful gastronomic potential. And they seem to scare people away, though everybody loves them if you ask them." And indeed, how does one not love Château de Myrat along a delicate fish dish or freshly caught prawns, served in a sunny harmony of chickpea cream and olive oil?

1. *In the controlled atmosphere of the barrel cellar, the wine waits many months for its ageing to be complete. The clock counts only hours.*

2. *The harvest reception zone at Château de Myrat: the facilities have little changed since the 19th century.*

3. *Château de Myrat takes on a remarkably intense colour after a few years.*

Chickpea Purée *with Gamberi Shrimp*

Fulvio PIERANGELINI
Gambero Rosso - San Vincenzo, Italy

SERVES 4

The chickpeas

½ cup (100 g) dried chickpeas
1 garlic clove
1 small sprig rosemary

The shrimp

1¾ pound (800 g) large fresh shrimp
(*gamberi*)
extra virgin olive oil
salt and freshly ground black pepper

For the chickpeas: Soak the chickpeas in cold water overnight.

The next day, cook the chickpeas with the garlic and rosemary in a generous amount of salted water. When soft, drain in a colander, reserving the cooking liquid. Discard the rosemary. Mash or blend the chickpeas into a purée, thinning it down with a little of the cooking liquid.

For the shrimp: Shell and de-vein the shrimp, removing the dark thread on the back. Steam the shrimp.

For the presentation: Divide the chickpea purée among 4 soup bowls.

Place the steamed shrimp on top. Drizzle with some extra virgin olive oil, and season with salt and pepper to taste. Serve warm.

CHÂTEAU DE MYRAT BY SERGE DUBS,
BEST SOMMELIER OF THE WORLD, 1989

One of the Great Classified Growths of Sauternes, with the appealing ability to surprise the palates of the most demanding tasters. A particularity of this wine is an oft-displayed light orange tint and a deep golden colour, which indicate the marvellous effects of botrytis and over-ripeness. Aromas of Corinthian grapes, dates, jammy kumquat, saffron and vanilla honey are sweet, suave, rich and ample. In the mouth there is unctuosity without heaviness, thanks to an underlying acidity, which brings out a dashing temperament and liveliness rooted in the château's location in this sector of Barsac.

CHÂTEAU DOISY DAËNE

SAUTERNES

VINEYARD SIZE	16 hectares
VINE DENSITY	7,000 stocks per hectare
AVERAGE AGE OF VINEYARD	40 years
AVERAGE PRODUCTION	3,000 cases
SOILS AND SUBSOILS	thin layer of clayey sand—"Barsac red sand"—covering a lightly fissurated limestone subsoil
GRAPE VARIETIES	Sémillon 89% Sauvignon 11%

A visit to Château Doisy Daëne inevitably brings hope, as you expect to find the answer to an enigma. You found the enigma in a glass where, for the first time, you saw the wine spinning, all golden and sprightly, with a masculine yet tender attack and an intense arpeggio of fresh citrus peel—citron, grapefruit, lime. Naturally, you adored it, but something kept eluding you. And since you are now going to meet the author of this wine, you will certainly get to the bottom of it. It is a case of now or never: you are counting on Denis Dubourdieu, a world-famous œnologist and the head of the brand new ISVV (Institute of Vine and Wine Sciences) in Bordeaux—the largest winemaking and wine-tasting research centre in the world—to tell you all. And so he will, with great kindness, much enthusiasm and many details.

Briefly, he will recall the history of the old Doisy estate, which was divided into three after the 1855 Classification, the name of its owner, Daëne, staying attached to the 16 hectares of Dubourdieu's property and the purchase of the estate by his grandfather in 1924 and its management by four generations of Dubourdieus (Denis's sons, Fabrice and Jean-Jacques, have joined the business, which he runs with his wife, Florence). He will mention the thorough cultivation of the vineyard, such an important feature to him, and show you the admirable Barsac red sand of the property, un-weeded, deeply ploughed and carefully earthed up. He will explain that the vine cropping is done not only in the air but also in the ground; the superficial root system must be trimmed so that the larger roots go seek their nutrients in the subsoil. He will add that his vines never see a drop of chemical weed killer and are only fed vegetable-based compost. And you will learn that *Botrytis cinerea* makes the grapes go crazy, deregulating their genome and increasing hundredfold their production of flavour precursors. The Doisy style, he says, is freshness without acidity, a pseudo-cooling sensation due to aromatic intensity, a distinctive toning-down

of the sugary perception and a typical citron-lemon-bergamot taste profile. Through this style, he identifies the mark of three generations of winemakers who brought it forward. Terroir, he says, is first and foremost a matter of taste definition. And how does the terroir convey that taste? "The most interesting wines always have a mystery at the core," he simply answers.

Either through the first wine or the *cuvée spéciale*—L'Extravagant de Doisy Daëne—or even the remarkable dry white wine of the estate, which takes on incredible truffle aromas at it ages, the Dubourdieu style is easy to grasp. It never clarifies the mystery but helps it to speak, boosts the flavour, lets the terroir express itself fully. Such is the true nature of state-of-the-art œnology; it does not separate man from Earth but, on the contrary, intensifies their mutual harmony.

According to Denis Dubourdieu, the best place to store a bottle of Sauternes is the refrigerator door. As you open it, the clinking of the glass annoys you—which makes it clear that you need to put in two bottles, not one—so you open the bottle and drink some of it. And when the bottles are empty, you replace them. And what is, according to him, the best time to drink Sauternes? The early evening, he says. You feel relaxed, a little hungry, your mind is free to enjoy the full Sauternes experience. Which is drinking it.

1. *"The best hour for tasting a Sauternes is the early evening", says Denis Dubourdieu, owner of Château Doisy Daëne. Tasting requires concentrated attention, but also a relaxed approach.*

2. *Château Doisy Daëne is a part of the former Doisy estate, one of the oldest wine properties in Barsac.*

3. *A door opens out onto the cellar, without revealing the secret that lies at the heart of great wines.*

Exotic Citrus and Jasmine Tea
"en gelée" Perfumed with Herbs

David KINCH

Manresa - Los Gatos (Ca), United States

SERVES 6

1½ cups (36 cl) Meyer lemon juice, from the ripest lemons possible

1 ounce (25 g) finest grade jasmine tea

1⅔ cup (40 cl) mineral water

¾ cup (170 g) sugar

½ cup (10 cl) lime juice

approximately 4 sheets leaf gelatine (8 g)

1 fresh yuzu

This is a deceptively simple dish in which one obtains complexity by finding the most varieties of different fruit and herbs at one"s disposal. It is worth the search.

Use as many different types of citrus as you can muster; for example: Meyer lemons, grapefruit, oranges, mandarins, satsumas, low-acid limes, etc. If you can find three different mandarins to compose this dish, it will only play better into the hands of the perfume and complexity of the Doisy Daène.

In California, the coast hills are filled with yerba buena, a wild mint with a haunting perfume. Use as many different mint-type herbs, both cultivated and wild as you can find; for example: lemon balm, marjoram, spearmint, peppermint, hyssop, yerba buena, etc.

For the infusion: The day before, squeeze enough Meyer lemons to obtain the 1½ cups (36 cl) of juice. Do not strain. Bring the juice to a simmer and add the jasmine tea. Remove the pot from the heat, cover the top with plastic wrap, and allow to cool to room temperature.

For the syrup: Make a syrup with the water and sugar. Allow to cool and then add the lime juice.

For the gelée: Soak the gelatine in approximately 1 cup (25 cl) of cold water to soften the sheets. Measure out exactly 1½ cups (350 ml) of the lime syrup. Combine with the tea infusion. Pour off approximately half the mixture and reserve. Remove the gelatine from the water and squeeze to remove excess moisture. Add the gelatine to the tea mixture and place over low heat. Stir until the gelatine has dissolved and then add it to the rest of the infusion. Allow to cool and set overnight.

The same day: Pick the smallest, most delicate leaves of the herbs. Soak and gently wash in a bowl of ice water, then remove and pat dry.

Peel and segment the various citrus fruits.

For the presentation: Arrange the citrus segments in an attractive manner at the bottom of a bowl. Gently stir the gelée as if you were breaking up delicate cheese curds. Spoon the gelée over the top of fruit. Garnish the gelée with the individual leaves of the various herbs. Grate the yuzu zest over the top and serve immediately.

CHÂTEAU DOISY DUBROCA

VINEYARD SIZE	3.3 hectares
VINE DENSITY	6 600 stocks per hectare
AVERAGE AGE OF VINEYARD	30 years
AVERAGE PRODUCTION	300 cases
SOILS AND SUBSOILS	red sand on a fissurated limestone bedrock
GRAPE VARIETIES	Sémillon 100%

The Doisy vineyard is one of the oldest wine estates in Barsac; some of it can be traced back to the 16th century. In the early 19th century, Jullien refers to it in his *Topography of All Known Vineyards* as one of the best wines of Haut Barsac. The wines of Doisy, he writes, "are remarkable for their body, their liqueurous quality, their opulence and their bouquet." Thus, the Doisy estate obtained quite naturally the rank of Second Classified Growth in 1855.

Soon after the classification, the hazards of inheritance caused Doisy to be divided into three parts. One part took the name of the Chevaliers de Védrines, who owned the place until 1846; another kept the name of Daëne, who owned Doisy at the time of the classification. The Dubroca family bought the 4 remaining hectares. In 1880, Miss Dubroca married Mr. Gounouilhou, the printer and publisher of the Bordeaux daily *La Petite Gironde*, who already owned the château Climens and was receiving Doisy Dubroca as a dowry. The two châteaux's destinies remained linked for more than a century, as Lucien Lurton bought both of them in 1971. Between 1992 and 2009, Doisy Dubroca was separated from its illustrious neighbour, but the Château Climens has temporarily taken over its management.

Doisy Dubroca is the smallest of the Doisys, but it has no reason to blush for it. Its terroir of Barsac red sands and Mindelian gravel on an asteriated limestone subsoil benefits from an excellent exposure, softly sloping to the southeast. Planted entirely with Sémillon, the vineyard enjoys abundant sunlight and good natural drainage. It also produces a second wine, Les Demoiselles de Doisy.

Although the hesperidated aromatic structure is a common character of the three Doisys, as is evident with Doisy Daëne and Doisy-Védrines each one of the three wines expresses its own personality in an assertive way. Doisy Daëne does it through an elegant bouquet of citron and grapefruit zest, and a fresh golden sensation that dazzles the mind and makes the wine a near-alchemical elixir. Doisy-Védrines, with a sunny expression of preserved citrus and orange peel, starts from the same base but directs the sensations towards an admirable brightness and notes of yellow peach. Doisy Dubroca, on this citrusy frame, develops warm notes of apricot with light touches of amaretto, particularly after some time. This wine is endowed with wonderful ageing qualities, and it needs a decade to reach its full almond-y dimension.

1. In the late 19th century, the four hectares of Château Doisy Dubroca belonged to the Gounouilhous, a family of press printers. The estate is now managed by the team of Château Climens.

2. The "smallest of the three Doisys" develops seductive notes of apricot and amaretto with age.

3. The vines grow on a typically Barsac terroir of ferruginous red sand on a limestone subsoil.

Caramel Apple,
Vanilla Ice Cream and Calvados

Peter GOOSSENS
Hof Van Cleve - Kruishoutem, Belgium

SERVES 4

The ice cream

2⅛ cups (50 cl) whole milk

3 vanilla pods, split length-wise

1⅛ cups (225 g) superfine sugar

about 12 large egg yolks
(240 g), about 1 cup

2⅛ cups (50 cl) heavy cream

The Calvados sabayon

3 egg yolks

3 tablespoons (45 g) superfine sugar

1½ teaspoons Calvados

⅓ cup (9 cl) dry white wine

1 vanilla pod, split length-wise

½ cup (100 g) whipped cream

The caramel

1 cup (200 g) superfine sugar

⅓ cup (8 cl) glucose

½ cup (10 cl) orange juice

1¼ cups (30 cl) heavy cream

The croustillant

1 scant cup (20 cl) water

2 cups (400 g) sugar

1 cup plus 1 tablespoon (135 g) flour

14 tablespoons (200 g)
unsalted butter (¾ stick)

2½ tablespoons pure vanilla extract

The crumble

14 tablespoons (200 g)
unsalted butter (¾ stick)

½ cup (100 g) cane sugar

⅔ cup (100 g) firmly packed brown sugar

1 teaspoon salt

1⅓ cups (175 g) flour

The apple cream

⅓ pound (140 g) diced Golden Delicious apple

⅛ cup (25 g) superfine sugar

1¾ teaspoons lemon juice

pure vanilla extract

⅓ gelatine leaf, soaked for 10 minutes in cold water

The jelly

3½ ounces (100 g) Boiron black currant pulp

2½ tablespoons (35 g) sugar

½ teaspoon agar-agar

1 gelatine leaf, soaked for 10 minutes in cold water

⅓ cup (7.5 cl) water

The garnish

4 Golden Delicious apples

zest of 1 lime

sugar syrup

For the ice cream: Make a crème anglaise with the milk, sugar and yolks. Boil the milk with the vanilla pods, cover and let infuse off the heat for 20 minutes. Whisk the yolks with the sugar until pale and creamy, add the hot milk, little by little, whisking all the while and cook over low heat, stirring, until the custard coats a spatula. Use the spatula to stir the custard in a to-and-fro movement to keep it smooth, and add the cream. Freeze in an ice-cream maker according to the manufacturer's directions.

For the Calvados sabayon: Mix all ingredients except for the whipped cream, and whisk the sabayon in a double boiler until it triples in volume. When cool, fold in the whipped cream.

For the caramel: Cook the sugar with the glucose and the orange juice. When nicely browned, add the cream slowly and mix well.

For the croustillant: Mix all the ingredients and spread them into a fine layer onto a silicone mat. Bake in a 350°F (175°C) oven for 10 minutes.

For the crumble: Mix all the ingredients and spread them into a fine layer on a baking sheet. Bake in a 400°F (200°C) oven for 15 minutes.

For the apple cream and the jelly: Mix all the ingredients except for the gelatine and boil them. Let cool slightly, add the drained and squeezed gelatine. Mix the preparation and pour it onto small plates. Refrigerate.

For the garnish: Cut out 16 apple balls using a melon baller. Caramelise them slightly. Cut the remaining lime zest into julienne and blanch it three times in boiling water; then cook it in sugar syrup. Shortly before serving, cut some apple into small cubes.

For the presentation: On each plate, drop a quenelle of vanilla ice cream. Beside the ice cream, place small portions of apple cream, Calvados sabayon, sugar crumble, caramel sauce and diced black currant jelly. Decorate with a vanilla croustillant, diced apple and the candied lime zest julienne.

CHÂTEAU DOISY DUBROCA BY VIRGINIA PHILIP,
BEST SOMMELIER OF THE UNITED STATES, 2002

Château Doisy Dubroca has a rare cépagement of 100 percent Sémillon, giving the wine a more rounded profile. Ripe notes of honey, apricot, peach and lemon on the nose with the addition of spice box nuances from the oak, make this wine easy to drink. Full-bodied and round, the wine has fresh fruit, jasmine and white peach on the palate. The oak profile carries over on the palate adding a bit of weight and texture. The acidity remains balanced, moving into the long, lingering palate with a hint of raciness and mineral.

CHÂTEAU DOISY-VÉDRINES

BARSAC

VINEYARD SIZE	27 hectares
VINE DENSITY	6,600 stocks per hectare
AVERAGE AGE OF VINEYARD	40 years
AVERAGE PRODUCTION	3,000 cases
SOILS AND SUBSOILS	red soil on a clay-limestone bedrock
GRAPE VARIETIES	Sémillon 80% Sauvignon 15% Muscadelle 5%

The Château Doisy-Védrines, in Barsac, is one of three wine properties that were created from the division of the Château Doisy, soon after the 1855 Classification had consecrated this large estate as Second Growth. The name of Védrines was given as a reference to the Chevaliers de Védrines, who were the owners of Doisy until 1846. They were followed by the Castéja family, who still own the Château Doisy-Védrines. Olivier Castéja manages the estate, which definitely has a charm of its own, with its lovely round-towered chartreuse, decorated inside in green and gold hues. As is often the case in Barsac, the vines start a few steps away from the château, right in front of it—20 hectares of Barsac red sands, all in one piece, on a clay-limestone subsoil. The planting is 80 percent Sémillon, 15 percent Sauvignon and 5 percent Muscadelle. A deuxième vin, Château Petit-Védrines, is also produced.

The purity of Barsac wines is a direct result of the quality of the harvest. To obtain these wonderful wines, a whole set of precautions is needed—the hiring of experimented harvesters; a painstaking harvesting process, with six to eight successive tries (selective pickings) in order to pick nothing but concentrated berries touched by a noble and pure botrytis; a gentle extraction of the must in low-pressure pneumatic presses; and finally a daily check of the fermentation in barrels to reach a perfect balance. Thus, the typicity of Château Doisy-Védrines makes it a consistent, structured, brilliant but not extravagant wine. Ideally served before a meal or alongside delicate foods, it is lively, joyful and intensely fruity. Ripe peach is a prominent note, yellow or white, fresh or preserved, with the slight bitter tang of antique, near-forgotten peach varieties. All of the aromatic range of the peach is expressed through the typical Doisy hesperidated, citrusy structure.

Indeed, the division of Sauternes estates throughout history has produced in some places a certain amount of dispersion in the vineyards, but it bears some interest for a curious wine taster. In a few cases, it allows the identification of a family style and highlights the magical quality of terroir—without, of course, revealing any of its deeper secrets. Thus, there is a definite "Doisy style," a special aromatic freshness based on citrus peel, where grapefruit and lemon dominate. A slight end-of-palate astringency elevates this typicity to the delicate bitterness of Thai pomelo, giving the wine a bright energy, which makes these wines ideal companions for Southeast Asian and South Chinese cuisines. Château Doisy-Védrines, a lovely bouquet of orange, Sicilian lemon and Asian pomelo zests in a golden, uplifting liqueur, is unmistakably part of the family.

However, with Sauternes and Barsac wines, nothing is ever as simple as it seems; wines born from such a complex harvesting process would never allow that. The expression of the terroir is one thing, the mark of the botrytis is another, but there is also an elusive criterion that should be taken into account—the mood of the wine. When you taste Doisy-Védrines on a hot, sunny spring day, an unexplained mystery lingers in your mind. You will never know whether the delicious sunshine you found in the glass was enhanced by that day's bright sunlight or if it would have been the same under a grey sky. Actually, you do know for sure it would still be there, intact, but you do not tell—you are only looking for an excuse to go back and taste some more the next time it rains.

1. The graceful, rustic chartreuse of Doisy-Védrines was built in the 18th century.

2. The purity of the wine depends on the quality of the harvest. Vine rows are checked up to six to eight times. At each trie, only the berries showing perfect botrytis are picked.

3. "Sunshine brews," as François Mauriac used to describe Sauternes wines.

Walnuts
with Dried Berries

René REDZEPI
Noma - Copenhagen, Denmark

SERVES 4

The walnut ice

2 cups plus 2½ tablespoons
(275 g) walnuts

½ cup (13.5 cl) heavy cream

¼ cup (5 cl) whole milk

⅓ cup (115 g) Trimoline
(inverted sugar)

⅓ cup (65 g) sugar

⅓ ounce (10 g) maltodextrin

½ teaspoon salt

⅛ ounce (2 g) sorbet stabiliser

The walnut powder

1 ounce (30 g) maltodextrin

3 tablespoons (45 g) walnuts

1½ teaspoons walnut oil

1 scant tablespoon confectioners' sugar

¼ teaspoon salt

The dried berries

2 ounces (50 g) freeze-dried
blackberries

1 quart (1 l) liquid nitrogen

The frozen milk

1 cup (25 cl) whole milk

1 cup (25 cl) heavy cream

For the walnut ice: Blanch the walnuts 4 times in boiling water and cool them down in ice water.

Heat up half the milk and add the sorbet stabiliser. Process all the other ingredients in a Thermomix, and then mix the two batches together. Pass through a fine-mesh sieve and freeze in Pacojet containers.

For the walnut powder :Blanch the walnuts four times and dry them in the oven for 30 minutes at 325°F (160°C). Thermomix until smooth. When cool, whisk into all the other components and mix well.

For the dried berries: Pour the berries into the liquid nitrogen and blend them in the Thermomix until you get a rough powder.

For the frozen milk: Mix the milk and cream and blend into a foam with an immersion blender, let the excess liquid in the foam fall down for 30 seconds, then scoop out the foam into the liquid nitrogen in order to freeze it. Crush the frozen "clouds" into a coarse powder and store in the freezer.

For the presentation: Process the walnut ice in a Pacojet ,and drop a few scoops into the centre of a frozen plate. Dump the frozen milk into the nitrogen very briefly and then sprinkle it on top of the ice cream along with the berry and walnut powders.

CHÂTEAU DOISY-VÉDRINES BY ÉRIC BEAUMARD,
SILVER MEDAL, BEST SOMMELIER OF THE WORLD, 1998

This wine is of an intense, bright yellow colour. The ample, delicate nose is remarkable for its bouquet where tropical fruits merge with citrus, light caramel and vanilla. A careful ageing makes the wine all the more charming and refined. The ample, sensuous, weightless mouthfeel is typical of the Barsac aerial typicity. The reasonably lengthy end-of-mouth persistency reveals lovely, clear-cut aromatic notes of candied pineapple, mango and toffee. Unmistakably, a true Barsac through its charm, freshness and seductive power, even at a young age.

CHÂTEAU D'ARCHE

VINEYARD SIZE	27 hectares
VINE DENSITY	6,600 stocks per hectare
AVERAGE AGE OF VINEYARD	45 years
AVERAGE PRODUCTION	4,000 cases
SOILS AND SUBSOILS	gravel and clay for both soil and subsoil
GRAPE VARIETIES	Sémillon 80% Sauvignon 20%

As you drive from Bommes, a short distance from Sauternes, this beautiful 17th-century chartreuse is easy to spot on the right-hand side of the road. Its elongated, one-level buildings surround a vast courtyard. Two square towers look over its seductive, simple shape, whose classic nobility is graced with a rustic touch. Set in enfilade, its rooms were ideally disposed to be converted into nine luxurious guest rooms. It would be, however, impossible to gaze at the château without admiring the surrounding landscape, an ancient vineyard growing on an exceptional terroir, on the soft, peaceful background of the Sauternes hills.

Before the French Revolution, the château was the property of the Comtes d'Arche, who gave it their name. Later, it passed through the hands of several successive owners, including the Dubédat and Bastit Saint-Martin families. The estate is now managed by a group of investors and directed by Jérôme Cosson, a dedicated winemaker.

The 40-hectare vineyard, including 27 hectares for the production of the classified growth, enjoys a full southern exposure, which insures that the grapes get the maximum amount of sunlight. The planting is composed of 80 percent Sémillon and 20 percent Sauvignon Blanc, the average age of the vines being 45 years. Some vine stocks, on the hilltop close to the château, even reach a venerable 100 years of age. Thick and gnarled, they still bear clusters of grapes whose highly concentrated juice goes into the *cuvée spéciale*. Various types of soils are found throughout the plots: gravel on hilltops, clay on hillsides and silts on the lower parts. This variety allows modulation of the blending according to the character sought in the wine—finesse from the silts, aroma from the clay, structure and vigour from the gravel.

Respect for the environment is a major concern at the Château d'Arche. "We have warm soils with a high draining power," says Cosson. "They warm up and cool down quickly. For quite a long time, we have been working in 'lutte raisonnée,' and we have managed to get rid of pesticides.

"The grapes are sorted at the vineyard, then we put them into antique vertical presses, which give clear musts needing very little decanting. The musts are preassembled in vats and tasted before we add yeasts and send them to ferment in oak barrels. To respect our wines' particular style, we never use more than one-third new barrels each year. We expect Château d'Arche to be delicate, precise and sharp, with a clear fruity expression."

Casson then refers to a recent scientific study; a substance secreted by the vine to fight the botrytis fungus, still present in the liqueur wines, is believed to protect against cardiovascular diseases. François Mauriac did not describe Sauternes as "liqueurs of sunshine" without good reason. Indeed the wines of Château d'Arche are packed with sunny sensations. The microcuvée obtained from old vines, Château d'Arche-Lafaurie, is a meditation wine whose aromatic palette includes dried hay, vanilla and sweet woodruff. Château d'Arche plays a similar tune with more emphasis on fruit—preserved peaches and apricots, melon preserves, ripe pineapple, honey and a spectacular finale of ginger and lemongrass. It is no wonder that the gourmets of Indonesia have adopted it as their pet French wine. Château d'Arche is a perfect companion for the archipelago's subtle cuisines—their long-simmered stews with coconut milk, palm sugar and sweet spices, and their savoury-sweet harmonies, not to mention the bounty of tropical fruit.

1. *This 17th-century elongated château, one of the loveliest in the Sauternais, is built on one level. Inside, nine guest rooms have been created.*

2. *Château d'Arche, through its beautiful aromatic framework, shows all the character of an opulent, powerful Sauternes.*

3. *Environment is a major concern at Château d'Arche. A full southern exposure ensures that the grapes get a maximal amount of sunlight. In some years, a cuvée spéciale is obtained from the oldest vines.*

The Bride's Egg,
"Grand Cru de l'Impératrice" Aquitaine Caviar

Michel GUÉRARD
Les Prés d'Eugénie - Eugénie-les-Bains, France

SERVES 4

The mussel-flavored custard

1½ teaspoons butter

1¼ tablespoons flour

½ cup (10 cl) mussel juice

½ egg yolk

The parsley chlorophyll

1 bunch flat-leaf parsley

½ cup (10 cl) whipped cream

½ tablespoons horseradish cream

salt and freshly ground black pepper

4 large eggs

½ ounces (100 g) smoked eel, diced

The fish jelly

½ cup (10 cl) juice from a tin of marinated mackerel

1 teaspoon agar-agar

1⅜ pounces (40 g) osetra caviar

8 green asparagus tips, cooked

For the mussel custard: Using a whisk, make a roux with the butter and flour. Bring the mussel juice to the boil and pour it over the roux, still whisking, and cook over low heat until thick and creamy. Add the half egg yolk and set aside.

For the parsley chlorophyll: Remove the stalks from the parsley and blanch the leaves in boiling salted water for a short moment. Drain, cool in ice water, drain again, and squeeze all water out. Blend the custard with the parsley, then delicately fold in the whipped cream to obtain a mousse. Taste and correct the seasoning, then add a little horseradish.

For the fish jelly: Boil the juice from the tinned, marinated mackerel with the agar-agar for 1 minute. Set aside.

Punch the eggs open and empty them. Wash the shells thoroughly, then dry them. Spoon the diced smoked eel into the egg shells and cover with the still liquid fish jelly. Set aside.

For the presentation: When the jelly has set, cover it with a thin layer of parsley chlorophyll, a few grams of caviar, another layer of parsley chlorophyll to reach the upper edge of the shell, and top with caviar.

Stick 2 small asparagus tips into each egg.

You may also serve this with a vegetable consommé and two buttered toast fingers, if desired.

CHÂTEAU D'ARCHE BY FRANCK THOMAS, BEST SOMMELIER OF THE WORLD, 2000

Château d'Arche enjoys a privileged situation in the heart of Sauternes—centrally located in the appellation's "golden triangle." Here, terraces of fine gravel, red sand and limestone provide ideal exposure to the nearby Ciron River. Noble rot develops easily here, saturating the grapes with elegance, complexity and balance. The wine is consistently powerful, with a soft and smooth character whose effect is heightened by a fine and harmonious freshness. Its complexity offers cooks the latitude to express their talents through the full extent of sweet and savoury combinations.

CHÂTEAU FILHOT

VINEYARD SIZE	62 hectares
VINE DENSITY	6,000 stocks per hectare
AVERAGE AGE OF VINEYARD	38 years
AVERAGE PRODUCTION	60,000 bottles
SOILS AND SUBSOILS	gravel, clay and sand on a clay bedrock
GRAPE VARIETIES	Sémillon 60% Sauvignon 36% Muscadelle 4%

Saying that the property is large would be an understatement. The landscaped park of the Château Filhot seems limitless, with clusters of trees punctuating a vast expanse of lawn that stretches in soft curves from the château to the older buildings—a farmhouse, a 16th-century dovecot and the cellar-vathouse unit. The whole place has a unique look and atmosphere, a feeling of poetic timelessness. Standing in front of the mid-19th-century château, which includes a monumental chapel, Count Henri de Vaucelles reads the landscape for you. His rich and unusual historical approach makes the visit fascinating.

"The Filhot estate," he says, "covers the whole southern part of the Sauternes commune. Although it was created around the mid-17th century, it got its name in 1709 when Romain de Filhot created it. Monsieur de Filhot was also famous for imposing the Sauternes appellation in replacement of the former 'vins de Langon' denomination. As for the wines of Filhot, they were known as 'Château Sauternes' until the late 19th century."

In 1840, Romain Bertrand de Lur-Saluces, who already owned the château since the French Revolution, united Filhot with another vineyard of his, Pineau du Rey, which now produces the second wine. He asked the architect Poitevin to build the château and the landscape architect Fisher to design the park, where the oldest trees probably remember the sumptuous parties and huntings of yesteryear. The property was acquired through marriage by the Durieu de Lacarelle family in 1935. The Count Henri de Vaucelles took over the management of the vineyard in 1972, and has been helped by his son, Gabriel, since 1996. "Our vines stretch to the south," says the Count, "in a crescent shape, around the park. We gave a few of our plots to the village of Sauternes to build the town hall and a few other facilities.

"Our 62 hectares of vineyards are still planted as was decided in the mid-19th century, 60 percent Sémillon, 36 percent Sauvignon and 4 percent Muscadelle, with vines of an average age of 38 years. I would describe our terroir of sandy gravel on a limestone subsoil as especially favourable to Sauvignon."

Monsieur de Vaucelles points out that the wines of Sauternes and Barsac were once developed in monasteries. "As natural stress fighters, these wines were much welcome after fasting periods, hence their success with the monks. The harvesting method, that painstaking selection of concentrated, noble-rotted grape berries, is also of clerical origin. Wherever there is a culture of liqueur wines— *tokaji aszú* in Hungary, *vin santo* in Italy, Austrian sweet wines—there is a direct link with the Church. Hunters, too, appreciated those wines for their restorative qualities. In the palombières, the forest shacks built for ring-dove hunting, Sauternes is still traditionally served with the hearty local fare. In the early 19th century, at the court of the czars, the Lur-Saluces succeeded in promoting Sauternes wines at the expense of Greek and Italian sweet wines, giving them access to international trade. But the rustic, earthy, monastic tradition of Sauternes is quite real and well worth studying."

Creamy, delicate and opulent, Château Filhot is a perfect match for the age-old palombières gastronomy, but its smoothness and complexity will make it an ideal companion for a lemon pie, a foie gras grilled on vine shoots, an aged Roquefort cheese or milky oysters. The vivacious tang of Sauvignon and the fragrance of Muscadelle merge to produce the uplifting sweetness loved by the happy monks of past centuries.

1. This extensive property, stretching south of the village of Sauternes, remained a property of the Lur-Saluces for a long time.

2. In the 19th century, much hunting and partying took place at Filhot, a glorious time that the château seems to remember.

3. A detail of the gardens.

Red-Braised Pork with Garlic
(Da Suan Hong Shao Rou)

Yu BO
Yu's Family Kitchen *(Yu Jia Chufang)* - Chengdu, China

SERVES 4

1⅛ pounds (500 g) boneless pork belly, with skin

¾ cup (150 g) rock sugar

⅔ ounce (20 g) dried longan fruit (fruit only, without stones)

1¼ cup (200 g) garlic cloves

3 teaspoons salt

a small piece of unpeeled ginger

1 spring onion

8 Sichuan pepper husks

This slow-cooked pork dish was originally cooked in the embers of a farmhouse fire. By the end of the cooking, the garlic has lost its pungency and melted away.

Cut the pork into 1³⁄₁₆-inch (3-cm) cubes and blanch in boiling water. Rinse and drain.

Peel the garlic cloves, keeping them whole. Use the flat of a cleaver blade to crush the ginger slightly, to release its flavour.

Place the pork in a clay pot with all the other ingredients and enough water to barely cover.

Bring gently to the boil, then cover with the lid and cook at an extremely low heat for 10 hours.

Serve with plain steamed rice, and other Chinese dishes, if desired.

CHÂTEAU FILHOT BY MARKUS DEL MONEGO,
BEST SOMMELIER OF THE WORLD, 1998

This historic property is well defined by a terroir that sets it apart from the neighbouring classified growths. Gravel soil on limestone produces a wine with pronounced mineral character, supported by expressive and elegant fruit. Château Filhot shows a restrained degree of softness, offering aficionados a more traditional style of Sauternes.

CHÂTEAU BROUSTET

BARSAC

VINEYARD SIZE	16 hectares
VINE DENSITY	7,100 stocks per hectare
AVERAGE AGE OF VINEYARD	30–35 years
SOILS AND SUBSOILS	gravel on asteriated limestone subsoil
GRAPE VARIETIES	Sémillon 70% Sauvignon 20% Muscadelle 10%

The 1855 Classification shows this château as part of an estate called Broustet-Nérac. Records show that, during the past centuries, the Broustet vineyard could be at times attached to the Château Nairac and at other times to the Château de Myrat. At the end of the 19th century, part of the vines of Broustet-Nérac went to Château Nairac, and the Fournier family bought the remaining part of the estate to install a cooperage on the premises. Some documents from the Bordeaux Chamber of Commerce show that the prototype of the Bordelaise barrel (of a capacity of 225 litres) was most probably created at Broustet.

In 1994, the Fourniers sold the estate to a talented winemaker named Didier Laulan. His family had been running the vineyard of nearby Château Saint-Marc for five generations. The beautiful terroir of Broustet had all it needed to seduce him, 16 hectares of reddish Barsac sand mixed with gravel on a limestone subsoil. It is said that topaz crystals mingle with the round white gravel stones in this light, well-drained, exceptional soil. This precious mineral bounty absorbs the heat during the day and radiates it back towards the grapes at night, thus helping the progress of noble rot and giving the berries the concentrated, roasted and spicy qualities that characterize the wine of Broustet. This also lies at the core of its fresh, brisk, energetic personality and its capacity for lengthy ageing. After a few years, the wine develops gorgeous aromas of conifer resin, fine leather, aged fruit preserves and rare wood.

It is not particularly easy to locate the Château Broustet in the maze of Barsac's small roads and pathways. You have to deserve it somehow. Didier Laulan does not mind this seclusion; he likes to work in peace and concentration, the very same concentration he pours into bottles in the form of a golden nectar, 10 percent Muscadelle, 20 percent Sauvignon Blanc and 70 percent Sémillon. "We are not dealing with just winemaking but a form of art," says Laulan. "Technology plays an important part in the making of red wines, but liqueur wines depend on the harvest at 95 percent. We depend completely on climate."

Laulan thus recalls the golden rule of Sauternes wines: harvest is the most decisive factor after natural weather and soil conditions, a quick and even evolution of botrytis, and morning mists alternating with dry, warm afternoons. Later, the skill of harvesters who inspect the rows up to six times to select the perfect berries is crucial. No further technology could then improve the quality of the must. When the berries reach the press, the chips are on the table. "I taste the must during the pressing," Didier explains. "If it tastes good, we've made it. Tasting is my only reference. Just like a family doctor who knows what is wrong by just looking at the patient."

The generous amount of Muscadelle gives an exotic and spicy touch to the wine of Château Broustet. Endowed with rich, jammy peach notes when young, these wines acquire their whole dimension after a few years and give out notes of preserved fruit, dried Syrian apricot paste, toasted sweet almond and raw bitter almond. After ten years of ageing, they reach the more abstract stage of meditation wines or cigar wines. Until then, though, the pairing of Château Broustet with foie gras, amaretto, almonds and spices offered in the following recipe has the simple clarity of a zen poem.

1. The vines of Château Broustet grow on a fine soil of ferruginous sand where gravel stones mingle with topaz crystals.

2. Formerly called Broustet-Nairac (or Broustet-Nérac), the estate leads an undisturbed life in the heart of the Barsac terroir.

3. 10 percent Muscadelle give the wine a distinctive aromatic delicacy, which evolves into elegant resinous, almondy notes.

Almonds and Foie Gras

Hans VÄLIMÄKI
Chez Dominique - Helsinki, Finland

SERVES 4

The milk

3⅓ cups (250 g) toasted almond flakes

1⅔ cups (40 cl) heavy cream

2⅔ cups (40 cl) whole milk

½ to ¾ teaspoon almond extract

The ice cream

3⅓ cups (80 cl) almond milk

scant ½ cup (45 g) milk powder

2½ teaspoons inverted sugar

2 ounces (40 g) ice cream stabiliser, such as Cremodan

¼ cup (80 g) glucose

The maltodextrin

1¾ ounce (45 g) maltodextrin

4 teaspoons almond oil

The fluid gel

3⅓ cups (800 g) almond milk

2 tablespoons agar-agar

salt

The foie gras snow

½ pound (250 g) foie gras, cleaned of veins and membranes

¾ cup (17.5 cl) water

salt

liquid nitrogen

The amaretto "Jello"

2⅛ cups (50 cl) amaretto

3 star anise

2 whole cloves

1 cinnamon stick

1 or 2 allspice berries

1½ tablespoons agar-agar

¼ ounce (6 g) gelling agent

salt

For the milk: Boil all the ingredients for the almond milk and let them infuse overnight, covered in plastic wrap.

For the ice cream: Boil the ingredients for the almond ice cream and cool it down. Freeze for 24 hours at 7.6°F (−22°C) and then process in a Pacojet or an ice cream machine.

For the maltodextrin: Put the maltodextrin into a blender and process, adding the oil slowly.

For the fluid gel: Boil the milk and add the agar-agar. Freeze and mix in a blender to make it smooth.

For the foie gras snow: Mix all the ingredients for the foie gras snow, except for the liquid nitrogen, and heat up in a Thermomix to 120°F (50°C). Strain and cool down to 80°F (28°C) and mix with a Bamix to make it smooth.

Pour liquid nitrogen into a metal bowl and mix with foie gras sauce. Whisk vigourously into snow. Please note that the foie gras snow needs to be prepared *à la minute*, i.e. just before serving.

Mix the "Jello" ingredients and boil until reduced to 1⅔ cup (40 cl) left. Add the agar-agar, gelling agent and salt and bring to the boil. Pour the mixture onto a metal sheet pan to cool. When set, cut into small cubes.

For the presentation: Using deep serving plates, or shallow soup bowls, place the amaretto "Jello" cubes and the fluid gel in the bottom. Place an almond ice cream quenelle on top, stack the almond maltodextrin and add the foie gras snow. Serve immediately.

CHÂTEAU BROUSTET BY YOICHI SATO, BEST SOMMELIER OF JAPAN, 2005

It's a shame that this wine is almost never seen in Japan! Its aromatic style makes it very adaptable, easy to enjoy with any dessert, without forgetting foods like foie gras and lobster in cream sauce. Many wine lovers swear by its long finish, garnished by touches of oriental spice.

CHÂTEAU NAIRAC

BARSAC

VINEYARD SIZE	17 hectares
VINE DENSITY	7,500 stocks per hectare
AVERAGE AGE OF VINEYARD	45 years
SOILS AND SUBSOILS	gravelly-sandy and loamy clayey soils on gravelly, marly-limestone and limestone subsoils
GRAPE VARIETIES	Sémillon 90% Sauvignon 6% Muscadelle 4%

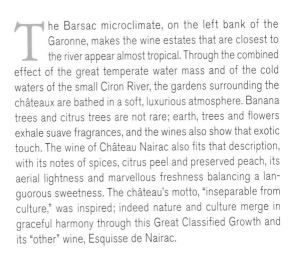

The Barsac microclimate, on the left bank of the Garonne, makes the wine estates that are closest to the river appear almost tropical. Through the combined effect of the great temperate water mass and of the cold waters of the small Ciron River, the gardens surrounding the châteaux are bathed in a soft, luxurious atmosphere. Banana trees and citrus trees are not rare; earth, trees and flowers exhale suave fragrances, and the wines also show that exotic touch. The wine of Château Nairac also fits that description, with its notes of spices, citrus peel and preserved peach, its aerial lightness and marvellous freshness balancing a languorous sweetness. The château's motto, "inseparable from culture," was inspired; indeed nature and culture merge in graceful harmony through this Great Classified Growth and its "other" wine, Esquisse de Nairac.

Château Nairac has been produced for nearly 40 years by the Tari-Heeter family. Nicole; her son, Nicolas; and her daughter, Eloïse devote their entire energy to the wine and speak about it with contagious passion. Barsac has some subtle geological idiosyncrasies, namely a subsoil of asteriated limestone that gives the wine a distinct minerality, although the amount of residual sugar is not different from that of other liqueur wines. Château Nairac is a faithful example of the Barsac appellation through its perfectly accomplished, voluptuous typicity.

The château was named after Élysée Nairac, a powerful Bordeaux trader who acquired this country estate in 1777. The vineyard had been in existence since the 17th century, as can be seen from details in the square courtyard and in the cellars, but the beautiful two-winged neoclassical chartreuse was built one century later by Jean Mollié, under the supervision of Victor Louis, architect of the Grand Théâtre de Bordeaux. The design of the French-style garden includes a play on perspective that makes the château's facade appear larger at a small distance—one of those architectural tricks that were much in style at the time. In a typically Barsac fashion, the vineyard starts right in front of the main building, like another garden.

"At Nairac," says Nicole Tari-Heeter, "it is easy to see how the living space was organised around wine-related activity. This configuration may be found everywhere in the Bordeaux region, but it is particularly visible in Barsac. Our vines, 45 years old on average, are comprised of 90 percent Sémillon, 6 percent Sauvignon and 4 percent Muscadelle, on 16 hectares of loam, sandy-gravelly in some places and clayey-gravelly with large pebbles in others."

"In Barsac," says Nicolas, "they say that Sémillon behaves like Sauvignon. And Muscadelle does well in Nairac. The clayey nature of the soils gives the wines a delicate, slightly lemony bitterness. The deeper note is almost tannic, with a very light salty touch. This light note gives complexity to the wine's sweetness and decreases the sugary feeling. What we try to express through the wine is the place itself, its soul, its terroir, as truthfully as possible. Back in the 1920s, Sauternes wines used to be served on buffet tables alongside Champagnes. I wish those days could be back!"

That was already a concern of Nicole Tari-Heeter's in the 1970s. The recipe cards she edited and published with the help of the greatest local chefs, such as Michel Guérard or Claude Darroze, were a perfect illustration of Sauternes' gastronomic versatility. These documents are now collectors' items, but the lobster you will find on the following page recalls the experience 30 years later.

1. A wine of great purity and luminosity— Château Nairac is a perfect companion for life's happiest moments.

2. The terroir mostly bears Sémillon vines, but Muscadelle does particularly well at Nairac.

3. The château was built in the late 18th century on a 17th-century base. From the French-style garden, the front facade appears larger than it actually is through a skilful play on perspective.

Roasted Breton Lobster
in Curry-Coconut Sauce

Alain SOLIVÉRÈS
Taillevent - Paris, France

SERVES 5

The lobsters

5 Breton lobsters,
1⅓ pounds (600 g) each

2 quarts (2 l) court-bouillon

celery root mousse

salted butter

The curry sauce

5 tablespoons (70 g) salted butter

1 lemon, chopped

1 orange, chopped

3½ ounces (100 g) tomato purée

1 onion, chopped

4 to 5 tablespoons (50 g) Madras curry powder

1 fresh coconut

2⅛ cups (50 cl) white chicken stock

1 bunch fresh basil

4½ tablespoons (60 g) butter

Espelette pepper

The crisps

1 Victoria pineapple

5¼ ounces (150 g) Malaga raisins

3 spring onions

celery leaves

tempura batter

For the lobsters: Cook the lobsters in a court-bouillon, timing 2 minutes for the tails and 7 minutes for the claws. Shell the lobsters and set the meat aside.

Grate the coconut and set the coconut water aside.

For the curry sauce: Chop the lobster heads and then brown them quickly in the butter. Add the lemon, orange, tomato purée and onion, and cook for 6 minutes. Add the curry powder and grated coconut. Deglaze with the coconut water.

Add stock to barely cover, then add the basil. Cook for 15 minutes, let steep for 10 minutes off the heat, then rub through a fine sieve.

Reduce the sauce until thick, then whisk in the butter. Season with Espelette pepper.

For the crisps: Cut the pineapple into large dice and dry in a low oven. Remove the seeds from the raisins and dry in the oven. Dip the onions and celery leaves in tempura batter and fry them in hot oil until crisp.

For the presentation: Lightly sauté the lobster in salted butter. In the middle of each plate, place a round cutter or ring and fill with celery root mousse. Add some around the warm lobster. Pour curry sauce over it, then decorate with the pineapple crisps, raisin crisps and onion and celery leaf tempura.

CHÂTEAU NAIRAC BY OLIVIER POUSSIER,
BEST SOMMELIER OF THE WORLD, 2000

This property is situated on a well-regarded terroir at the south of Barsac on the right bank of the Ciron River. It produces a wine in which a delicate expression of candied aromas is joined with a rich texture. With a constant emphasis on quality worthy of the greatest wines, the Tari-Heeter family decided not to produce any Nairac in 2000 and 1984 due to an absence of botrytis. We salute their commitment.

CHÂTEAU CAILLOU

BARSAC

VINEYARD SIZE	13 hectares
SOILS AND SUBSOILS	a clay layer with patches of red sand resting on an asteriated limestone bedrock
GRAPE VARIETIES	Sémillon 90% Sauvignon Blanc 10%

The Château Caillou, in Barsac, has belonged to the same family for exactly a century. The estate was purchased in 1909 by Joseph Ballan, the grandfather of the present owner, Marie-José Pierre, who manages the estate with her husband Michel. Since Caillou entered the family, three successive generations of the family have followed one another at the head of the château and surrounding vineyards, 18 hectares of typically Barsacais soil, red ferruginous-clayey sands on a limestone bedrock, similar in composition to the soils of nearby Château Climens. Out of the whole surface, the Sauternes Classified Growth is produced on 13 hectares from 90 percent Sémillon and 10 percent Sauvignon Blanc.

Although this is not a very large château, it is easy to spot at a distance in the Barsac countryside. The Château Caillou is one of the most interesting and peculiar of all châteaux in the Bordeaux region. Its two very sharp towers covered in slate and chalky white walls make it recognizable at one glance. A good example of the famous mid-19th century *troubadour* style, which is a common sight in the region—châteaux like Rayne Vigneau, Palmer or Pichon-Longueville come to the mind. Caillou is, however, one of a kind. The main stone building seems to date back to the late 18th or early 19th century, but the two brick and stone towers were added a few decades later to achieve a romantic "castle" appearance that chartreuse owners found desirable in those days. Entering the estate through the main gate, you may admire Caillou from its frontal aspect, indisputably the grandest, especially in sunny weather when the pure white walls shine in an almost blinding manner. The towers give the building a proud, decided look, which does not impair the grace of the facade, where a central clock is framed by rhythmically disposed windows and half-moon-shaped oculi below the roof.

The interior of the château is decorated in a pure 1930s style, interestingly untouched. A beautiful glass door set in a crisscross bronze frame leads into an elegant entrance hall, adorned with streamlined ironwork. The main elements of the remarkable Art-Deco main room are a stucco bas-relief on the mantelpiece and a stunning bay window—the only opening in an otherwise blind back facade—which offers a view on the vineyards in a typical chartreuse fashion.

The whole setting expresses the worship of past generations, love for the land and respect for the family roots. In that context, the wine of Château Caillou tastes remarkably exotic. The excellent soil and the careful attention devoted to the harvest and winemaking can be praised for that. Sixty percent of the must ferments in stainless-steel vats and 40 percent in oak casks. Aging is carried out for 18 to 24 months, depending on the requirements of each vintage, the casks being renewed by 60 percent each year. Notes of ripe yellow fruit—peach, plum, and especially mango and pineapple—are a remarkable characteristic of Château Caillou. Tropical fruits are its signature. The choicest cuvées ("cuvées prestige") are slightly less exuberant but more structured, offering lovely citrusy notes and resting on a slightly resinous, honey-tinged acidic frame. Whatever the vintage, the aromatic structure is always splendid.

1. A detail from an old-fashioned vertical press.

2. Château Caillou is easy to spot—its peculiar, chalk-white silhouette has a character of its own.

3. Depending on the vintage, the ageing may last as long as 24 months.

Duck Foie Gras
with Amazon Green Peppercorns and Apricot

Heinz WINKLER

Rezidenz Heinz Winkler - Aschau im Chiemgau, Germany

SERVES 6

The foie gras

1 whole duck liver

pinch of confectioners' sugar

2 tablespoons ruby Port

1 tablespoon reduced white Port

salt

The peppercorn purée

1 scant cup (180 g) Amazon green peppercorns preserved in brine

1 gelatine leaf (2 g)

1 rectangular-shaped brioche

The Port jelly

1¼ cups (30 cl) consommé stock

2 tablespoons reduced Madeira

2 tablespoons reduced ruby Port

3 gelatine leaves (2 g)

apricot purée

salt

For the foie gras: Separate the lobes of the duck liver and de-vein them. Marinate the liver in the sugar, salt, ruby Port, white Port and Madeira. Gently squeeze the lobes together to compress the liver, roll the liver in aluminum foil and refrigerate for 24 hours.

For the peppercorn purée: Soak the 4 leaves of gelatine in cold water, then drain. Blend the peppercorns at high speed until smooth. Heat the puréed peppercorns, add 1 leaf of the soaked gelatine and stir until dissolved. Strain through cheesecloth and set aside at room temperature.

Cut the brioche length-wise into 1-inch-thick (1-cm) slices, lay them between non-stick sheet pans and bake them into a 350°F (180°C) oven until crispy. Let cool, and set aside.

For the Port jelly: Bring the consommé to the boil, add the Madeira, Port and salt to taste. Add the remaining gelatine and stir to dissolve. Refrigerate half of the resulting liquid and keep the other half at room temperature.

Cover a sheet pan with aluminium foil. Lay the brioche slices onto it in a 6 x 4-inch (15 x 10-cm) rectangle. Take the foie gras out of the refrigerator and cut it length-wise into 1-inch-thick (1-cm) slices. Lay these slices onto the brioche, leaving no margin. Using a spatula, spread a very thin layer (¹⁄₂₄ inch, 1 mm) of peppercorn sauce onto the foie gras. Cover with another layer of foie gras.

Cut off a 24-inch-long (60-cm) sheet of aluminum foil, fold it in two length-wise, then in two again in order to obtain a thin strip. Wrap this strip around the foie gras and secure it with a paper clip. Using a spoon, spread a ⅛-inch (3-mm) layer of warm Port jelly onto the part of the foie gras that is not covered by foil. Refrigerate for 2 or 3 hours.

For the presentation: Take the foie gras out of the refrigerator and remove the aluminum strip. Heat a knife blade and cut the foie gras into 2 x ¾-inch (5 x 2-cm) rectangles. Place the foie gras on serving plates. Finely chop the Port jelly and scatter it over the foie gras. Serve with apricot purée.

CHÂTEAU CAILLOU BY SERGE DUBS,
BEST SOMMELIER OF THE WORLD, 1989

So beautiful and attractive in its yellow-gold appearance, with a crystal glint that fascinates sweet-wine lovers. Expressive and evocative of very ripe pineapples, yellow peaches and sultana raisins, there's just a hint of subtle over-ripeness, which is the wine's signature. This is a precious, delicious, joyous treat. Mellow and harmoniously sugared, with a very attractive and delicate sweetness, this wine knows how to entice and delight.

CHÂTEAU SUAU

BARSAC

VINEYARD SIZE	6.5 hectares
VINE DENSITY	5,500 stocks per hectare
AVERAGE AGE OF VINEYARD	40 years
SOILS AND SUBSOILS	clayey gravel
GRAPE VARIETIES	Sémillon 80% Sauvignon 20%

" I once swam in a Sauternes vat, at the Flower Festival. It is a very pleasant feeling of lightness, as if you were swimming in sugar." You would take Corinne Dubourdieu's word without hesitation if she told you that she fills her bathtub with Château Suau every morning. After all, Poppaea Sabina did bathe in ass's milk every day and Cleopatra would gobble up pearls as others do oysters. Beautiful women have always had a kinship with rare and precious substances. Besides, nothing in Sauternais should be a cause for amazement; nothing there is ever too golden, too delicious or too sensuous. The inner sunshine that their wines weave into life compensates for the hardship involved in extracting three drops of juice from overripe grapes. Difficulty has to be useful for something—for instance, a certain amount of excessiveness. That explains why a swim in a Sauternes vat sounds like a very normal thing to do. "Sauternes is a wine," says Dubourdieu, "that expresses femininity above all. A woman's wine. For that matter I believe it should be made by women only." There, it has been said.

A well-deserved tribute to the sensuality of noble-rot wines, to this erotic touch that plays such a crucial part in the peculiar magic of Sauternes wines. The estate of Château Suau—a lovely, simple chartreuse; a cool, shady garden—is in perfect harmony with this womanly spell. So is its history, which takes us back to Élie de Suau, a councillor at King Louis XIV's *Grande Chambre*, who gave his name to the property. It is probable that he acquired it as dowry from his wife, Anne de Tarnaud, who herself had gotten it as a gift from her lover, Mr. de Lur-Saluces.

When it was inscribed into the 1855 Classification, the Suau estate was managed by the Pédesclaux family, who already owned the château of the same name in Pauillac. If you read the description of that other château in this book you will notice that there, too, women are at the helm. The deeper streams of family traditions seem to run through land proper-ties as they run through people's psyches, and that also concerns the wines. Could this be a clue to understanding some of the mystery lying in Great Growths? That is beyond the scope of this book. Suffice it to say that the Suau vineyard covers 6.5 hectares on the Barsac commune, with 80 percent Sémillon, 20 percent Sauvignon. This latter grape variety, reputedly tricky and moody but so rewarding in terms of fragrance, does well in this soil and makes up a generous part of the planting, bringing lovely muscatel aromas, a unique roundness and delicately sweet fruit notes.

As should be expected, the wines of Château Suau are bursting with womanliness. They have the opulent, summery richness, no irresolution, no shallow vanity but freshness and energy showing through a complex framework of flowers, ripe fruit, peach and honeysuckle. As a perfectly accomplished Barsac, Château Suau lends itself to an extensive range of pairings, equally at ease alongside a Chinese or Thai dinner or with fresh, crunchy vegetables spiced with a caramel almond sand, the only essential condition being a perfect flavour harmony radiating from both the recipe and the wine.

1. The vines of Château Suau stretch on six and a half hectares near the banks of the Garonne.

2, 3. Details of the chartreuse and its garden.

Asparagus
in Spicy Caramel

Roberta SUDBRACK
Roberta Sudbrack - Rio de Janeiro, Brazil

SERVES 8

8 fresh white or green asparagus

¼ pound (100 g) sourdough bread (pain au levain), at least 2 days old

⅓ cup (1¾ ounces) (50 g) peeled whole almonds

7 tablespoons (100 g) unsalted butter

2 crushed red pepper flakes

⅛ cup (25 g) sugar

assorted fresh leaves and blossoms: beet, cilantro, carrot flower, purple basil, anise flower

fine sea salt

fleur de sel

For the asparagus: Clean the asparagus and gently remove the peel.

For the caramel: Cut the bread into small cubes and slice the almonds into fine flakes.

Melt the butter, and when it is very hot, add the bread, almonds and sugar. Gently fry the bread cubes and almond flakes until they are crispy and golden. Remove from heat, drain the bread and almonds in a sieve, reserving the butter, and set aside. Place the fried bread and almonds in a food processor, add some of the reserved butter and pulverize until the mixture turns into a loose paste. Add the red pepper flakes and a pinch of salt. Pulverize the paste again. Pass it through a fine sieve to get a caramel consistency, and set aside in a double boiler.

For the presentation: Cook the asparagus in boiling salted water until they are *al dente*. Place the asparagus in warmed dishes. Arrange the caramel on top of the asparagus and garnish with leaves and blossoms. Finish the dish with a sprinkling of fleur de sel and serve.

CHÂTEAU SUAU BY ANDREAS LARSSON, BEST SOMMELIER OF THE WORLD, 2007

Produced in a historical estate today under the direction of Corinne Dubordieu, the wines have gained in terms of concentration, purity and finesse, and the recent vintages have been splendid. In the 2005 I noted quiet, deep golden colour, a waxy and honeyed nose and young sweet fruit. Immense structure on the palate, sweet and viscous, yet fresh and structured with a refreshing citrus-peel bitterness and a very long finish.

CHÂTEAU DE MALLE

VINEYARD SIZE	27 hectares
VINE DENSITY	6,600 stocks per hectare
AVERAGE AGE OF VINEYARD	47 years
AVERAGE PRODUCTION	6,000 cases
SOILS AND SUBSOILS	sandy gravelly soil; some swelling clay in the subsoil
GRAPE VARIETIES	Sémillon 70% Sauvignon 27% Muscadelle 3%

Your first glimpse of Château de Malle will not fail to dazzle you, especially on a clear morning, when the sun gives a glorious sheen to the stone facade. The fact that this fairytale château is the birthplace of a great liqueur wine adds to the wonder. The alchemical process that is the making of a Sauternes wine appears in a more acute manner. And as you gradually discover the whole place through its gorgeous architecture, its spectacular interior decor and finally its royal wine, you become certain that Malle is, above all, a style, expressed through each one of its parts.

Count Pierre de Bournazel, who has devoted his heart and soul to the château and the vineyard, has succeeded in preserving the antique character of the house without making it stiff and museum-like. The picturesque baroque style presents a warm and welcoming atmosphere. Since the death of Pierre de Bournazel in 1985, his wife runs the estate with the help of their sons, Paul-Henry, Antoine and Charles.

With its Mansard roofs and its curious "à l'impériale" tower domes in a depressed bulb shape, Malle is a beautiful example of late mannerist French architecture, balanced by the classic perfection of its shapes. The architect remained anonymous, but an Italian touch may be felt throughout the building, particularly in the Florentine terraced gardens rising at the back, beyond a flat garden laid out in the French style. Jacques de Malle, a president of the Bordeaux parliament, probably had this Italian style in mind when he ordered the building of the château in the early 17th century. However, the long ownership of the Lur-Saluces family and of their Piedmontese roots certainly helped to impart an italiante atmosphere to the place.

Winemaking is an ancient tradition here. Jacques de Malle, back in the 1600s, already kept a cellar diary and decided on the date of the harvest. The 27 hectares of clayey gravel on a siliceous subsoil that are devoted to the Sauternes Classified Growth stretch onto the communes of Fargues and Preignac, with a planting of 70 percent Sémillon, 27 percent Sauvignon and 3 percent Muscadelle. After the grapes are pressed, the must is decanted for about 10 hours, then the fine lees are reintroduced into it and the must goes into the barrels to ferment. The wine is aged for 20 to 24 months in one-third new oak barrels in the beautiful old-style cellar.

The style of Château de Malle tells only one story—art and pleasure stand above all; opulence is nothing without beauty; and the values of courage and military art are also appreciated as long as they bear the ornaments of chivalry and elegance. Such is the heritage of the Malle and Lur-Saluces families. The wine of Malle is voluptuous, rich, ample and exotic, with notes of preserved pineapple and beeswax. It speaks of history and of a centuries-old culture with a stylish, theatrical end-of-mouth note that irresistibly reminds one of the small open-air theatre that was built at one end of the garden. Without a doubt, small plays and sketches were acted here, as shown by some written documents in the château's archives. So do the amazing *trompe-l'œil* life-size wooden silhouettes that were painted in the early 18th century to be used for the set design. They can be seen on the walls, adorning them with their enigmatic presence, or even sitting by a fireplace, glancing at you seductively. These unusual figures have a fascinating presence, echoing the wine's aristocratic elegance and the mystery that Sauternes wines always conceal under the many layers of their complex aromas.

1. Behind the Mannerist château, geometrical French-style flowerbeds are drawn between the facade and an Italianate terraced garden.

2. A voluptuous wine, Château de Malle offers precious aromas of apricot, honeysuckle and sugared apple.

3. Each room of the château has many surprises in store. This old home has been miraculously preserved.

Roquefort Cheese in Apple Jelly, *Crispy Roquefort Toast*

Vincent ARNOULD
Le Vieux Logis - Trémolat, France

SERVES 8

The apple jelly

8 bertane apples (a local variety; use other apples if unavailable)

leaf gelatine (see recipe; count 1 g of gelatine for 100 g of apple juice)

The mousse

¼ pound (105 g) Roquefort cheese plus a few cubes for decoration

⅓ cup (75 cl) chicken stock

⅓ cup (7.5 cl) heavy cream

The toast

walnut-raisin bread

unsalted butter

1 banana

a few sprigs of chervil, arugula and curly chicory

walnut oil vinaigrette

chopped walnuts

freshly ground black pepper

For the apples: Peel the apples and cut three ¼-inch (5-mm) slices on either side without reaching the core. Reserve the cores. Cook the apple slices in a dry non-stick pan over low heat, then let them cool.

Soak the gelatine in cold water for 10 minutes.

For the apple jelly: Pass the apple cores through a juicer and let the juice rest until decanted. Strain the juice and bring it to a boil. Strain again. Add the drained gelatine, mix and let cool.

For the roquefort mousse: Crumble ⅛ pound (75 g) of the Roquefort in a blender. Bring the chicken stock to a boil and pour it onto the Roquefort. Blend, let cool, then add the cream. Strain the mixture, then pour into a siphon. Add one gas cartridge and check the texture. Keep refrigerated.

For the toast: Cut the bread into ¼-inch (5-mm) slices. Spread a little butter over them. Add a fine layer of bananas, sliced as thinly as you can manage. Scatter crumbled Roquefort over them. Bake for 5 to 8 minutes in a very hot oven until crispy.

For the presentation: Put three apple slices in each serving bowl. Add apple jelly to reach the top of the apples, and refrigerate until set.

Season the chervil, arugula and chicory with a little walnut vinaigrette. Cut the remaining Roquefort into pieces.

Just before serving, shake the siphon, and spread the mousse onto the 3 apple slices. Add a few chopped nuts, the Roquefort, and the herbs and season with pepper. Place the Roquefort toast on the side of the plate.

CHÂTEAU DE MALLE BY VIRGINIA PHILIP,
BEST SOMMELIER OF THE UNITED STATES, 2002

The nose is unctuous with notes of honeysuckle, apricot and baked apples. Just a hint of oak teases the nose. On the palate, the wine is full-bodied. The notes of apricot, honeysuckle and ripe Golden Delicious apple carry over on the palate with well-balanced acidity and that hint of oak and mineral. The wine can age for many years, depending on the vintage.

CHÂTEAU ROMER DU HAYOT

SAUTERNES

VINEYARD SIZE	12 hectares
VINE DENSITY	6,500 stocks per hectare
AVERAGE AGE OF VINEYARD	30 years
AVERAGE PRODUCTION	2,000 cases
SOILS AND SUBSOILS	sandy-gravelly on a clay-limestone subsoil
GRAPE VARIETIES	Sémillon 70% Sauvignon 25% Muscadelle 5%

The Romer estate, in Fargues, was created in the 17th century by the de Montalier family. In the late 18th century, its wine was known as Château Montalier-Romer. In 1833, the property was sold to the Comte de La Myre-Mory, the husband of Louise de Lur-Saluces. When Louise died, the vineyard was divided between their five children. Shortly before World War II, Mr. du Hayot bought two-thirds of the vineyard. During the 1960s, the remaining part was exploited in tenant farming by his son, André du Hayot, before it could be purchased and the estate reunited.

During the 1970s, the construction of the Autoroute des Deux-Mers motorway posed a direct threat to the property. After struggling fiercely to save the entire estate, du Hayot had to face a heartbreaking decision: keep the vineyard or keep the buildings, including the château. The château and the cellars disappeared; the vineyard remained, and the existence of this Sauternes 1855 Great Classified Growth was preserved.

Following this event, du Hayot bought a large number of vineyard plots in the communes of Sauternes and Barsac, building up, year after year, a small viticultural empire of 87 hectares, under the brand name of Vignobles du Hayot.

Today, the Vignobles du Hayot are directed by Fabienne du Hayot and Catherine Boyer, André's daughters, assisted by Markus, Fabienne's husband, both the technical manager and creator of the brand's graphic communication. Each of the wines is developed according to its personality and history, but "conceptual" blends are also devised, like "2 de Romer du Hayot" and "Delicius de Romer du Hayot," which in some way play the part of second wines for the classified growth. Four other Sauternes liqueur wines are also produced.

Château Romer du Hayot is made at the Château d'Andoyse, one of the brand's Barsac estates. The winemaking buildings have generous fermenting and ageing capacities because of the large number of different wines produced on the premises. The vines for the Classified Growth are located in Fargues, on 12 hectares of sandy gravel planted with 70 percent Sémillon, 25 percent Sauvignon and 5 percent Muscadelle. The average age of the vines is 30 years and the harvest is done entirely by hand, in successive tries. The fermentation is carried in thermoregulated vats, followed by 36 months of ageing in oak barrels.

The typically Sauternes notion of balance and delicacy is carefully respected and promoted by the Vignobles du Hayot. Château Romer du Hayot is remarkable for its deep amber colour, of a decided golden hue even in youth, and for its spring-like flowery character, lined by fruity pineapple and pear notes. After a few years, this wine gives out notes of toasted almond, pear preserves and Seville orange marmalade. Old vintages even lean towards aged rum or Armagnac, raw spiced cane syrup and cigar box. Whatever the age of Château Romer du Hayot, its finish is never devoid of freshness, with a touch of acidity.

"We like to cultivate a balanced character in this wine," says manager Patrick Sorin. "Our soils are worked with respect to the best viticultural traditions, with integrated pest control. And we hold on to Muscadelle for its fragrance, which makes a difference. One never knows the evolution of botrytis in advance, but in the years when Muscadelle does well, the wine is indeed very fresh and aromatic."

1. The vineyard of Château Romer du Hayot is located in Fargues, but the wine is made in Barsac.

2. The Vignobles du Hayot—a view of the barrel cellar.

3. The bottle cellar.

Nougat Mousse, Chocolate-Raspberry Coulis, Lime Mousse

Claus-Peter LUMPP
Bareiss -Baiersbronn, Germany

SERVES 6

The nougat mousse

1¼ ounces (35 g) nougat

2⅓ ounces (65 g) white chocolate

1 egg

pinch of sugar

cocoa liqueur

1.3 g leaf gelatine

⅔ cup (16 cl) heavy cream

The tulips

¼ cup (65 g) brown sugar

2 egg whites (50 g)

¼ cup (30 g) flour

⅓ cup (20 g) cocoa powder

3 tablespoons melted unsalted butter

the seeds from a portion of a vanilla pod

The chocolate sablé

3 tablespoons sugar

4 tablespoons (50 g) softened unsalted butter (½ stick)

pinch of salt

1 large or extra-large egg yolk (25 g)

1½ tablespoons almond powder

¾ cup plus 1 tablespoon (100 g) flour

⅛ cup (10 g) cocoa powder

The raspberry marzipan

¼ cup (80 g) almond paste (70% almond)

3 tablespoons raspberry preserves

2 teaspoons lime juice

2 teaspoons raspberry brandy

The chocolate-raspberry coulis

½ cup (100 g) sugar

⅛ cup (4 cl) water

5 tablespoons (70 g) unsalted butter

¼ cup (60 g) raspberry coulis

¼ ounce (6 g) milk chocolate (40% cocoa)

marinated raspberries

sugared thyme

a few shreds of candied lime zest

ginger ice cream

raspberry sorbet

lime mousse

For the nougat mousse: Melt the nougat and white chocolate in a double boiler. Soak the gelatine in cold water for 10 minutes. Beat the eggs and sugar over the heat. Then, off the heat, add the cocoa liqueur and the drained gelatine. Fold in the cream.

For the tulips: Mix all the ingredients for the tulips to form a dough.

Roll out the dough cut it into 2 x 4-inch (5 x 10-cm) rectangles and bake them for 7 minutes in a 350°F (180°C) oven.

For the chocolate sablé: Beat the sugar, softened butter and salt into a light foam, then add the egg yolks and the remaining ingredients. Let cool. When cool, spread the dough into a thin layer on a lined baking sheet. Cut out 2½-inch (6-cm) disks and bake them for 7 minutes at 350°F (180° C).

For the raspberry marzipan: Mix all the ingredients together and pour them into a piping bag. Set aside until serving time.

For the chocolate-raspberry coulis: Place the chocolate in a bowl. Melt the sugar and cook it into a pale-coloured caramel. Deglaze with water, add the butter and mix well. When you obtain a thick paste, add the raspberry coulis and strain the mass over the chocolate.

For the presentation: Place some coulis in the middle of each plate, add some nougat mousse and top with a tulip. Garnish with marinated raspberries, sugared thyme and candied lime peel.

In six soup bowls, place a chocolate sablé and top it with raspberry marzipan and marinated raspberries. Add a little warm coulis and shape the ginger ice cream into small quenelles. On the side, serve some raspberry sorbet and lime mousse in a small cup.

CHÂTEAU ROMER DU HAYOT BY ÉRIC BEAUMARD, SILVER MEDAL, BEST SOMMELIER OF THE WORLD, 1998

The luminous golden yellow colour suggests a precocious maturity. The rich, straight nose is already expressive and delivers melliferous notes of candied white fruit. The attack is rich and generous. In mid-palate, the wine shows a clear, tender aromatic profile and a rich, slightly heavy texture. The persistency remains average. This Sauternes, in 2004, expresses itself with frankness and simplicity. A little extra minerality and freshness would not be superfluous.

CHÂTEAU ROMER

SAUTERNES

VINEYARD SIZE	3 hectares
VINE DENSITY	6,600 stocks per hectare
AVERAGE AGE OF VINEYARD	15 years
AVERAGE PRODUCTION	4,000 bottles
SOILS AND SUBSOILS	gravelly and clayey-gravelly
GRAPE VARIETIES	Sémillon 90% Sauvignon Blanc 5% Muscadelle 5%

As is the case with Climens, Suau, Clos Haut-Peyraguey and La Tour Blanche, Château Romer is managed by a woman. Like the mythical unicorn, Sauternes wine seems to like female hands. In return for the loving care it receives from its great priestesses, it appears to have a special beauty treatment in store for them: it lights them up, makes them blossom out, gives them a special shine and a mysterious charm. And Sauternes ladies master the sacred language of this golden wine; they are familiar with its luminous and voluptuous virtues, its joy potential. This is how Anne Farges, owner and manager of the Château Romer, appears to you as she leads you through her tiny vineyard where very young vines cover a visible surface. Indeed, on six Great Classified Growth hectares, only three are now planted in vines. Little by little, she replants her plots. Farges's target is to re-create the growth on its entire original surface. So this is a case of rebirth: a vineyard is being regenerated.

Château Romer likes discretion. A small distance away from the Château de Malle, its signpost is half concealed by tree branches. If you do see it and follow the direction it points out, you will discover the recently replanted plots before stopping at the gate of a beautiful, rustic 18th-century farmhouse tucked in a lush garden. Masses of wisteria, potted lemon trees give it the look of a Mediterranean hideaway and symbolically foreshadow the wine's aromas. A grey cat leaps over the wall to run home. The whole building, centred around its garden courtyard, seems like an island amidst the vines.

The Romer estate used to belong to the Count de La Myre-Mory, then to the Count de Beaurepaire-Louvagny, and has been the property of the Farges family since 1911. Farges took it in her hands in 2002, putting an end to a period of tenant farming. This young woman, trained as a historian, was not even 40 yet when she fell in love with the place. Soon, her agricultural diploma in her pocket, her house sold, she set out to bring this much under-exploited vineyard to fruition.

The terroir, though small, is of first-rate quality. Its light sandy-gravelly soil is planted with 90 percent Sémillon, the remaining 10 percent being half Muscadelle and half Sauvignon Blanc. Avoiding the use of herbicide, she treats the vineyard by deep ploughing, side-shoot removal and leaf stripping to get the finest possible grapes. After the *tries* are done in the vineyard, the berries are thrown into a small hydraulic press. The must ferments in barrels after a 24-hour debourbage in vats, then the wine is aged between 12 and 18 months. Instead of the traditional bottle sizes, Farges uses 50-cl bottles that are very convenient for a liqueur wine.

The peaceful atmosphere of this little corner of the Sauternais seems to seep into the wines of Château Romer. Fruity, flowery, fresh and delicious, they do not touch the ground. These very balanced wines inspire confidence and comfort to the drinker. They require delicate food pairings with crunchy textures and a balance of acidity, sugar and spices. You instantly think of Southeast Asian cuisines—Vietnamese, Laotian, or Thai—and you dream of serving crispy Vietnamese spring rolls alongside one of Farges's precious bottles. It also has to be said that beyond all traditional pairings, these wines are perfectly adapted to contemporary, streamlined, conceptual cuisines, based on a play of tastes and textures.

1. *The smallest Great Classified Growth château in Sauternes has the charm of a romantic farmhouse.*

2. *The cellars open out directly onto a shady garden.*

3. *The wine has a delicate, clear-cut style and a flowery-fruity lightness that does not touch the ground.*

100% Cotton Foie

Bruno OTEIZA & Mikel ALONSO
Biko - Mexico City, Mexico

SERVES 10

The foie gras mousse

¾ pound (350 g) foie gras

2⅛ ounces (60 g) cream cheese

¼ cup (60 g) jocoque
(a type of Mexican fermented milk,
which you may replace with sour cream,
crème fraîche, or thick yogurt)

salt

ginger powder

liquorice powder

The vinaigrette

3 tomatoes

¼ cup (50 g) heavy cream

1 tablespoon olive oil

½ teaspoon sherry vinegar

salt

30 romaine lettuce leaves
a cloud of ethereal white cotton candy

For the foie gras mousse: Grill the foie gras briefly on both sides, then blend it with the cheese, the jocoque and the spice powders and refrigerate.

Remove the ribs from 30 lettuce leaves. Set aside.

When the mousse is hard enough to wrap, take 1 tablespoon (15 g) of the mousse and wrap it in each lettuce leaf. Each roll should be 1½ inches (4 cm) long.

For the vinaigrette: Peel and seed the tomatoes. Finely dice them and blend them with the other ingredients for the vinaigrette.

For the presentation: On each serving dish, place 3 wraps of lettuce and foie, and near each wrap draw a line of tomato creamy vinaigrette. Top each wrap with a little ethereal cloud of white cotton candy.

CHÂTEAU ROMER BY FRANCK THOMAS,
BEST SOMMELIER OF EUROPE, 2005

Situated in the south of the Sauternes appellation, Château Romer's vines are more often touched by noble rot than properties on the other side of the Garonne river. With a style more supple and less profound than found elsewhere in Sauternes and Bommes, and perhaps less mineral than Barsac, Château Romer's wines show a quintessential fruitiness from their earliest youth. Their classic, ethereal character makes them equally suited to traditional food and more adventurous pairings.

CHÂTEAU LAMOTHE

SAUTERNES

VINEYARD SIZE	7.5 hectares
VINE DENSITY	7,400 stocks per hectare
AVERAGE AGE OF VINEYARD	40 years
AVERAGE PRODUCTION	1,300 cases
SOILS AND SUBSOILS	sandy gravel on a deep clay-limestone subsoil
GRAPE VARIETIES	Sémillon 85% Sauvignon 10% Muscadelle 5%

On the top of one of the highest gravel hills in the Sauternes region, overlooking the Ciron River, the fine terroir of Lamothe has passed through many hands and was divided more than once. It finally got divided into two in the 19th century: up to this day, two different Lamothe estates share the hill. Lamothe-Guignard on the north side and, to the south, Lamothe-Despujols, 8 hectares purchased in 1961 by Jean Despujols. Since 1989, the estate has been managed by Guy, his son, and Marie-France, his daughter-in-law.

The place is simple and rustic, with a quiet and peaceful atmosphere. The château, a low, elongated 16th-century building with an angular round tower, leans upon the remains of a Merovingian fort to which the property owes its name (*mothe* being an old word for a medieval fortified hilltop). This *castrum* has seen a lot pass by, from the Saracen invasions in the 8th century and the Norman raids of the 9th to the combats of the Hundred Years War, when it was used as a watchtower by the lords of Fargue and Budos. Behind the farm, in a tree-planted enclosure, the remains of the fort may still be seen; their square shape appears clearly.

Château Lamothe covers 7.5 hectares of vineyard, planted with 85 percent Sémillon, 10 percent Sauvignon and 5 percent Muscadelle. The soil is warm, well drained and cooled by abundant winds—all factors helping to hasten the maturity process and to give the wines power and balance. The vines are old, more than 40 years of age on average.

"We work in the old-fashioned way," says Guy Despujols. "We graft with carefully selected shoots cut from our own vines, a technique which insures that our plants will perfectly adapt to the terroir." He points out that the layout of the vine rows is also traditional, one wider row alternating with three narrower ones to allow space for the manure carts. The harvest is done manually, with five or six successive tries, and the must is extracted through a lengthy process through a pneumatic press: two pressings are done every 24 hours, each one lasting from 4 to 6 hours. A careful decanting is then performed in underground vats, and the must from each pressing is selected after tasting and grading. The ageing begins with five months on the lees and regular batonnage, and continues in barrels. The wine is bottled 26 months later. Such painstaking work explains the remarkable silky quality of Château Lamothe, a wine that offers hawthorn and lime blossom fragrances and notes of honey pastry, pineapple and apple roasted with sugar.

The way Château Lamothe is commercialised is another particularity of the place. Despujols, who believes in local initiative to help develop and promote the image of regional wines, runs a small wine shop in the village of Sauternes. There, among other wines, he sells his own, both the Classified Growth and the second wine, Les Tourelles de Lamothe. Any visitor may gather information on great liqueur wines and tips on how to serve them. "These wines are meant to be drunk with meals," says Despujols. "They should achieve a balance in the mouth. And their aromatic stability is so great that a bottle of Sauternes may be kept uncorked in a refrigerator. This fact deserves to be better known!"

1. A view on the angular tower of Château Lamothe, a country-style château built in the 16th century.

2. In the Sauternais, latesummer morning mists help the botrytis to settle in.

3. The wine requires up to 26 months of ageing.

Veal Kidney with Sea Urchins
and Morel Mushrooms

Carlo CRACCO
Cracco - Milan, Italy

SERVES 2

1 veal kidney

1 scant tablespoon olive oil

3 tablespoons (40 g) unsalted butter
for cooking kidneys and morels

1 garlic clove, finely chopped

Maldon sea salt

¼ pound (80 g) fresh sea urchin roe

¼ pound (100 g) fresh morel
mushrooms, thoroughly cleaned

¼ cup (5 cl) meat jus
(or reduced veal stock)

For the kidney: Sauté the whole kidney for
5 minutes in a non-stick pan with a little oil.
Add the butter and garlic, and cook for
4 minutes Remove from the heat and let the
kidney rest for 5 minutes to render its juices.

Slice the kidney thinly and place the slices in
a circle shape on a sheet of parchment paper.
Add a little olive oil and Maldon sea salt. Drop
the sea urchin roe all over the kidney, cover
with aluminum foil and bake for about 4
minutes in a 325°F (163°C) oven.

In a pan, quickly sauté the morels with a little
olive oil, butter and some Maldon sea salt,
keeping them al dente.

For the presentation: Place the kidney on warm
serving plates, cover with the morels, sprinkle
a little jus over the plate and serve.

GRAND CRU CLASSE EN 1855

VIN   WINE

Château Lamothe

SAUTERNES
APPELLATION SAUTERNES CONTRÔLÉE

PRODUIT DE FRANCE   **2005**   PRODUCT OF FRANCE

CHÂTEAU LAMOTHE BY MARKUS DEL MONEGO,
BEST SOMMELIER OF THE WORLD, 1998

*Time is an important element in this growth. Time and patience
allow this great wine to acquire all its finesse and complexity.
Time plays a role in the vineyard, too; the average age of the vines
is older than 40 years, guaranteeing concentrated flavours in the
wine. Discreet in its youth, it develops an aromatic richness, joining
yellow fruit with the light mineral character that is the mark of
a classic Sauternes.*

CHÂTEAU LAMOTHE-GUIGNARD

SAUTERNES

VINEYARD SIZE	18 hectares
VINE DENSITY	6,600 stocks per hectare
AVERAGE AGE OF VINEYARD	34 years
AVERAGE PRODUCTION	2,800 cases
SOILS AND SUBSOILS	gravelly and clayey-gravelly soils on a limestone subsoil
GRAPE VARIETIES	Sémillon 90% Sauvignon 5% Muscadelle 5%

The estate of Château Lamothe-Guignard shares with Château Lamothe-Despujols one of the best gravel hills of the Sauternes region, which still bears at the top the remains of an early medieval fort dating from the Merovingian period. The fort may be seen close up on the "other" Lamothe vineyard This beautiful hill, long ago, used to be one single estate called La Mothe-d'Assault. Since it was created in the 16th century, its eventful history has been punctuated by frequent changes of owner, which at times led to land division. Today, Lamothe remains divided in two, Lamothe-Despujols covering 8 hectares on the southern part of the hill while Lamothe-Guignard stretches to the north and northwest on 32 hectares, including 18 dedicated to the Sauternes Great Classified Growth. The estate is named after the brothers Philippe and Jacques Guignard, who acquired it in 1981."When we took over the property," the brothers say, "this terroir produced a wine from which a very small quantity was bottled. We rebuilt and restructured this vineyard, remodelled the chais, and gave back to the wines of this estate their Grand Cru Classé excellence."

The vineyard of Château Lamothe-Guignard comprises two different entities. The main terroir is located on several gravelly plateaux on the top of the hill; the other one goes down to the north and northwest on clayey-gravelly slopes. The whole constitutes a superbly exposed and well-drained vineyard, with a unique charm of its own. Looking north from the hilltop, the view over the surrounding hills is enchanting, with the chalky line of Château La Tour-Blanche shining in the distance and crowning the landscape. This is one of the most beautiful and soothing panoramas in the Sauternais.

Ninety percent Sémillon, 5 percent Sauvignon and 5 percent Muscadelle make up the planting of this beautiful terroir. Add to that some excellent climatic and pedologic conditions, a rigorous winemaking approach and the devotion to quality shown by the Guignard brothers, and you will understand why such an exceptional Sauternes is made here. Two old-fashioned vertical presses and one horizontal pneumatic press are used to extract the must; the ageing is carried on for 12 to 15 months in barrels, and the bottling is done 20 months after harvest.

Château Lamothe-Guignard may not be the most media-exposed of all Sauternes, but it has its aficionados all over the world, many of the 50 or so trading companies that distribute the wine. Aside from this international dimension, the Guignard brothers, very aware of the great ageing capacity of their wines, directly sell some of their older vintages right at the property.

A masculine, generous wine resting on an assertive aromatic framework, with the added palatal tang of a seductive resinous touch, Château Lamothe-Guignard gives out more freshness than sweetness. "We are less liquorish than many other Sauternes," the two brothers point out. The concentrated, roasted notes in the wine are not burdened by any syrupy excess, as shown by the beautiful vintages of 2002—smooth and woody, with great acidic structure—and 2004, with tropical fruit and a lengthy ending of citrus zest. One thinks of the old traditional pairing of Sauternes and oysters, which used to be popular and has now become almost obsolete. This is a wine that invites us to revive that tradition, perhaps extending it to high-character seafood like sea urchin, violet (sea squirt), raw sardine marinated in a little sugar or brown crabmeat.

1. A powerfully aromatic wine is slowly maturing in barrels. Philippe and Jacques Guignard worked hard to restore this great classified growth to its rightful quality level.

2. A view of Château Lamothe-Guignard.

3. In the cellars.

Crispy Seared Foie Gras
and Star Fruit in a Sweet and Sour Broth

Chris SALANS
Mozaic - Bali, Indonesia

SERVES 5

The foie gras

1⅛ pound (500 g) raw duck foie gras

1 cup (125 g) finely sliced shallots

3 tablespoons fresh thyme leaves

The spiced syrup

1 cup (250 ml) water

½ cup (100 g) sugar

1½ teaspoons coriander seeds

⅛ ounce (2.5 g) star anise

⅛ ounce (4 g) cinnamon stick

½ vanilla bean, split in half length-wise

1 whole clove

1 piece of orange peel

1 piece of lemon peel

The garnish

½ pound (250 g) carambola
(baby star fruit)

½ pound (250 g) star fruit

The broth

1 cup (25 cl) carambola
(baby star fruit) juice

1 cup (25 cl) chicken stock

sea salt and freshly ground black pepper

sprigs of any fresh herb

For the foie gras: Slice the foie gras into 5 pieces. De-vein and refrigerate.

Just before serving: Sear the foie gras until crispy on both sides. Remove from the pan. Add the sliced shallots and thyme leaves to the pan with all the foie gras fat. When cooked, place the shallots on top of the foie gras and season with sea salt. Reserve the pan with the fat.

For the spiced syrup: Bring all the ingredients for the spiced syrup to a boil. Meanwhile slice the carambola into bite-size pieces, add them to the spiced syrup and simmer for a few minutes until tender. Refrigerate for at least 24 hours.

For the garnish: Make star fruit chips, slicing them thinly, dipping them in simple syrup and drying them on a silicon mat until crispy (about 1½ hours) in an oven at 175°F (80°C).

For the broth: Pour the carambola juice, the chicken stock and ½ cup (10 cl) of the syrup from the poached carambola into the pan with the foie gras fat. Season with salt and pepper to taste.

For the presentation: Reheat the poached carambola. Place a few pieces of the carambola in the centre of a hot bowl. Place the cooked foie gras on top of the carambola. Pour the broth around the foie gras. Top the foie gras with a star fruit chip and a fresh herb sprig.

CHÂTEAU LAMOTHE-GUIGNARD BY YOICHI SATO,
BEST SOMMELIER OF JAPAN, 2005

This wine, a word, is complex—the perfect description for this wine. Not only is it sweet and unctuous but it has a delicate acidity and spicy notes. From its fresh and instant aromatic expression when first sipped, to the remarkable length, which continues on the palate long after the wine has left the mouth, the pleasure offered here is long-lasting. When drinking this wine, I enjoy taking note of how it evolves in the glass throughout the course of an evening.

INDEX OF THE CHÂTEAUX

MÉDOC, GRANDS CRUS CLASSÉS IN 1855

CHÂTEAU D'ARMAILHAC
33 250 PAUILLAC
Tel + 33 (0) 5 56 73 20 20
Fax + 33 (0) 5 56 73 20 33
www.bpdr.com

CHÂTEAU BATAILLEY
33 250 PAUILLAC
Tel + 33 (0) 5 56 00 00 70
Fax + 33 (0) 5 57 87 48 61
domaines@borie-manoux.fr

CHÂTEAU BELGRAVE
33 112 SAINT-LAURENT MÉDOC
Tel + 33 (0) 5 56 35 53 00
Fax + 33 (0) 5 56 35 53 29
www.dourthe.com

CHÂTEAU BEYCHEVELLE
Route des Châteaux
33 250 SAINT-JULIEN BEYCHEVELLE
Tel + 33 (0) 5 56 73 20 70
Fax + 33 (0) 5 56 73 20 71
www.beychevelle.com

CHÂTEAU BOYD-CANTENAC
11 route de Jean Faure
33 460 MARGAUX
Tel + 33 (0) 5 57 88 90 82
www.boyd-cantenac.fr

CHÂTEAU BRANAIRE-DUCRU
33 250 SAINT-JULIEN
Tel + 33 (0) 5 56 59 25 86
Fax + 33 (0) 5 56 59 16 26
www.branaire.com

CHÂTEAU BRANE-CANTENAC
33 460 MARGAUX
Tel + 33 (0) 5 57 88 83 33
Fax + 33 (0) 5 57 88 72 51
www.brane-cantenac.com

CHÂTEAU CALON SÉGUR
33 180 SAINT-ESTEPHE
Tel + 33 (0) 5 56 59 30 08
Fax + 33 (0) 5 56 59 71 51
calon-segur@calon-segur.fr

CHÂTEAU DE CAMENSAC
Route de Saint-Julien
33 112 SAINT-LAURENT MÉDOC
Tel + 33 (0) 5 56 59 41 69
Fax + 33 (0) 5 56 59 41 73
www.chateaucamensac.com

CHÂTEAU CANTEMERLE
33 460 MACAU
Tel + 33 (0) 5 57 97 02 82
Fax + 33 (0) 5 57 97 02 84
www.cantemerle.com

CHÂTEAU CANTENAC BROWN
33 460 MARGAUX
Tel + 33 (0) 5 57 88 81 81
Fax + 33 (0) 5 57 88 81 90
www.cantenacbrown.com

CHÂTEAU CLERC MILON
33 250 PAUILLAC
Tel + 33 (0) 5 56 73 20 20
Fax + 33 (0) 5 56 73 20 33
www.bpdr.com

CHÂTEAU COS D'ESTOURNEL
33 180 SAINT-ESTÈPHE
Tel :+ 33 (0) 5 56 73 15 50
Fax + 33 (0) 05 56 59 72 59
www.estournel.com

CHÂTEAU COS LABORY
33 180 SAINT-ESTÈPHE
Tel + 33 (0) 5 56 59 30 22
Fax + 33 (0) 5 56 59 73 52
cos-labory@wanadoo.fr

CHÂTEAU CROIZET-BAGES
Rue de la Verrerie
33 250 PAUILLAC
Tel + 33 (0) 5 56 59 01 62
Fax + 33 (0) 5 56 59 23 39
www.domaines-quie.com

CHÂTEAU DAUZAC
Avenue Georges Johnson
33 460 MARGAUX
Tel + 33 (0) 5 57 88 32 10
Fax + 33 (0) 5 57 88 96 00
www.chateaudauzac.com

CHÂTEAU DESMIRAIL
28 Avenue de la Vème République
33 460 MARGAUX
Tel + 33 (0) 5 57 88 34 33
Fax + 33 (0) 5 57 88 96 27
www.desmirail.com

CHÂTEAU DUCRU-BEAUCAILLOU
33 250 SAINT-JULIEN
Tel + 33 (0) 5 56 73 16 73
Fax + 33 (0) 5 56 59 27 37
www.chateau-ducru-beaucaillou.com

CHÂTEAU DUHART-MILON
33 250 PAUILLAC
Tel + 33 (0) 5 56 73 18 18
Fax + 33 (0) 5 56 59 26 83
www.lafite.com

CHÂTEAU DURFORT-VIVENS
33 460 MARGAUX
Tel + 33 (0) 5 57 88 31 02
Fax + 33 (0) 5 57 88 60 60
www.durfort-vivens.com

CHÂTEAU FERRIÈRE
33 bis rue de la Trémoille
33 460 MARGAUX
Tel + 33 (0) 5 57 88 76 65
Fax + 33 (0) 5 57 88 98 33
www.ferriere.com

CHÂTEAU GISCOURS
10 route de Giscours
33 460 LABARDE
Tel + 33 (0) 5 57 97 09 09
Fax + 33 (0) 5 57 97 09 00
www.chateau-giscours.fr

CHÂTEAU GRAND-PUY DUCASSE
4 Quai Antoine Ferchaud
33 250 PAUILLAC
Tel + 33 (0) 5 56 59 00 40
Fax + 33 (0) 5 56 59 36 47
www.cagrandscrus.com

CHÂTEAU GRAND-PUY-LACOSTE
Domaines.françois-Xavier Borie
33 250 PAUILLAC
Tel + 33 (0) 5 56 59 06 66
Fax + 33 (0) 5 56 59 22 27
dfxb@domainesfxborie.com

CHÂTEAU GRUAUD LAROSE
33 250 SAINT-JULIEN
Tel + 33 (0) 5 56 73 15 20
Fax + 33 (0) 5 56 59 64 72
www.gruaud-larose.com

CHÂTEAU HAUT-BAGES LIBÉRAL
33 250 PAUILLAC
Tel + 33 (0) 5 57 88 76 65
Fax + 33 (0) 5 57 88 98 33
www.hautbagesliberal.com

CHÂTEAU HAUT-BATAILLEY
Domaines François-Xavier Borie
33 250 PAUILLAC
Tel + 33 (0) 5 56 59 06 66
Fax + 33 (0) 5 56 59 22 27
dfxb@domainesfxborie.com

CHÂTEAU HAUT-BRION
135 Avenue Jean Jaurés
33 608 PESSAC Cedex
Tel + 33 (0) 5 56 00 29 30
Fax + 33 (0) 5 56 98 75 14
www.haut-brion.com

CHÂTEAU D'ISSAN
33 460 MARGAUX
Tel + 33 (0) 5 57 88 35 91
Fax + 33 (0) 5 57 88 74 24
www.chateau-issan.com

CHÂTEAU KIRWAN
33 460 MARGAUX
Tél : + 33 (0) 5 57 88 71 00
Fax + 33 (0) 5 57 88 77 62
www.chateau-kirwan.com

CHÂTEAU LA LAGUNE
33 290 LUDON-MÉDOC
Tel + 33 (0) 5 57 88 82 77
Fax + 33 (0) 5 57 88 82 70
www.chateau-lalagune.com

CHÂTEAU LA TOUR CARNET
Route de Beychevelle
33 112 SAINT LAURENT MÉDOC
Tel + 33 (0) 5 56 73 30 90
Fax + 33 (0) 5 56 59 48 54
www.bernard-magrez.com

CHÂTEAU LAFITE-ROTHSCHILD
33 250 PAUILLAC
Tel + 33 (0) 5 56 73 18 18
Fax + 33 (0) 5 56 59 26 83
www.lafite.com

CHÂTEAU LAFON-ROCHET
Lieu-dit Blanquet
33 180 SAINT-ESTÈPHE
Tel + 33 (0) 5 56 59 32 06
Fax + 33 (0) 5 56 59 72 43
www.lafon-rochet.com

CHÂTEAU LAGRANGE
33 250 SAINT-JULIEN
Tel + 33 (0) 5 56 73 38 38
Fax + 33 (0) 5 56 59 26 09
www.chateau-lagrange.com

CHÂTEAU LANGOA BARTON
33 250 SAINT-JULIEN
Tel + 33 (0) 5 56 59 06 05
Fax + 33 (0) 5 56 59 14 29
www.leoville-barton.com

CHÂTEAU LASCOMBES
1 Cours de Verdun
33 460 MARGAUX
Tel + 33 (0) 5 57 88 70 66
Fax + 33 (0) 5 57 88 72 17
www.chateau-lascombes.com

CHÂTEAU LATOUR
Saint-Lambert
33 250 PAUILLAC
Tel + 33 (0) 5 56 73 19 80
Fax + 33 (0) 5 56 73 19 81
www.chateau-latour.com

CHÂTEAU LÉOVILLE BARTON
33 250 SAINT-JULIEN
Tel + 33 (0) 5 56 59 06 05
Fax + 33 (0) 5 56 59 14 29
www.leoville-barton.com

CHÂTEAU LÉOVILLE-POYFERRÉ
33 250 SAINT-JULIEN
Tel + 33 (0) 5 56 59 08 30
Fax + 33 (0) 5 56 59 60 09
www.leoville-poyferre.fr

CHÂTEAU LYNCH-BAGES
33 250 PAUILLAC
Tel + 33 (0) 5 56 73 24 00
Fax + 33 (0) 5 56 59 26 42
www.lynchbages.com

CHÂTEAU LYNCH-MOUSSAS
33 250 PAUILLAC
Tel + 33 (0) 5 56 00 00 70
Fax + 33 (0) 5 57 87 48 61
domaines@borie-manoux.fr

CHÂTEAU MALESCOT SAINT-EXUPÉRY
33 460 MARGAUX
Tel + 33 (0) 5 57 88 97 20
Fax + 33 (0) 5 57 88 97 21
www.malescot.com

CHÂTEAU MARGAUX
33 460 MARGAUX
Tel + 33 (0) 5 57 88 83 83
Fax + 33 (0) 5 57 88 31 32
www.chateau-margaux.com

CHÂTEAU MARQUIS D'ALESME
1 route de Labégorce
33 460 MARGAUX
Tel + 33 (0) 5 57 88 71 32
Fax + 33 (0) 5 57 88 35 01
www.chateau-marquis-dalesme.fr

CHÂTEAU MARQUIS DE TERME
3 Route de Rauzan
33 460 MARGAUX
Tel + 33 (0) 5 57 88 30 01
Fax + 33 (0) 5 57 88 32 51
www.chateau-marquis-de-terme.com

CHÂTEAU MONTROSE
33 180 SAINT-ESTÈPHE
Tel + 33 (0) 5 56 59 30 12
Fax + 33 (0) 5 56 59 71 86
www.chateau-montrose.com

CHÂTEAU MOUTON
ROTHSCHILD
33 250 PAUILLAC
Tel + 33 (0) 5 56 73 20 20
Fax + 33 (0) 5 56 73 20 33
www.bpdr.com

CHÂTEAU PALMER
33 460 MARGAUX
Tel + 33 (0) 5 57 88 72 72
Fax + 33 (0) 5 57 88 37 16
www.chateau-palmer.com

CHÂTEAU PÉDESCLAUX
33 250 PAUILLAC
Tel + 33 (0) 5 56 59 22 59
Fax + 33 (0) 5 56 59 63 19
www.chateau-pedesclaux.com

CHÂTEAU PICHON-
LONGUEVILLE
33 250 PAUILLAC
Tel + 33 (0) 5 56 73 17 17
Fax + 33 (0) 5 56 73 17 28
www.pichonlongueville.com

CHÂTEAU PICHON-
LONGUEVILLE COMTESSE
DE LALANDE
33 250 PAUILLAC
Tel + 33 (0) 5 56 59 19 40
Fax + 33 (0) 5 56 59 26 56
www.pichon-lalande.com

CHÂTEAU PONTET-CANET
33 250 PAUILLAC
Tel + 33 (0) 5 56 59 04 04
Fax + 33 (0)5 56 59 26 63
www.pontet-canet.com

CHÂTEAU POUGET
11 route de Jean Faure
33 460 MARGAUX
Tel + 33 (0) 5 57 88 90 82
www.chateau-pouget.com

CHÂTEAU PRIEURÉ-LICHINE
34 Avenue de la 5ème République
33 460 MARGAUX
Tel + 33 (0) 5 57 88 36 28
Fax + 33 (0) 5 57 88 78 93
www.prieure-lichine.fr

CHÂTEAU RAUZAN-GASSIES
1 rue Alexis Millardet
33 460 MARGAUX
Tel + 33 (0) 5 57 88 71 88
Fax + 33 (0) 5 57 88 37 49
www.domaines-quie.com

CHÂTEAU RAUZAN-SÉGLA
1 rue Alexis Millardet
33 460 MARGAUX
Tel + 33 (0) 5 57 88 82 10
Fax + 33 (0) 5 57 88 34 54
www.chateaurauzansegla.com

CHÂTEAU SAINT-PIERRE
Domaines Henri Martin
33 250 SAINT-JULIEN
Tel + 33 (0) 5 56 59 08 18
Fax + 33 (0) 5 56 59 16 18
www.domaines-henri-martin.com

CHÂTEAU TALBOT
33 250 SAINT-JULIEN
Tel + 33 (0) 5 56 73 21 50
Fax + 33 (0) 5 56 73 21 51
www.chateau-talbot.com

CHÂTEAU DU TERTRE
Avenue de Ligondras
33 460 ARSAC
Tel + 33 (0) 5 57 88 52 52
Fax + 33 (0) 5 57 88 52 51
www.chateaudutertre.fr

SAUTERNES GRANDS CRUS CLASSES IN 1855

CHÂTEAU D'ARCHE
33 210 SAUTERNES
Tel + 33 (0)5 56 76 66 55
Fax + 33 (0)5 56 76 64 38
www.chateaudarche-sauternes.com

CHÂTEAU BROUSTET
33 720 BARSAC
Tel + 33 (0)5 56 27 16 87
Fax + 33 (0)5 56 27 05 93
www.chateau-broustet.com

CHÂTEAU CAILLOU
33 720 BARSAC
Tel + 33 (0)5 56 27 16 38
Fax + 33 (0)5 56 27 09 60
www.chateaucaillou.com

CHÂTEAU CLIMENS
33 720 BARSAC
Tel + 33 (0)5 56 27 15 33
Fax + 33 (0)5 56 27 21 04
www.chateau-climens.fr

CHÂTEAU COUTET
33 720 BARSAC
Tel + 33 (0)5 56 27 15 46
Fax + 33 (0)5 56 27 02 20
www.chateaucoutet.com

CHÂTEAU DOISY DAËNE
33 720 BARSAC
Tel + 33 (0)5 56 62 96 51
Fax + 33 (0)5 56 62 14 89
www.denisdubourdieudomaines.com

CHÂTEAU DOISY-DUBROCA
Château Climens
33 720 BARSAC
Tel + 33 (0)5 56 27 15 33
Fax + 33 (0)5 56 27 21 04
contact@chateau-climens.fr

CHÂTEAU DOISY-VÉDRINES
33 720 BARSAC
Tel + 33 (0)5 56 27 15 13
Fax + 33 (0)5 56 27 26 76
doisy-vedrines@orange.fr

CHÂTEAU FILHOT
33 210 SAUTERNES
Tel + 33 (0)5 56 76 61 09
Fax + 33 (0)5 56 76 67 91
www.filhot.com

CHÂTEAU GUIRAUD
33 210 SAUTERNES
Tel + 33 (0)5 56 76 61 01
Fax + 33 (0)5 56 76 67 52
www.chateauguiraud.com

CHÂTEAU LAFAURIE-
PEYRAGUEY
33 210 BOMMES
Tel + 33 (0)5 56 76 60 54
Fax + 33 (0)5 56 76 61 89
www.lafaurie-peyraguey.com

CHÂTEAU LAMOTHE
19 rue Principale
33 210 SAUTERNES
Tel +33 (0)5 56 76 67 89
Fax +33 (0)5 56 76 63 77
www.lamothe-despujols.com

CHÂTEAU LAMOTHE-GUIGNARD
33 210 SAUTERNES
Tel 05 56 76 60 28
Fax 05 56 76 69 05
www.chateau-lamothe-guignard.fr

CHÂTEAU LA TOUR BLANCHE
33 210 BOMMES
Tel + 33 (0)5 57 98 02 73
Fax + 33 (0)5 57 98 02 78
www.tour-blanche.com

CHÂTEAU DE MALLE
33 210 PREIGNAC
Tel + 33 (0)5 56 62 36 86
Fax + 33 (0)5 56 76 82 40
www.chateau-de-malle.fr

CHÂTEAU DE MYRAT
33 720 BARSAC
Tel +33 (0)5 56 27 09 06
Fax +33 (0)5 56 27 11 75
myrat@chateaudemyrat.fr

CHÂTEAU NAIRAC
33 720 BARSAC
Tel +33 (0)5 56 27 16 16
Fax +33 (0)5 56 27 26 50
www.chateau-nairac.com

CHÂTEAU RABAUD-PROMIS
33 210 BOMMES
Tel + 33 (0)5 56 76 60 52
Fax + 33 (0)5 56 76 63 10
rabaud-promis@wanadoo.fr

CHÂTEAU DE RAYNE VIGNEAU
33 210 BOMMES
Tel + 33 (0) 5 56 59 00 40
Fax + 33 (0) 5 56 59 36 47
www.cagrandscrus.com

CHÂTEAU RIEUSSEC
33 210 FARGUES
Tel + 33 (0)5 57 98 14 14
Fax + 33 (0)5 57 98 14 10
www.lafite.com

CHÂTEAU ROMER
33 210 FARGUES
Tel +33 (0)5 56 63 24 04
Fax +33 (0)5 56 63 24 05
www.chateau-romer.com

CHÂTEAU ROMER DU HAYOT
33 720 BARSAC
Tel + 33 (0)5 56 27 15 37
Fax + 33 (0)5 56 27 04 24
www.vignobles-du-hayot.com

CHÂTEAU SIGALAS-RABAUD
33 210 BOMMES
Tel + 33 (0)5 56 21 31 43
Fax + 33 (0)5 56 78 71 55

CHÂTEAU SUDUIRAUT
33 210 PREIGNAC
Tel + 33 (0)5 56 63 61 90
Fax + 33 (0)5 56 63 61 93
www.suduiraut.com

CHÂTEAU SUAU
33 720 ILLATS
Tel +33 (0)6 81 56 42 57
Fax +33 (0)5 56 62 47 98
chateau-archambeau@wanadoo.fr

CHÂTEAU D'YQUEM
33 210 SAUTERNES
Tel + 33 (0)5 57 98 07 07
Fax + 33 (0)5 57 98 07 08
www.yquem.fr

CLOS HAUT-PEYRAGUEY
33 210 BOMMES-SAUTERNES
Tel + 33 (0)5 56 76 61 53
Fax + 33 (0)5 56 76 69 65
www.closhautpeyraguey.com

For all informations:

CONSEIL DES GRANDS CRUS
CLASSÉS EN 1855
1 cours du XXX juillet
33 000 BORDEAUX
Tel + 33 (0)5 56 48 47 74
Fax + 33 (0)5 56 79 11 05
www.grand-cru-classe.com

INDEX OF THE CHEFS

DENMARK
Tel. +45 3296 3297
www.noma.dk

Heinz REITBAUER 140
Steirereck
Am Heumarkt 2A
A-1030 Vienna
AUSTRIA
Tel. +43 (1) 713 31 68
Fax +43 (1) 713 31 68 - 2
http://steirereck.at/wien/meierei

Michel RICHARD 164
Citronelle
3000 M Street NW
Washington, DC 20007
UNITED STATES
Tel. +1 202 625 2150
Fax +1 202 339 6326
www.citronelledc.com

Eric RIPERT 72
Le Bernardin
155 West 51st Street
(near Seventh Avenue)
New York, NY 10019
UNITED STATES
Tel. +1 212 554 1515
Fax +1 212 554 1100

Joël ROBUCHON 38
La Table de Joël Robuchon
16 avenue Bugeaud
75116 Paris
FRANCE
Tel. +33 (0)1 56 28 16 16
Fax +33 (0)1 56 28 16 78
www.joel-robuchon.com

Michel ROUX 84
Le Gavroche
43 Upper Brook Street
London W1K 7QR
UNITED KINGDOM
Tel. +44 (0) 20 7408 0881
Fax +44 (0) 20 7491 4387
www.le-gavroche.co.uk

Chris SALANS 376
Mozaic
Jalan Raya Sanggingan
Ubud 80571 Bali
INDONESIA
Tel. +62 361 97 57 68

Fax +62 361 97 57 68
www.mozaic-bali.com

Yoshinori SHIBUYA 108
La Bécasse
Ginsenyokobori Bldg. 1F
4-6-2 Kouraibashi Chuou-ku
Osaka 541-0043
JAPAN
Tel. +81 (0)6 4707 0070
Fax +81 (0)6 4707 0027

Anthony SICIGNANO 228
The Breakers
One South County Road
Palm Beach, FL 33480
UNITED STATES
Tel. +1 561 655 6611
Fax +1 561 655 3577
www.thebreakers.com

Manjit SINGH GILL 260
Bukhara
ITC Hotel Maurya Sheraton & Towers
Diplomatic Enclave Sardar Patel Marg
New Delhi 110 021
INDIA
Tel. +91 (0)11 26112233
Fax +91 (0)11 26113333
www.itcportal.com

Christian SINICROPI 316
La Palme d'Or
Hotel Martinez
73 La Croisette
06400 Cannes
FRANCE
Tel. +33 (0)4 92 98 73 00
Fax +33 (0)4 93 39 67 82
www.hotel-martinez.com

Alain SOLIVÉRÈS 348
Taillevent
15 rue Lamennais
75008 Paris
FRANCE
Tel. +33 (0)1 40 74 20 20
Fax +33 (0)1 40 74 20 21
www.taillevent.com

Roberta SUDBRACK 356
Sudbrack
Rua Lineu de Paula Machado 916
Jardim Botanico, Rio de Janeiro

BRAZIL
Tel. +55 21 3874 0139
www.robertasudbrack.com.br

Jacques THOREL 88
L'Auberge Bretonne
2 place Duguesclin
56130 La Roche-Bernard
FRANCE
Tel. +33 (0)2 99 90 60 28
Fax +33 (0)2 99 90 85 00
www.auberge-bretonne.com

Michel TRAMA 188
Les Loges de l'Aubergade
52 rue Royale
47270 Puymirol
FRANCE
Tel. +33 (0)5 53 95 31 46
Fax +33 (0)5 53 95 33 80
www.aubergade.com

Michel TROISGROS 104
Troisgros
Place Gare
42300 Roanne
FRANCE
Tel. +33 (0)4 77 71 66 97
Fax +33 (0)4 77 70 39 77
www.troisgros.fr

Charlie TROTTER 52
Charlie Trotter's
816 West Armitage
Chicago, IL 60614
UNITED STATES
Tel. +1 773 248 6228
Fax +1 773 248 6088
www.charlietrotters.com

Hans VÄLIMÄKI 344
Chez Dominique
Rikhardinkatu 4
00130 Helsinki
FINLAND
Tel. +358 (0)9 612 7393
Fax +358 (0)9 612 4422 0
www.chezdominique.fi

Marc VEYRAT 152
La Maison de Marc Veyrat
(temporarily closed)
13 vieille route des Pensières
74290 Veyrier-du-Lac

FRANCE
Tel. +33 (0)4 50 60 24 00
Fax +33 (0)4 50 60 23 63
www.marcveyrat.fr

Jean-Georges VONGERICHTEN . . . 304
Jean-Georges
1 Central Park West
New York, NY 10023
UNITED STATES
Tel. +1 212 299 3900
Fax +1 212 299 3908
www.jean-georges.fr

Tetsuya WAKUDA 312
Tetsuya's Restaurant
529 Kent Street
Sydney, NSW 2000
AUSTRALIA
Tel. +61 2 9267 2900
Fax +61 2 9262 7099
www.tetsuyas.com

Heinz WINKLER 352
Residenz Heinz Winkler
Kirchplatz 1
83229 Aschau im Chiemgau
GERMANY
Tel. +49 8052 1799 0
Fax +49 8052 1799 66
www.residenz-heinz-winkler.de

Chan YAN-TAK 68
Lung King Heen
Four Seasons Hotel, 8 Finance Street
Central, Hong Kong
CHINA
Tel. +852 3196 8888
Fax +852 3196 8899
www.fourseasons.com/hongkong

Alexander ZAITSEV 256
Pushkin
Boulevard Tverskoy 26a
Moscow 103009
RUSSIA
Tel. +7 495 739 00 33
www.cafe-pushkin.ru

BIBLIOGRAPHY

Anthony Barton and Claude Petit-Castelli, *La Saga des Barton*. Paris: Manya, 1991.

Asa Briggs, *Haut-Brion, An Illustrious Lineage*. London: Faber & Faber, 1994.

Nicholas Faith, *Château Margaux*. Paris: Flammarion, 2004.

Bernard Ginestet, *Je suis le marquis de Terme*. Bordeaux: Éditions William Blake & Co., 1999.

Bernard Ginestet, *Saint-Julien*. Paris: Nathan, 1984.

David Haziot, *Château Pichon-Longueville Comtesse de Lalande, la passion du vin*. Paris: La Martinière, 2007.

Aurélie Labruyère, *Palmer*. Bordeaux: Mollat, 2008.

Dewey Markham, Jr., *1855, Histoire d'un classement des vins de Bordeaux*. Bordeaux: Féret, 1997.

Dewey Markham, Jr., Cornelis Van Leeuwen and Franck Ferrand; forewords by Jean-Paul Kauffmann and Hugh Johnson, *Bordeaux, Grands Crus Classés 1855–2005*. Paris: Flammarion, 2005.

Richard Olney, Pierre Rival and Francis Mayeur, *Yquem*, Paris, Flammarion, 2007.

René Pijassou, *Château Rauzan-Ségla, la naissance d'un grand cru classé*. Paris: La Martinière, 2004.

René Pijassou and Didier Ters, *Gruaud-Larose*. Paris: Stock, 1997.

Nicolas de Rabaudy, *Château Kirwan, histoire d'une renaissance*. Paris: Stock, 1995.

James Seely, *Great Bordeaux Wines*. London: Pallas Athene, 1986; new edition, 1998.

Tastet and Lawton, *De l'air du temps*, 2 vol. Bordeaux: Éditions Confluences, 2006–7.

ACKNOWLEDGMENTS OF THE CONSEIL DES GRANDS CRUS CLASSÉS IN 1855

The purpose of this book is to create a perfect harmony between the exceptional wines selected by the famous 1855 Classification of Bordeaux wines and the recipes of the greatest chefs worldwide. The Conseil des Grands Crus Classés en 1855 (Médoc & Sauternes) wishes to thank the La Martinière publishing house, and particularly Corinne Schmidt, Aude Mantoux, Nathalie Chapuis and Sophie Compagne, for their availability and their commitment to this beautiful book.

We also wish to thank the author, Sophie Brissaud, the photographers Cyril Le Tourner d'Ison, Guy Charneau and Iris L. Sullivan, as well as the authors of the introductory texts, Jancis Robinson and Nick Lander, and Jacques Dupont, who wrote the foreword.

Warm thanks to Riedel, Bernardaud and Christofle for their support.

Special thanks to Alexandra Arquey.

ACKNOWLEDGMENTS FROM THE AUTHOR

I wish to thank everyone connected with this project for honouring me with their trust.

Éditions de La Martinière: Aude Mantoux and Nathalie Chapuis.

Conseil des Grands Crus Classés de Médoc et de Sauternes: Philippe Castéja and Sylvain Boisvert.

For their hospitality and precious help, my warmest thanks to: Pierre Lurton and Valérie Lailheugue (Château d'Yquem); John Kolasa and Sandrine Bégaud (Château Rauzan-Ségla); Thierry Budin (Château Grand-Puy-Ducasse); Eric Albada Jelgersma, Alexander Van Beek and Laure Bastard (Châteaux Giscours and Le Tertre); Isabelle and Alfred Tesseron (Château Pontet-Canet); Éric Larramona (Château Lafaurie-Peyraguey); Emmanuel Cruse (Château d'Issan); Aline Baly (Château Coutet); Anne-Françoise and Jean-Philippe Quié (Châteaux Rauzan-Gassies and Croizet-Bages); Xavier Planty and Didier Galhaud (Château Guiraud); Philippe Castéja (Châteaux Lynch-Moussas and Batailley); Dominique Befve (Château Lascombes); Mr. and Mrs. Patrick Maroteaux (Château Branaire-Ducru); Bérénice Lurton-Thomas (Châteaux Climens and Doisy-Dubroca); Nicole, Eloïse and Nicolas Tari-Heeter (Château Nairac); Lucien Guillemet (Châteaux Boyd-Cantenac and Pouget); Céline and Jean-Pierre Foubet (Château de Camensac); Jean-Michel Cazes (Château Lynch-Bages); Denis Lurton (Château Desmirail); Lise Latrille, Louis Ballande and Justin Onclin (Château Prieuré-Lichine); Ludovic David (Château Marquis de Terme).

Also my warmest thanks for their precious help and much-appreciated welcome: *Médoc and Pessac:* Charles Chevallier and my guide to Lafite and Duhart-Milon (Châteaux Lafite Rothschild, Duhart-Milon and Rieussec); Frédéric Engerer (Château Latour); Corinne Mentzelopoulos, Johana Loubet and Paul Pontallier (Château Margaux); Baronne Philippine de Rothschild, Cécile Loqmane and Hervé Berland (Châteaux Mouton Rothschild, d'Armailhac and Clerc-Milon); HRH Prince Robert de Luxembourg, Turid Hoel Alcaras and Alain Puginier (Château Haut-Brion); Anthony Barton (Châteaux Léoville Barton and Langoa Barton); Didier Cuvelier (Château Léoville Poyferré); Gonzague Lurton (Château Durfort-Vivens); Jean Merlaut (Château Gruaud-Larose); Corinne Saussier-Conroy and Henri Lurton (Château Brane-Cantenac); Christian Seely (Châteaux Pichon-Longueville and Suduiraut); Gildas d'Ollone (Châteaux Pichon-Longueville and Comtesse de Lalande); Bruno Borie (Château Ducru-Beaucaillou); Géraldine Marquay and Jean-Guillaume Prats (Château Cos d'Estournel); Jean-Bernard Delmas, Lorraine Watrin and Nicolas Glumineau (Château Montrose); Nathalie Schÿler and Philippe Delfault (Château Kirwan); Bruno Eynard (Château Lagrange); Jean-Luc Züger and Gilles Pouget (Château Malescot Saint-Exupéry); José Sanfins (Château Cantenac-Brown); Thomas Duroux (Château Palmer); Caroline Frey and Jérôme Juhé (Château La Lagune); Denise Capbern-Gasqueton (Château Calon-Ségur); Claire Villars-Lurton and Jeanne Girardot (Châteaux Ferrière and Haut-Bages-Libéral); Philippe de Laguarigue (Château Marquis d'Alesme); Jean-Louis Triaud (Château Saint-Pierre); Nancy Bignon-Cordier and Jean-Pierre Marty (Château Talbot); Anne Le Naour (Château La Tour-Carnet); Michel Tesseron (Château Lafon-Rochet); Philippe Blanc (Château Beychevelle); François-Xavier Borie (Châteaux Haut-Batailley and Grand-Puy-Lacoste); Christine Lurton-de Caix (Château Dauzac); Patrick Jestin, Nathalie Schwartz and Antoine Gonzalez (Château Belgrave); Sandrine Arroyo (Château Pédesclaux); Bernard Audoy (Château Cos Labory); Philippe Dambrine (Château Cantemerle). *Sauternes and Barsac:* Corinne Reulet (Château La Tour Blanche); Martine Langlais-Pauly (Château Clos Haut-Peyraguey); Patrick Eymery (Château de Rayne-Vigneau); Pierre Montégut (Château Suduiraut); Philippe Déjean (Château Rabaud-Promis); Mr. de Lambert des Granges (Château Sigalas-Rabaud); Xavier de Pontac (Château de Myrat); Florence, Denis and Fabrice Dubourdieu (Château Doisy-Daëne); Olivier Castéja (Château Doisy-Védrines); Jérôme Cosson (Château d'Arche); Henri and Gabriel de Vaucelles (Château Filhot); Didier Laulan (Château Broustet); Mr. and Mrs. Pierre (Château Caillou); Corinne Dubourdieu (Château Suau); Paul-Henri de Bournazel (Château de Malle); Anne Fargue (Château Romer); Patrick Lopez (Château Romer du Hayot); Guy Despujols (Château Lamothe); Philippe and Jacques Guignard (Château Lamothe-Guignard).

Special thanks to Vincent Gross, Boris Chapuis, Marc Sibard, Dewey Markham, Alain Dejean, Mr. and Mrs. Jean-Paul Barbier and my friends and family for putting up with both my presence and my absence (and sometimes absent-mindedness) during months of searching and writing.

Sophie Brissaud

Coco Jobard wishes to address her warmest thanks to her cooking assistant Nicolas Matveieff and to everybody who helped her for the photos of the chefs' recipes by graciously providing her with prestigious ingredients:

Caviar by Petrossian (PR: Bernadette Vizioz)
18 boulevard de Latour-Maubourg
75007 Paris
Tel : 01 44 11 32 22
www.petrossian.fr

Foie gras by Dupérier
www.duperier.fr

Spices and seasonings by Terre Exotique
www.terreexotique.fr

The butchers
Christian Lelann
242, bis rue des Pyrénées
75020 Paris

Christophe Le Bourdais
77 ter rue de la Tombe Issoire
75014 Paris

The Pays d'Oc Farm-raised Lamb
www.agneau-pays-oc@groupe-unicor.com

Marie Paule Meunier
www.pouletdebresse.fr

Sophie Bartkowski
for lending the cotton candy machine

Claude Location
31 avenue de Chennevières
94420 Le Plessis-Trévise
www.claude-location.fr

For dishes, cutlery and chinaware:
Bernardaud
www.bernardaud.fr
Christofle
www.christofle.com
Riedel
www. riedel.com

and:
Asiatides
www.asiatides.com
Astier de Villatte
www.astierdevillatte.com
CFOC (La Compagnie d'Orient et de la Chine)
www.cfoc.fr
Emery&Co
www.emeryetcie.com
La Fleur de Badiane
www.lafleurdebadiane.com
Gedimat
www.gedimat.fr
Intérieur lin
www.interieurlin.com

Le Jacquard français
www.le-jacquard-français.fr
Kitchen Bazaar
www.kitchenbazaar.fr
Marie Papier
www.mariepapier.fr
Mise en demeure
www.miseendemeure.fr
Moline
www.tissus.moline.com
Nobilis
www.nobilis.fr
Gilles Nouailhac
www.gillesnouailhac.com
Matflor
www.matflor.com
Mora
www.mora.fr
Red Halo
www.redhalo.zoomshare.com
Rouge du Rhône
www.rougedurhone.com
Staub
www.staub.fr
Alexandre Turpault
www.alexandre-turpault.com

Nathalie Nannini would like to thank Oliver Howard, painter and interior decorator.

CHÂTEAU LAFITE-ROTHSCHILD
Yannick ALLÉNO

CHÂTEAU LATOUR
Éric BRIFFARD

CHÂTEAU MARGAUX
Pierre CARRIER & Pierre MAILLET

CHÂTEAU MOUTON ROTHSCHILD
Joël ROBUCHON

CHÂTEAU HAUT-BRION
Alain PASSARD

CHÂTEAU RAUZAN-SÉGLA
Heinz BECK

CHÂTEAU RAUZAN-GASSIES
Charlie TROTTER

CHÂTEAU LÉOVILLE-POYFERRÉ
Paul BOCUSE

CHÂTEAU LÉOVILLE BARTON
Marc HAEBERLIN

CHÂTEAU DURFORT-VIVENS
Per BENGTSSON

CHÂTEAU GRUAUD LAROSE
Chan YAN-TAK

CHÂTEAU LASCOMBES
Eric RIPERT

CHÂTEAU BRANE-CANTENAC
Nils HENKEL

CHÂTEAU PICHON-LONGUEVILLE
Fergus HENDERSON

CHÂTEAU PICHON LONGUEVILLE COMTESSE DE LALANDE
Michel ROUX

CHÂTEAU DUCRU-BEAUCAILLOU
Jacques THOREL

CHÂTEAU COS D'ESTOURNEL
Jean-Georges KLEIN

CHÂTEAU MONTROSE
Éric FRÉCHON

CHÂTEAU KIRWAN
Neil PERRY

CHÂTEAU D'ISSAN
Michel TROISGROS

CHÂTEAU LAGRANGE
Yoshinori SHIBUYA

CHÂTEAU LANGOA BARTON
Wai Kwan CHUI

CHÂTEAU GISCOURS
Thomas KELLER

CHÂTEAU MALESCOT SAINT-EXUPÉRY
Gérard RABAEY

CHÂTEAU BOYD-CANTENAC
Hyo Nam PARK

CHÂTEAU CANTENAC BROWN
Bernard & Guy RAVET

CHÂTEAU PALMER
Christian LE SQUER

CHÂTEAU LA LAGUNE
Arnaud BIGNON

CHÂTEAU DESMIRAIL
Heinz REITBAUER

CHÂTEAU CALON SÉGUR
Nobu MATSUHISA

CHÂTEAU FERRIÈRE
Kobe DESRAMAULTS

CHÂTEAU MARQUIS D'ALESME
Marc VEYRAT

CHÂTEAU SAINT-PIERRE
Luisa MARELLI VALAZZA

CHÂTEAU TALBOT
Alvin LEUNG DESMON

CHÂTEAU BRANAIRE-DUCRU
Michel RICHARD

CHÂTEAU DUHART-MILON
Anne-Sophie PIC

CHÂTEAU POUGET
Nicola & Pierluigi PORTINARI

CHÂTEAU LA TOUR CARNET
Jannis BREVET

CHÂTEAU LAFON-ROCHET
Alain PÉGOURET

CHÂTEAU BEYCHEVELLE
Léa LINSTER

CHÂTEAU PRIEURÉ-LICHINE
Michel TRAMA

CHÂTEAU MARQUIS DE TERME
André CHIANG

CHÂTEAU HAUT-BATAILLEY
Éric PRAS

CHÂTEAU GRAND-PUY DUCASSE
Normand LAPRISE